Case Management in Human Service Practice

A Systematic Approach to Mobilizing Resources for Clients

Marie Weil
James M. Karls
and Associates

Case Management in Human Service Practice

Jossey-Bass Publishers

San Francisco • Washington • London • 1985

CASE MANAGEMENT IN HUMAN SERVICE PRACTICE
A Systematic Approach to Mobilizing Resources for Clients
by Marie Weil, James M. Karls, and Associates

Copyright © 1985 by: Jossey-Bass Inc., Publishers
433 California Street
San Francisco, California 94104

&

Jossey-Bass Limited
28 Banner Street
London EC1Y 8QE

Library of Congress Cataloging in Publication Data

Weil, Marie (date)
Case management in human service practice.

(The Jossey-Bass social and behavioral science series)
Includes bibliographies and index.
1. Social work administration—United States.
2. Social case work.   I. Karls, James M. (date)
II. Title.   III. Series.
HV91.W43   1985   361.3 '2 '068   84-47999
ISBN 0-87589-631-6 (alk. paper)

Manufactured in the United States of America

The paper in this book meets the guidelines for
permanence and durability of the Committee on
Production Guidelines for Book Longevity of the
Council on Library Resources.

JACKET DESIGN BY WILLI BAUM

FIRST EDITION

Code 8521

The Jossey-Bass
Social and Behavioral Science Series

This book is dedicated to
Ruth Perkinson Overby and Alton Kermit Overby
who have been exemplars of
compassion and strength
for their daughter

Preface

The use of case management systems and techniques is rapidly increasing in the human services. The growing interest in these applications of case management results from (1) a heightened concern within agencies for service accountability, (2) advances in computer systems technology, which have enabled human services agencies and institutions to use sophisticated management information systems, and (3) the increasing frequency with which federal, state, and local policies have mandated case management systems to account for services to clients, the use of service resources, and program costs and benefits. Because of these developments, human services programs must improve their quality and make the delivery of their services more accountable. Not only can case management systems help to increase the effectiveness of decision making within programs, but they can also aid in maximizing the use of a community's resources for dealing with social problems and assisting people in need.

Despite the rapid development of technology and various systems approaches to case management, little has appeared in the management literature that discusses the concepts and procedures necessary to develop appropriate case management models for

ix

human services. This book is intended to meet that need by
presenting the theoretical and methodological base of case management systems and the state of the art in operations and technology
of case management in human services. The book develops and
explicates appropriate and effective models and systems of case
management for the major fields of human services practice: child
welfare, aging, mental health, physical disability, health, and
developmental disability. Such a presentation, uniting model development, theory building, and planning strategies, has not been
available for human services administrators and providers. The
presentation here is intended to inform human services administrators, managers, and practitioners of the knowledge base, methods,
and techniques they need to develop or adapt a case management
system to their field and program setting.

The book will thus meet a major need for human services
administrators, managers, clinicians, and students preparing to
enter these fields. It presents theory and methods of case management; it describes case management model development in a variety
of fields; it illustrates inherent tensions; and it details guidelines for
developing and tailoring a case management system to specific
program needs. The book will be useful for service planners,
administrators, managers, and practitioners in all human services
fields. It can also serve as a text for graduate courses in case
management, service design, and administration and will be valuable in a variety of professional disciplines, including public
administration, medical and health services administration, social
service administration, social work, and human services management and administration.

Perspective on Case Management

The authors present case management as a coordinating
function, albeit with therapeutic facets. The essential elements of
case management are client identification, assessment of need,
service planning, service coordination and linking, and the monitoring and continuous evaluation of the client, of service delivery,
and of available resources. Client and class advocacy are considered

integral to the case management process. Client advocacy denotes speaking on behalf of and working for a client's benefit to ensure that quality services are provided. Class advocacy denotes working to provide general policy and service benefits for a particular target population. The goal of case management in the human services is to resolve the client's problems in the most effective way possible within the constraints of the service program.

Many human services providers, especially clinicians but also some managers, view case management procedures and systems with trepidation or cynicism. Many of them believe that the technology is of value to confirmed bureaucrats but of questionable worth to clients and staff. The authors take the position that good case management is an essential element of good clinical practice.

Administrators and funding sources often view service efficiency and cost-effectiveness as their central concern; practitioners, however, are more likely to emphasize the quality of services and intensive care for clients. The result is that the case management process often becomes the ground for a classic battle between cost-effectiveness and treatment-effectiveness. This book confronts this ubiquitous organizational tension and demonstrates the benefits to agency, clients, and staff of carefully considered and appropriate case management approaches.

The dichotomy between cost-effectiveness and treatment-effectiveness is, we hold, a false one. Quality service requires the effective and caring provision of services to clients *and* the cost-effective delivery of services so that targeted populations can be served adequately. Administrative users of management systems need to come to terms with the effectiveness issue; staff and managers need more effective and responsive models as well as training in efficiency and cost-effectiveness. The realities of service management require the dual focus on effectiveness and efficiency. If case management systems are designed to provide useful feedback to practitioners for service planning, then they can knowledgeably work toward cost-effective use of limited resources.

This volume focuses on the development of case management systems at the local level. Although there are many issues that relate to state and national coordinating and information management systems, local service networks are the foundation on which such large systems are built. Most of the existing literature deals with large-system coordination such as state plans, presents case management practices in one field, or details the development of particular systems through case studies. However, an overview of general case management issues and a description of case management program development at the local level for a variety of human services fields have been lacking. This volume addresses that need. This book is attuned to the needs of local-level planners, administrators, and providers of case management services as well as students in the related fields. However, it will also be of assistance to regional and state planners in their roles as consultants to and monitors of local systems.

Organization of the Book

This book illustrates how to address concerns for effectiveness and efficiency in ways that will be accountable for administrators and meaningful for practitioners. In many respects, the agency and staff are clients of the case management system, just as persons needing service are clients of the agency. Therefore, case management systems must be designed to meet the information needs of staff as well as of administrators and funding sources. This volume presents strategies to meet these needs.

This book is divided into three parts. Part One, "Knowledge Base of Case Management," presents the history of case management, describes the models and essential components of case management systems, and discusses the development of its conceptual and theoretical bases. Part Two, "Working with Specific Populations: Case Management in Major Areas of Practice," presents the policies, practice methods, and techniques of case management in six major fields of human service practice. Part Three, "Developing Case Management Systems: Issues and Implications for Practice," provides guidelines for developing case management systems tailored to the needs of specific programs and discusses professional and educational issues in case management practice.

In each part emphasis is placed on the concerns shared by both administrators and practitioners for effectiveness and efficiency in providing services to clients. Thus Chapter One describes the evolution of case management including the inescapable tension between service quality and service efficiency; discusses the service ideology, goals, and objectives of case management systems; and analyzes the roles necessary for an effective case management system and the general skills needed for case management practice. Chapter Two addresses the structure and processes of case management programs. It describes the functions and general process of case management, delineates and analyzes the models of case management practice, and discusses variations in practice based on organizational setting. The increasingly sophisticated procedures for information management and computerized reporting and feedback are presented along with the developing methods of accounting for service quality and effectiveness and management of information. Performance issues and supervision concerns are analyzed.

Chapter Three explicates principles of organizational theory involved in developing appropriate case management systems in human services programs. Intra- and interorganizational behavior patterns are analyzed, and micro- and macrosystem interaction issues are delineated. Chapter Four analyzes evaluation for decision making and program accountability in case management programs. Evaluation models and methodologies are examined with regard to their strengths and weaknesses in accounting for program quality and effects.

Chapters Five through Ten in Part Two describe and illustrate the case management systems, methods, and techniques used in six major human services fields: child welfare, the elderly and their families, the elderly in long-term care, the chronically mentally ill, the developmentally disabled, and independent living programs for people with physical disabilities. Each of these six chapters examines the theoretical approach and definitions of case management relevant to one of these fields of practice. Each reviews guiding policy issues and describes effective case management models and programs. Issues of role performance, collaboration, and specific methods and techniques of case management are analyzed for each field of practice. Special training, educational needs, and consumer advocacy issues related to each field are explored. Expected future trends in case management practices are described within each chapter. Although the populations treated in the book are quite varied, they are united in their vulnerability and their need for skilled services in case coordination, advocacy, and counseling.

Chapter Five analyzes the changing practice models in the child welfare system and explores the implications of permanency planning for dependent children and for programs and staff. Case management related to direct work with dependent children in their homes, in foster care, or in residential treatment is discussed along with methods of working with birth parents to maximize the possibilities of family reunification. Interactions between public social service agencies, the court system, and voluntary sector programs are examined and the changing roles of case managers in child welfare are explored.

Chapters Six and Seven deal with the elderly. Chapter Six presents a model of case management practice that focuses on working with family members and the elderly person and on assisting them in some case management functions. The value of the family-oriented model and particular roles for case managers in this field are considered. The issues of case management for the elderly in long-term care facilities are presented in Chapter Seven, and the special issues of interprofessional collaboration, intersystem communication, and long-term case management are analyzed.

In Chapter Eight the special needs of chronically mentally ill persons living in community settings are explored. Issues related to deinstitutionalization and the scarcity of community treatment and support resources for this population are examined. Differential models of work with this population are analyzed and community settings are considered.

Chapters Nine and Ten deal with the complex problems of disability. For children and adults who are developmentally disabled, a model of teaching families to become case managers is presented. Considerable emphasis is placed on teaching families how to become advocates and service coordinators for a disabled family member. The special issues of working with clients whose mental functioning constitutes a problem with regard to independence and self-determination are explored, and the history of services and care for the developmentally disabled is documented. Chapter Ten presents a model of case management in independent living programs for people with physical disabilities that is rapidly growing in popularity. Issues of service access, advocacy, and variability of service needs are analyzed as well as the community-based structure of independent living programs. The case management approach in programs following this model is strongly oriented toward assisting the client in becoming her or his own case manager. Part Two thus offers an in-depth view of current and exemplary models, as well as methods of case management in the major practice fields of human service.

Chapter Eleven in Part Three discusses common themes and issues in developing case management systems; analyzes the benefits and constraints of various models; and provides guidelines for designing, implementing, and evaluating workable, responsive, and appropriate case management systems that can be tailored to suit specific programs. Chapter Twelve summarizes issues and directions in case management practice; analyzes professional, educational, and service delivery issues; and suggests ways to demonstrate that concerns for service effectiveness and service efficiency can be complementary rather than divergent.

We believe this book describes the methodological state of the art in the practice of case management in the human services. We hope that it will stimulate research and model testing to address further the concerns for service quality and efficiency. The discussion of methods, models, and planning strategies will be useful guidelines for developing or revising case management programs in established and emerging fields of human service. This volume is the first to document the development of programs and to evaluate models of case management in various fields of human service and to analyze generic issues pertaining to planning, organizing, and evaluating case management programs.

We wish to acknowledge the expertise and creativity of our contributors and to thank them for their cooperation in developing this book. We thank Vicki Reiber, Cathy Harlan, and Nettie Mowery for their assistance and support in preparing the manuscript. Special acknowledgment goes to Ruth Britton, librarian of the School of Social Work of the University of Southern California, who was indefatigable in reference and research assistance, and to Charles B. Weil, Jr., for drafting the artwork for the book. Finally, we wish to thank our families for their forbearance and understanding during the book's preparation. With unbounded appreciation we acknowledge the support of Charles and David and Mary and Paul.

March 1985   Marie Weil
                                          Los Angeles, California

                                          James M. Karls
                                          Sausalito, California

Contents

Part Two: Working with Specific Populations: Case Management in Major Areas of Practice

Part Three: Developing Case Management Systems: Issues and Implications for Practice

The Authors

Marie Weil is associate professor in the School of Social Work at the University of Southern California. She joined the faculty there in 1977, immediately after receiving the D.S.W. degree from the Graduate Center of the City University of New York. She was awarded an M.S.W. degree in community organization from the University of Pennsylvania (1967) and a B.A. degree in philosophy from the University of North Carolina at Chapel Hill (1963).

At the University of Southern California, Weil teaches organizational and group behavior, administration, and community organization. She specializes in the field of services for families and children and in the connections between social work and the law. Her current consultation focuses on organizational and staff development in social service agencies and in the evaluation of human services programs. She has held a variety of administrative and planning posts in the social services, including deputy director of a municipal housing authority; deputy director of a state office of economic opportunity; and project director at the University of Southern California, at the Hunter College School of Social Work (City University of New York), and at Lehigh University.

Weil's major research interest is in practice and policy issues relating social work and the law, particularly issues of confidentiality and interprofessional collaboration. She has been involved with several research projects relating to service needs of minority and vulnerable populations and has been involved in continuing research on learning models for professional education and management.

Weil is the coauthor of *Child, Family, Neighborhood: A Master Plan for Social Service Delivery* (1982) and *Teaching Clinical Social Work: An Instructor's Manual* (1982). Her administrative and research articles have been published in such journals as *Social Service Review, Administration in Social Work, Administration in Mental Health, Social Development Issues,* and *Social Casework.* She has authored chapters in books on voluntarism and social work, social work with Southeast Asian refugees, and service integration for troubled families. Currently she is at work on a book on community organization practice and on research on children, families, and the courts.

James M. Karls is currently chief of the manpower development branch of the state of California's department of mental health. In this capacity he has been the director of several National Institute of Mental Health–funded research projects exploring the use and development of personnel, including case managers, in the state's mental health care system.

He is the former assistant director and director of the state of California's Mental Health Training Center, a postgraduate and continuing education program for mental health personnel in Southern California. There he developed training programs for human service personnel, including one in case management.

Karls is the immediate past president of the California chapter of the National Association of Social Workers. He has been a member of the faculty at the Graduate School of Welfare, University of California, Los Angeles, where he taught courses in case management principles and practices, which led to the development of this book. He has also taught at the School of Social Welfare, University of California, Berkeley, and at the University of California, Santa Barbara. He received a D.S.W. degree from the University of Southern California (1977). He was awarded an M.A. degree in social work from the School of Social Service Administration, University of Chicago (1950) and a B.A. degree in psychology from Loyola University of Chicago (1949). He currently resides with his wife and son in Sausalito, California.

Kathleen Burch Caires is a clinical social worker with the Glendale Adventist Medical Center, Glendale, California. Formerly she was coordinator of parent programs for the Lanterman Regional Center for the Developmentally Disabled in Los Angeles.

Rachel Downing is a consultant on geriatric social work and in private practice with the elderly and their families. Formerly she was a research associate at the Rehabilitation Research and Training Center on Aging, Rancho Los Amigos Medical Center, University of Southern California.

Ron Honnard is a research analyst for the Planning, Development, and Quality Assurance Bureau of the Los Angeles County Department of Mental Health.

June Isaacson Kailes is executive director of the Westside Community for Independent Living in Los Angeles, a nonresidential, public benefit corporation providing support services that enable people with physical disabilities or sensory impairments to live independently.

Rosalie A. Kane is a social scientist with the Rand Corporation and is affiliated with the University of California, Los Angeles/University of Southern California Long-Term Care Gerontology Center.

Alex J. Norman is associate professor of social welfare at the Graduate School of Social Welfare, University of California, Los Angeles, and a consultant for organizational development.

Susan J. Wells is principal investigator, Project on Decision Making in Child Protective Services, National Legal Resource Center for Child Advocacy and Protection of the American Bar Association,

Washington, D.C.; formerly she was postdoctoral fellow, Department of Mental Hygiene, School of Hygiene and Public Health, Johns Hopkins University.

George H. Wolkon is regional director, Los Angeles County Department of Mental Health, and associate professor, Department of Psychiatry and the Behavioral Sciences, University of Southern California.

Case Management in Human Service Practice

A Systematic Approach to Mobilizing Resources for Clients

1

Historical Origins and Recent Developments

Marie Weil, James M. Karls

Case management as a process of service coordination and accountability has a century-long history in the United States. It has evolved from the dual concerns to provide quality service coordination and to deliver human services in an efficient and cost-effective manner. The tensions related to this dual focus continue to be problematic for many case managers. Placing case management in its historical context and analyzing the framework of philosophical underpinnings, goals, and objectives clarifies the importance of the dual functions of case management and illuminates the complex roles, tasks, and skills necessary to provide effective and efficient services to vulnerable populations.

The use of case management systems and techniques in the human services is increasing rapidly. The emergence of case management over the last decade has had a major effect on how social, medical, and mental health services are offered. Case management is a developing method of service coordination and accountability in the human services. In essence, it is a series of actions and a process to assure that clients of human services systems receive the services, treatment, care, and opportunities to which they are

1

entitled. It is also a means of accounting for service delivery and the expenditures of funds and resources in providing services to vulnerable target populations. Although case management has been described in a variety of ways, the simplest definition is that *case management is a set of logical steps and a process of interaction within a service network which assure that a client receives needed services in a supportive, effective, efficient, and cost-effective manner.*

Throughout its history, case management has had dual sets of goals—one set related to service quality, effectiveness, and service coordination and the other set related to goals of accountability and cost-effective use of resources. Given the perennial dilemma that the service needs of vulnerable populations inevitably exceed the program, staff, and funding resources of human services systems, the equitable allocation of resources as well as coordination of resources remain constant concerns for both direct service case managers and program administrators.

When dealing with clients, the direct service case manager concentrates on providing continuity of service in a way that fits a client's needs and is a justifiable use of service resources (Benjamin and Ben-Dashan, 1982; Weissman, Epstein, and Savage, 1983). The case manager assumes many roles but underlying them is the primary role of "problem solver who acts with and on behalf of clients to assist them to function as independently as possible" (Grisham, White, and Miller, 1983, p. 6). In general then, the "case management function is designed to coordinate the range of services needed . . . in order to assure accountability, continuity of care, accessibility, and efficiency. . . ." (Levine and Fleming, 1984, p. 1).

Synonyms for case management are "service coordination" and "service integration"; the most precise synonym is "client-level service coordination" (Grisham, White, and Miller, 1983). This service coordination for each client is itself a means of service delivery that must account for the effectiveness and efficiency of services to clients, organizations, and funding sources. The primary relationship is between the client and the case manager, but both people will relate to other direct service providers or vendors. In addition, the case manager and occasionally the client will relate to agency administrators (Boserup and Gouge, 1980). Describing this complex system of interrelationships identifies elements of the service network. Case management is an "essential function of a service delivery system"; it gives focus to a definable order of program events and staff responsibilities (Boserup and Gouge, 1980, p. 1). The sine qua non of a case management program is the clients (target population) in need of services and assistance and the "human service network which is utilized for the formal service provision" (Ford, 1983, p. 2).

In practice, case management is a method of placing responsibility for service planning and delivery and system coordination on a person (or a team) who works with the client and frequently his or her family in an ongoing relationship to develop an appropriate service plan, to assure access to services, to monitor service delivery, to advocate for client needs, and to evaluate service outcomes. The major roles assumed by the case manager are those of case coordinator, counselor, and client advocate (Downing, 1979). Increasingly these three roles are seen as a means of empowering the client as well as assuring the provision of services. Advocacy is a means of speaking for and representing the needs of a client. Empowerment builds on and moves beyond advocacy as a facilitating process that enables clients to speak and work effectively for their own needs (Solomon, 1976).

Case management has evolved from the needs of an increasingly complex society and correspondingly complex human services system. Currently called case management, the concept has been used for over a hundred years in the United States under a variety of names, including case coordination, service integration, service coordination, and social service exchange. Occasionally the notion has been subsumed under definitions of social casework. Case management is both a concept and a process. As a concept, it is a system of relationships between direct service providers, agency administrators, and clients. As a process, case management is an orderly, planned provision of services intended to facilitate a client's functioning at as normal a level as possible and as economically as possible. At the core of case management is the question of what is the most effective, most expeditious, and most cost-effective method of restoring a client to a state of equilibrium, that is, ideally to a state where the client can arrange for his or her own care through the existing health and social services institutions of our society.

Historical Antecedents and Development

The roots of case management in the United States can be traced as far back as 1863. The state of Massachusetts in that year established the nation's first board of charities in an effort to coordinate public human services and to conserve public funds used in the care of the poor and the sick. From this earliest reporting one can sense the internal tension of different case management approaches. The desire was to assist the poor but also to guard the public coffers. This tension appears throughout the history of case management. It expresses both the traditional Judeo-Christian value to aid the poor and the homeless and the social stigma that is all too often attached to receiving charity. The desire to provide for people in need is inextricably linked to the duty to use scarce financial and staff resources as efficiently as possible so that the neediest and the largest possible number of the target population can be served. Political or service philosophies sometimes overstress one side of the effectiveness-efficiency equation, but demands for service quality and accountability for resources and service delivery indicate that the balance between the two must be maintained.

Two basic kinds of service coordination can be identified in the early history of the human services. Both early settlement houses and the Charity Organization Societies were involved in case coordination, albeit for different purposes and to different degrees. Settlement houses, such as Jane Addams's Hull House, the Henry Street Settlement in New York, and the University Settlement in Philadelphia were greatly involved in documenting family, immigrant group, and social and neighborhood problems. The case management system was rudimentary—but effective. It consisted of index card files listing each family's needs and involvements; the socialization, recreation, and vocational training groups for children and adults; and the neighborhood issues and environmental problems. Early settlement workers were involved in case and service coordination and advocacy for immigrant and low-income families and in group and community development projects. Service coordination in the settlement movement tended to focus on advocacy and organizing, thus stressing the value of service development and quality service delivery to immigrant populations.

Charity Organization Societies (COSs) concentrated on the efficiency side of the case management equation. The COS movement began in 1877 and became the dominant force in human services by the last decade of the nineteenth century (Lewis, 1973). They held sway until the 1920s, providing services for the poor but stressing, in the language of their day, the need to deliver services efficiently and cost-effectively. The COS movement was the first major effort at interagency cooperation and coordination and can be viewed as the forerunner of today's United Way and sectarian federations of agencies.

The COSs registered client families to ensure the rational and "scientific" administration of charitable relief. The registration bureau kept records on needy families, and these records were cross-checked to assure that a family did not receive two food baskets from different organizations. The focus was charitable but stressed efficiency and the elimination of the redundant use of resources. In fact, many COSs stressed efficiency to such an extent that their staff primarily had a detective role, sniffing out and eradicating fraud (Lewis, 1973). This was case coordination geared to the needs of the service network in contrast to the settlement movement's emphasis on service development and coordination for needy populations.

Thus, although the term *case management* is relatively new, the concern to provide carefully coordinated services for clients of social and human services and to account for service provision and the use of resources has its roots in the record-keeping methods developed in these early movements. Case management issues appear quite early in the social services literature. The social services registry or exchange was the earliest of the formal coordinating mechanisms. Carter states that its purpose was simple and clear: "to prevent cheating and duplication of assistance to the needy poor" (Carter, 1978, p. 2).

However, social services pioneer Mary Richmond broadened the notion of social investigation and indicated needs for more demanding and client-oriented forms of interagency cooperation. In the 1901 *Proceedings of the National Conference on Charities and*

Correction, Richmond described the proliferation of services and the duplication of effort caused by a lack of communication and coordination among the human services agencies of the time:

> It is not enough for charities to refrain from saying disagreeable things about each other; it is not enough for them to make commercial contracts, dividing the burdens of investigation of relief. . . . Real cooperation implies the hearty working together of those who are striving with convictions held in common toward some definite object. . . . We have already seen that this definite object should be the restoration [of the recipient] . . . to a position of independence [Richmond, 1901, pp. 308–309].

In the same article, Richmond diagrams the "forces with which the charity worker may cooperate" (Figure 1) and presents a model that could easily be applied to case management with troubled families more than eighty years later (Richmond, 1901, p. 300).

Richmond's approach clearly fits our present concept of service coordination and is an early conceptualization of case management. Another early leader in social services development and social and business administration was Mary Parker Follett. In Boston she was involved in innovative services through the Boston School Centers. She wrote in *Creative Experience* (1924) and *Dynamic Administration* (1942) about organizing and managing services.

As noted by White (1980), early service pioneers such as Joseph Tuckerman, Jane Addams, and Mary Richmond contributed a strong value orientation to early efforts in case management. Their focus was concern for the client. The "worth of the individual" was the cardinal value, and they supported "direct contact with, and knowledge of those they served and the importance of individualized 'treatment' and of working 'with' clients toward self-support and self sufficiency" (Grisham, White, and Miller, 1983, p. 5).

Figure 1. Mary Richmond's 1901 Model of Case Coordination.

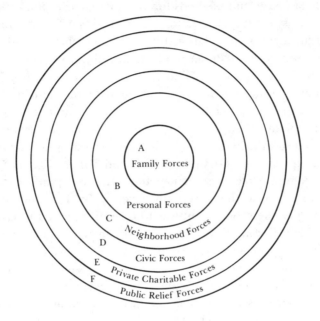

A. Family Forces
  Capacity of each member for
    Affection
    Training
    Endeavor
    Social development

B. Personal Forces
    Kindred
    Friends

C. Neighborhood Forces
    Neighbors, landlords, tradesmen
    Former and present employers
    Clergymen, Sunday-school teachers,
      fellow church members
    Doctors
    Trade-unions, fraternal and benefit
      societies, social clubs, fellow-workmen
    Libraries, educational clubs, classes,
      settlements, and so on
    Thrift agencies, savings banks, stamp-
      savings, building and loan associations

D. Civic Forces
    School teachers, truant officers
    Police, police magistrates, probation
      officers, reformatories

Health department, sanitary inspectors
  factory inspectors
Postmen
Parks, baths, and so on

E. Private Charitable Forces
    Charity organization society
    Church of denomination to which
      family belongs
    Benevolent individuals
    National, special, and general
      relief societies
    Charitable employment agencies
      and work-rooms
    Fresh-air society, children's aid
      society, society for protection
      of children, children's homes, and so on

    District nurses, sick-diet kitchens,
      dispensaries, hospitals, and so on
    Society for suppressing vice, prisoner's
      aid society, and so on

F. Public Relief Force
    Almshouses
    Outdoor poor department
    Public hospitals and dispensaries

Richmond, Addams, and their followers "developed professional standards and methods for systematic collection of information; stressed the importance of trained staff and volunteers; encouraged working relationships with members of other disciplines; and stressed understanding the objectives, methods, and services of other agencies. This led to the development of the case conference, a significant case management mechanism bringing multidisciplinary specialists together to discuss and plan for clients. This problem-solving device necessitated a comprehensive assessment to determine what was needed and who should be involved in providing services" (Grisham, White, and Miller, 1983, p. 5).

A number of case-management-like programs have waxed and waned over the past eighty years. By the mid 1920s the community chest movement was in operation, which was followed by the social planning councils and agency federations. These coordinating agencies were organized to use the welfare resources of communities more effectively (Carter, 1978). Also in the mid 1920s, the newly formed child guidance clinics were experimenting with a team model of service delivery and case coordination. These teams utilized the skills of psychiatrists, social workers, and psychologists and were client-centered forms of case management (Carter, 1978).

Following World War II, Los Angeles pioneered in developing one-stop, multiservice centers to assist veterans in their return home. These centers were staffed by out-stationed representatives of the major public and private service agencies (Carter, 1978). Another significant effort in case management was reported in *The Multiproblem Family Treatment Project* from a St. Paul, Minnesota, project (Birell and others, 1952). Here the initial study finding that 6 percent of the families in the community utilized 50 percent of the public services led to the development of a case management and treatment approach that successfully expedited services, reduced costs, and improved the condition of families. The staff of the project reported that through intensive, family-centered work and aggressive case management, the so-called multiproblem families made significant gains in family functioning (Overton, Tinker, and associates, 1957).

Client-level coordination (that is, case management) came into its own during the 1950s and 1960s, particularly in services for the handicapped and families with internal deviant behavior such as child abuse or juvenile deliquency. During this period the brokerage and advocacy roles of both workers and clients developed with an increasing awareness of individual rights to services and resources so strongly emphasized in the Community Action Programs of that time. Coordination in the early 1970s was aimed at administrative and management levels. Later legislation focusing on specific populations, including the frail elderly, spurred the development of case management programs as we know them today [Grisham, White, and Miller, 1983, p. 5].

Bertsche and Horejsi (1980, p. 94) note that "in the 1950s . . . case coordination became a central concern to those attempting to develop more effective approaches to the multiproblem family. As a result, the use of case conferences as a coordinating device became commonplace." More recent developments derive from the civil rights movement and the War on Poverty programs of the 1960s and 1970s, which changed the passive recipient of service, the "patient," into the active participant, the client or consumer. A mid 1970s demonstration program in New York City designed to integrate and coordinate services for troubled families, the Lower East Side Family Union (LESFU), sought to empower parents and to provide support and service integration through interagency service contracts. These contracts clearly specified that the LESFU worker was the case manager and specifically documented the services and timetables to be met by agencies and the clients. This proved to be a powerful model of case management, one that operated on the basis of both a structured, written contract and a high level of interaction among the participating agencies. The contracts and subsequent documentation of service provision proved to be useful in encouraging collaboration and were felt by clients to be an empowering experience (Weissman and Weil, 1978).

The emphasis on empowerment and consumerism has had a significant impact on worker-client relationships. The focus on empowerment increased joint planning between workers and clients. It also increased worker activity on behalf of clients and heightened worker responsibility to assure access to services that clients requested. The forces of the broad-scale consumer movement of the 1960s and 1970s pressed for direct accountability to consumers for service quality and for governmental action to increase protection of service consumers. Concomitant with these changes was a growing concern for service efficiency on the part of administrators and funding sources. New governmental regulations mandated clearer program accountability and documentation of efficient use of public funds. The case manager or resources coordinator was created by law, but unlike the COS detectives, the coordinator was restrained by law to adhere to rules of confidentiality and clients' rights. The Education for All Handicapped Children Act (Public Law 94-142), enacted in 1975, first formalized a type of case management approach in the nation's school system. Subsequent federal and state legislation has formalized case management for the elderly (the Older Americans Act), the mentally ill (the Community Mental Health Centers Act), and the developmentally disabled (Developmentally Disabled Assistance and Bill of Rights Act, Public Law 94-103).

Today's human services system displays an array of case management models and an accompanying array of case managers and service coordinators. The trend is clearly for expanded use of the case management concept and process. The emergence of case management in the last decade is, as can be seen from this brief history, a reemergence and formalization of an approach to practice and coordination that dates back 100 years in the United States.

The history of case management is best correlated with the industrialization and urbanization of our society and the growth in size and structure of our country's health and social services systems. As a natural consequence of an increasingly complex human services system, case management reflects the human needs and problems of postindustrial society. Case management is a synergism evolving from the concern for humane care of the troubled, disabled, or sick individual combined with concern for the scientific management and conservation of community resources. It seems fair to speculate that case management would not exist if human problems were singular or simple, if they could be resolved with a single intervention, and if the needed interventions were readily available and inexpensive. Most human problems are complex and often chronic. The complexity of individual needs coupled with the complexity of services necessitates a clearly worked out case management approach to assure that clients receive quality services.

Framework for Case Management

Case management has become an increasingly important topic as at-risk populations such as the chronically mentally ill and the developmentally disabled have participated in the movement for deinstitutionalization and moved into community-based systems of care. An examination of the target populations considered in this book indicates that case management is a paramount service objective when the client population is vulnerable or at risk.

For any target population, case management begins with an analysis of client vulnerability and need. The framework for case management tasks and processes is formed by anchoring service philosophy, service objectives, professional values, and worker roles and functions to the analysis of the client population's needs. These essential issues will be discussed in this book as components of the generic process of case management in all fields. The impact of technical and operations considerations on the design of case management systems will also be described.

The process of case management is most important in work with vulnerable populations. Vulnerability refers to conditions that limit the opportunities or independence of clients or that shape their basic life-style. Vulnerability comes in many forms. Children by virtue of their dependence on adults for food, clothing, shelter, guidance, education, support, and love are a vulnerable population. Children must rely on adults to fulfill their basic physical, emotional, and psychological needs. Many older Americans are vulnerable with regard to health care, fiscal resources, and living arrangements. Although many senior citizens can maintain an independent life-style, thousands are in need of skilled health care, support services, and social services. For both of these populations, vulnerability is due to life stage.

When individual needs for care, growth, or support cannot be met by natural support systems, social, health, or mental health services must be provided. Human services programs are thus mediating structures between individuals in need and society; when natural family and community support systems fail, these mediating structures provide for service, advocacy, and basic needs. Case management is the process that provides access to and coordinates needed services. Most often a member of a vulnerable population will need a variety of services; case management ensures that services are provided supportively and with respect for the client. Services should assist in healing or growth and not be degrading, endangering, or chaotic. All professionals involved in case management would do well to attend to a central element of the Hippocratic oath: "Do no harm."

Case management, then, is needed by people whose emotional, physical, or psychological well-being is endangered. Case management is needed for children whose families have not been able to provide adequately for their growth and development or whose parents or guardians have been abusive or neglectful. The well-being of children who have suffered abuse or neglect depends on the interaction and collaboration between the social services system and the family and juvenile court system. The developing policies of permanency planning support a case management process that mandates supportive and rehabilitative services for families so that children can be returned to their parents in an environment that is at least minimally supportive of growth and development. Where reunification is not advisable or feasible, case management under permanency planning must terminate in a timely fashion the rights of parents to the custody of their children and initiate the adoption process so that the children can have a permanent home and a supportive environment. Sensitive and skilled case management is needed in this complex process so that children are not further traumatized.

Older persons with major health, mental health, or disability problems need case management to assure that they receive the services, resources, and care that they require. Isolated older persons may also need a continuous relationship with a case manager as a basic element of social support. In case management with the elderly, needs must be accurately assessed and clients must be introduced to appropriate services.

Other vulnerabilities are due to mental instability or chronic mental illness, mental retardation or other developmental disabilities, chronic health problems, or physical handicaps that impair an individual's ability to live and work independently. In these situations, individuals (and sometimes their families) need case management to locate needed services and to assure that an appropriate and supportive plan is developed and carried out.

The large size and varying needs for service in vulnerable populations indicate that case managers must also serve a gatekeeping function. That is, they must scrupuously screen in those who need services and must carefully determine eligibility and screen out people who do not fit within the target population or whose service needs are not congruent with the capabilities of the service network. Some case management systems will have a specific focus on the most needy, troubled, or debilitated members of the target population whereas others may be designed to provide services to those more likely to respond to rehabilitative efforts. Professional ethics and values as well as societal values and policies shape the focus of service for vulnerable populations.

Any case management system will reflect prevailing social attitudes toward the client population. The development of programs that "mainstream" handicapped children into general public education classes rather than special classes reflects a societal value as well as a social policy. The requirement to husband scarce resources carefully reflects another value and a responsibility for case managers and program supervisors and administrators: the responsibility of applying scarce resources where they will contribute to the desired case management system outcome. There is a tension related to focusing on either the most needy or the most likely to be successfully rehabilitated in a vulnerable population. Professionals in human services may well be responsible for targeting service integration for one subgroup or the other, but they should not cease to pursue the rehabilitation or care and rights of all members of their target population. The need for equitable application of resources and for professionals to be involved in policy development for their service population underscores not only the responsibility of developing cost-effective means of service delivery but the need for a commitment to social justice for members of society who are at risk.

Philosophy for Case Management. A successful case management system needs more than procedures and a general process for coordinating services. It must also be grounded in a philosophy that delineates the relationships between clients and workers and between clients and the system and a philosophy of how and why agencies should and can work together for the benefit of clients. Without such a service philosophy or ideology, it will be extremely difficult for the system to focus on clients' needs and to solve service integration and resource problems. A traditional value of social work is the worth and dignity of the client. Because many clients of case management programs have suffered severe hardships, impairments, or disabilities, it is very important that workers be able to articulate and believe in the integral worth and dignity of each client and the client population. A second basic value is the need for workers to subscribe to a concept of mutual responsibility, that is, the responsibility to human beings for each other (Dromi and Weil, 1984).

From these two primary values are derived supporting values for case management practice: participation of clients in decision-making processes, self-determination, and the empowerment of clients (Dromi and Weil, 1984). Because many clients of case management programs have serious vulnerabilities, it is crucial that staff have a sense of hope about them. Although total independence is the general goal, some clients with severe problems such as mental illness, developmental disabilities, or other impairments will not be able to achieve a fully independent life; however, setting realistic goals and establishing a sense of the possibilities of growth for all human beings or for humane care are necessary components of the philosophy of all case management systems. Lamb (1982) cautions that some chronic mental health clients may not be able to handle the pressures to become fully active and that therapists should be aware of the bind in which they can put clients through their own ambition. Children with severe developmental disabilities will not "grow out of" the problem and greatly need supportive care.

Levine and Fleming (1984, p. 8) provide the following philosophical ground rules for developing case management programs:

1. The needs of individual clients are unique and wide ranging and vary over time; therefore, the system must be flexible.
2. Clients can function in the community when provided with varying degrees of support and should be encouraged to function as independently as possible.
3. Clients should be encouraged to assume an active, rather than passive, role in the case management process.

4. Case management is not a time-limited service, but rather is ongoing and provides clients with what they need, when they need it, and when they want it for as long as necessary.

Goals and Objectives for Case Management Systems. The most basic goal of any case management program is to provide the best possible quality of service as efficiently and as cost-effectively as possible. Structurally, case management systems are composed of three elements: service effectiveness, service efficiency, and cost-effectiveness. The interaction of these elements in shaping case management tasks and service integration methods is illustrated in Figure 2.

It may be helpful to bear in mind that the strength of a triangle is the tension inherent in its construction. For a case management program to be effective and to survive, each of the structural elements must be attended to. The focus should be on the client and

Figure 2. Structural Elements of Case Management.

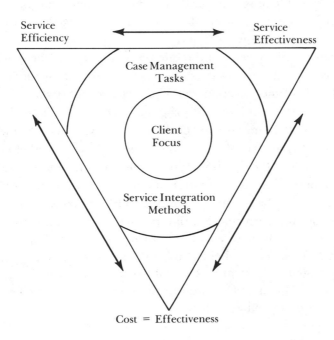

the development of service integration, but none of these structural elements can be overlooked without imperiling the program.

Goals state the desired outcomes of a service plan or a program, and objectives state the means that will be employed to meet the goals. Case management programs need to have goals and objectives directed to all three of the structural elements at both the direct service coordination level for individual clients and at the program level for the entire population being served. As a means of evaluating the effects and effectiveness of programs, these goals and objectives directed toward service effectiveness and efficiency and cost-effectiveness need to be stated in ways that are observable or measurable. Other objectives of a case management system pertain to system maintenance and development and to client needs and service development.

At the microlevel or individual-client level of service delivery, specific (and measurable) goals and objectives must be set for each client. However, one common goal should be to enable the individual to function as independently as possible, or to have a high standard of supportive care if independence is not a feasible goal (Levine and Fleming, 1984). To accomplish that goal, objectives will need to specify measurable means of increasing the continuity of service and of integrating services according to each client's need. The accountability goals at the microlevel relate to assuring that a client receives the services she or he needs and that those services are provided in a timely fashion and on a cost-effective basis.

At the macrolevel or program level, specific goals and objectives will be needed for both the quality of service and the accountability aspects of case management practice. On the quality assurance side of the equation, system objectives include (1) encouraging a productive collaboration among agencies and programs that are part of the service network; (2) building consensus within the network for definition of primary client needs and methods for solving or dealing with client's problems; (3) structuring work to benefit staff as well as clients; and (4) building and maintaining a case management system that is stable enough to provide support for clients and dynamic enough to promote growth and change in organizations as well as in clients.

With regard to accountability, case management systems will need measurable goals and objectives that relate to (1) defining and implementing cost-effective services; (2) developing adequate information and reporting procedures; (3) establishing the appropriate technology to support management information and cost accounting systems; and (4) establishing a measurable system for management by objectives.

In addition, the case management program will need specified goals and objectives dealing with the service delivery processes of client assessment, service planning and implementation, monitoring and evaluation. At the program level, measurable objectives will also be needed to evaluate client benefits and system interaction. Evaluations might be carried out internally or by contracting with an independent agency.

Roles. The selected set of roles that a case manager takes on in any system largely determines the nature and emphasis of service integration and coordination. A role is an expected set of behaviors within a specific context (Biddle, 1979). The set of roles adopted by the case manager is the primary focus here, but these roles are enacted in the context of agency functions and positions. Each of the following essential agency positions has some responsibility in case management:

1. *Administrator.* Responsible for overall program accountability (service effectiveness, service efficiency, and cost-effectiveness). May be involved in the design of the case management system and the negotiation of contracts that specify functions, responsibilities, and decision-making authority.
2. *Planner.* May be a member of staff or a consultant. Responsible for analyzing the service network, service needs, and gaps in service and for designing the case management system to fit the needs of the target population, service network resources, the means of operation, and the accountability for services.
3. *Manager.* Responsible for seeing that the case management system operates. May be at level of middle management or first-line management. Responsible for identifying and correcting problems in task accomplishment and interactional processes.

4. *Evaluator.* May be combined with planner or administrator or may be a separate role depending on the size of the program. Essentially responsible for analyzing the overall effectiveness and efficiency of the program. Should be on-line from the beginning of program development so that research and evaluation can be built into the program design.

5. *Case manager or direct service coordinator.* Essential, ongoing case management role that is organized around the service needs of a specific client. Typically has a caseload and is responsible for moving clients through the service system. Must be concerned with planning services to clients, coordinating service delivery, and monitoring and evaluating the effects and effectiveness of the service.

Direct service case managers then adopt various roles. The set of roles assumed by the case manager can be quite complex. As Levine and Fleming (1984) note, the set of roles carried out in a particular program depends on the target population, the types of services available, the model of coordination and decision making, and the expectations of the program. The case manager provides information and feedback to the people occupying the positions listed above and assumes the vital responsibility of assuring that clients receive and benefit from services. Various authors (Downing, 1979; Kemp, 1981; White, 1983; Grisham, White, and Miller, 1983; and Weissman, Epstein, and Savage, 1983) have discussed and emphasized the particular roles or role sets needed in case management practice. Figure 3 presents the configuration of service provision roles that case managers need to assume. Each role is essential, but the primary focus of the roles differs. Some, such as advocate or broker, focus most directly on specific client needs. Some, including consultant, community or service organizer, and colleague or collaborator, focus primarily on intervention in the service network and interaction with the staff from other agencies. Other roles such as evaluator and record keeper focus most directly on the case management system itself.

As can be seen in Figure 3, a large number of roles is required

Figure 3. Service Provision Roles of Case Managers.

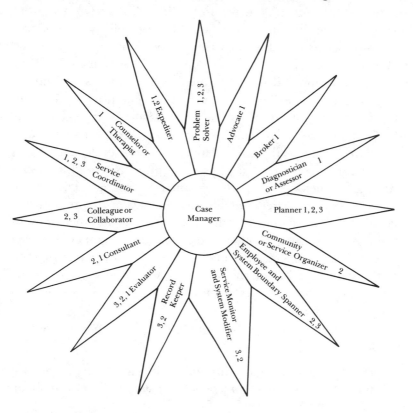

1. Major responsibility to client
2. Major responsibility to service network
3. Major responsibility to case management program

The first number listed with each role indicates the major focus of role responsibility to either (1) the client, (2) the service network, or (3) the case management program itself. When more than one focus of responsibility is noted, the second and third numbers indicate an important function but not the primary area of role responsibility.

to make case management an effective service. The combination of these roles in a workable model for interaction with clients, the service network, and the case management system is the most complex task facing the case manager. Although different systems emphasize different roles, it would be difficult indeed to carry out a case management program if any of these roles were not performed somewhere within the case management system. In many case management programs, the individual case manager will be expected to assume all the illustrated roles; in others, specialized staff may take on part of such functions as planning, evaluating, and record keeping. Establishing role clarity is critical for the effectiveness of a case management program. Program administrators and case managers need to have a common understanding of the specific role set required in their program and need to ensure that other agencies participating in the case management system, their staff, and the clients of the case management program are cognizant of roles assumed by the case managers and their responsibilities as advocates for clients and boundary spanners between agencies. The case manager is an employee of one specific program, but the nature of his or her work requires intervention in the operations of other agencies as they perform services for clients of the case management program.

The major responsibilities of these service provision roles are as follows:

1. *Problem solver.* "Acts with and on behalf of clients to assist them to function as independently as possible" (Grisham, White, and Miller, 1983, p. 6).
2. *Advocate.* Represents clients and helps them speak for themselves.
3. *Broker.* Arranges for and sets conditions for service delivery.
4. *Diagnostician or assessor.* Analyzes client's situation, needs, and system arrangements that will facilitate or impede service delivery; recommends services and initial plans for care.
5. *Planner.* Designs case plans, treatment, service integration, and agency collaboration to meet the needs of clients and the service network.
6. *Community or service organizer.* Develops arrangements to facilitate interagency cooperation and coordination and/or plans for needed services with agencies and citizens.
7. *Employee and system boundary spanner.* Occupies a specific position to provide service coordination; must move beyond

the agency to develop coordination and collaboration with agency members of the service network.

8. *Service monitor and system modifier.* Keeps track of what goes well and what does not in case management and in the interagency collaboration process. Studies effects on a particular client and on the overall target population and service network. Identification of problems is key to correcting them.

9. *Record keeper.* Documents what happens to clients and to case service coordination, agency interaction, and interagency coordination efforts.

10. *Evaluator.* Analyzes effectiveness of services for individual clients, for the caseload, and for the service network.

11. *Consultant.* Analyzes organizational or client problems and develops strategies to solve them.

12. *Colleague and collaborator.* Develops productive working relationships within the service agency and service network to help accomplish tasks.

13. *Service coordinator.* Sees that things work, that client needs and provided services mesh, and that monitoring, feedback, and evaluation take place.

14. *Counselor or therapist.* Provides support, mental health interventions, and consultation to assist clients in decision making and planning.

15. *Expeditor.* Secures cooperation, carries out tasks, and analyzes results (Weissman, Epstein, and Savage, 1983).

The successful performance of these case management roles depends on support from the leaders of the case management program and from cooperating agencies and on the case manager's ability to master the specific knowledge and skills required to accomplish the complex tasks of case management.

The service provision roles described will generally fit most fields of human services practice. However, there may be additional roles that are field specific. For example, in health settings, in addition to the roles described, case managers may act as health educators and health monitors and may even administer medication and monitor patients' reactions to drugs and other treatments.

In some case management programs, the critical role for the professional case manager will be that of supervisor. If programs typically use paraprofessionals, program aides, student interns, or volunteers, the supervisory role will carry responsibility for the quality and accountability of the service. If the professional role is that of supervisor, she or he will be responsible for ensuring that staff follow the procedures, policies, and practices of the program; that clients receive adequate service in terms of quality and timeliness; and that workers effectively carry out their roles of service provision and accountability.

In addition to their roles as service providers, case managers also have multiple roles related to accountability and cost-effectiveness. This role set includes: (1) gatekeeper (eligibility determination and service access); (2) information manager; (3) resource manager and conservator; (4) record keeper; (5) contract monitor; and (6) cost and service monitor. The case manager inevitably adopts a gatekeeping role in determining an individual's eligibility for service. They also monitor continued eligibility if status is subject to change. Most significantly, case managers control client's access to needed service resources.

As information managers, they transmit information to clients and to agencies in the service system. Frequently this information relates to accountability. Information is a source not only of knowledge but also of power in a service system. As a resource manager and conservator, the case manager is responsible for judicious and equitable use of the components of the service system and other entitlements. If service resources are scarce, the decision to provide one client with a full range of services may well mean that other clients receive fewer types of service or diminished quality of service. Conservation of resources refers also to service system maintenance.

In keeping records, the case manager documents service use, service problems, and cost-benefit information. Records may be used by program evaluators to determine the efficiency of the case management program itself and of constituent agencies. The record-keeping function whether accomplished by note taking, formal typed reports, or a computer-assisted, interactive information system is the backbone of any case management program, for it provides the documentation of service delivery in terms of both quality assurance and fiscal accountability.

Acting as a contract monitor, a case manager may oversee the provision of services and the allocation of the resources and costs of other programs. For example, in child welfare programs, a case manager from a public protective service unit may oversee and monitor the services of a residential treatment center in which dependent children are placed. Monitoring may relate to the carrying out of contracted services for one or more specific clients or may involve a specialized function in monitoring contracts and grants. The bottom line in accountability is the monitoring of service costs within the case management program itself, through the service network and as illustrated perhaps through formal contracts for service provision. As a cost and service monitor, a protective service worker from the public sector may be responsible to assure that private agencies in the case management system are actually providing the services they claim to provide in a timely, appropriate, and cost-effective fashion. Frequently case managers will carry many of these responsibilities, and in large service systems, specialists may be responsible for aggregate record keeping, information management, and cost accounting. In filling these roles, case managers are protecting the public coffers or husbanding the resources of voluntary sector agencies and programs. Thus in the service provision and accountability roles, each case manager is a microcosm of the historical tension between service quality and service costs. If the case manager is able to see the necessity of both roles and understand that without the accountability functions, the service provision functions would be greatly weakened, then he or she will be able to balance these two role sets in a constructive and productive manner that can benefit both clients and programs.

Tasks and Skills. As the descriptions of roles in case management imply, people working as case managers need the knowledge and skills to perform varied tasks. Some tasks relate primarily to the client, others to the maintenance of the case management system, and still others to the facilitation of the service network. Many of these tasks can be derived directly from the role descriptions. There are other basic tasks that relate to carrying out the process of case management. Bertsche and Horejsi (1980, pp. 96–97) conducted research to identify these basic tasks through intensive interviews with skilled case managers. As a result of their study they classified thirteen basic tasks for case coordination:

1. complete the initial interviews with the client and his or her family to assess the client's eligibility for services;
2. gather relevant and useful data from the client, family, other agencies, and so on to formulate a psychosocial assessment of the client and his or her family;
3. assemble and guide group discussions and decision-making sessions among relevant professionals and program representatives, the client and his or her family, and significant others to formulate goals and design an integrated intervention plan;
4. monitor adherence to the plan and manage the flow of accurate information within the action system to maintain a goal orientation and coordination momentum;
5. provide "follow-along" to the client and his or her family to speed identification of unexpected problems in service delivery and to serve as a general troubleshooter on behalf of the client;
6. provide counseling and information to help the client and his or her family in situations of crisis and conflict with service providers;
7. provide ongoing emotional support to the client and his or her family so they can cope better with problems and utilize professionals and complex services;
8. complete the necessary paperwork to maintain documentation of client progress and adherence to the plan by all concerned;
9. act as a liaison between the client and his or her family and all relevant professionals, programs, and informal resources involved in the overall intervention plan to help the client make his or her preferences known and secure the services needed;
10. act as a liaison between programs, providing services to the client to ensure the smooth flow of information and minimize conflict between the subsystems;
11. establish and maintain credibility and good public relations with significant formal and informal resource systems to mobilize resources for current and future clients;

12.   perform effectively and as a "good bureaucrat"
      within the organization to be in a position to
      develop and modify policies and procedures
      affecting clients and the effectiveness of the
      service delivery system; and
13.   secure and maintain the respect and support of
      those in positions of authority so their influence
      can be enlisted on behalf of the client and used,
      when necessary, to encourage other individuals
      and agencies to participate in the coordination
      effort.

Subsequent chapters of this book will address the specific
knowledge bases, skills, and tasks needed to be an effective case
manager in specific fields of human services practice. There are,
however, some general skills for case management that apply to all
fields. Skills are typically categorized in relation to people, data, and
things. Most jobs will have aspects that relate to all three categories.
Case management tasks and roles demand high skill levels with
both data management and intervention and interaction with other
people. Clinically a variety of skills are needed to work with the
client in assessing need, planning for services, and seeing that
services are provided. This is a major area of skill for case managers.
Equally as important is the ability to intervene effectively with
other professionals in the service network to contract for, assure
access to, and monitor services that clients receive. Interprofessional
collaboration requires major skills in negotiating, planning, monitoring, group facilitating, and decision making (Weil, 1979).
Effective collaboration with members of other professions and
vocations also requires an understanding of the values, knowledge
base, and service orientation of each occupational group (Weil,
1977). As Grisham, White, and Miller (1983) have noted, the major
skills in case management are those of a problem solver able to work
with and relate to problems in technical, clinical, and service design
areas. Kane (1975) identified skill needs in personal flexibility and
a positive orientation toward intake, referral, and information-
sharing processes. Downing (1979) highlighted skills in counseling,
coordinating, and advocacy. Bertsche and Horejsi (1980) highlight:
(1) clinical skills such as crisis intervention and mediation methods;
(2) system intervention skills related to policy analysis, consultation, and organizational change; and (3) data management skills

related to record keeping, preparing written reports, and writing behavioral objectives. For case managers, learning to use data management skills in the service of and for the benefit of vulnerable clients is a key skill and one that effectively merges the dual focus on accountability and quality of service.

Suggested Readings

Benjamin, M., and Ben-Dashan, T. "Case Management: Implications and Issues." In C. Sanborn (Ed.), *Case Management in Mental Health Services*. New York: Haworth, 1982.

Bertsche, A. V., and Horejsi, C. R. "Coordination of Client Services." *Social Work*, March 1980, pp. 94–98.

Lamb, H. R. "Therapists–Case Managers: More Than Brokers of Service." *Hospital and Community Psychiatry*, 1980, *31*, 762–764.

McGowan, B. G. "The Case Advocacy Function in Child Welfare Practice." *Child Welfare*, 1978, *57*, 275–284.

Overton, A., and Tinker, K., and associates. *The Casework Notebook*. St. Paul, Minn.: Community Chest and Councils, 1957.

Ozarin, L. "The Pros and Cons of Case Management." In J. Talbott (Ed.), *The Chronic Mental Patient*. Washington, D.C.: American Psychiatric Association, 1978.

Stein, T. J. "Macro and Micro Level Issues in Case Management." In National Conference on Social Welfare, *Case Management: State of the Art*. Final report to Administration on Developmental Disabilities. Washington, D.C.: U.S. Department of Health and Human Services, April 15, 1981.

Weissman, H. *Integrating Services for Troubled Families: Dilemmas of Program Design and Implementation*. San Francisco: Jossey-Bass, 1978.

Weissman, H., Epstein, I., and Savage, A. *Agency-Based Social Work: Neglected Aspects of Clinical Practice*. Philadelphia: Temple University Press, 1983.

References

Benjamin, M., and Ben-Dashan, T. "Case Management: Implications and Issues." In C. Sanborn (Ed.), *Case Management in Mental Health Services*. New York: Haworth, 1982.

Bertsche, A. V., and Horejsi, C. R. "Coordination of Client Services." *Social Work,* March 1980, pp. 94–98.

Biddle, B. J. *Role Theory: Expectations, Identities, and Behaviors.* New York: Academic Press, 1979.

Birell, W. J., and others. *Multiproblem Family Treatment Project.* St. Paul, Minn.: Wesley J. Birell and Associates, 1952.

Boserup, D. G., and Gouge, G. V. *The Case Management Model: Concept, Implementation, and Training.* Athens, Ga.: Regional Institute of Social Welfare Research, 1980.

Carter, G. "Service Coordination: Recycling of Tested Concepts." In *Case Coordination and Service Integration Projects: Client Impact, Program Survival, and Research Priorities.* Los Angeles: Social Policy Laboratory, Andrus Gerontology Center, University of Southern California, 1978.

Downing, R. *Three Working Papers* ("An Exploration of Case Manager Roles: Coordinator, Advocate and Counselor," "Issues of Client Assessment in Coordination Programs," and "Client Pathway"). Los Angeles: Social Policy Laboratory, Andrus Gerontology Center, University of Southern California, 1979.

Dromi, P., and Weil, M. "Social Group Work Values: Their Role in a Technological Age." Paper presented at the 6th Annual Symposium of Social Work with Groups, Chicago, October 1984.

Follett, M. P. *Creative Experience.* New York: Longman, 1924.

Follett, M. P. *Dynamic Administration: The Collected Papers of Mary Parker Follett.* (H. Metcalf and L. Urick, Eds.) New York: Harper & Row, 1942.

Ford, K. "Process and Tasks in Developing a Management Information System in a Case Management Agency." Unpublished paper, School of Social Work, University of Southern California, May 1983.

Grisham, M., White, M., and Miller, L. S. "An Overview of Case Management." MSSP Evaluation Unit, University Extension, University of California, Berkeley, April 29, 1983.

Kane, R. *Training for Teamwork.* Manpower Monograph No. 9. Syracuse, N.Y.: Syracuse University School of Social Work, 1975, pp. 16–26.

Kemp, B. "The Case Management Model in Human Service Delivery." In E. Pan, T. E. Backer, and C. L. Vash (Eds.), *Annual*

Review of Rehabilitation. Vol. 2. New York: Springer, 1981.

Lamb, H. R. *Treating the Long-Term Mentally Ill.* San Francisco: Jossey-Bass, 1982.

Levine, I. S., and Fleming, M. *Human Resource Development: Issues in Case Management.* Baltimore: Center of Rehabilitation and Manpower Services, University of Maryland, 1984.

Lewis, V. S. "Charity Organization Society." In *Encyclopedia of Social Work.* (16th ed.) Vol. 1. Washington, D.C.: National Association of Social Workers, 1973.

Overton, A., and Tinker, K., and associates. *The Casework Notebook.* St. Paul, Minn.: Community Chest and Councils, 1957.

Richmond, M. E. "Charitable Co-Operation." In I. C. Barrows (Ed.), *Proceedings of the National Conference of Charities and Correction.* Boston: George H. Ellis, 1901.

Solomon, B. B. *Black Empowerment: Social Work in Oppressed Communities.* New York: Columbia University Press, 1976.

Weil, M. *Practicum in Law and Social Work: An Educational Program in Interprofessional Education.* Ann Arbor, Mich.: University Microfilms, 1977.

Weil, M. "Interprofessional Work in Adoptions Practice: Collaboration and Beyond." *Social Work Papers,* 1979, *15,* 46–54.

Weissman, H. H. *Integrating Services for Troubled Families: Dilemmas of Program Design and Implementation.* San Francisco: Jossey-Bass, 1978.

Weissman, H., and Weil, M. "Successes and Failures in Integrating Services and Helping Families." In H. H. Weissman, *Integrating Services for Troubled Families: Dilemmas of Program Design and Implementation.* San Francisco: Jossey-Bass, 1978.

Weissman, H., Epstein, I., and Savage, A. *Agency-Based Social Work: Neglected Aspects of Clinical Practice.* Philadelphia: Temple University Press, 1983.

White, M. "Toward a Conceptual Framework for Case Coordination Program Designs: Lessons from the Past, Guidelines for the Future." Unpublished doctoral dissertation, School of Social Work, University of Southern California, June 1980.

White, M. "Decision Determinants in MSSP Client Movement." Unpublished manuscript, MSSP Evaluation Unit, University Extension, University of California, Berkeley, January 1983.

2

❧❧❧❧❧❧❧❧❧❧❧❧❧❧❧

Key Components
in Providing Efficient
and Effective Services

Marie Weil

The essential functions of case management are present in some form in all case management programs. These functions are carried out by case managers through involvement with the client and collaborative work with agencies and programs in the service network. Figure 1 presents the progression of functions necessary to effectively deliver services to clients from vulnerable populations. The eight basic case management functions are (1) client identification and outreach, (2) individual assessment and diagnosis, (3) service planning and resource identification, (4) linking client to needed services, (5) service implementation and coordination, (6) monitoring service delivery, (7) advocacy, and (8) evaluation. As the figure illustrates, the case management process is a means of problem solving for each client through a series of logically connected steps involving service planning, delivery, and evaluation.

To complete the basic problem-solving process, the case manager is continually involved with the client and with the

Figure 1. The Functions and Process of Case Management.

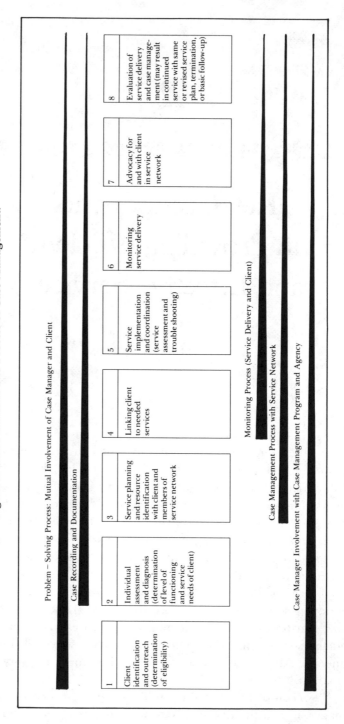

Problem – Solving Process: Mutual Involvement of Case Manager and Client

Case Recording and Documentation

1	2	3	4	5	6	7	8
Client identification and outreach (determination of eligibility)	Individual assessment and diagnosis (determination of level of functioning and service needs of client)	Service planning and resource identification with client and members of service network	Linking client to needed services	Service implementation and coordination (service assessment and trouble shooting)	Monitoring service delivery	Advocacy for and with client in service network	Evaluation of service delivery and case management (may result in continued service with same or revised service plan, termination, or basic follow-up)

Monitoring Process (Service Delivery and Client)

Case Management Process with Service Network

Case Manager Involvement with Case Management Program and Agency

agency sponsoring the case management program. These major interactions are supported by three component processes necessary to carry through the eight functions. Case managers must be involved in *(a)* recording and documenting the case; *(b)* monitoring service delivery and monitoring the client; and *(c)* interacting with agencies involved in the service network. These supportive processes provide information and feedback that enable the case manager to take corrective, problem-solving action. Each of the basic eight functions is necessary to assure effective, efficient services for clients.

> Case management is not an event; it is a process which is flexible and should be tailored to meet local needs and demands. While the activities are relatively standard, case management may take on dramatically different shades of emphasis depending upon such factors as: the richness and nature of services available in a specific locale; how the inventory of services is controlled; the geography of the area in which case management operates; the existence of other case management systems . . . ; purchase of service capability; and the value system which informs the behavior of case managers" [National Conference on Social Welfare, 1981, p. 20].

Client Identification and Outreach. Any case management program must first identify its target population and individual clients within this population. The client or the client's family might request service, or another agency in the service network might see a need for specific services and case management (Levine and Fleming, 1984). In many programs, whether a potential client is eligible for inclusion in the case management program is determined in the initial interview (Boserup and Gouge, 1980; Stein, 1981). Some populations in need of case management services, particularly the chronically mentally ill, do not actively seek them. Levine and Fleming (1984) point out that this fact places a responsibility on the case manager to be "aggressive and creative" in reaching out to potential clients. These authors note that homeless mentally ill persons "can be encouraged to secure case management services when these services are offered on-site in soup kitchens. Case management services can also be 'marketed' when mentally ill persons apply for Social Security Disability Income" (p. 10).

Individual Assessment or Diagnosis. This assessment determines the course of case management for the individual. In this assessment, the worker establishes a relationship with the client and develops the data base that will be used for subsequent service planning. The worker carefully determines the client's level of functioning, social supports, service needs, and attitudes toward service. Because case management frequently deals with vulnerable and abused or overprotected populations, it is important that the case manager assess not only the client's current level of functioning but also his or her probable "highest level of functioning" (Levine and Fleming, 1984, p. 10). For clients of the mental health system, this may require information on the client's highest level of functioning before the client's mental health crisis and involvement with the mental health system. For other populations, such as those with developmental disabilities or physical handicaps who state an interest in developing independent living skills, the assessment should include current functioning levels, aspects of the environment that may have hindered the development of skills and responsibilities, and the probable level of functioning that is possible with supportive services and training in independent living skills.

The case manager may carry out the clinical assessment or rely additionally or exclusively on assessments by other professionals. The client should always be actively involved in the assessment process. If clients perceive case management as a shared problem-solving process, they will be much more involved in their own assessment, service planning, and growth. Although the case manager may use several information sources about the client, such as "hospital or agency records, court proceedings, family, friends, and therapists," it is essential to bear in mind that "these sources should be used only with the knowledge and consent of the client" (Levine and Fleming, 1984, p. 11).

The format and emphasis of an assessment depend on the general needs of the target population, the specific needs of the client, and the client's present and possible functioning. Assessments may be done by an individual, compiled from a variety of sources, or completed by an interdisciplinary team. Some problem areas require a team (Scott and Cassidy, 1981). However this responsibility is divided, it is important that the case manager be actively involved in an assessment. The importance of assessing functioning and need accurately gives weight to the argument favoring the professional training of case managers. Finally, the decisions made in the concluding assessment will determine the type of service plan developed and the degree of case manager involvement in service delivery and monitoring.

Service Planning and Resource Identification. The comprehensive service plan states the steps and issues involved in service delivery, monitoring, and evaluation. It is based on information obtained in the assessment. Because resource identification should be an integral part of service planning, the case manager needs to know what services exist that can help meet a client's needs. If an ideal plan is developed but most resources are lacking in the system, the plan cannot be carried out. In some settings the case manager is the primary service planner for the client; in other settings, a treatment team may be responsible for service planning. Even if the case manager is not the principal planner, he or she should be highly involved in the planning process and see that clients are involved as much as possible in developing the service plan (Intagliata, 1982; Marlowe, 1982). Involving the client in the planning process can be a major step in advocacy.

Although the particulars of service plans vary greatly, several items are necessary:

1. clearly defined priority areas for needed services;
2. within each of these areas, short- and long-term measurable objectives which can be used to evaluate client progress;
3. specific actions which must be taken to reach these goals;
4. agencies to which client will be referred and, if possible, specific individuals within those agencies who will be contacted;
5. realistic time frames for completing activities; and

6. identification of potential barriers to service utili-
    zation and delivery (for example, admission crite-
    ria, client attitudes or resistance, nonexistent
    services) and proposed solutions to these prob-
    lems [Levine and Fleming, 1984, p. 13; see also
    Kemp, 1981; Bradfield and Dame, 1982].

Linking Clients to Needed Services. Connecting clients to
services that they need is a critical function in case management.
Especially since many populations needing case management are by
definition vulnerable and sometimes unable to make service connections themselves, the case manager's handling of this role usually
determines the style and tone of interaction with the service network. Linking is not simply making a referral—"it requires doing
whatever is necessary to get the client to the service" (Levine and
Fleming, 1984, p. 13). The case manager may have to transport the
client physically or make sure that the client is transported to the
service agency and even go through the other agency's intake
process with the client. These concrete services are sometimes
viewed as nonprofessional, but they are essential in making sure
that clients get the services they need. In some agencies paraprofessionals, interns, or case aides go with a client signing up for services
or assist the client in intake at another agency. If the case manager
does not personally perform this function, he or she must see to it
that the function is carried through. This linking role often differs
from the classic view of the mental health professional role.
According to Lamb (1980, 1982), seeing that linkage occurs is a basic
element in clinical practice. Several discussions of case management
stress the linkage function almost to the exclusion of the clinical
function. In some programs, clinicians handle assessment and
diagnosis, and the case manager handles linkage and follow-up
(Caragonne, 1983).

To make the linking function work, the case manager may
have to use both formal and informal mechanisms (Bradfield and
Dame, 1982). Examples of formal mechanisms include "interagency
agreements that spell out the roles and responsibilities of each
agency, admissions criteria, and other provisions for agency collaboration on behalf of clients" (Levine and Fleming, 1984, p. 13).
Typical informal mechanisms include "working agreements or

understandings between the staff of different programs and are often critical to a successful referral" (p. 14). Formal arrangement for service and the clout of the case manager and his or her agency are needed to see that the linkage function works effectively. *Clout* is the power to see that an agreement is carried through. Numerous studies of case management indicate that this power is essential to case management success (see Chapter Eight of this book; also Grisham, White, and Miller, 1983). In addition to the formal sanction and agreements for service, case managers need personal skills in communication, negotiation, and interprofessional collaboration.

Service Implementation and Coordination. Implementation is most simply getting the work done through the service plan and established procedures. *Coordination* is defined as arranging something "in the proper relative position" or carrying out a complex task through "harmonious adjustment or interaction" (*American Heritage Dictionary,* 2d ed., under the entry "coordination"). For case management purposes, coordination involves seeing that the service plan is carried out and that the agency interactions and service delivery benefit the client and are in accordance with service agreements. Much of the literature on case management overlooks this process and merely assumes it. However, the complexity of service delivery requires that this process not be taken for granted. Implementing a service means that the case manager follows up on the service plan and linkage and sees to it that a planned service is carried out. Usually the case manager will not provide most of the basic services; instead he or she will be working with the client and coordinating services. Coordination entails troubleshooting in the service network as the client's service plan is implemented. Coordination can range from the mundane, such as resolving the problem that two needed services are available only on Thursday afternoons, to the complex, such as getting two agencies that have not previously collaborated to work together to serve clients of the case management agency.

Getting all the pieces of the service plan in place so that they are carried out in a logical sequence is the heart of service coordination. The case manager must make sure that items in the service plan are carried out and attend to the interpersonal and interprofessional aspects of the services. Careful documentation and record keeping are important elements of coordination, as are formal and informal meetings with professionals and service providers. Maintaining a close relationship with the client is also critical to service coordination. A client's experiences with an agency may be quite different from the experiences of visiting professionals. Clients' reactions to service provision and service coordination are important variables in the case management process.

The degree of power inherent in coordinating adds to its importance. Formal and informal agreements are frequently basic parts of a case management program, but the authority to cut through impending regulations, to set up more responsive procedures, or to change how agencies relate to each other or their clients requires authority. The degree of authority vested in the case management program and in the case manager will be a major factor in the success or failure of any case management program.

Monitoring Service Delivery. The general definition of *monitor* is to oversee or supervise or "to scrutinize or check systematically with a view to collecting certain specified categories of data" (*American Heritage Dictionary,* 2d ed., under the entry "monitor"). In case management, monitoring is a core function that is often difficult to carry out. "The objectives of the monitoring function are to assure that the client is receiving the expected services and that these services are necessary and appropriate for the client. This requires that the case manager maintain ongoing contact with both the client and the service provider" (Levine and Fleming, 1984, p. 14). Performing this function requires that the case manager be involved with the client while the client is participating in other services and programs. If a sound relationship with the client has been established, monitoring can be accomplished without undue stress. The client needs to understand that the case manager is not maliciously getting involved in the client's private affairs but is making sure that things are going as well as possible and that any problems in service delivery are resolved.

The difficult part of monitoring is to oversee the work of staff in other agencies and programs. Supervision is typically an administrative process tied into program and worker evaluation. Administrative sanctions are likely to apply if a worker does not fulfill job tasks in ways that seem appropriate to the agency's mission and goals. However, staff in contracted service agencies often view the case management program goals as extraneous to their own. Consequently, the case manager who is monitoring a contracted service may be viewed as an intruder. Authority and clout are essential for effective service monitoring. To find out what is going wrong is necessary but not sufficient; it is critical for the client's well-being that the case manager be empowered to intervene to get service delivery back on track.

Weissman, Epstein, and Savage (1983, p. 103) graphically describe monitoring and coordination as the most difficult parts of case management, but they do note that requests for ordinary service can usually be met without major difficulty. However,

> The request for extraordinary service, such as the waiving of eligibility requirements, will often be resisted. Nevertheless, it is a common experience to have other agencies, other departments, and other professionals promise to deliver services and not come through, for a variety of reasons: other priorities emerge from their department and agencies; they do not understand the overall pattern of a particular client's needs and how they fit into it; they are negligent, or in some cases indifferent; or they choose to interpret rules and procedures rigidly.
>
> The problems of monitoring are obvious. How does the case manager gain the authority to order a doctor or nurse to do something? How does a case manager get the authority to ensure that the city housing department provides an apartment? How does a case manager ensure that educational remediation is given when promised?

It helps if the case manager is skilled in interprofessional collaboration and competent in expediting problems; however, all the charisma in the world will not improve poor services or compensate for an agency's refusal to perform a needed service. Here the case management system and its administrators must come to the aid of the case manager. Although solving problems in service delivery is not likely to be simple, several steps can be taken in the case management program to assure that difficulties can be worked out. When service network leaders are committed to case management and interagency cooperation, written agreements or contracts can grant the case manager and the case management program authority to intervene in another program. Within a multiservice center, all staff involved are likely to be close enough and under the same authority so that problems can be resolved. Some programs use a variant of matrix management, which cuts across task boundaries. Where possible it is useful to develop agency contracts. This will automatically take place if the case management agency pays for specific services, but even if there is not a financial contract, it is often possible to work out interagency agreements that facilitate case management monitoring.

Other strategies are to use interagency teams to plan, implement, and monitor all services in the network. Such teams can be powerful advocates for clients and monitors of the system. A less formal strategy is the time-honored case conference. At such a conference, service providers discuss the case, individual goals, and the overall goals for the client. This process can lead to informal agreements on providing services and selecting structures to work out problems. In this instance, "the particular service providers come to an interprofessional agreement that is dependent on the goodwill and professional concern that develops out of the group process" (Weissman, Epstein, and Savage, 1983, p. 104).

A more formal way of monitoring services is to use a dual-contract system: an interagency contract that spells out basic roles and responsibilities and a specific contract for each client. Working out such contracts involves meeting with all service providers, drafting a contract specifying the responsibilities of each agency or worker, and having the assigned worker and an administrator sign the agreement (Weissman and Weil, 1978). Having various staff members participate in the contracting process lowers the threat to each agency's autonomy. The process involves negotiation and renegotiation. If a representative worker decides not to sign such a contract, problems will have to be handled through administrative mediation. In some agencies, such as the Lower East Side Family

Union, clients have been involved in the contract negotiation and also signed the final document, thereby agreeing to participate in services (Weissman and Weil, 1978). Involving the client in this process can be a step toward empowerment and a very direct form of advocacy, and it also involves him or her in evaluation (Scott and Cassidy, 1981).

Monitoring is obviously extremely complex because it can encounter so many organizational obstacles. It is critical to ensure cooperation but important not to undermine the "basic autonomy of the cooperating organizations and professions" (Weissman, Epstein, and Savage, 1983, p. 103). Specific problems related to interorganizational and interprofessional coordination include (1) challenges to the status system among professionals, (2) disagreements over the needs of the target population and strategies for problem solving, and (3) divergent professional cultures and values regarding the good of the client (Kahn, 1974). Whenever a case manager crosses organizational or program boundaries to monitor services, it may be viewed as a threat or a challenge to the inspected agency's judgment. The monitor must use collaborative skills to assure service delivery and must monitor agency cooperation as well as client progress. The goal of monitoring is to provide information to evaluate "the client's progress toward meeting the objectives of the service plan" and to indicate problems in service delivery that may necessitate changes in the plan (Levine and Fleming, 1984, p. 14). The monitoring function is also extremely useful in providing information that can be used to evaluate the operations of the case management system itself.

Advocacy. An advocate is a supporter or defender of another; the role requires that the advocate speak for the client. Advocacy is particularly important in case management because many of the vulnerable populations served have not had fair access to services, have been assumed to be unsuitable for services, or have been poorly served in both policy and programs. Because many clients are dependent, advocacy must be emphasized in case management.

In case management, advocacy must be carried out at two levels: (1) the case level, where the case manager presses for the needs and best interests of a client, and (2) the systems level, where the case manager lobbies, negotiates, mediates, and works for system changes that will benefit the entire target population. Thus the case manager must be able to move from considering the plight of an individual to examining and seeking redress for all people who have such problems. Saul Alinsky used to tell a story about social workers and other well-intentioned people who pulled drowned or nearly drowned people out of a river without going upstream to see who was pushing them in (Alinsky, 1979). Going upstream to stop the carnage—advocacy—is essential in case management.

Advocacy is usually (but not always) assumed to be an adversarial process and thus is an area of risk for the case manager. Other functions of case management call for close collaboration and cooperation with the staffs of various agencies. Collaboration and cooperation sound like peaceful processes in which one tries to construct win-win situations, that is, situations that are mutually beneficial to all staff members and clients. Advocacy is necessary when collaboration has not worked. Other staff members often perceive advocacy as a very aggressive, adversarial activity, and they typically respond by saying "What do you mean, I'm not doing my job?" or "Who are you to say that my agency isn't serving clients effectively?" Because of this tension, the advocate must have a clear strategy; she or he must be willing to cancel contracts but only when more moderate attempts have failed. The risk is evident: You can't beat people over the head, tell them to be nice, and expect them to be so. In particular, a case manager cannot expect the collaborative activities of other case management phases to be unaffected by advocacy activities. "One cannot be in continual disagreement and conflict on one set of issues and expect others to cooperate on others" (Weissman, Epstein, and Savage, 1983, p. 148).

Middleman and Goldberg (1974, p. 73) recommend a strategy for advocating clients' needs ethically and effectively without destroying the collaborative system needed to execute case management: the principle of least contest. They illustrate the role progression from conferee (when there is substantial agreement on what is to be done) to broker (laying out and arranging for what needs to be done). If these roles fail, the worker must become an advocate for the client.

The community organization literature from social work also supports the least-contest strategy. Brager and Specht (1973) discuss a range of approaches escalating from education, to persuasion, to bargaining, to campaign tactics, and finally to direct-contest tactics only when other means have failed. This range of tactics exists because, regardless of the outcome of the current client situation, the case manager will have to come back and work with these same agencies and staff persons on other cases. "If you can persuade someone, then why mediate? If you can mediate, then why fight with them?" (Weissman, Epstein, and Savage, 1983, p. 105; see also Middleman and Goldberg, 1974).

Effective advocacy requires logical analyzing of problems and selecting a strategy that maximizes the possibility of achieving the desired change. Yet as McGowan (1978, p. 281) notes: "It also demands sensitivity, flexibility, and imagination, qualities that reflect the skill and style of the individual worker." The logical process for resolving problems through advocacy involves answering the following questions (McGowan, 1978, p. 280):

1. What is the source of the problem?
2. What is the appropriate target system?
3. What is the objective?
4. What is the sanction for the proposed intervention?
5. What resources are available for the intervention?
6. How receptive is the target system?
7. With whom should the intervention be carried out?
8. At what level should the intervention take place?
9. What methods of intervention should be employed?
10. What is the outcome?

To answer these questions, case managers need a firm knowledge of (1) the client, (2) the case management agency, (3) the broader service network making up the case management system, (4) the workings of other bureaucratic agencies, and (5) "knowledge of community resources" (Weissman, Epstein, and Savage, 1983, p. 164).

Weissman, Epstein, and Savage (1983) offer a helpful approach for carrying out advocacy functions and using the case management system rather than dismembering it. In this approach, based on Homans's principles of exchange theory (1958), problematic advocacy situations are viewed as exchange relationships. That is, it is easier to approach someone with something to exchange rather than with a club to force them into submission. The exchange might be of resources, time, assistance, or simply rewarding cooperative staff by recognizing their productive work. Exchange involves an investment in a relationship "in the hopes of some return or reward" (Weissman, Epstein, and Savage, 1983, p. 148).

Thus, advocacy can be practiced as a form of exchange whereby people who provide a client with a needed service or resource receive a reward in exchange. "The rewards and costs of advocacy are affected by (1) what one wants; (2) the procedure that one uses to get it; and (3) the structures that one uses" (Weissman, Epstein, and Savage, 1983, p. 148). The rewards given must be of value to the agencies participating in the case management system and their individual workers. Weissman, Epstein, and Savage (1983, p. 148) note that "if advocacy is to be successful, the rewards must outweigh the costs."

Evaluation. Just as advocacy in case management must be carried out on two levels, so must evaluation. Case managers need to be directly involved in evaluating services for their clients and their clients' progress and problems. Case managers also need to participate in the overall evaluation of the case management system. What happens to individual clients and particular types of clients is important to a system evaluation. Involvement in a system evaluation can help pinpoint problems in providing services to specific clients.

Plans and formats for evaluating each case and a total system need to be incorporated into the planning of a case management system. These formats should be of direct use to individual case managers as well as to specialized program evaluators and administrators.

The principal means of feedback and system correction is to issue reports throughout system development and at certain points during operations. Evaluation can identify programs or procedures that need to be modified. It formalizes the monitoring function by collecting, analyzing, and distributing data on the case management program. Frequent reports on a client's progress and the system's operation can keep a system on track, prevent goal displacement, and ensure that the system is focused on the well-being and needs of the target population.

For the individual client, continual monitoring can provide periodic summary evaluations that might result in the following: (1) a redefinition of needs and service goals, requiring a revised service plan; (2) a confirmation that all is going well and that the service plan should remain in effect as written; (3) an identification of problems in the service plan that indicate a need for closer monitoring, problem solving, or advocacy; (4) the recognition that the client's needs for service have been met or that she or he no longer needs continuous case management services (in this instance, the case manager might meet with the client periodically as a consultant); or (5) basic service needs have been met so that only occasional follow-up is needed rather than intensive involvement in a case management system.

The evaluation role completes the process of case management and may lead to reassessment and service planning if needs or situations have changed for specific clients. For the case management system, evaluation is necessary for survival as well as improvement. Throughout the case management process, the case manager will relate to the client, acting in the roles described in Chapter One. In acting as a counselor and advocate for the client, the case manager will often be involved as an educator, problem solver, and coordinator of both formal and informal support.

Models for Case Management Programs

The case management process can be carried out using any of several service models. It is important that a new case management program adopt a service model that is appropriate to its clients and its service network. Regardless of the model adopted, all case managers are responsible for three basic types of service: (1) direct work, such as counseling clients and perhaps their families; (2) coordinating services, such as working with other professionals and service providers on behalf of clients; and (3) advocating for (and with) clients for access to services, creating needed services, and assuring the appropriateness and quality of services.

A practice model is a working design for conducting services and case management. It represents the functioning of the service network and illustrates roles, functions, and supporting structures. The model for any case management system will include a design for services and indicate how case management functions will be carried out. It should define the roles of the staff, the responsibilities of the staff of different agencies, and the ways case managers will relate to clients and their families. It should also illustrate the planned interactions of the components of the service network and the structure, sequence, and process of carrying out case management activities.

A wide variety of models for case management practice have been presented in the literature. Some are quite specific and detailed; others are general. In addition to client needs and staff capabilities, factors influencing the choice of a case management model include financial resources, the scope of the service network for the target population, public and political attitudes toward the problems of the target population, and legislation, legal mandates, and policy guidelines and regulations. Levine and Fleming (1984, p. 17) point out that case management may be "performed by individuals or by teams; by a primary therapist or by case management specialists; by paid staff or by volunteers; by professionals trained in the core disciplines or by indigenous workers." Although a great variety of models are present in the literature, the following discussion describes the models that seem most promising.

Three essential categories of models seem to be emerging in practice: (1) case management provided by professionals in the human services or by specially trained paraprofessionals, (2) case management provided by nonprofessionals who have a special relationship with clients, and (3) comprehensive service centers that provide case management. Three major models prevail in the first category: (1) the generalist case manager or broker model, (2) the primary-therapist-as-case-manager model, and (3) the interdisciplinary team model. In the second category we find: (1) family (often parents) as case managers, (2) a supportive care case manager, and (3) the volunteer case manager. The comprehensive service center model for case management seems to be becoming more popular and is appropriate when clients reside in and receive core services. Such models are found in institutionalized settings, such as inpatient programs for developmentally disabled children and adults, community residential settings for people coping with chronic mental health problems, and community-based programs for the frail elderly. Some residential drug abuse treatment and rehabilitation programs also provide case management. As Figure 2 illustrates, whatever the model for case management, the primary responsibility of the case manager remains constant: to connect the client to the service network and provide coordination of needed services.

Figure 2. Case Management Model Options.

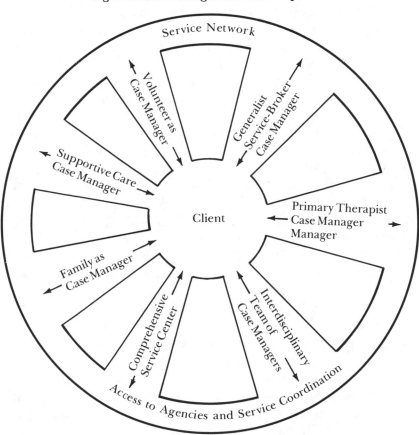

Generalist Model. In this model, which is extensively covered in the literature, the case manager is a professional responsible for service coordination for an individual client or a set of clients. Such case managers might come from disciplines such as social work, nursing, public welfare, psychology, human services, or vocational rehabilitation. As Levine and Fleming (1984, p. 17) note, of all of the case management models, this one most closely resembles "the traditional social casework model." This generalist carries on all the case management functions and provides the basic direct service, coordination, and advocacy necessary in all case management programs.

Generalist implies a jack-of-all-trades, and accordingly, the generalist case manager acts as a broker and carries out a variety of functions. The generalist carries the client through the entire case management process: intake, planning service coordination, and evaluation. The workload is determined by the size of the caseload rather than by specialized function.

Bradfield and Dame (1982) and the report from the Minnesota Department of Public Welfare (1980) indicate the following advantages of the generalist model: (1) Each client has a single person to work with regarding treatment planning and service issues; (2) staff are less likely to feel that they are in a routine because they perform various functions; (3) staff autonomy is encouraged; and (4) one person is accountable for each client.

Levine and Fleming (1984, p. 19) cite a particularly effective generalist model in which a broad array of community services are offered that are relatively accessible.

Although professional-level staff are usually used in this model, in some instances, such as the family intervention program of the Lower East Side Family Union, workers with bachelor's degrees carry out complex case management functions under the direction of highly skilled clinical and service delivery specialists with master's degrees (Weissman and Weil, 1978).

The Family Union, operating on the Lower East Side of Manhattan, was located in an area of New York where the target population was families with multiple problems whose children were being considered for out-of-home care. This area had numerous human services agencies, and service network members contracted with the Family Union to provide specified services to Family Union clients (Weissman, 1978). Although obtaining services could be difficult for needy individuals, the Family Union Program developed useful and workable access mechanisms through contracts (Weissman, 1978).

The generalist model is sometimes described as a broker approach, in which the case manager arranges access and service coordination, making necessary connections between the client and programs in the service network. This model does offer flexibility in personnel and supervisory arrangements, and often case management duties are carried out either by bachelor's- or master's-level staff trained in one of the human services.

Primary Therapist as Case Manager. In contrast to the generalist model, in the primary therapist model the case manager's relationship to the client is primarily therapeutic. This fact restricts who can fill this role. The case manager–primary therapist will probably be a master's-degree social worker, psychologist, or psychiatrist. Case management functions are undertaken as a part of or an extension of therapeutic intervention. Lamb (1980, 1982) is one of the strongest proponents of this model, maintaining that the case management functions are an integral part of the basic responsibilities of a competent therapist.

The therapeutic relationship should be founded on trust and on the therapist's knowledge of the client's concerns and problems. Although Lamb (1982) notes that a paraprofessional might perform such activities as escorting a client to apply for benefits, he holds that a highly trained clinician who is the client's therapist should be the case manager. This model implies that the case manager–primary therapist will have graduate training, most likely in psychology, social work, psychiatry, or psychiatric nursing.

The primary benefit of this model is that the client has one person to relate to concerning treatment, service access, and case coordination. For clients with limited functioning abilities, the possibility of having one person to depend on for assistance can be both useful and comfortable. In many small programs and communities, the primary-therapist–case-manager model may be necessary, even if not preferred. Small service systems have few professionals, and they are likely to have constant face-to-face contact with most of their clients. In these situations, this model can operate on a basis of mutual exchange of resources among programs, which can be both functional and beneficial to all participants.

The problem most often cited in this model is that many therapists seem to feel that case management is a secondary activity to therapeutic work. When therapy is seen as the major responsibility, it is critical to assure that all case manager–primary therapists are skilled in case management and give case management high priority as an ongoing part of their duties. An additional question raised by several authors is whether the professional programs that train therapists provide them with appropriate skills for effective case management (Schwartz, Goldman, and Churgin, 1982). In many ways, the primary-therapist-as-case-manager model is extremely enticing, because it stresses the power of the therapeutic relationship.

This model may be the ideal, and it is sound when the system and staff support it. However, the other models may have developed because the primary therapist often neglects his or her role as case manager. Where system accountability is a legal responsibility as well as a professional ethic, the service system must assure that all case management functions are carried out and that treatment, coordination, and advocacy are carefully evaluated.

Interdisciplinary Team Model. The interdisciplinary team model of case management is based on the concept of an interdisciplinary, specialized team in which each member has a particular responsibility for service activities in their special area of expertise (Brill, 1976). In team models of case management, each case manager carries out a specific case management function or set of functions. In combination, the activities of these specialized case managers constitute a complete case management process. The case loads of these specialists are built around a particular case management function. The team might divide responsibilities by activity, such as intake, service linkage to residential programs, service access, and case monitoring.

An alternative structure for a case management team uses professionals from a variety of fields who provide case management for the particular service that they provide. In such a team model,

Brill (1976) notes that one person is often the "first among equals" in the amount of work with the client; consequently, a social worker, therapist, or nurse might function rather like the generalist case manager but work in very close collaboration with an ongoing interdisciplinary team. McMahan and associates (1982) describe a team model in which a social worker is responsible for a client's movement through the service system. This person works with an interdisciplinary group of professionals, each of whom provides a specific service to the client and is accountable for that function; the social worker is responsible for the sequence and coordination of service delivery. This model closely fits Brill's basic concept of an interdisciplinary, collaborative team that is involved in service planning and decision making, where each team member provides his own specialized service as part of an agreed-upon treatment plan, and one member of the team maintains primary responsibility for assuring service coordination.

In this model of team collaboration, it is particularly important that the person responsible for service coordination, who may or may not be the team leader, have skills in group facilitation and decision making, as well as clinical and technical skills. Social work training at present is the likeliest human services discipline to provide education in these areas though nursing programs also increasingly include this content.

Where team members are strongly commited to client well-being, the team can provide high-quality service through mutual planning and problem solving (Weil, 1982). Teams can become a support system for the involved professionals and a way of avoiding burnout and sharing responsibility for difficult cases. When dealing with severely troubled or disabled members of the target population, Intagliata and Baker (in press) point out that the team support system might be very valuable. Research indicates that the team approach can provide better continuity of care and improve planning and the integration of services in treating chronic patients (Test, 1979).

However, the group interaction that the team model offers as a prime virtue also poses its greatest potential weaknesses. When team members are not committed to client well-being and system intervention, responsibility may be shirked or denied. As a result, lines of responsibility can become blurred, and accountability for service effectiveness may be evaded. To prevent this form of "passing the buck" (or, more likely, passing the client—or keeping the buck and passing the client), it is important that team members receive training in their collaborative, planning, coordinating, and evaluative roles. If team members are not so trained, they may not know how to perform competently in this major area (Kahn, 1974; Weil, 1977; Mailick and Ashley, 1981).

In addition to training in collaboration tactics, it is important that team members develop clear lines of communication and reporting among themselves and between clients and the service network (Minnesota Department of Public Welfare, 1980). Clear, frequent communication can assist in identifying problems early and in enhancing the possibility of taking corrective action on behalf of the client in any part of the service network. Combining the roles of collaboration with safeguarding and advocating clients' rights is particularly challenging (Weil, 1979). Decisions must be made about when to "challenge the norm of cooperation and consensus and take an independent position in advocacy for their client" (Mailick and Ashley, 1981).

Another problem that the team model poses is that clients must negotiate with a variety of people about their services. Lamb (1980) and others (Turner and Shifren, 1979) have noted that this may pose extra difficulties for the severely troubled client.

If team members cannot plan, coordinate, and evaluate services effectively, the client may be lost in an unaccountable morass. However, when the team functions well, the total benefit to the client can be greater than the sum of the individual services. The value of the team model to clients and to its professional members should not be underestimated. But if the team model is to be successful, careful structuring of roles, reporting procedures, and communication functions and procedures are essential, as is specific training in collaboration and service coordination.

Comprehensive Service Center Model. In the comprehensive service center model for case management, service centers provide comprehensive services, including social and emotional support, vocational training, and residential facilities. Such programs may serve clients with chronic mental health problems, residents of live-in programs or institutions for people with developmental disabilities, or residents of Independent Living Centers, which serve people with physical disabilities or long-term health care programs. Planned long-term group placement for adolescents in foster care might also fit this model. Typically, the comprehensive service center provides basic services for residents and case management to aid clients in gaining access to services from other agencies. This type of program is often rehabilitative, for example, residential programs for chronic mental patients or clients who have had problems with drug abuse. Such rehabilitation programs often serve a major resocialization function and operate almost as a surrogate extended family to provide support and corrective emotional experiences for clients (Hays, 1982). Case management in such comprehensive service centers is typically handled by staff members who have several residents in their case load. Both professional and paraprofessional staff are likely to carry out case management functions.

The benefits of this model for case management stem from the staff person's multiple interventions with clients, wherein case management is viewed as a basic service function. Often mutual self-help between clients and an advocacy function are built into such programs, which can help clients take on some case management responsibilities for themselves. Obviously, the model is limited because it can only be applied in a comprehensive service center, but it can be a strong force for the continuity of care and for case management. Most important, it may also help clients to master independent living skills and more socially productive and personally fulfilling life-styles.

Case Management by Nonprofessionals. The previous models for case management employ professionals or staff members, but other case management models are developing wherein the roles of these people are diminished. These models are not as conceptually evolved and have been subject to little empirical testing, but they bear watching and may prove useful in planning for empowerment or in dealing with funding cutbacks. What is needed in case management by nonprofessionals, such as family members, clients themselves, or volunteers, is the necessary training so that these nonprofessionals can carry out case management and advocacy functions in ways that maximize client benefits and establish productive collaboration with program and staff.

Family Model of Case Management. In Chapter Nine, Caires and Weil present an exciting model in which parents are trained to be case managers for their developmentally disabled children. In discussing case management for the frail elderly, Downing in Chapter Six notes the trend toward using adult children of elderly persons as case managers. She cites the tremendous effect that families can have on the quality of service and the continuity of care if they have been trained in case management processes and have appropriate staff with whom to interact and consult. In California, challenging and exciting steps have been taken to assist families in case management and advocacy for developmentally disabled children. In addition to the model described by Caires and Weil, a specialized training program, Fiesta Educativa, has operated for several years. This program provides special training for Hispanic parents of children with developmental disabilities, acquaints them with the service system, and shows them how they can help in treatment planning and service coordination for their children (Weil, 1981).

In these models of family case management, the intent is to develop a professional-parental partnership where the parents have access to staff to work out service delivery problems and to consult about changing conditions in their child or the service network. However, in this model the professional has not abandoned the essential function of assuring service quality.

Despite exciting examples of case management by families of clients, an unfortunate fact is that families often become case managers for troubled, disabled, or dependent members by default (Levine and Fleming, 1984). When this occurs, it usually indicates that the case management responsibility has never been properly structured as a staff role or has been abandoned. As noted by Levine (1984), families may well be assuming too much responsibility for service coordination. Families are usually not trained to handle these responsibilities and many learn by trial and error—a costly and frustrating experience. Levine and Fleming (1984, p. 20) note that often "families feel that this role is not appropriate and that an unfair burden has been placed upon them . . . and are typically not prepared to meet the service needs" of the disabled member. The complexity of most human services systems is difficult for many professionals to negotiate and may seem like hopeless mazes to families.

There is considerable merit in the notion that training in case management and advocacy for their disabled or vulnerable family member can be an empowering experience for families. Professionals and policy makers need to examine how families can appropriately take on some duties of case coordination or other responsibilities, but they must also develop carefully structured training and support systems so that families can carry out such tasks effectively. Although increasing a family's involvement in service planning, coordinating, monitoring, and evaluating is a laudable goal and in accordance with assuring the civil and social rights of vulnerable populations, it would be legally and morally reprehensible for professionals to abandon their official accountability and quality assurance responsibilities. What is needed is effective service coordination and advocacy partnership among clients, their families, and professional case managers.

Supportive Care Model. Levine and Fleming (1984, p. 21) discuss the supportive care model of case management operating in Rhinelander, Wisconsin (Thwing and Cannady, 1979; Cannady, 1982). This model has usually been used in rural communities, but it has also been used in an inner-city area in Chicago. The model is founded on the belief "that the psychological and support needs to maintain the chronically mentally ill in the community exists within their natural neighborhoods and citizenry; moreover, given support structure and guidance, citizens can deliver direct mental health services and link clients with other necessary community supports in an effective and economical manner" (Levine and Fleming, 1984, p. 21).

Supportive care workers are selected to work as case managers for clients of the mental health system from the general population. Each worker receives specialized training and is assigned to work with one client; rarely will more than one client be assigned to a supportive care worker (Levine and Fleming, 1984, p. 21). Ongoing monthly training sessions that focus on psychological awareness and functioning and service delivery are held as part of the supervisory process. These workers are paid to perform these services and are under contract to local human services agencies (Levine and Fleming, 1984).

This model is based on the importance of community involvement in mental health and advocacy. The paid supportive care workers are primarily responsible for relating to the client and developing linkages to services. The model distributes tasks but maintains legal and program obligations with the mental health system. Some functions, such as case review, are shared with the agency, and the agencies retain some formal aspects of evaluation.

A variation on the supportive care model used with patients of the mental health system was a program funded by the Department of Housing and Urban Development (HUD) in Wilmington, Delaware, during the late 1960s and early 1970s. Given a major HUD demonstration grant, the "Wilmington System" was set up to be a demonstration management, social services and cost-effectiveness program. The Housing Authority of Wilmington set up as part of the Wilmington System a demonstration program of social and community services called "Resident Services" (Wilmington Housing Authority, 1972). Under this program, which had a program director with an M.S.W., a social worker with a bachelor's degree, and a home economist as supervisors, residents of the public housing projects were hired as case aides, community workers, and home economics aides to assist in case finding and case management for families with social and health services problems (Weil, 1975).

The case aides, who were titled "family support workers," located families in the housing projects who were in need of services. They performed an intake interview for potential clients and, after reviewing a family's needs and problems with their supervisor, developed linkages to needed services. In addition, these workers often accompanied families to the social and health agencies to see that services were received. They served as advocates for clients and monitored services by checking with clients to see if they got results and were satisfied. They also contacted agencies to see what steps could be taken by the housing authority and other agencies to improve services for low-income and elderly clients.

This program proved to be very successful; it received positive recognition from tenants' groups, citizens, political organizations, and the mayor of Wilmington, and it was regarded as a helpful, mediating service by public and private agencies (Wilmington Housing Authority, 1972; Weil, 1975). Unfortunately, despite the program's success, HUD decided it was not going to be involved in the social services business. Although significant collaborative relationships among agencies lasted and several family support workers assumed positions in social agencies and Office of Economic Opportunity programs, momentum was lost, and the mediating case management system was not able to sustain itself without organizational sanction and resources.

The Volunteer Case Manager Model. This final model also depends on a workable partnership with the staff of the agency responsible for case management. A number of mental health programs have adopted models in which volunteers assist clients who have recently been released from state facilities. In Rochester, New York, the Compeer program assigned community volunteers to work in supportive relationships on a one-to-one basis with either an adult or a child who had been a client of the state mental health system. Volunteers can provide support, assistance in transportation, and concrete services for people who are returning to community life from institutional settings (Folkenberg, 1982).

The Montgomery County, Maryland, Mental Health Association has used social work students in master's programs to serve part of their internship as case managers for chronic mental patients. In this program, the students are supervised by a professional field supervisor, who assists them in systems negotiation, direct work with clients, and monitoring services. The interns have proved effective in coordinating services for clients (Bramhall, 1983).

In the child welfare field, several demonstration programs in different parts of the nation have used volunteers as case managers under guardian ad litem programs with the family or juvenile court. A guardian ad litem is a guardian for a child who is going through legal processes that will determine the child's future status. The term connotes a guardian or overseer of the process and is intended to assure that an objective party, that is, someone who has no vested interest but the well-being of the child, oversees the various professionals from legal, social, and health agencies who are involved with the child. One benefit of the volunteer guardian ad litem program is that it opens up to public scrutiny the process of what happens to children in court. It gives the child someone with whom to have a trusting relationship while major decisions are made about the child's future. These volunteers act as supporters and friends of the child, oversee legal processes to see that the child's interests are represented fairly, and discuss and plan the child's future with legal and social work professionals.

Volunteers can be extremely helpful "junior partners" (Lauffer, 1978), but it is critically important here, as with paraprofessionals, that those people who are legally and professionally responsible for case management not shirk their responsibility for the well-being of clients. Volunteers can be a zestful boost to a system, aiding clients and staff alike, but it is unfair to clients and to volunteers to expect volunteers to carry the major responsibility for a client's well-being. It is critically important when using volunteers as supports in a program that they have a clear understanding of roles—their own and the professional's—and that they are adequately trained for their duties and receive necessary supervision.

Each of the seven models of case management discussed can be used effectively to promote client well-being. The way the model operates will be greatly affected by the agency setting of the case management program and by the skills and role emphasis of the case manager. Implementation of the models will also vary based on whether there is a full-scale, comprehensive service network for the population, a smaller number of services that can effectively be coordinated, or a minimal service system (Boserup and Gouge, 1980). Figure 3 illustrates that any of the models may exist at any one of these levels of comprehensiveness.

Case Management Settings

The organizational setting strongly influences how a case management system will operate. By its nature case management for a vulnerable population is sufficiently complex that organizational

Figure 3. Case Management Models for Human Services Programs.

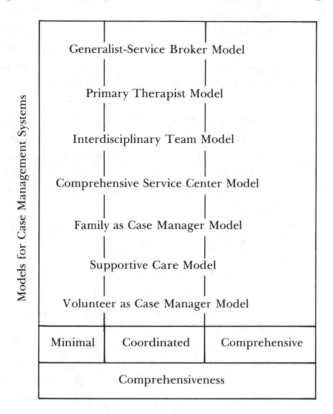

arrangements (such as service structure, a hierarchical form of decision making, and a division of labor, as well as what defines the mission and socially sanctioned goals) are essential to a fully functioning case management system. The size, scope, and structure of an agency will affect the design of case management and largely determine what case management functions are emphasized. Steinberg and Carter (1983) describe eight major categories of agency settings that might house and sponsor a case management program: a freestanding agency, a special unit in a planning agency, a special unit in an information and referral agency, a special unit in a direct service agency, a special unit in an institution or multifunctional agency, a consortium or federation, and membership associations.

Although there may be other settings, these constitute the likeliest settings for case management programs.

Freestanding Agency. A freestanding agency in this sense is an agency exclusively devoted to a case management program that has its own board of directors. The agency has a high degree of autonomy, with decisions based primarily on board and staff interests and perhaps secondarily on constraints imposed by funding grants. The risks in developing a new free standing program relate to the need to establish credibility with the service community and with potential clients. A freestanding agency has the benefit of not being seen as competing with the service-providing agencies in the network. However, because it has a single purpose, it can face "cash flow problems and consequent interruptions in service" (Steinberg and Carter, 1983, p. 38). A freestanding agency has the flexibility of being able to pursue funds from a variety of sources but the vulnerability of having to alter programs to reflect changes in funding priorities (Steinberg and Carter, 1983).

Special Unit in a Planning Agency. This is a very typical model. Here the case management project is a special unit housed in a larger social planning or health planning agency. Visibility is an advantage, but other problems that the planning agency has with service providers may be blamed on the case management unit.

Special Unit in an Information and Referral Agency. Accommodating the case management program in an information and referral agency can have many advantages for a case management program. If the agency's purpose is information and referral, it will already be connected with agencies in the service network. Because it does not offer direct therapeutic, health, or social services, it will not be viewed as threatening by agencies that do provide such services. Generally information and referral (I&R) agencies are seen as serving all types and classes of people rather than one income stratum or one type of stigmatized population. I&R agencies have long been involved in identifying gaps in service and participating in planning to meet changing community needs (Steinberg and Carter, 1983). Difficulties are likely to arise in securing and maintaining an adequate funding base. An I&R agency that begins a case management program will probably need to specify one or a very few target populations for this service, because it is quite difficult to have specialists for all of the possible target populations. Many case management programs have evolved to serve the particular needs of a segment of the population that is large enough to warrant services. Numerous case management programs for senior citizens are lodged in I&R agencies (Steinberg and Carter, 1983).

Special Unit in a Direct Service Agency. The most common setting for case management programs is probably a direct service agency. Case management units are housed in child welfare agencies, family service agencies, and home health agencies. An advantage to this arrangement is that many such agencies are well established with the target population and the community; however, when "the case coordination program becomes the purchaser of services and the monitor of other services providers, it may be criticized for its overlapping roles or conflict of interest" (Steinberg and Carter, 1983, p. 40).

Special Unit in an Institution or Multifunctional Agency. Examples of institutions or multifunctional agencies housing case management programs include a multipurpose agency serving children and families or the elderly or a hospital unit that serves discharged patients and others in their homes. These programs may well take on the credibility of the host agency, but Steinberg and Carter (1983, p. 41) report that "many front-line practitioners and administrators of such units report difficulties in gaining acceptance within the larger, host institution for the roles of case managers and the extra resources required for a case management program." Consequently, people developing a program in a multifunction agency must ensure that they have the sanction and support to make their program effective.

Consortium or Federation. Programs set up as consortiums or federations are relatively rare because of the complexity of arrangements. Typically, the most successful ones have combined a variety of agencies and university departments that have obtained funding to develop a research and demonstration program (Steinberg and Carter, 1983, p. 42). Perhaps the most visible of these types of programs are in long-term care gerontology centers. Although such programs are usually quite prestigious and can attract top-quality service and research staff, there may be problems in developing ongoing operations. The marriage of convenience undertaken with sincere interest to get the dollars may prove to be problematic when service delivery complications or personnel details intrude into the grand scheme of research and development. Continuity can also be a problem, since such programs usually result from securing major public or private grants. Plans to develop an ongoing base of support and structure must be included at the inception of the program.

Membership Associations. Steinberg and Carter (1983) consider membership associations with case management programs "somewhat hypothetical"; typical groups are labor unions, leagues of senior citizens, guardian ad litem programs in child welfare, and tenant councils. These organizations are often quite effective in securing services for members, but their case management systems are informal. We may see more of this type of case management in the more formalized settings of health maintenance organizations (Steinberg and Carter, 1983).

Bases of Authority. The social sanction for case management programs may come through legislation, incorporation into the private voluntary service sector, research and demonstration grants, or membership associations. Public mandate or private incorporation are the obvious major bases of authority and sanction. Legislatively mandated case management programs are discussed in the following chapters on child welfare, the elderly, mental health, developmental disability, and people with physical disabilities. Administrative regulations specifying how states and local authorities should enact the legislation follow the legal mandate. States and municipalities may also enact laws that set up case management systems; these acts must complement federal mandates. In addition to legislated authority, courts sometimes create case management systems indirectly by designating guardians ad litem to oversee children who are dependents of the court or public guardians who make sure that former clients of mental hospitals or developmental disability institutions obtain follow-up services (Steinberg and Carter, 1983).

The voluntary sector consists of private agencies operating under the authority of an incorporated board of directors. The types of voluntary agencies involved are limited only by one's imagination and sources of funding. Developing areas of service in this sector are shelters for battered women and their children, which are now joining established services for child abuse and neglect, home health, family counseling, health care, and mental health care. Voluntary agencies can usually develop innovative demonstration programs and have often tested service ideas, such as homemaker programs, before they were adopted by public agencies. Voluntary agencies are supposed to represent the common welfare through a board of directors. The board acts with authority gained from incorporation as a nonprofit corporation, through a religious body, or from membership in a national or worldwide organization (Steinberg and Carter, 1983). Whereas public agencies must meet legislated standards for service, the voluntary sector has created national accrediting bodies such as the Family Service Association of America and the Child Welfare League.

A strength of the voluntary sector is its freedom to innovate. Frequently private agencies are attractive work sites for professionals, who feel that a private agency provides more autonomy than a large public bureaucracy. Usually these agencies also have strong links to the volunteer community, which lends credibility and becomes a source for fund raising. Increasingly, however, the freedom of the voluntary sector is being limited by funding constraints. In many fields, agencies have increasingly sought government funds, and, inevitably, he who pays the piper calls the tune. The choice must be made about whether to raise funds to meet full operating expenses without government assistance or whether to adapt programs to meet government regulations in order to obtain public funding. Many private agencies make purchase-of-service arrangements with public agencies; in such cases, the public agency generally has the primary responsibility for case management.

Information Management and Accountability

The rapid increase in the use of case management systems, both governmentally mandated and voluntarily implemented by service agencies and institutions, has resulted from concerns for both quality of service and cost-effectiveness. The increase has developed not only out of a need to be accountable to the public and to funding bodies for service costs and effectiveness but also as the result of the development of computer-based systems of information management. As noted earlier, human services programs have always had some system of organizing and using information to plan and evaluate services. However, computer technology has made such systems more complex and more powerful—both in substance and in application.

The most important thing for administrators and case managers to know when setting up management information systems (MISs) is what information they want, what it represents, and how it will be useful to the agency in monitoring clients, services, and costs and benefits. The current technology is quite sophisticated but unfortunately not yet able to inform about many of the issues important to administrators and case managers. For example, it is very easy for a computer to count the number of clients and contacts and to analyze the use of funds but not to analyze service quality and effectiveness. If efficiency (and therefore good performance) is judged (as is happening in some agencies) simply by who has the most client contacts, the very purpose of service may be grossly neglected. The staff person with many contacts may in fact be working only at a very superficial level, whereas workers with fewer contacts may well be employing the planning, coordination, and monitoring necessary to significantly help the client.

In discussing information management in the human services, Gruber (1981, p. 235) notes that ideally MISs "are designed to deliver timely, accurate and comprehensive information. . . . Thus for example, an MIS can easily 'track' and locate clients as they move through and between systems. It can answer the question, 'what is the unit cost of an hour of adult outpatient service as compared to the same services for a child?' or it can provide administrators with data on staff activities even down to hourly counseling sessions." The critical question, however, is what information is needed, by whom, for what purposes, and how it can be used to improve service quality and efficiency. Systems can be state-of-the-art yet not collect information necessary to decision making and evaluation in case management. Unless the real information needs for both case and system decision making are met, a computerized MIS may undermine service effectiveness and displace goals out of a misconceived notion of efficiency. A second danger posed by computerized MISs is the misuse of confidential data, resulting in serious breaches of privacy and civil liberties (Gruber, 1981). Only data that are really needed should be collected in computerized data bases.

An MIS is "an organized set of data gathering and processing procedures designed as a supportive tool for managers" (Gruber, 1981, p. 236). Thus, MISs are extremely important in large case management systems, such as state mental health programs or county child welfare systems, but they must meet the coordination and evaluation needs of the programs. Such programs must keep track of chronic patients in board and care facilities or of children in foster homes and residential treatment centers. It is quite problematic if MISs are designed to meet the informational needs of only administrators and planners. Case managers have other specific informational needs. Increasingly, an MIS can be designed to support the service monitoring, coordination, and evaluation conducted by the direct case manager. Such an MIS can become a tool in organizing work and decision making rather than just a ritual offering of information to the data-hungry computer. A continuing issue in case management is the development of computer-based information systems that truly support case management practice.

The developing technology of computer-assisted information management systems will be a boon to case managers in their responsibilities for documenting and monitoring services. Where carefully designed, MISs can greatly reduce the time required to carry out reporting functions. Such a system can also speedily pinpoint problems in implementing service plans, so that case managers can invest their service monitoring time in solving problems rather than simply identifying service delivery deficiencies. Where interactive computer systems are operating in several agencies participating in the case management program, they can greatly assist service monitoring and troubleshooting, speed up the process of feedback, and provide the timely information needed to take corrective action to deal with problems in service delivery for clients.

More efficient means of managing and reporting information will be welcome to staffs of most human services programs. Appropriate design and introduction of computerized systems will be discussed in Chapter Eleven, but it is important to note at the outset that introducing a computer-assisted MIS often represents a radical change in agency procedures and management technology. Staff are much more likely to readily accept the technological changes if "(1) the change is seen as needed and useful by members of the staff; (2) the change simplifies the work process; (3) the change saves agency resources; and (4) the change is seen as helping people do their jobs" (National Conference on Social Welfare, 1976).

Well-designed MISs can assist in and improve the decision-making processes in human services programs (Schoech, 1982). Computerized systems can enable agencies, administrators, and staff to use and interpret the "massive amounts of data and information they now collect" (Schoech, 1982, p. 21). Schoech holds that "by improving an organization's data and information management efforts, decision making throughout all its levels will be improved" (Schoech, 1982, p. 21).

The pressure and need to develop more functional means of case monitoring, cost accounting, and record keeping for case management programs will continue. The service efficiency and cost-effectiveness aspects of service planning and delivery are the necessary corollary to service quality. The balance of these essential elements is best explained as a basic part of accountability and good management of resources. Case management programs should be accountable to funding sources, to boards, administrators, staff, and service consumers. The American Public Welfare Association (1977, p. 34) defines accountability in two ways that are critical to case management systems:

1.   "Program" accountability—that is, responsibility for the philosophy, substance, and quality of programs—requires the performance of such functions as *(a)* consumer participation in planning, evaluating, and revising the content of programs; *(b)* the provision of relevant and understandable public information; *(c)* measurement of the quality of services; *(d)* measurement of consumer satisfaction with services; *(e)* periodic evaluation of the results of programs within the context of other social economic indicators; and *(f)* evalua-

tion of the results obtained by focusing on target populations or on special problems or conditions.

2. "Technical" accountability—that is, responsibility for the procedures involved in management of
the social services system—involves such functions as *(a)* the planning process . . . ; *(b)* the
negotiation and monitoring of contracts for the
purchase of services; *(c)* the reporting of program
data (for example, which groups received which
services, at what cost, in what geographic areas);
and *(d)* the auditing of fiscal transactions.

These perspectives on accountability connect very well to the
dual focus of case management on program effectiveness and
program efficiency. As computerized management of data and
accountability systems become more prevalent, four trends are
appearing that underscore the concerns for accountability and
efficient program management: *"(a)* the move to quantify services,
(b) the focus on program outcomes, *(c)* the push for service
integration, and *(d)* recent mandated planning and evaluation"
(Schoech, 1982, p. 42). These trends complement the concerns for
service quality.

Conclusion

The practice of case management is growing in various
human services settings. This book discusses several major applications of case management in the human services in the 1980s. The
service areas chosen—mental health, health, developmental disability, aging, physical disability, and child welfare—are those in which
case management has shown the most growth in recent years.

Of the controversies about case management discussed in the
following chapters, one of the most prominent is the effort by
legislators, administrators, and policy makers to use it exclusively
as a cost control device in an era of cutbacks in government funding.
The idea of cost containment is preeminent and has created a
climate in which efforts to control the use of public resources often
takes priority over helping clients. Despite—or perhaps because
of—the intention of most care providers to provide good and
efficient service, there is a resentment of this climate, which

challenges the autonomy and the authority of the human services professional and severely limits services available to clients.

Another troublesome issue, that of inadequate service resources, is identified by Lourie (1978) and by several authors in this book: "Even after we agree on the nature of a problem to be solved . . . we do not have systems in place to guarantee that needs are met" (Lourie, 1978, p. 8). The best case management systems cannot make up for services missing in the service network.

The issue of scarcity of resources for services and for case management programs is addressed in several later chapters. Other problems discussed later include staffing, supervision, and staff performance in case management. Case management programs are experiencing such growth in technological methods that new information management methods are constantly being developed.

It is a methodology currently experiencing productive and challenging growing pains. Careful resolution of the efficiency-effectiveness dichotomy, which can be assisted by computer technology, will increase the power and utility of case management programs as service planning, monitoring, and accountability systems.

Case management can now boast an increasing body of knowledge. A framework for practice is now established, and there is a growing consensus on methodology. The following chapters of this book examine general issues and explore practice models and methods in specific fields. The final chapters present guidelines for developing case management systems and discuss future directions for case management.

Suggested Readings

Gruber, M. L. (Ed.). *Management Systems in the Human Services.* Philadelphia: Temple University Press, 1981.

Johnson, P. J., and Rubin, A. "Case Management in Mental Health: A Social Work Domain?" *Social Work,* 1983, *28* (1), 49–55.

Levine, I. S., and Fleming, M. *Human Resource Development: Issues in Case Management.* Baltimore: Center of Rehabilitation and Manpower Services, University of Maryland, 1984.

National Conference on Social Welfare. *Case Management: State of the Art.* Final report, Grant No. 54-P-71542/3-01, submitted to the Administration on Developmental Disabilities, U.S. Department of Health and Human Services, Washington, D.C., April 15, 1981.

National Institute of Mental Health. *The Design of Management Information Systems for Mental Health Organizations: A Primer.* Series FN No. 5 (formerly Series C No. 13). DHHS Publication No. (ADM) 80-333. Washington, D.C.: U.S. Government Printing Office, 1980.

Schoech, D. *Computer Use in Human Service Organizations.* New York: Human Sciences Press, 1982.

Steinberg, R. M., and Carter, G. W. *Case Management and the Elderly: A Handbook for Planning and Administering Programs.* Lexington, Mass.: Heath, Lexington Books, 1983.

Weissman, H., Epstein, I., and Savage, A. *Agency-Based Social Work: Neglected Aspects of Clinical Practice.* Philadelphia: Temple University Press, 1983.

References

Alinsky, S. D. "Of Means and Ends." In F. M. Cox, J. L. Erlich, J. Rothman, and J. E. Tropman (Eds.), *Strategies of Community Organization.* Itasca, Ill.: Peacock, 1979.

American Public Welfare Association, Committee on Social Services. "Policy Statement on Personal Social Services." *Public Welfare* (Special), 1977, *35* (2), 32–36.

Boserup, D. G., and Gouge, G. V. *The Case Management Model: Concept, Implementation and Training.* Athens, Ga.: Regional Institute of Social Welfare Research, 1980.

Bradfield, E., and Dame, F. *Community Support Systems: Planning and Implementation.* Report on the Rural Mental Health Training and Consultation Programs. Community Counseling Services, Huron, S.D., 1982.

Brager, G., and Specht, H. *Community Organizing.* New York: Columbia University Press, 1973.

Bramhall, M. "Case Management Program." Unpublished manuscript, Montgomery County Mental Health Association, Kensington, Md., 1983.

Brill, N. I. *Team Work: Working Together in the Human Services.* Philadelphia: Lippincott, 1976.

Cannady, D. "Chronics and Cleaning Ladies." *Psychosocial Rehabilitation Journal,* 1982, *5* (1), 6–19.

Caragonne, P. "A Comparative Analysis of the Twenty-Two Settings Using Case Management Components." Case Management Research Project, School of Social Work, University of Texas, Austin, 1980.

Caragonne, P. *A Comparison of Case Management Work Activity and Current Models of Work Activity Within the Texas Department of Mental Health and Mental Retardation.* Report for the Texas Department of Mental Health and Mental Retardation, Austin, April 1983.

Folkenberg, J. "Compeer Provides Help for Patients Returning to Community." *ADAMHA News,* 1982, *8* (20), 1–5.

Grisham, M., White, M., and Miller, L. S. "An Overview of Case Management." MSSP Evaluation Unit, University Extension, University of California, Berkeley, April 29, 1983.

Gruber, M. L. (Ed.). *Management Systems in the Human Services.* Philadelphia: Temple University Press, 1981.

Hays, P. "Models of Case Management for the Chronically Mentally Ill." In J. Marlowe and R. Weinberg (Eds.), *Proceedings of the 1982 Florida Conference on Deinstitutionalization.* Tampa: University of South Florida, 1982.

Homans, G. "Social Behavior as Exchange." *American Journal of Sociology,* 1958, *63,* 597–606.

Intagliata, J. "Improving the Quality of Community Care for the Chronically Mentally Disabled: The Role of Case Management." *Schizophrenia Bulletin,* 1982, *8,* 655–674.

Intagliata, J., and Baker, F. "Factors Affecting the Delivery of Case Management Services for the Chronically Mentally Ill." *Administration in Mental Health,* in press.

Kadushin, A. *Supervision in Social Work.* New York: Columbia University Press, 1978.

Kahn, A. J. "Institutional Constraints to Interprofessional Practice." In Helen Rehr (Ed.), *Medicine and Social Work.* New York: Prodist, 1974.

Kemp, B. "The Case Management Model in Human Service Delivery." In E. Pan, T. E. Backer, and C. L. Vash (Eds.), *Annual Review of Rehabilitation.* Vol. 2. New York: Springer, 1981.

Lamb, H. R. "Therapists-Case Managers: More Than Brokers of Service." *Hospital and Community Psychiatry*, 1980, *31*, 762-764.

Lamb, H. R. *Treating the Long-Term Mentally Ill*. San Francisco: Jossey-Bass, 1982.

Lauffer, A. *Social Planning at the Community Level*. Englewood Cliffs, N.J.: Prentice-Hall, 1978.

Levine, I. S. *Developing Community Support Service Programs: A Resource Manual for Family Groups*. Washington, D.C.: National Alliance for the Mentally Ill, 1984.

Levine, I. S., and Fleming, M. *Human Resource Development: Issues in Case Management*. Baltimore: Center of Rehabilitation and Manpower Services, University of Maryland, 1984.

Lourie, N. V. "Case Management." In J. Talbott (Ed.), *The Chronic Mental Patient: Problems, Solutions, and Recommendations for a Public Policy*. Washington, D.C.: American Psychiatric Association, 1978.

McGowan, B. G. "The Case Advocacy Function in Child Welfare Practice." *Child Welfare*, 1978, *57*, 275-284.

McMahan, L., and associates. "Case Management/Systems and Strategies." Unpublished manuscript, Department of Training, State of California, Sacramento, 1982.

Mailick, M. D., and Ashley, A. A. "Politics of Interprofessional Collaboration: Challenge to Advocacy." *Social Casework*, 1981, *62* (3), 131-137.

Marlowe, J. "The Functions of Case Management." In J. Marlowe and R. Weinberg (Eds.), *Proceedings of the 1982 Florida Conference on Deinstitutionalization*. Tampa: University of Florida, 1982.

Middleman, R., and Goldberg, G. *Social Service Delivery: A Structural Approach to Social Work Practice*. New York: Columbia University Press, 1974.

Minnesota Department of Public Welfare. "Case Management." *Minnesota Community Support Project Newsletter*, 1980, *3* (4), 1-10.

National Conference on Social Welfare. *Expanding Management Technology and Professional Accountability in Social Service Programs*. Final report, The Task Force on the Organization and Delivery of Human Services: The Public, Private, and Consumer Partnership. Columbus, Ohio: National Conference on Social Welfare, 1976.

National Conference on Social Welfare. *Case Management: State of the Art.* Final report, Grant No. 54-P-71542/3-01, submitted to the Administration on Developmental Disabilities, U.S. Department of Health and Human Services, Washington, D.C., April 15, 1981.

Platman, S. R., and others. "Case Management of the Mentally Disabled." *Journal of Public Health Policy,* September 1982, pp. 302–314.

Schoech, D. *Computer Use in Human Service Organizations.* New York: Human Sciences Press, 1982.

Schwartz, S. R., Goldman, H. H., and Churgin, S. *Manpower Issues in the Care of the Chronically Mentally Ill.* Sacramento: Department of Mental Health, State of California, 1980.

Schwartz, S. R., Goldman, H. H., and Churgin, S. "Case Management for the Chronically Mentally Ill: Models and Dimensions." *Hospital and Community Psychiatry,* 1982, *33* (12), 1006–1009.

Scott, R., and Cassidy, K. "The Case Management Function: A Position Paper." Unpublished manuscript, New Jersey Division of Mental Health and Hospitals, Trenton, 1981.

Solomon, B. B. *Black Empowerment: Social Work in Oppressed Communities.* New York: Columbia University Press, 1976.

Stein, T. J. "Macro and Micro Level Issues in Case Management." In National Conference on Social Welfare, *Case Management: State of the Art.* Final report to Administration on Developmental Disabilities, U.S. Department of Health and Human Services, Washington, D.C., April 15, 1981.

Steinberg, R. M., and Carter, G. W. *Case Management and the Elderly: A Handbook for Planning and Administering Programs.* Lexington, Mass.: Heath, Lexington Books, 1983.

Steinberg, R. M., Carter, G. W., and White, M. "National Survey of Current Case Coordination Programs for the Elderly: Preliminary Findings." Paper presented at the 32d annual meeting of the Gerontological Society of America, Washington, D.C., November 24, 1979.

Steindorff, S., Lannon, P., and Soldano, B. "Case Management

Evaluation: A Review of Factors and Findings in New York." Unpublished manuscript, School of Social Work, Columbia University, undated.

Test, M. "Continuity of Care in Community Treatment." In L. I. Stein (Ed.), *Community Support Systems for the Long-Term Patient*. San Francisco: Jossey-Bass, 1979.

Thwing, E., and Cannady, D. "Community Support Care." Unpublished manuscript, Human Service Center, Rhinelander, Wis., 1979.

Turner, J. C., and Shifren, I. "Community Support Systems: How Comprehensive?" In L. I. Stein (Ed.), *Community Support Systems for the Long-Term Patient*. San Francisco: Jossey-Bass, 1979.

Weil, M. "Social Services in a Housing Authority Setting." Unpublished manuscript, Hunter College School of Social Work, City University of New York, New York, 1975.

Weil, M. "Practicum in Law and Social Work: An Educational Program in Interprofessional Education." Unpublished doctoral dissertation, Hunter College School of Social Work, City University of New York, 1977. (Available from University Microfilms, Ann Arbor, Mich.)

Weil, M. "Interprofessional Work in Adoptions—Collaboration and Beyond." *Social Work Papers*, 1979, *15*, 46–54.

Weil, M. "Report on Fiesta Educativa." Unpublished manuscript, School of Social Work, University of Southern California, 1981.

Weil, M. "Research on Issues in Collaboration Between Social Workers and Lawyers. *Social Service Review*, 1982, *56*, 393–405.

Weissman, H. *Integrating Services for Troubled Families*. San Francisco: Jossey-Bass, 1978.

Weissman, H., and Weil, M. "Successes and Failures in Integrating Services and Helping Families." In H. Weissman, *Integrating Services for Troubled Families*. San Francisco: Jossey-Bass, 1978.

Weissman, H., Epstein, I., and Savage, A. *Agency-Based Social Work: Neglected Aspects of Clinical Practice*. Philadelphia: Temple University Press, 1983.

Wilmington Housing Authority. *The Wilmington System*. Wilmington, Del.: Wilmington Housing Authority, 1972.

3

Applying Theory to Practice: The Impact of Organizational Structure on Programs and Providers

Alex J. Norman

This chapter presents the basic concepts in general systems theory and discusses case management from an open systems perspective. Mayer's models of social systems are related to case management; micro- and macrolevels, structure, and integrative mechanisms are discussed. Kuhn's model of organizational analysis is also applied to case management. His concepts of detector, selector, and effector are related to interorganizational and intraorganizational systems analysis of case management programs. Miles' models of management styles, the traditional model, human relations model, and human resources model, are described and applied to case management. Weisbord's organizational model is discussed and related to case management programs and organization. The chapter closes with a discussion of the potential assistance general systems theory offers for developing case management into a discrete field of practice.

The case management process facilitates a client's progress through service coordination and sequencing within a network of human services programs. This process assures that the services are comprehensive and compatible with the client's program of recovery or maintenance. Systems (organizations) interact with each other in an effort to provide a common good—needed services to a specific client group, whether it is the frail elderly, the developmentally disabled, the chronically ill, or others. At direct service levels, case management is often confused with casework or considered a process alien to good clinical work. Both of these views pose significant risks for clients. Since most case managers come from professions with a clinical emphasis, they overlook two important factors that influence the case management process: the framework from which services are provided and the impact of the organizational structure on those services. These factors affect client progress and satisfaction, the network of relations, and the resources that make up the case management system.

This chapter is intended to clarify these organizational factors and to address the issues surrounding them as a way of examining the various roles of case managers and clarifying the implications for fields of practice. First, case management will be viewed from an open systems perspective, and the interactions within the system as a whole will be detailed. The effect of organizational structure will then be analyzed, and the ideologies of case management will be examined, as will the case manager's role in monitoring the system for effectiveness. Finally, some practical implications for human services providers in general and case managers in particular will be discussed.

An Open Systems Perspective

Incorporated in a general systems approach is the concept of holism. *Holism* in this context means that the parts of the system are interrelated and interdependent; the system has a basic need to adapt, survive, and maintain some state of equilibrium; and communications, feedback, and control are essential for the system to survive (von Bertalanffy, 1968). Although the concept of holism is borrowed from the biological study of organisms, these concepts apply to organizations as systems. General systems theory originated as a means of synthesizing scientific knowledge from many fields. The concept of synthesis, the combining of separate elements to create a coherent whole, has become dominant in explaining the interrelationships of the components of systems and predicting outcomes based on the value of the components parts to the system as a whole. To apply general systems theory to an analysis of case management in organizations, we must first determine the boundaries of the system in question. Relationships among agencies, institutions, and informal networks must be examined. The unit of analysis cannot be the single agency but rather the network of formal organizations and informal social systems that influence client behavior and well-being.

Case management systems as open systems depend upon the goals that result from interactions with the social, economic, and political environments. For example, changing social norms have focused attention and concern on the problems of elderly people, children with developmental disabilities, and children who have been sexually abused. In response to the appeals by advocates for these groups, legislators have developed social policies that mandated services and created organizations to serve at-risk populations such as area agencies on aging or regional centers for the developmentally disabled. The organization that is developed or modified to serve these special needs is viewed as an open system in which such environmental elements as consumers, professional groups, constituent bodies, and political bodies influence program goals and outcomes. When the wishes of these groups change, the organization must accommodate them.

Case management itself is an outgrowth of constituent and environmental demands for more comprehensive, better coordinated, and more appropriate services for individuals and groups in need. As the complexities of the needs of vulnerable populations gained recognition, it became apparent that no single discipline or profession provided the services and resources needed for complete care. To create an interlocked, synergistic system of care, services, resources, and supports dealing with the major needs of client groups must be brought together. Therefore, casework, which is a one-to-one approach, was augmented by case management, which coordinates services. The case management role enlarges the scope of direct service provision by emphasizing the practitioner's responsibility to connect clients to a variety of essential services and to coordinate the sequencing of those services.

Human services organizations are classified as social systems (Boulding, 1956) with an open relationship to the environment. In the same sense that constructs of general systems theory represent a systematic search for laws and order in the universe, social systems theorists have been searching for an "order of order" for human services organizations. This chapter will discuss the most significant contributions that theories of social systems provide for case management operations and functions.

One of the most significant contributions is the work of Robert Mayer (1972), who analyzed the work of four principal theorists and developed five distinct models of social systems that can be used by social welfare planners. Mayer used three variables: (1) system level, which refers to the unit of analysis; (2) structure, which indicates how the elements are arranged to interact; and (3) integrative mechanisms, which refer to what holds the system together. Using this framework, he analyzed the works of Parsons (1951), Ramsoy (1963), Blau (1964), and Warren (1967). From their work, he constructed five models or types:

1. microcollectivity, where the basic elements of the system are individual actors and role incumbents;
2. complex macrosystems, whose constituent elements, social systems, are treated as subsystems;
3. the exchange system, where the constituent elements are individual actors voluntarily attracted to each other because they expect an exchange of rewards or resources;
4. the interorganizational field, whose elements, formal systems (organizations or institutions), act independently of a centralized authority; and
5. the ecological system, where all the other models are incorporated into an interactive whole in which the constituent ele-

ments are individual actors, organizations, or systems with no element having authority or power over any other.

Table 1 lists the models in Mayer's analysis. Two of the five models described by Mayer are particularly important to the case management process because they represent settings in which case managers are likely to operate: complex macrosystems, which include bureaucracies, and interorganizational fields, which include formal organizations like the United Way, health departments, and voluntary agencies. Another model, microcollectivity, is important because it represents a client system with which case managers must interact as a system and not as an individual client.

Complex macrosystems such as bureaus in a department of public social service often have subsystems of their own, yet they themselves are subsystems of some larger system, such as a county government department. A case manager in a child protective services unit could have within the case management system the resources of a bureau of social services, an office of foster home placement, the conciliation court, the bureau of assistance payments, and the district attorney's office, all working on behalf of a neglected or abused child. In this example, the services are all parts of a county government system, but some parts, such as the conciliation court, may have separate system status themselves while others are components of the department of public social services. These various bureaus and service units should collaborate to support the health and safety of the child. The organizational aspects of case management in examples like this are complex but have the benefit of a single macrosystem authority, the county government, that is empowered to settle subsystem disputes and make policy decisions.

Case management within the interorganizational field occurs between formal systems or organizations that are generally independent or quasi-independent. For example, if we add to the previous scenario that the mother as well as the child was victimized by an abusive and battering father, the case management system would also include a shelter for battered women from the voluntary service sector. This shelter would have its own board and organizational structure. In addition, the case management system should

Table 1. Social Systems Planning Model.

Model	System Level (unit of analysis)	Structure of Elements (interaction patterns)	Integrative Mechanisms
Microcollectivity (family, friendships, support groups)	Individual actors in a system of action	Division of labor and distribution of rewards and duties among elements of the system	Shared goals and values
Complex macrosystem (bureaucracies)	Social system; subsystems	Number of differentiated subsystems; distribution of power among subsystems	Shared goals and values: referee subsystems, contracts, arbitration
Exchange system (relationships between friends or colleagues)	Individual actors attracted to each other by an expected exchange of rewards	Undifferentiated relationship patterns based on equal status or differentiated relations based on control of rewards and resources	Shared goals and values: mutually satisfying rewards, negotiated contracts
Interorganizational field (health department, voluntary agencies, United Way, federations of agencies)	Formal systems	Independent operations; quasi-independent discretionary power	Dependence on a common resource base, temporarily shared goals and values; centralized resource or leadership subsystem
Ecological system (dense urban neighborhoods, market system)	Formal and informal social system	Undifferentiated relationship patterns based on equal status and interdependence or differentiated relations based on varying influence over common resources	Common resource base; reciprocity

Source: Adapted from Mayer, 1972.

include involvement with women's advocacy groups such as coalitions opposing the battering of women and an agency from the voluntary sector to provide counseling services to men who batter. Although these interacting agencies may share goals and values, their interdependence is derived from relying on a common resource base that is external to the county public service system. Integrative mechanisms for these interorganizational systems are more difficult to set in place because of the autonomy of the individual formal organizations involved.

Analysis of Social Systems

Although the models or types of organizational social systems are differentiated, they are more similar than dissimilar. Alfred Kuhn (1974) has illustrated essential elements of a "logic of social systems" in his book of the same name. His logical model is composed of three elements that any controlled and successfully adaptive social system must use. The relationship between these elements that detect information, select preferences, and affect behavior is illustrated in Figure 1. The detector deals with information within the system, the selector deals with values or preferences within the system, and the effector produces a behavioral result from the system. An organization is a complex social system and the elements indicate the influence of information and value preference on intraorganizational behavior. Decisions and power are strong determinants of the outcomes and behavior within organizations. Kuhn defines *decision* as a response selection under conditions of uncertainty; a manager can never have all the information needed to make the best decision. He defines *power* as the ability to acquire desired things from others. With these definitions, decisions determine the direction and nature of organizational behavior, whereas power determines the operating values and goals of the organization.

Kuhn's model can be applied to interorganizational behavior where parallel elements of communication, transaction, and organization replace the intraorganizational detector, selector, effector functions. The logical connection between Kuhn's essential functional elements for organizational and interorganizational behavior are illustrated in Figure 1.

Figure 1. Essential Functions of Organizational and Interorganizational Behavior (based on Kuhn's *Logic of Social Systems*).

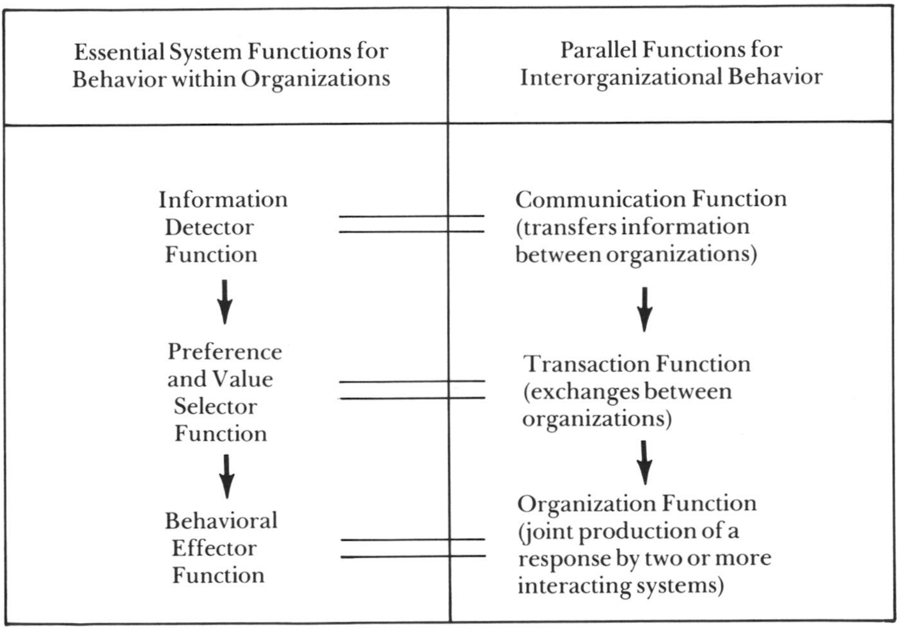

Essential System Functions for Behavior within Organizations	Parallel Functions for Interorganizational Behavior
Information Detector Function ⟶	Communication Function (transfers information between organizations) ↓
Preference and Value Selector Function ⟶	Transaction Function (exchanges between organizations) ↓
Behavioral Effector Function ⟶	Organization Function (joint production of a response by two or more interacting systems)

The model can be used to analyze the behavior of an individual within an organization (microlevel), to analyze behavior within an organization (macrosystem), or to analyze interactions between two or more complex organizations (interorganizational field).

Case management systems can be analyzed using either approach, depending on whether the system is a complex macrosystem or an interorganizational field. In the complex macrosystem example of a child protective services unit, the case manager fulfills the detector function and seeks information about the environment, both internal and external regarding the client's treatment program and the client's problem in general. Questions such as what resources are available, where they are located, how accessible they are, what the extent of the problem is, and what the trends in treatment are provide the case manager with knowledge about the internal and external environment and are labeled a *knowing* function.

In fulfilling the selector function, the case manager screens information to ensure that it is congruent with the values and preferences of the system. Within bureaucracies, where the administrative preference is for interacting with internal subsystems, there is a risk that valuable information about community processes and resources for dealing with a problem might be screened out, having a negative effect on the case management system. Because of this internal processing of information, the selector function is a *wanting* function according to Kuhn. Decisions about what information is valued and used or devalued and discarded determine the nature and direction of case management system behavior.

The effector function guides the actions of the case manager within the environment after the decision about what information to use has been made. The effector function is one of *doing*—doing on behalf of or with the client to improve or maintain a certain level of life functioning. The effect of the case manager's actions is determined by his or her power or ability to influence elements in the system. Consequently, the type or kind of services provided in a case management system may be a function of the decisions made about what information is used in internal processing, whereas the extent of services provided might be determined by the ability of actors in the system to exert power over each other.

When the case management system is located in an interorganizational field, the analysis is based on interactions between the organizational systems involving the communication of information, the transactions of valued things, and the organization of actions and outputs. When a worker in a child protective services unit is managing a case that includes a mother and child who are victims of a husband and father who batters them, other dimensions are added to the case, given that the value preference of the case management system is to keep the family intact where rehabilitation is feasible. One of the major service resources, domestic violence shelters, is external to the public service organization employing the case manager and is another formal organization with a less complex structure. In addition, the troubled family is another social system, a microcollectivity that must be part of the interactions of the case management system. The interaction between the family and the shelter must be analyzed, along with interactions between other nongovernmental agencies or organizations and agencies within the governmental structure.

For example, if the court assigns jurisdiction for services to the public child protective services unit, a case manager will be appointed there. If the domestic violence shelter provides psychosocial counseling and seeks other services and resources (such as housing and day care) for the mother and child, the worker performing these functions will be a case manager. If the father is involved in counseling or rehabilitative services he may have a case manager also.

Because of the interorganizational nature of this case management system, the system must be analyzed in terms of the communications and transactions between agencies. What type of information is shared by case managers and other staff providing direct services to the family members? What other elements in the system have access to that information? What kind of information is not shared? These types of questions give clues to the detector/selector function of each element and what the values and preferences are.

Transactions between the case management subsystems are analyzed by their value content. The domestic violence shelter might want to keep the location of its facility confidential and have a policy against counseling batterers there. A United Way agency might offer a counseling room where the social worker from the shelter can meet with the father. A sympathetic savings and loan association might offer a meeting room where helping professionals can conduct group sessions with men who batter. These examples illustrate the interdependence among the agencies participating in the case management system.

Another area where elements in the case management system are interdependent is in the organization of actions and output. Organizational behavior and outputs, which Kuhn calls "effectuations," are analyzed with respect to the joint actions or cooperative ventures between two or more agencies in the case management system. Assuming that the transactions between the agencies prove helpful to the case management process and that the client system improves dramatically, county government at the prompting of the protective services unit and the other involved agencies might be persuaded to continue the arrangement discussed earlier on a contract basis. The domestic violence shelter will continue providing services on a stabler basis. The United Way might provide facilities for counseling male batterers and fund an additional social worker for the shelter. Such activities strengthen the loosely coupled relationships between formal organizations by increasing their common dependence upon needed resources for the common good.

Case Management Systems and Organization Structures

A particular application of general systems theory to the study of complex organizations is the sociotechnical approach, which holds that people and processes are inseparably intertwined in organizations. Though developed in industrial organizations where the technology is mainly machinery, tools, and equipment (Woodward, 1958; Emery and Trist, 1965; Miller and Rice, 1967), the sociotechnical view has since been applied to human services organizations, where the technology is human skills and knowledge (Miles, 1975; Weiner, 1982). This approach focuses on the work group and stresses the interrelationships between the technology used, the organizational environment, the attitudes and beliefs of the workers, and the organizational form. Case management systems as open systems must react to the different demands from and changes among these elements as well as to the effect that the elements have on each other.

Researchers have validated Woodward's (1958) earlier contentions that the organizational setting, particularly the technology employed, can shape human behavior (Burns and Stalker, 1971; Trist, 1963). One consequence of these findings is that case management roles differ in particular case management systems depending on the changes in any of the elements in the sociotechnical system. For example, where workers have a strong belief that family involvement is a critical aspect of case management, as is increasingly true in work with developmentally disabled children and with the elderly, that belief will cause major changes in the structure of case management roles and will lead to a partnership with the family in planning services. Where an interagency team bears case management responsibilities, the process of service planning and the structure of work will be quite different from situations in which a single case manager works with a variety of agencies to secure needed services for clients. The public or private auspices of case management work will affect the patterns of agency interaction and will frequently determine whether there is a central decision-making structure or a pattern of voluntary cooperation. The authority of the juvenile or family court, for example, is a critical determinant in child welfare where the thrust of timely decision making with regard to permanency planning mandates specific periodic reviews and decisions regarding custody and guardianship of dependent children. Increasingly, the type of technology used in information management, which ranges from sophisticated, inter-active, computerized case monitoring to often unsophisticated pen and paper reporting systems, determines the type of information collected and the timeliness of information sharing among agencies. The particular configuration of roles and responsibilities for case management in any program will depend on the unique interactions of its sociotechnical system.

Equally significant in determining differences in case management systems are client needs. As the fields of practice chapters in Part Two of this volume illustrate, case management is employed with very different client populations under quite diverse conditions. In independent living programs for people with physical disabilities, for example, the service goal is to enable the client to become his or her own case manager in contrast to programs serving older persons suffering from senility or the results of Alzheimer's disease where the deterioration in mental functioning makes it impossible for the individual client to take responsibility for service integration. Because the target group's needs will significantly shape the types of service and the membership of the service network, there will be no single most efficient form of organization appropriate for managing all resources and services. Therefore, we should expect to see a variety of case management models emerge that are adapted to the particular needs of specific client populations and specific service systems and technologies. Regardless, however, of the dynamics and technology of a particular situation, the case manager's role is to ensure that the service and support elements are compatible, whether the system is a single, complex macrosystem or an interorganizational field. Figure 2 shows the relationships between elements in a sociotechnical system used in case management and illustrates the characteristics of the subsystems. The central relationship is between the case manager and the client, but this relationship is shaped in significant ways by the particular aspects of the social and technical subsystems of the organization.

**Figure 2. Interaction and Relationships of Elements
in Case Management Systems.**

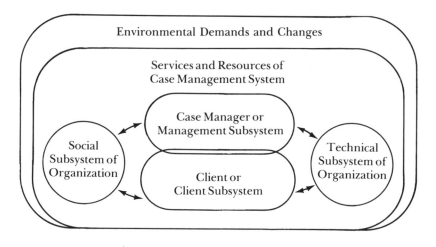

Characteristics of Social Subsystems of Formal Organizations	Characteristics of Technical Subsystems of Formal Organizations
Work group factors Organizational climate Communications Motivation Cooperation Participation Job satisfaction Human resource development	Technology Work flow Task configurations Task relationships Role configuration Job feedback Procedures Policies Guidelines

An Ideological Perspective on Case Management

Since the structure of an organization can shape human behavior within the organization, it follows that case management behavior is also influenced. In human services organizations, that influence is manifested in how service and resource providers view clients or the client system. These views determine the nature of the interaction between clients and the case management system. Thus, labels like "worthy poor" or "truly needy" reflect social or political perceptions of vulnerable population groups that are designated as clients or recipients. Societal views of specific target populations are reflected in the language and labels applied to the population itself and used to describe the nature of their relationship to the service network. Some societal views reflect negative stereotypes or social fear or stigma. Terms such as *crazy* or *dummy* clearly illustrate societal devaluation of client populations with mental illnesses or developmental disabilities. In this society, with its emphasis on individualism and power, people who are dependent in any way on society suffer some social stigma. Labels such as *crippled child* or *wheelchair-bound* illustrate negative stereotypes of persons with physical disabilities. Professional case managers sensitive to the needs of target populations will not use or sanction such negative labels. Along with their stigmatized clients, professionals have advocated a recognition of their common humanity and the elimination of pejorative labeling of vulnerable populations.

Terms used to describe the relationship between the target population and the service system are indications of socially ascribed status or occasionally self-chosen status. The term *recipient* is typically used when the client population and the service they receive are subject to widespread social stigma, such as clients of income maintenance programs. Throughout the human services sector, social and economic factors affect those receiving services. When a person both has a low income and is physically disabled, for example, the stigma is compounded. The most frequently used term in human services for those who receive services is *client*. It connotes a relationship of dependence on the case manager in relation to professional knowledge and access to resources but generally has no negative connotation. The term *consumer of services* is used where development of increased client independence is the major service goal as in independent living programs. It connotes a more egalitarian relationship between the client and the professional in which the client is seen as a partner in service planning and integration. Since all populations closely tied to case management programs are vulnerable, they risk being devalued and viewed as less than fully human as a result of their dependent status. The degree of dependence or the social acceptance of the problem or disability will affect how society views clients and the network of services provided for them. Service providers need to be sensitive to the issue of status ascribed to the client group by society and the possible parallel status ascribed to themselves as service providers. Case managers need to be aware of issues related to client status and societal labeling or even labeling within the service network. Although case managers' perceptions are not usually codified in a full-blown ideology, their views about the client population's needs and aspirations influence both decision making and behavior in the case management system. In combination, case managers' values, concepts, and beliefs about their clients form the basis of advocacy for client needs.

Raymond Miles (1975) has provided a framework for examining case management from an ideological perspective. Based upon his own research on public-sector and private-sector organizations and a synthesis of the works of prominent organization theorists, Miles categorized three styles or models of management based on assumptions about individuals, the task of the manager, and the expectations of the worker. We shall not explain these styles in detail here but only attempt to summarize important concepts that can be related to styles of case management. The case manager's style of relating to clients is likely to reflect both organizational style and the case manager's own perceptions of authority, communication, and participation.

The Traditional Model. The traditional model is an extrapolation and synthesis of social Darwinian views of individuals, classical economists' interpretations of Judeo-Christian beliefs about work, and the views of the scientific management movement. In this model, the manager's style is based on the assumptions that work is inherently distasteful to people and that the money received as a reward is more important than the work being done. The manager believes that few people can carry out duties without being closely supervised in a strict but fair environment and that worker tasks should be routine and should be simplified into repetitive, easily learned operations. Hence workers are expected to tolerate work if the pay is decent, the boss is fair, and they produce according to established standards. Orderliness and stability in the work process and rational authority based on capability are important features of the relationships between managers and subordinates.

In this model, the manager has an active role overseeing a worker in a reactive role. Case managers using this model are likely to view clients in the system as incapable of contributing to the case management process because of physical or psychological disabilities, a lack of knowledge and skills in organizational processes, or other factors. In contrast, case managers play an active role in helping clients receive available services by exacting resources from other human services delivery systems. Little is expected of the client except to "get better" or "maintain a level of functioning" that is acceptable to decision makers in the system. It is assumed that clients will cooperate passively with professionals.

This approach is typically found in large bureaucratic institutions such as public income maintenance programs or in structures with several hierarchical levels. Communication tends to occur vertically and mostly downward, and there is little or no collaboration between horizontal units. This practice model is likely to be found in veterans hospitals, general hospitals, and large municipal and county departments.

The Human Relations Model. The human relations model is a reaction against the traditional model. Managers and scholars who use this second model are quick to point out the problems in developing an emotionless work force similar to automatons. Yet the approach does carry over significant aspects of the traditional approach, principally its rationality and hierarchical aspects. Proponents of this approach contend that people are more than mindless machines and that morale and production suffer unless certain basic needs are recognized. In this model, people's desires to feel useful, important, recognized, and that they belong are viewed as being more important than money in motivating them to work. The manager's tasks are to make each worker feel useful and important, keep the workers informed, listen to their objections, and allow them some self-direction and self-control on routine matters. By sharing information, satisfying basic social needs, and being involved in routine decision making, the workers are expected to be less resistant to authority and more cooperative. Emphasis on informal groups, hierarchical communication, and nonmonetary rewards are important facets of this approach.

In this model, the manager's role is less of an overseer and more of a mediator between the hierarchical structure and the work force, and the manager is primarily interested in work efficiency and effectiveness. The worker is more active, but in matters of little consequence. Case managers using this model usually see client involvement as useful on routine items but inappropriate or intrusive on issues perceived to be of a more professional nature. Clients are given a more active role than in the traditional model, but the major emphasis is on the case manager manipulating the system's resources on behalf of the client while keeping the client informed of the process.

Settings where this approach is common are those quasi-public and quasi-private organizations set up through social legislation designed to bring services closer to the community. Some examples are centers for the developmentally disabled, community mental health centers, and area agencies on aging. These organizations typically model themselves after large bureaucracies or recruit their staffs from large institutions.

The human resources model is an extension of the human relations model. It is based on the theories of human needs and development. The assumptions of the traditional model are rejected; instead, followers of this model contend that people want to seek meaningful goals that they help to set and are more creative, self-directed, and self-controlled than their jobs demand. The major task of the manager is to unleash these untapped human resources to help accomplish the organization's goals. This is done by creating an environment in which workers contribute to the limits of their abilities and are encouraged to participate on all important matters. The increase of influence, self-direction, and self-control for workers is expected to increase operating efficiency and, as a by-product, job satisfaction. The purpose of this approach is to improve organizational performance, and so it differs significantly from the other approaches.

In this model, the manager is a developer of human potential as well as of the organization's other resources. The worker is an active participant in the problem-solving and decision-making processes. Case managers using this model interact with the client as an informed consumer, consistently share information with the client, and include the client in decision making. The case management role here facilitates the development of the client through collaboration, decision making, and resource development. The client system becomes an additional resource in the treatment program. The major difference between this approach and the others is its emphasis on an abundance rather than a scarcity of organizational and environmental resources and an intentional inclusion of the clients and supportive systems in decision making, service, and advocacy.

This approach is likely to be found in organizations where the hierarchy is flattened out and where communication is encouraged and is horizontal as well as vertical. This approach is generally found in newly formed human services organizations at the community level, such as women's health centers, domestic violence shelters, centers for independent living, community counseling centers, and family planning organizations. Frequently these emerging service agencies develop from social change and advocacy movements, and the resulting service organizations strongly reflect constituent and client advocacy issues.

Agencies based on a particular theory rarely exist as pure types in actual practice. Contingency theorists hold that there is no one best way to organize or complete a task (Lawrence and Lorsch, 1967). Good case management systems may primarily employ one of these models or combine them. We can determine a good case management system by assessing whether its operations are effective and efficient. Since effectiveness is measured against purpose, case managers should constantly scan the system to ensure it is achieving its goals efficiently. Case managers must constantly monitor, revise, adapt, and fine-tune the system on the client's behalf.

The Diagnostic Model. Weisbord (1976) has developed a diagnostic model that has been adapted here for use by case managers to examine the relationships that might be problematic within a system. The model is offered in the form of guidelines for practitioners and administrators who take a developmental approach to case management.

1. The purposes or goals of the case management system should be related to environmental demands and consistent with organizational values.
2. The structure of roles should be determined by the purposes. As in engineering models, form follows function.
3. The system of rewards and consequences should support the purpose and structure of the case management system.
4. The "helpful mechanisms" (the systems, procedures, and policies) must be congruent with the purposes, structure, and reward system and should be updated and revised as necessary.
5. Relationships should be based on what components in the system are necessary to achieve the purposes given the current structure, reward system, and helpful mechanisms. Adequate systems ensure that the proper elements are coordinated with each other.
6. Evaluation should focus on answering the question "How efficiently and effectively did the system perform considering the goals and resources available?"

Using this model, the case manager performs a leadership function in detecting the demands and constraints of the environment and by feeding this information into the service delivery system. He or she also initiates whatever action is necessary to keep the system in balance.

Implications for Fields of Practice

The final product is often only as complete as the development of the product or the ability to interpret its advances. Case management as a field of practice is still in an early stage of development. The use of general systems theory to analyze the

various organizational forms of case management is a recent phenomenon. The specific approaches to case management described
here are also developing forms of practice in human services
organizations.

Large-scale political and economic factors affect the delivery
of human services. Bell (1973) has identified trends in postindustrial
societies, such as the tight money market and the reduced role of
government at every level, that have already had profound effects on
human services organizations and their clients. Other trends are not
as easy to discern. However, futurists like Toffler (1980) and
Naisbitt (1982) describe international and national movements that
will seriously affect professional service givers and their clients. For
example, both men agree that institutions of the future will be
decentralized and that groups exogenous or external to the institutions' hierarchical structure will be more involved in decision
making. At the same time, they see trends away from institutions
and toward networking, self-help, and mutual aid. These trends
favor the human resources model of case management over the
earlier models. The implications of these trends are far-reaching for
professionals in case management and must be considered if organizations are to be built that are viable for the long term.

Case management demands a broader systems orientation for
professionals who have generally had a clinically oriented education. Thus, case managers must think in much broader terms in
planning for their clients' welfare than must the institutions that
employ them and the agencies with which they interact. Informal
networks and arrangements are important to the client and must be
considered as part of the resource system. The case manager must
consider separate parts of a whole and their interrelationships and
interactions, concentrating more on synthesis and less on analysis
of the parts. The unit of analysis must shift from the host institution of the case manager to the entire arrangement of services,
resources, and supports that comprises the case management system.
The demand in the kinds of systems we have described here calls for
the skills of a generalist, not a specialist.

Joint problem solving must take place in interdisciplinary
collaboration within case management systems. At the same time,
collaboration is needed at the community level to ensure that all

resources are tapped and that needed resources are generated. As we become more oriented toward self-help, professionals will find it helpful to serve as technical consultants to individuals and groups involved in case management. Professional schools can assist the case management institutions by developing collaboration models and conducting research to build knowledge, test theories, and evaluate programs. Scholars in the human services fields need to be involved with each other and with agencies in developing and testing frameworks for collaborative case management practice. Case management is going to expand in the next two decades. It is critical that practitioners, administrators, and scholars integrate professional values with case management procedures and shape the technology of case management so that effective service for vulnerable clients is coupled with efficient means of service delivery.

Suggested Readings

Kuhn, A. J. *The Logic of Social Systems: A Unified, Deductive, System-Based Approach to Social Science.* San Francisco: Jossey-Bass, 1974.

Mayer, R. R. "Social Systems Models by Planners." *Journal of the American Institute of Planners,* 1972, *38* (3), 130–139.

Meyer, M. W., and Associates. *Environments and Organizations: Theoretical and Empirical Perspectives.* San Francisco: Jossey-Bass, 1978.

Porter, L. W., Lawler, E. E., III, and Hackman, J. R. *Behavior in Organizations.* New York: McGraw-Hill, 1975.

Stein, H. D. (Ed.). *Organization and the Human Services.* Philadelphia: Temple University Press, 1981.

Weiner, M. E. *Human Services Management: Analysis and Applications.* Homewood, Ill.: Dorsey Press, 1982.

References

Bell, D. *The Coming of Post-Industrial Society: A Venture in Social Forecasting.* New York: Basic Books, 1973.

Blau, P. M. *Exchange Power in Social Life.* New York: Wiley, 1964.

Boulding, K. E. "General Systems Theory—The Skeleton of Science." *Management Science,* 1956, *4,* 197–208.

Burns, T., and Stalker, G. M. *The Management of Innovation.* London: Tavistock, 1971.

Emery, F. E., and Trist, E. L. "The Casual Texture of Organizational Environments." *Human Relations,* 1965, 18 (1), 21–32.

Kuhn, A. J. *The Logic of Social Systems: A Unified, Deductive, System-Based Approach to Social Science.* San Francisco: Jossey-Bass, 1974.

Lawrence, P. L., and Lorsch, J. W. *Organizations and Environment.* Cambridge, Mass.: Harvard University Press, 1967.

Mayer, R. R. "Social Systems Models by Planners." *Journal of the American Institute of Planners,* 1972, *38* (3), 130–139.

Miles, R. E. *Theories of Management: Implications for Organizational Behavior and Development.* New York: McGraw-Hill, 1975.

Miller, E. J., and Rice, A. K. *Systems of Organizations: The Control of Task and Sentient Boundaries.* London: Tavistock, 1967.

Naisbitt, J. *Megatrends: Ten New Directions Transforming Our Lives.* New York: Warner Books, 1982.

Parsons, T. *The Social System.* New York: Free Press, 1951.

Ramsoy, O. *Social Groups as Systems and Subsystems.* New York: Free Press, 1963.

Toffler, A. *The Third Wave.* New York: Morrow, 1980.

Trist, E. L. *Organizational Choice.* London: Tavistock, 1963.

von Bertalanffy, L. *General Systems Theory: Foundations, Development, Applications.* New York: Braziller, 1968.

Warren, R. L. "The Interorganizational Field as a Focus of Investigation." *Administrative Science Quarterly,* 1967, *12,* 396–419.

Weiner, M. E. *Human Services Management: Analysis and Applications.* Homewood, Ill.: Dorsey Press, 1982.

Weisbord, M. R. "Organizational Diagnosis: Six Places to Look for Trouble with or Without a Theory." In Black Petrella Associates, *Organization and Group Studies.* San Francisco: Black Petrella Associates, 1976.

Woodward, J. *Management and Technology.* London: H. M. Stationery Office, 1958.

4

Evaluation for Decision Making and Program Accountability

Ron Honnard, George H. Wolkon

Basic issues associated with the use of program evaluation in case management programs are identified in this chapter. A number of strategies for developing evaluation systems using the community mental health system as a point of reference are presented and a conceptual approach applicable to a range of settings is developed. The components of the Balanced Service System (BSS) are described, as well as the quality assurance dimension of six case management models: provider focus, role focus, service focus, client focus, goal focus, and mixed focus. Authority for evaluating programs is seen as administrative, legal, fiscal, and clinical. Strategies for developing program evaluation are related to the authority base and to organizational and political issues. Suggestions are provided for selecting program evaluation models and devising strategies for implementing them.

In 1978, the President's Commission on Mental Health recommended case management as an effective mental health procedure. The federal government has mandated case management through the Rehabilitation Act, Social Services Title XX, the Education for All Handicapped Children Act, and the Developmentally Disabled Assistance Act. Case management is an integral part of the community support program of the National Institute of Mental Health and of the balanced service system model of the Joint Hospital Accreditation Committee. Some states, including California, have also mandated case management. Many professionals have extolled it as a new concept. Many other professionals have proclaimed case management as a good, necessary, and extremely useful concept that they have been practicing for years but under different names: aftercare, making referrals, providing continuing care, performing casework, and dealing with the whole person.

With such enthusiastic and widespread testimony, such strong political backing, and the great proliferation of case management programs, why is there even a hint of a need to evaluate this panacea? Although there is a broad consensus that case management is needed, we argue that case management evaluation is also needed. The major stimulus for the argument is that case management has different meanings for people who are saying case management is needed, for people who are doing it, and for people who are declaring that more case management should be done. We know that given different definitions of case management, some definitions are probably better; that is, they describe operational procedures and goals in a more effective or efficient manner than other definitions under specified conditions. We also know that the term *evaluation* has different meanings for different people.

A major difference exists between case management programs as generally defined here and the earlier, more traditional mental health programs. Namely, case management programs cross over administrative boundaries to ensure that the client obtains needed services at the appropriate time from wherever the services are available. Traditional programs tend to operate within their own administrative hierarchies. One of the case manager's more difficult and complex tasks is to reduce the barriers in crossing administrative lines in order to obtain services for the client. This issue does not exist for traditional programs or for integrated team approaches to treatment. The complications of crossing administrative boundaries creates unique challenges not only for implementing case management programs but also for evaluating them.

Case management program development seeks to establish an integrated set of functions that helps individual clients obtain services when they are needed or to press for services that do not exist or are low in quantity or quality in order to establish a viable comprehensive continuum of care. The former function has been variously labeled case management, linking, and monitoring. The latter function has been and is still called advocacy, community action, change intervention, and political action.

When professionals extol the virtues of case management, do they mean only the function of facilitating service delivery to individuals, or do they include advocacy? If we assume that only the former is meant, is this enough of a definition of case management? Have we now eliminated the need to clarify the program and its evaluation? No. Programs differ in any number of ways: the type of clients, the nature of services available in the community, the organization of those services, the nature of the case management program (including the role, skill level, and authority of the case managers), and the nature of the case manager–client interaction.

The different types of case management models are usually characterized by who delivers the service and what type of function is provided. On one extreme is the model in which a primary therapist performs the case management function. The primary therapist refers, links, monitors, and evaluates the patient's progress in a coordinated, comprehensive service program. The primary therapist in this model is a professional with high status and skills. This model is explicitly described by Lamb (1980). A modified model is described by Peterson, Wirth, and Wolkon (1979), wherein the ward chief (a psychiatrist) develops an aftercare plan, that is, plans an appropriate referral. A caseworker (a nonprofessional) makes the appropriate phone calls, completes the necessary paperwork, and, most important, prepares the patient for the referral, then follows up to assure that the referral is successfully completed.

On the other extreme is what has been called the broker model of case management. The case manager is a service manager, or broker, who identifies client's needs, knows community resources, and matches the two through appropriate referrals. The broker monitors the results and updates the comprehensive service plan but does no direct treatment. Both the primary therapist model and broker model attend to the basic task of facilitating the individual client in obtaining needed services in a timely manner. The task is necessary when the needed services are not available under one administratively coordinated, comprehensive service system such as a long-term hospital.

A third model of case management has been proposed (Polak, Kirby, and Deitchman, 1979) that, in our minds, is not case management but rather a fully integrated mental health service delivery system. A team of mental health experts is assigned responsibility for a small geographical area. They provide all necessary services in the community, and, if hospitalization is needed, the team provides the professional services in the hospital. Indeed, such an administratively coordinated, comprehensive service system eliminates the need for a separate case management program. Utilizing the term for such services merely confuses an already vague and unclear term and emphasizes the need for a clear and explicit definition of case management.

These three models have in common the task of assuring that the patient gets to the next program in the treatment process. At that point, a new agency or new primary therapist may take over case management responsibilities, or the responsibility may remain with the patient's original or last case manager. Such distinctions must, of course, be explicit in the plans and procedures of the case management program and are among the aspects of the program that should be evaluated. In addition, first-line practitioners in all three models have hands-on information concerning gaps and inadequacies in available community services. They should have a channel to communicate such information so that action can be taken. This channel is another aspect to be evaluated.

Case Management Program Evaluation

When we attempt to describe a program and say that the program works, we are doing an evaluation, whether we like it or not. When we decide to make a program change, the decision is based on an evaluation, whether we like it or not. And when we tell our clients that a particular program is the best program for them, we have done an evaluation of the program relative to the needs of the client. We do these evaluations in good faith, using the best information available.

In this context evaluation is the application of the most appropriate scientific methodology to provide systematic and objective, or at least unbiased, information to management to help in decision making and in providing information for program accountability. Such evaluation research is essential for good management. Indeed, good managers and good clinicians use such information as much as possible whether or not they call it evaluation. They may call it assessment, feedback, planning, or just plain decision making. Whatever the name, they analyze the situation in as much detail as possible with as much systematic data and as many facts as possible before they act. They may or may not have a staff to help gather and analyze the information. If such a staff exists, they may or may not call it an evaluation staff.

The first step in any evaluation is to describe the independent variable or the intervention, what it is that is to be evaluated— namely, the program or particular aspects of interest in the program. We shall define a *program* as the combined social, psychological, and physiological interactions—the influences and relationships among patients, staff, and community elements involved in the provision of case management. In evaluating a case management program completely, all factors that can influence the program should be taken into account. Obviously, this cannot be done, because we do not know all the factors. If we did know them all, we probably could not specify them precisely enough to obtain reliable and valid measures. Even if we could identify and measure the relevant variables, we probably would not have the time, money, or staff to accomplish the task. Thus, we must select from the myriad of potential variables those which we think are most important.

The definition of *important* depends on the purpose of the evaluation. Is the evaluation for planning, reporting to the board or funding agency, or seeking new funds? Is it for improving efficiency or effectiveness or making suggestions to correct a known weakness in the program? Is it for making clients more satisfied or preventing burnout of staff? Is it for reducing the use of hospitals, improving referral processes, or documenting the need for additional services in the community? Each of these purposes might require classifying different variables as being important. Importance depends not only on the purpose of the evaluation but also on the perceptions of reality, theoretical frameworks, assumptions, philosophy, knowledge, and values of the definer of importance. In most cases the definer is the director of the program, who usually has appropriate input from others.

Given a list of important variables, some may have to be eliminated because of the availability of information related to the important variables; the cost, effort, and skill needed to obtain the information; or the amount of interference with the ongoing service program that collecting such information entails. Nothing is easy; there is no ideal world; compromise is necessary.

In order to maximize the utility of the evaluation, it is frequently advisable to have an expert in evaluation research involved from the beginning to the end of the evaluation effort. This expert should be familiar with case management and become thoroughly familiar with the program to be evaluated. The evaluator's technical suggestions concerning interview schedules, instrument development, sample selection, evaluation design, statistical analyses, and even the writing of the results may prove extremely useful.

The first set of questions to be answered in any kind of evaluation is the same as the first set of questions that are answered by any competent manager establishing a case management program: What functions are provided by the case management program? Who or what kinds of persons should provide them? On what or whom should they be focused? It should be remembered that the goals of case management programs are to help a client obtain needed services at the appropriate time in order to improve the client's functioning, prevent regression, reduce the use of more expensive services (such as hospitalization), and improve the quality of the client's life. Any particular program may have different priorities and may include other goals.

The functions that seem necessary in any case management program are: the identification of case management clients, the assessment of those clients, the planning of coordinated and comprehensive service programs, and the implementation of plans by linking clients with or referring clients to appropriate services or facilities in a timely fashion. Also needed are monitoring the progress of clients, and evaluating clients in relation to current and planned services and advocacy. Other functions that may be necessary are education or counseling at-risk individuals and their families about community support services; the identification and documentation of gaps in services, inadequate services, and service system resistances to case management; training and consulting with non-mental-health-trained care providers (such as board and care providers); and resource location and development. These functions need not be performed by the same person or even by the same agency, but they all should be performed when needed and in a coordinated manner.

It is the task of the program manager and of the evaluator, at different times and under different circumstances, to specify which functions are to be performed by which agency and which agency personnel. The manager plans for and implements services and then attempts to see that the services are provided according to the plan. It is this latter aspect that is called evaluation. The utility and sophistication of the evaluation depend on the training, experience, and other characteristics of the person conducting the evaluation. Given the importance of program description, how does an evaluator go about describing the program, making value judgments about it, and, most important, making recommendations for program improvement?

Evaluation Tasks and Methods

First the evaluator should obtain systematic, objective, explicit, and preferably quantifiable information on the program's goals, policies, procedures, and division of labor. This can be accomplished by any of the following methods: observing the program in action; interviewing policy makers, boards, directors, managers, and staff; and examining written material such as policy and procedure manuals, budgets, organizational charts, job descriptions, and interagency agreements, especially in agreements describing the authority of case managers over any other agencies with which they deal (Altschuler and Forward, 1978). Which methods are used and how detailed the evaluation is are determined by the purpose of the evaluation, the time and budget allocated to the evaluation, and the skill levels and approaches of the evaluators. With such information, it can be determined whether a program is actually following the policies and procedures that were originally defined. If it is not, it may be recommended that the policies and procedures be changed or the supervision of the program be improved. Essential to an evaluation is the existence of a standard against which to measure performance.

A benchmark of great importance to program planners, administrators, and evaluators is the staffing standard, that is, the number of case managers needed in a particular program and the skill levels they need. One service model (Legislative Work Group, 1981) recommends 8.6 case managers and 2.6 support staff for every 400 clients, who would receive 4,800 units of service per year. Thus each case manager would have a caseload of 50 clients. The skill levels of staff are not specified in the model, nor are the functions of the case managers. In this model, each client receives one case management unit of service about once a month. It is clear from the infrequency of contact that these case managers are not the primary therapists; if primary therapists are the case managers, they must be able to distinguish their different functions and record them separately in order to ascertain if the model is being followed. Thus, although this model does not specify the role, function, and responsibilities of the case manager, the staffing pattern in the model imposes constraints to be considered when defining the functions of case managers.

A different staffing standard was developed for a public guardian case management program (Public Guardian, 1982). It states, "The conservator shall make provisions for the conservatee in the community to be seen for case management purposes at a frequency sufficient for the conservator to be informed of the conservatee's problems, needs, and progress with a minimum of one face-to-face contact each month during the first three months of conservatorship in the community and at least quarterly thereafter" (Public Guardian, 1982, p. 12). Given the task or model of case

management in a particular program, the administrator and evaluator must ask if the staffing pattern, frequency of contacts, and
budget make sense. The crucial question is: Do the tasks assigned
to a case management program make sense, given existing community services?

Classifications of Program Evaluations

One useful way to classify program evaluations is by the time
segment that is evaluated. Is it before the intervention (prior to
seeing the client), during the intervention, or after? Simply put, is
the evaluation of the input into the program how the program is
implemented, or the outcome of the program? Does the evaluation
require measurements or information obtained at one or more
points of time? Zusman and Wurster (1975) have classified evaluation studies into the simple categories of before, during, and after
interventions.

Before studies measure an agency's preparation for providing
case management services. They involve the examination of agency
resources, plans, organization, and management techniques.
Among the analytic techniques for before studies described in the
literature are structure evaluation (Donabedian, 1966), effort evaluation (Suchman, 1967; James, 1969), and system evaluation (Etzioni,
1969). This last type of study is generally the quickest and easiest
to carry out. In structural or input evaluation, the program is
described. A description by itself, however, is not an evaluation.
Description is necessary but not sufficient for an evaluation. To be
an evaluation, a description must be compared with some standard
(ideally, an explicit standard of quality of excellence). Effort evaluations (Suchman, 1967) describe what resources are being expended
in a program in a particular time period. These studies generally
focus on staffing patterns, including training, the number of hours
worked, budget, and the number and kind of production units.
These kinds of studies are sometimes classified as before studies and
sometimes as during studies.

During studies focus on the service process itself and take
place while the services are being provided. Terms such as process

evaluation (Suchman, 1967) and formative evaluation (Aiken, 1972; Scriven, 1972) have been used to describe such studies. Examples include an examination of the case manager–client interaction or of the relationship between the case management agency and other community agencies involved in the case management system. Other areas that might be studied by process evaluations are determining whether a program was implemented as intended or determining if previously defined standards of care have been applied. During studies require a detailed, intimate examination of the program itself.

After studies focus on what occurs after a program. Such studies generally determine whether an intervention benefited clients. These are generally called outcome evaluations when the participants in the program are studied and impact evaluations when the social indicators in the community are studied (Suchman, 1967). After studies attribute what occurs after the program to the program itself. Thus, even in this type of evaluation, a good description of the program is essential.

Structural Evaluations. The concept of structure in a program applies not only internally (such as a program's organization and staffing and the size of its caseload) but also externally (such as the community resources available to case management clients). For example, are there adequate living facilities, recreational facilities, medical services, financial resources, mental health treatment facilities, or vocational rehabilitation services? Without such resources, case management services in the client's behalf cannot be provided at all or can be provided too infrequently to meet the client's needs. When resources are lacking, the advocacy aspect of case management becomes important. Indeed, adequate community resources are necessary (but not sufficient) for a viable case management program. Although structural evaluations are widely used because they are simple to perform, easy to quantify, inexpensive, and fairly valid for comparing agencies within the same categories, they clearly do not help meet the goal of quality care. Therefore, they probably should not be considered as definitive evaluations.

Effort or Input Evaluations. These evaluations focus on what kinds and how much effort is expended in case management, including the number and type of staff utilized, the budget, and defining and counting work units. Factors evaluated in this approach include the number of case management client visits, case management contact hours, the number of referrals, the number of cases open, the number of clients currently involved in the case management system compared to the number of people in the community eligible for the service, and the number of clients successfully completing the case management plan or a part thereof. Another factor that is analyzed in effort or input evaluations is the ratio of case management contact hours to total case management program hours. With this ratio, the time spent in client contacts can be compared with in-service training, staff development, and any other activities.

As part of a pilot case management program, Honnard (1983) evaluated the relationship between client contact hours and total case management hours (including the time spent in administration and referral source development). He predicted that the ratio of client contact hours to administrative hours would increase with program duration and staff experience. However, an analysis of the case managers' time and activities revealed that this did not occur. The time spent in administration (approximately 50 percent) remained relatively constant during the course of the program. Studies to determine the reasons for this finding disclosed that the time allocated for preprogram development, training, and interpretation and for establishing an interagency referral network was not sufficient. Thus, increased contact with community agencies in the form of administrative time was necessary to ensure a flow of clients into the program.

Although client contact hours did not increase over time, program utilization did. Presumably, increased utilization could be attributed to the continued emphasis on establishing a referral network within the region. Analysis of the ratio of average caseload to program capacity (based on a standard of forty clients per case manager) provides a measure of this effect. Ratios were determined for periods just after program initiation, ten months into the program, and just before program termination (sixteen months). The ratios obtained were 0.62 at program initiation, 0.77 at program midpoint, and 1.10 before program termination. These data appear to confirm increased program utilization over time.

As noted, effort or input evaluation often includes statements of the number of cases opened, of patient visits, of contact hours, or of referrals. Agencies commonly interpret an increase in one or more of these variables as an improvement in service. A critical set of assumptions underlies this type of evaluation, namely, that case management expenditures and activities accomplish something desirable and that the amount accomplished is related to the amount of effort expended.

Process Evaluations. Process evaluations examine what happens during treatment rather than before or after treatment. They are used to determine if "good case management" is being applied (Carmichael, Small, and Regan, 1972, p. 42). Process evaluations study the extent to which accepted case management practices are used in meeting client needs. However, the definition of good case management practices is problematical. Is it determined by the program's policies and procedures manual, by comparison with other programs already deemed successful by experts, by systematic empirical research, or by what is written in the professional literature? The definition used, as in all evaluation studies, should be mutually determined by the program management and the evaluator. All methods of collecting reliable and valid data relevant to the particular process issue should be considered, including interviewing staff and clients, observing actual interactions, and reading charts. Whatever the source of data, appropriate sampling techniques and well-constructed instruments (such as interview schedules, observation recordings, and content analyses) are necessary.

In the study previously described, Honnard (1983) systematically observed the case manager–client interaction to ascertain if the actual process of case management followed the program plan (policies and procedures). In this program, case management was defined in terms of a brokerage model, in which the case manager functioned as a service manager who identified client needs, used agency services, referred the client to appropriate units, continually monitored the client's progress, and updated the service plan. Contrary to the program's definition, observation of the program's process revealed that the case managers were functioning as intake workers whose primary activity was linking the clients with treatment units within the mental health system. They were not able to monitor the client's progress continuously.

In this instance, the communication to management described the findings and offered explanations for the findings. It also recommended that management reexamine the task and function of the case management program in light of available services in the community to see whether the program description should be changed or whether the staff should be following the policies and procedures. On the other hand, an auditor who made the same findings might report that the program does not comply with its own policies and procedures and therefore recommend that funding be cut off. Since the functions and goals of an audit are different from those of a program evaluation, they should always be made explicit.

Linking Function Evaluations. A major part of most case management programs is the linking function, or referring clients from one agency to another. Referrals seem a simple and mundane activity, yet failures in the referral process have been a concern for decades. Clearly defining the linking function for all agencies participating in the case management system is one recent attempt to overcome the problem. Indeed, for many years professionals have blamed clients for not following through on referrals, for noncompliance, or for just not being motivated. This is especially true of chronic mental patients. Wolkon (1968) found that 70 percent of the patients referred from psychiatric hospitals to community-based social rehabilitation centers did not complete the referrals. He then examined the records of the intake workers to ascertain if the workers' interventions were related to the results of the referral process. He later examined the characteristics of clients who completed and did not complete referrals (Wolkon, 1970). The data for these studies were descriptions of the case manager–client interaction as reflected in the clinical charts. The intake workers were professional social workers and the researcher assumed that the clinical records would include specific content that reflected diagnostic, evaluative, and client-worker interactive processes providing guidance for clinical treatment. Unfortunately, it was not possible to systematically categorize record material in ways that illuminated the character of client-professional interaction. In contrast to the variability of recording regarding client-professional interaction, data about when contracts were made and how they were made was systematically recorded.

The author concluded that hospital discharge represented some form of crisis, and thus crisis theory (Caplan, 1963) could be applied. One of the basic tenets of crisis theory is that the closer in time the intervention is to the crisis, the greater its effect. It was therefore hypothesized that the closer the intake contact was to the day of hospital discharge, the more effective the referral would be. The data supported the hypothesis; 52 percent of the clients seen within seven days of hospital discharge began the rehabilitation program, 33 percent contacted between seven and fourteen days began rehabilitation, and 16 percent contacted more than two weeks after discharge began rehabilitation. Analysis of the patients' charts also revealed that having the client visit the rehabilitation center was more than twice as effective as contacts by telephone, which themselves were twice as effective as contacts through the mail.

Despite the correlations in the findings, here was a set of initial data that could be used as a standard for implementing referral procedures. In addition, several sets of data (what the intake workers did, the characteristics of the clients who completed referrals, support provided by outpatient and family service settings [Wolkon, 1972], and crisis theory itself) led to the proposal that a necessary but not sufficient condition for successful crisis intervention was the satisfaction of the client's dependency or affiliative needs. Acting on this principle led to even more successful linkages (Wolkon, 1974).

These principles were applied later in establishing a hospital aftercare program by training caseworkers to make appointments for patients with community-based resources as soon after discharge as possible. Of course, the clinics were not always able to make early appointments. Systematic data were collected in this program to test the effectiveness of the principles; again and again, the principles were confirmed (Wolkon, Peterson, and Rogawski, 1978). The data were analyzed in greater detail to ascertain if the application of these principles was as effective with patients who had different characteristics. They were not. The principles were significantly more effective with nonwhite than with white persons (Wolkon and Peterson, 1980).

Outcome Evaluations. Outcome evaluations determine the extent to which a program or intervention accomplishes its goals and how much it has influenced the target illness, problem, or behavior. Outcome evaluations in a case management program determine how much the program improves the functioning of the client, enhances the quality of the client's life, reduces the use of more intensive and expensive treatment facilities by the client, and increases the amount and quality of services in the community (the advocacy function). As has been pointed out, all input and process evaluations are assumed to be related to accomplishing the goals of the entire case management program. Whatever the outcome measures are, the underlying point of an outcome evaluation is to attribute the obtained results to the case management program.

The best approach to an outcome evaluation is the classical experimental design wherein clients are randomly assigned to receive, to not receive, or to receive variations of the case management program. Random assignment with large numbers of persons improves the likelihood that the characteristics of the clients in each group will be about the same. If data are collected about the characteristics of the clients, then the assumption of similar characteristics can be empirically checked. Unwanted differences can be controlled by statistical methods, such as by controlling selected variables or using an analysis of covariance. If equivalent groups are randomly exposed to different interventions during the same time period, any measures taken after an intervention can reasonably be attributed to the intervention (in this instance, case management).

Another approach to outcome evaluation has been called impact evaluation (Suchman, 1967; James, 1969). In this approach, the focus of the evaluation is not on the persons who participate in the case management program but rather on the impact of the program on the community, that is, on social indicators. If the case management program is focused on a geographical or catchment area and one of the goals is to lessen hospitalizations, then an impact study might look at the hospitalization rate of the catchment area before and after the case management program was implemented. If the target of the case management program is the chronic patient, an appropriate criterion variable would be rehospitalization.

To examine the impact of the advocacy aspect of case management, the comprehensiveness and adequacy of services before and after a case management program was introduced might be appropriate comparisons. Stronger findings of the impact of case management could be revealed in a study comparing two similar catchment areas—one in which a case management system was introduced and one without a case management program. Given the realities of environmental and policy changes, such as funding cuts, which may occur during an evaluation, the importance of having two catchment areas to compare is obvious. Even with severe funding cuts that might grossly limit services, the catchment area with a case management program might still provide better service coordination among the limited service resources than an area without such a program. However, if no comparison catchment area is used, it may simply appear that the case management program was ineffective. Such factors may have more effect on the outcome variables than the intervention under investigation. For example, funding cutbacks in the public sector may decrease the comprehensiveness and adequacy of services in a community despite an active advocacy program.

Another type of impact evaluation has been termed adequacy of performance (Suchman, 1967; James, 1969). In the initial planning for a case management program, the number of persons in the community who need case management (both incidence and prevalence) should have been estimated and the proportion of the need that the new program would satisfy should have been stated. At some point after the program has been implemented, the proportion of the total need that the program is satisfying should be determined. Is the ratio between the amount of case management provided to the amount needed approaching the total community need or the program goal?

The final type of after evaluation is cost-benefit analysis. The common sense of these words is compelling. Are the benefits of the program worth the costs? How can responsible administrators not answer this most reasonable question? How can programs be funded without a statement that the benefits are worth the costs?

Such statements are usually based on logic and values, not data. In cost-benefit analyses, a cost in dollars for attaining a particular benefit is compared with the dollar value of those benefits. However, defining benefits in a meaningful way and assigning dollar values to these benefits, such as an improved quality of life or improved skills in daily living, pose heroic challenges. However, costs can be associated with treatment programs before and after the case management intervention. If clients obtain jobs, wages can be used as the dollar value of benefits; in addition, the savings to the welfare rolls or social security disability funds and the increase in collectible taxes can also be calculated as benefits. Dollar costs can be attributed to the service program despite the fact that there are many different accepted cost-accounting and allocation methods.

Technological Issues

It is difficult to determine the course or courses of positive findings, particularly of client-centered outcome evaluations. One of the functions of case management is to assure that the clients obtain appropriate treatment, not necessarily to deliver it. Perhaps the positive findings are due to the treatment that the clients received rather than to case management. Would the client have received the treatment had the case management program not existed? If there are comparison groups in the study design for whom the same kinds of treatment facilities were available, then the question can be examined and answered with some confidence. If treatment histories were available for similar clients with the same community resources before case management was established in the community, a partial answer to the question may be possible. The assumption underlying the proliferation of case management programs is that clients do not otherwise take advantage of available treatment resources and so do not function in the community to their capacity or frequently regress to the point of needing hospitalization again and again. Is this assumption justified?

Another problem with client-centered program evaluation is in obtaining a study sample. Ethics forbid withholding what is believed to be the best treatment from an individual for research purposes. Frequently, although control is assumed over the entire operation—the program, the staff, and the clients—no such control exists (Wolkon, 1971). Honnard (1983) reported a specific relevant example. Program management had agreed to assign clients randomly to a case management condition and a control group (in this case, a non-case-management condition). The plan was quickly abandoned because of a lack of referrals to the program and an inability to establish a pool of eligible case management clients. Ethics and the administrative necessity of having a full caseload prohibited the establishment of the randomly assigned control group. A compromise design was then set up wherein the comparison group was selected at random from a pool of patients who lived in the same geographical region and who matched the case management participants on several variables thought to be related to the outcome variable of subsequent hospitalization.

An outcome study of a case management program is usually more difficult than an outcome study of other programs. In addition to the problems of definition, measurement, design, control, time, and expense is the problem that a case management program is geared to helping the client make use of a variety of other needed and available services. The problem of defining when a client completes or should complete a case management program is unclear. Usually the target groups of case management programs are the chronically ill. These are patients for whom a lifetime of treatment of one kind or another is the best prognosis. One of the functions of case management is to minimize the intensity and expense of the needed treatment. If case management is a lifelong program, how can its outcome be measured? What constitutes an after study?

Few case management programs have criteria for discharge from the program; what criteria do exist vary from program to program (Roessler and Mack, 1974; Human Services Coordination Alliance, 1976; Solberg, 1980; Hammake, 1983). Clients, of course, withdraw from programs whether staff wants them to or not. If one evaluates only those clients who choose to terminate, one has a self-selected, or biased, sample. Such a sample may be useful for certain purposes, but it is not useful for a general program evaluation. How can an outcome study be done?

One method is to take an arbitrary time period for each client and examine his status at the end of, for example, one year in the program or his status at different points during the year. The status description may include such variables as symptomatology, the level of functioning in different areas (skills of daily living, social functioning, relationships with the family, and vocational functioning), the type of treatment needed and/or used, the quality of life, and any other variable specified in the goals of the program. The evaluation of such interventions should include the client's self-report of progress, which is valid in its own right. However, this should be distinguished from satisfaction with services, which also has its own validity.

Assuming that we have a systematic, reliable, and valid description of clients before and one year after entering a case management program (or a description of case management activities over a year), we must ask if the effort expended in the case management program is worth it. The descriptions so painstakingly collected have to be put into context. They must be compared with something. The context and nature of the comparison should be specified before the evaluation is begun. If a randomly assigned control group exists, the case management group and the control group are compared. The same would be done if a matched comparison group was used as a control. With either type of comparison group, the amount of change in each of the groups can also be compared. That is, did one group change (regress or improve) more than the other group?

When no specific comparison group is in the initial study design, the findings of the case management program can be compared with findings of programs in the literature. Such a comparison is much weaker than a built-in comparison, but it is substantially better than no comparison at all. In addition to or in combination with these methods, another technique is using the clients as their own control in preprogram and postprogram measures. If a goal of the case management program is to reduce the use of inpatient facilities, the amount of time spent in hospitals the year before entering the case management program should be compared with the time so spent in hospitals the year after entry into the program. If the variables used in the evaluation include the reduction of symptomatology, then preprogram and postprogram measures on this variable should be obtained and compared.

Another question can be raised about after studies. Should results be observable or measurable one year later or two, three, five, or ten years later? What length of time is of concern to the evaluators, to management, to the funding authorities, to the profession, to the science of rehabilitation, and to public policy? Since we have cited program improvement as one major function of evaluation research, we must make a special comment. Namely, the longer the follow-up is after the clients' involvement, the less likely that the program will be the same as when the clients participated; therefore, the less the evaluation has to say about improving the existing program. Of course, if data are collected that are related to theory, useful hypotheses may evolve that can be tested through future program changes.

Let us now move from problems to more positive aspects. Since *Time* magazine declared the computer as "Man of the Year" in 1983, no discussion of research and no discussion of improving the management of programs can take place without discussing automated data systems. Computers can manipulate data and report it faster than manual methods, especially if the data base is large. Computer systems, however, are expensive. They require a major capital expenditure for development and installation. Although it is beyond the scope of this chapter to explore under what conditions a case management program should have an automated data system, we do want to describe the use of an existing automated management information system (AMIS; if necessary, please ask a French-speaking friend for the friendly meaning of this acronym) for case management purposes.

The Los Angeles County Department of Mental Health implemented an AMIS in 1982. This department delivers over one million units of service each year, initiates over 100,000 episodes of treatment each year, and has a variety of programs ranging from acute inpatient care to long-term socialization programs for a population of over 7.5 million people (3 percent of the U.S. population). The relevant characteristics of the AMIS are as follows:

1. Information is entered when an episode of treatment is opened, when a unit of service is delivered, and when an episode is closed. The information includes who delivered what kind of service, when, to whom, where, and for how long.

2.   Each client has a unique AMIS number wherever he or she re-
     ceives services in the system. (The department has over 100 loca-
     tions throughout the county.)
3.   Information is entered daily from over fifty terminals through-
     out the county.
4.   Information on a client is available on the terminals as soon
     as it is entered into the terminal.
5.   Reports are produced monthly.
6.   Ad hoc reports are available as needed.

What does all this have to do with case management and its
evaluation? Two of the major functions of most case management
programs are linking the client to appropriate services and monitoring the client's progress. For example, the client may be referred
to a particular agency by the case manager and, under ideal
circumstances, the client calls the case manager after completing the
referral and says: "It is a wonderful place; I'll continue to go there."
In the same ideal world, the receiving agency calls the referring
source (in this instance, the case manager), gives thanks for the
referral, and gives a status report. The ideal world, however, seldom
exists. How, then, does the case manager find out the results of the
referral efforts? Are additional intervention efforts needed to help
the client obtain needed services? The case manager could call the
agency or the client. However, both are time-consuming activities,
especially if the only purpose is to ascertain if the client kept the
appointment. A more efficient method is to ask a computer terminal
the day after the appointment. (For this to work, the agency must
have entered the data into the terminal when the service was
delivered.) In this way the case manager can easily find out the
results of the referral intervention and take any follow-up action
that is necessary.
    Whether an automated information system is useful in a
particular case management program is an important management
question, but it is beyond the scope of this chapter. However,
evaluations of case management programs should look for a functional equivalent of such a routine monitoring system; follow-up
interventions should exist whether they are automated or manual.

Conclusion

The evaluation of a case management program is complex and challenging. Within case management and program evaluation, there are several models and procedures to consider, each with its own merits and limitations. Each model and procedure also has a natural constituency; managers, boards, and funding agencies may prefer organizational data; consumers may prefer client-reported outcome data; and case managers may prefer process-oriented data. These different groups are likely to assign different values to the different models and procedures (Lebow, 1982). Evaluators may prefer certain research methodologies and certain theories. The challenges of integrating the various points of view, priorities, values, and philosophies in conducting evaluation research in case management are great. The rewards for analysts who work on successful evaluations more than compensate for the difficulties. The real beneficiaries of successful evaluation research are the clients, who will participate in more effective programs in the future.

Suggested Readings

Aiken, R. C. "Evaluation Theory Development." In C. H. Weiss (Ed.), *Evaluating Action Programs: Readings in Social Action and Evaluation.* Boston: Allyn & Bacon, 1972.

Altschuler, S. L., and Forward, T. "The Inverted Hierarchy: A Case Manager Approach to Mental Health Services." *Administration in Mental Health*, 1978, 57, 57–68.

Bachrach, L. L., and Lamb, H. R. "Conceptual Issues in the Evaluation of Deinstitutionalization." In G. J. Stabler and W. R. Tash (Eds.), *Innovation Approaches to Mental Health Evaluation.* New York: Academic Press, 1982.

Lamb, H. R. "Guiding Principles for Community Survival." In H. R. Lamb and Associates, *Community Survival for Long-Term Patients.* San Francisco: Jossey-Bass, 1976.

Scriven, M. "The Methodology of Evaluation." In C. H. Weiss (Ed.), *Evaluating Action Programs: Readings in Social Action and Evaluation.* Boston: Allyn & Bacon, 1972.

Suchman, E. *Evaluation Research*. New York: Russell Sage Foundation, 1967.

References

Aiken, R. C. "Evaluation Theory Development." In C. H. Weiss (Ed.), *Evaluating Action Programs: Readings in Social Action and Evaluation*. Boston: Allyn & Bacon, 1972.

Altschuler, S. L., and Forward, T. "The Inverted Hierarchy: A Case Manager Approach to Mental Health Services." *Administration in Mental Health*, 1978, 57, 57–68.

Caplan, G. "Emotional Crisis." In A. Deutch and H. Fishbein (Eds.), *The Encyclopedia of Mental Health*. Vol. 2. New York: Funk and Watts, 1963.

Carmichael, H. T., Small, S. M., and Regan, T. F. *Prospects and Proposals: Lifetime Learning for Psychiatrists*. Washington, D.C.: American Psychiatric Association, 1972.

Donabedian, A. "Evaluating the Quality of Medical Care." *Milbank Memorial Fund Quarterly*, 1966, 44, 166–203.

Etzioni, A. "Two Approaches to Organizational Analysis: A Critique and a Suggestion." In H. C. Schulberg, A. Sheldon, and F. Baker (Eds.), *Program Evaluation in the Health Fields*. New York: Behavioral Publications, 1969.

Hammake, R. A. "Client Outcome Evaluation of the Statewide Implementations of Community Support Services." *Psychosocial Rehabilitation Journal*, 1983, 7 (1), 2–10.

Honnard, R. "Case Management Pilot Project: Report on the Implementation of SB 951." County of Los Angeles, Department of Mental Health E & R Papers, November 1983, 11 (4), 1–21.

Human Services Coordination Alliance. "Case Accountability: Care Management, Service Provision Reporting, Service Outcome Assessment." *Project Share Executive Summary*. Louisville, Ky., September 1976.

James, G. "Evaluation in Public Health Practice." In H. C. Schulberg, A. Sheldon, and F. Baker (Eds.), *Program Evaluation in the Health Fields*. New York: Behavioral Publications, 1969.

Lamb, H. R. "Therapist–Case Managers: More Than Brokers of

Services." *Hospital and Community Psychiatry*, 1980, *31*, 762–764.

Lebow, J. "Models for Evaluating Services at Community Mental Health Centers." *Hospital and Community Psychiatry*, 1982, *33* (12), 1010–1014.

Legislative Work Group. *A Model for California Community Mental Health Programs*. Sacramento, Calif.: Legislative Work Group, 1981.

Peterson, C. L., Wirth, B., and Wolkon, G. H. "Utilization of Paraprofessionals in a Mental Health Continuing Care Program." *Health and Social Work*, 1979, *4* (3), 64–81.

Polak, P. R., Kirby, M. W., and Deitchman, W. S. "Treating Acutely Psychotic Patients in Private Homes." In H. R. Lamb (Ed.), *New Directions in Mental Health Services: Alternatives to Acute Hospitalization*, no. 1. San Francisco: Jossey-Bass, 1979.

Public Guardian, Los Angeles County Interagency Agreement, Los Angeles County Department of Mental Health, 1982.

Roessler, R., and Mack, G. "Services Integration Second Year Report: Statement of Issues, Research Methodology, and Experimental Case Management Procedures: Social and Rehabilitation Service." *Project Share Executive Summary*. Washington, D.C.: September 1974.

Scriven, M. "The Methodology of Evaluation." In C. H. Weiss (Ed.), *Evaluating Action Programs: Readings in Social Action and Evaluation*. Boston: Allyn & Bacon, 1972.

Solberg, A. "The Effects of Intensive Post-Hospital Follow-Up Services: A Controlled Study." Unpublished manuscript, Acute Psychiatric Unit, Fresno County, Calif., Department of Health, 1980.

Suchman, E. *Evaluation Research*. New York: Russell Sage Foundation, 1967.

Wolkon, G. H. "Effecting a Continuum of Care: An Exploitation of the Crisis of Psychiatric Hospital Release." *Community Mental Health Journal*, 1968, *4*, 63–73.

Wolkon, G. H. "Characteristics of Clients and Continuity of Care into the Community." *Community Mental Health Journal*, 1970, *6*, 215–221.

Wolkon, G. H.. "Consent, Cooperation and Control in Rehabilitation Research." In R. O'Toole (Ed.), *Organization, Management and Tactics of Social Research.* Cambridge, Mass.: Schenckman, 1971.

Wolkon, G. H. "Crisis Theory, the Application for Treatment and Dependency." *Comprehensive Psychiatry,* 1972, *13,* 459–464.

Wolkon, G. H. "Changing Roles: Crisis in the Continuum of Care in the Community." *Psychotherapy: Theory, Research and Practice,* 1974, *11,* 367–370.

Wolkon, G. H., and Peterson, C. L. "Characteristics of Clients, Staff Interventions and the Continuum of Care." *Journal of Community Psychology,* 1980, *8,* 256–260.

Wolkon, G. H., Peterson, C. L., and Rogawski, A. S. "The Implementation of a Psychiatric Continuing Care Program." *Hospital and Community Psychiatry,* 1978, *29,* 254–256.

Zusman, J., and Wurster, L. (Eds.). *Program Evaluation: Alcohol, Drug Abuse, and Mental Health Services.* Lexington, Mass.: Heath, 1975.

5

Children and the
Child Welfare System

Susan J. Wells

This chapter discusses theoretical and conceptual issues of particular importance in child welfare case management. It analyzes
guiding policies, regulations, and major models for case management in this field; highlights exemplars of effective programs to
indicate effective innovations in child welfare case management;
and examines issues of professional role, team work, and collaboration within human services agencies and with health and family
court systems. It also outlines skills required of effective case
managers, as well as training and education needs. Discussions of
consumer advocacy issues, current problems, and future directions
for practice conclude the chapter.

Child welfare is a system of services, both public and private,
that safeguards the well-being of children and their families. When

Note: This work was made possible by the Region 9 Child Welfare
Training Grant, supported by Grant OHD 90-CT-1965 from the Children's
Bureau, Department of Health and Human Services. Portions of this paper
are taken from a paper written for publication by the National Child
Welfare Training Center.

family breakdown threatens the health or welfare of a child, public agencies, private agencies, or proprietary care may be part of the intervention effort. Every state has a public agency mandated to protect children at risk. Public child welfare services may be housed in public welfare, an umbrella agency, or a separate child welfare department. Responsibility for administering and supervising services varies from total local control to state control (U.S. Department of Health, Education and Welfare, 1977).

Some private, nonprofit agencies have an organizational mandate to deliver preventive or protective services. They provide outreach to vulnerable families or work cooperatively with the public agency to provide services to a common clientele. Private agencies may also receive grants to develop a child welfare program or enter into contracts with the state or county to provide services to public agency clients.

In proprietary care, clients hire licensed therapists, lawyers, or other professionals to provide some child welfare service. Proprietary agencies operate on a for-profit basis.

The public protective service agency, mandated by the state to protect children from harm, is a fundamental component of the child welfare system. Referrals to protective services are primarily concerned with neglect, abuse, or the absence of a caretaker. Other common reasons for referral are children's status offenses, behavioral problems, or mental or physical illness that requires care beyond the parents' capacity (Jenkins and Schroeder, 1980). Protective service has long been regarded as the bottom line of service delivery. Only when the family and community have failed and the child is in clear danger will the public agency intervene.

In spite of this residual approach to child welfare, there have been many efforts to provide positive environments and experiences for children. The settlement houses, child labor laws, well-baby clinics, and Head Start are examples of nationwide efforts to adopt a preventive program. Recent federal legislation (Public Law 96-272) and state enactments (such as California SB-14) have increased efforts to prevent families from breaking up and to encourage broken families to reunite.

Currently the child welfare system is comprised of a great number of community services. Child protection often involves the police, hospitals, public health, juvenile court, the school system, family agencies, the public prosecutor and public defender, public welfare, homemakers, probation and parole, volunteers, and the public protective agency. Child welfare services also include daycare, foster care, institutional care, and adoption.

Daycare is the provision of care for children outside the home for part of the day. It is most often used by working parents, but it can also alleviate stress in children with abusive or neglectful parents or provide stimulation and learning opportunities that a child would not otherwise receive. Incidents of physical and sexual abuse of children in daycare centers has focused parental, governmental, and media attention on the quality of care and licensing in this burgeoning field of service (Alston, 1984). Since the proportion of working mothers with children under the age of six is approaching 50 percent, daycare services as a component of child welfare and family services are becoming increasingly important (Fox, 1984; Miller, 1984).

Substitute care (foster care, group homes, institutions, and adoption) protects children from harm, provides respite for parents with severely ill children, supplies treatment services that are not available in the home, and administers care to children whose parents are not willing or able to do so. Children who are adjudged delinquent or incorrigible may also be placed in substitute care. The rising rate of births among teenagers, which creates a high-risk category for child abuse, has escalated the need for service programs that teach parenting skills to teenage mothers and the fathers of their babies (Miller, 1984). Innovative programs also provide support and counseling for grandparents involved in child care (Williams, 1984).

Two critical problems in providing child welfare services are interagency coordination and the orderly and timely progression of a case through the system. These issues are particularly important in child protection, where mismanagement can result in years of multiple placements or the death of a child. Case management is regarded as a way to reduce confusion, to enhance accountability, and to provide quality services to children and their families.

Definition and Theoretical Basis

Case management is the process of shepherding the client through the service delivery system by following a standardized

series of activities designed to facilitate decision making, goal
planning, intervention, and evaluation (Jurkiewicz, 1980). The
goals of case management are to maximize the quality of service,
access community resources, and maintain an accountable, cost-
effective service delivery system. Case management can be described
as "obtaining the entire range of services needed by people with
multiple problems" (Steinberg, 1978, p. 1). In addition, it is a
process of "interconnected steps . . . [that] constitute a framework
for activities and tasks in the agency/worker/client relationship"
(Regional Institute of Social Welfare Research, 1977, p. 5).

In child welfare, the intraagency aspects of case management
are emphasized. One training manual defines case management as
a "client-centered, goal-oriented strategy for case assessment and
service delivery" (U.S. Department of Health, Education and Welfare, 1978, p. 133). The worker negotiates appropriate services for
the client, improves access to them, and promotes compatibility and
coordinates service provision. There is less stress on direct service
delivery and more on case monitoring, regular case review, improved record keeping, and regular reviews of the service agreement
(U.S. Department of Health, Education and Welfare, 1977).

The theoretical framework for case management practice in
child welfare consists of a basic knowledge of human behavior and
the social environment, knowledge of generic social work practice,
and issues specific to child welfare. Critical to such a practice are
skills in observation, data gathering, assessment, and decision
making. Special knowledge necessary to sharpening these skills
include assessment of parents' potential for violence and their
ability to provide minimal care for children. Knowledge about
children's and parents' reactions to separation, loss, and deprivation
are also basic to decision making. Whether a child is placed in
substitute care is determined by weighing the chance of imminent
harm to the child if he is left in his home against the certain trauma
of placement.

Goal planning, contracting, and the intervention process are
influenced by the authoritative role of protective services and the
auxiliary involvement of the court and possibly the police. The
theoretical framework must include not only the formulation of
observable goals and contract writing but also the use of authority

in helping relationships. In addition to clinical knowledge of assessing child and family interactions, the theory for professional action in child welfare must include knowledge about the child welfare, family court, and health systems, which are integrally involved in the issues of dependency, abuse, and neglect. Practitioners need to master theory and intervention skills related to organizations and interprofessional collaboration and advocacy as well as direct service and assessment (Weil, 1979, 1982).

Intervention in child welfare is shaped by the concept of permanency planning. Permanency planning is an approach to service delivery that assures the "best interests of the child" (Goldstein, Freud, and Solnit, 1973) by guarding against unwarranted, erratic placements and foster care drift (Maluccio and Sinanoglu, 1981). Foster care drift refers to the endless wandering of a child through the foster care system without a plan to return the child to her home and without prospects for adoption. Losing the child in the system is often the result of fuzzy planning, inadequate record keeping, and lack of a means to monitor children who enter foster care. This movement toward permanency planning is accompanied by the belief that many children who were thought to be unadoptable can find permanent homes. Permanency planning is often considerd synonymous with case management, but it actually involves more than substitute care—it refers to the processing of all cases through the child welfare system.

Every protective service worker and many other workers involved in child welfare must know juvenile court procedures, rules of evidence, laws regarding the protection of children, methods for presenting testimony, and the parameters of state intervention (Weil, 1982). Case managers in child welfare also need to know crisis intervention and how to deal with family violence.

Recent research into the effectiveness of intervention has focused on reuniting natural parents and their children in foster care. Some concepts integral to this effort are frequent contacts between the worker and parents and an emphasis on the use of behavioral theories in intervention and on the concept of timeliness. Timeliness pertains to the time between a report and an investigation, the time between the first contact and the beginning of treatment, and the total time in process (Berkeley Planning Associates, 1977; Stein, Gambrill, and Wiltse, 1978).

Policy

Child welfare policy suffers from the lack of a broad national plan. States differ widely in their laws and their organization of services. Although some laws have improved the system by requiring a standardized procedure for tracking children in care, other policies have diminished the quality of service delivery. A 1977 study found that cutbacks, hiring freezes, and funding regulations were having a marked effect on child welfare. The cutbacks limited who was eligible for services and the types of services that were readily available (U.S. Department of Health, Education and Welfare, 1977). The shift in federal funding to state block grants has greatly altered the structure of funding and marked a retreat from a unified national policy.

Permanency planning was promoted at the federal level by the passage of Public Law 96-272, the Federal Adoption Assistance and Child Welfare Act. Signed into law in 1980, the law sets down prerequisites for service delivery, including the use of written case plans and a mandatory case review system. The law stresses preventing placement, promoting family reunification, and providing assistance for families who adopt children with special needs. Public Law 96-272 also altered the federal reimbursement structure to deemphasize foster care and to support prevention, reunification, and adoption. The law sets forth requirements for case planning and case reviews for children in foster care as well as for services to be provided that will prevent the need for foster care. One example of the tighter connection between funding and service design can be found in new provisions made under Title IV-E of the Social Security Act. Federal reimbursement for foster care or adoption assistance for individual children is now contingent on a judicial determination that reasonable efforts have been made to prevent placement and to reunify the family (Allen, Golubock, and Olsen, 1983).

Several states have also adopted case management policies or implemented demonstration projects to facilitate permanency planning. In 1976, California passed the Family Protection Act, which selected two counties as sites for a new approach. Some of the major provisions were to provide for time-limited, comprehensive services to prevent placement and to reunify families of children already in placement. These provisions included six-month court reviews of all dependent children except those in court-approved long-term care and legal counsel to all minors at all stages of juvenile court proceedings (California Department of Social Services, 1981).

Following the documented success of the Family Protection Act Project (funded in California in 1976 under the Family Protection Act), which matched demonstration programs in San Mateo and Shasta counties against control programs in two counties matched for general population characteristics (Sacramento and Humboldt), the California legislature enacted SB-14 in 1982. This legislation provides five key services: emergency response, family maintenance, family reunification, permanency planning, and adoption. The emergency response program requires a twenty-four-hour response capability to calls or reports of child abuse emergencies that includes screening and an initial determination of service needs. The family maintenance program is intended to provide supportive services to families caring for children and to prevent out-of-home placement. In this program services can be provided only to families whose children are at risk of abuse or neglect. One six-month period of service can be provided with a maximum of two service extensions for three months each. Services in this program are out-of-home respite care, counseling, teaching and demonstrating of home and child care, emergency shelter care, parent training, and transportation of parents to services.

The family reunification program is geared to rehabilitating families so they can solve problems and meet the growth needs of children. The children of families in this program are put in placement, and intensive services are given to parents to give them support and to help them develop parenting skills and accept and carry out adult responsibilities so their children can be returned to safe and functioning homes (Brown, 1984). In addition, the legislation made standards for removing children from their homes more stringent and focused on the reunification of families as a major service goal. This program limits voluntary placement to six months. The maximum period of court-ordered placement with the family reunification program is eighteen months, and a court or administrative case review is mandated each six months. Visits between the parent or parents and child are required during this period, so a major staff responsibility is to facilitate and monitor these visits and to maintain the bonds between the child and his or her family. Services included in the family reunification program are counseling, emergency shelter care, parent training, and transportation. To participate in these programs, families must sign service agreements with the agency.

When efforts to reunify a family fail, permanency planning becomes the service goal. Included in this process is the legal process of terminating parental rights. The focus of service shifts to developing alternative, permanent arrangements for the child and eliminating foster care drift. The permanency planning program is designed to assure a permanent and supportive environment for the child through adoption, legal guardianship, or planned long-term placement. The child has no contact during this period with his or her own parents but is visited in the foster care setting by agency case management staff. Optimally, a joint assessment to determine the most appropriate long-term plan for an individual child is conducted by an adoption worker and a foster care worker (Brown, 1984). A permanency planning hearing is required by the end of eighteen months. In long-term placement, the public agency monitors the well-being of the child. Case management responsibilities where legal guardianship is the plan of choice are more nebulous, although some case management oversight seems necessary to assure the care and safety of the child (Brown, 1984). Through adoption, a new family is created. Prospective adoptive parents and the child participate in intensive assessment and counseling before the adoption is approved. When the adoption process is completed, the family has no official, continuing tie to the child welfare agency. However, demands by adoptive families are increasing for postadoptive counseling to deal with the particular problems of adjustment and development that they experience (Brown, Finch, Northen, Taylor, and Weil, 1982).

The SB-14 legislation increases services to families to prevent disruption. It also emphasizes reunification services and imposes restrictions on the time allowed for deciding whether to terminate parental rights in order to assure children a permanent home and a supportive environment.

The California agencies implementing this legislation face both fiscal and procedural problems. The crucial issue is adequate funding to provide the range of intensive, supportive services that are mandated. Adequate funding is also necessary to maintain the caliber of staff needed for these complex programs and to hire enough staff to provide adequate service and allow careful decision making. The sheer volume of responsibility in family intervention has escalated over the last few years. In California and throughout the nation, child abuse referrals have risen drastically. As the impetus toward permanency planning gathers strength, adoption referrals are also on the increase (Children's Services Task Force, 1984). Court calendars are also being overwhelmed by the necessity to schedule permanency planning hearings for cases already in the child welfare system (Blakeley, 1984).

Comparable efforts to strengthen services and case management procedures have been undertaken in other states. In South Carolina, advocacy groups pushed for and attained periodic case review (Chappel, 1975). New York instituted the New York judicial review of foster care (Festinger, 1976).

Case Management Models and Effective Programs

Case management models are constructed according to the client pathway through services that represent the steps of the social work process. Boserup (1978) developed a model for case management in protective services that is shown in Figure 1. Boserup developed each phase in detail, using charts to depict decision points and service alternatives.

Models for interagency coordination vary widely according to community needs and context. Figure 2 presents Helfer's (1974) design, which illustrates case management on a case-by-case basis and at the community level. Each of the major components (A, B, and C) of his model represents part of a team effort by several agencies. For example, identification and diagnosis may be the task of police, protective services, the hospital, schools, or public health

Figure 1. Case Management Model.

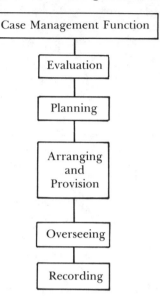

Source: Boserup, 1978, p. 27.

nurses. Long-term treatment may be handled by protective services, family service agencies, or other community resources. The interaction of these teams is coordinated on the case level and at the community level.

Most case management models have been developed from experiences in demonstration projects. Although one cannot overgeneralize from demonstrations that target specifically defined clienteles under special administrative arrangements, the two projects described here implemented exemplary case management practices. In Oregon, a cooperative undertaking involving the permanency planning project, the state Department of Children's Services, and the court system was implemented in five counties to place children back in their own homes or to free them for adoption (Emlen and others, 1978). The children selected for the project had been in placement for at least one year and were considered unlikely to return to their own families. After two years, 27 percent of the 509 children involved were returned to their own homes and 52 percent were adopted or awaiting adoption.

Figure 2. Helfer's Interagency Coordination Model.

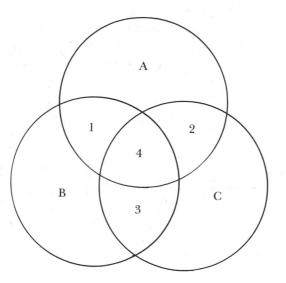

Major components	Functions
A. Identification and diagnosis	1. Case coordination
B. Long-term treatment	2. Professional training and recruitment
C. Education, training, and public relations	3. Public and professional education
	4. Program coordination

In this project, legislative requirements were an enforceable statute on the termination of parental rights and a body of case law on appellate decisions. Successful work with the court also required access to expert testimony, worker skills in documenting evidence and taking cases to court, and active participation of judges and all lawyers including expert supervision and consultation, caseloads under twenty-five per worker, resources for search procedures, and a goal orientation toward permanency planning. Direct service was facilitated by screening cases for permanency planning and by developing a client pathway that required highly skilled decision making and intervention procedures. For any permanency planning effort to be successful, alternatives to foster care must be available.

The Alameda project (Stein, Gambrill, and Wiltse, 1978) was also concerned with finding permanent homes for children. The project managers and staff used a behavioral approach with a system of record keeping, contracting, and planning to ensure observable and measurable changes in parental behavior, mutual planning between staff and parents, and agency accountability. They also systematically attended to intervention throughout the client pathway by emphasizing assessment, decision making, goal planning, and intensive work with the natural parents. They used both a control group and an experimental group with a sample of ninety-nine families. The control group was served through the customary agency channels; 30 percent were restored to their natural parents, 10 percent were candidates for adoption, and 60 percent went into long-term foster care. In the experimental group under the behavioral approach, the respective figures were 48, 20, and 21 percent.

Professional Roles and Collaboration

The professional orientation of case managers in child welfare varies greatly. For children in placement, the public agency is the responsible party and is likeliest to assume a coordinating role. For clients who receive service in their home, any number of people may perform the case management function. In Helfer's model, doctors, nurses, nonprofessionals, and public agency workers can find themselves in the coordination role either through formal arrangements or informal happenstance. Although Helfer's approach can be very functional, especially in small communities, one research study suggests that case management efforts may be more successful if they are housed in public protective service agencies (Berkeley Planning Associates, 1977).

Case managers negotiate and work with a myriad of other professionals and community people. These relationships require perceived equality; however, case managers must demonstrate their expertise or else they can lose their managerial role. Any case can involve a wide variety of agencies whose functions conflict with one another at times. A strong manager will help guide the intervention and ensure unity of goals and plans.

The professional roles of the case manager are well described by Downing (1979). She outlines the roles of the counselor, coordinator, and advocate. The counselor may provide casework services to facilitate client engagement in the service delivery system. If the case manager is the public agency worker, he or she may provide therapeutic services or arrange for them through another agency. The coordinator accesses available services that are not readily available. The public agency worker also serves as a symbol of authority, helping the family while fulfilling the mandate of the state to protect the child. Some child welfare agencies believe that assigning the helping and authority roles to different workers is better for the client. Another school of thought supports combining these roles in one worker, arguing that the family can accept both authority and aid from the same person. Role strain may be an inescapable part of case management in child welfare. Advocacy is a form of intervention through which the worker actively supports and argues for the needs of the client. The worker may initially speak for clients, representing their wishes and needs, but work to enable clients to press their own causes (Weil, 1979). Advocacy in child welfare is extremely complex as the child and parents may each desire different outcomes. At times the worker will have to make court recommendations on behalf of a child that do not represent the child's own preference.

A treatment team often performs the essential service functions in child welfare. Team functioning provides a way not only to share the burden of serving clients with severe problems but also to share decision making. In child protection, the latter benefit has often been cited, since the burden of making decisions affecting the life of a child is not borne by a single worker. Through teamwork and sound group discussions, workers can be more confident of considering all aspects of a case. Although such decisions are always a matter of judgment, it is critical to assure that all case components, both strengths and risks, have been weighed. Treatment teams open up issues for debate and, through individual team members' expertise and knowledge, can broaden or strengthen the basis for judgment (Weil, 1982).

Role strain may result from conflict between managing cases and helping people, which creates tension regarding professional identity. The variations in expertise and status attached to each role and how one spends one's working hours are major factors in a social worker's self-image. Many people become social workers expecting to be heavily involved with counseling or treatment. Yet in many agencies, particularly in large urban areas, treatment is contracted to other agencies, and the most basic case management procedures occupy the public agency worker's day (Ten Broek, 1980).

Case Management Practices

Berkeley Planning Associates evaluated eleven demonstration projects in child welfare services between 1974 and 1977. They concluded that excellence in case management practice was difficult to assess, but the following practices were most strongly associated with overall quality: response to incoming reports in one day; frequent contact between the case manager and the client, ideally once a week; use of consultation from outside the agency; the same case manager following a client from the client's entry into the program; and involvement of the client in service over six months. Other factors related to high quality were recontacting the reporting source for more information, using multidisciplinary review teams, and following up clients after termination of service.

A small caseload size (under twenty) and over six months in process were the only case management factors associated with a positive outcome in the treatment of parents. Positive outcome here meant an increased awareness of child development, more constructive ways of handling anger, a more positive self-image, accomplishing the treatment goal, and reducing or eliminating recidivism. Another factor related to a positive outcome was the provision of lay services in conjunction with professional supervision.

The authors of both the Alameda project report (Stein, Gambrill, and Wiltse, 1978) and the local welfare services assessment manual (Children's Bureau, 1979) emphasize the importance of standardized record keeping, the use of teamwork, establishing observable indicators of desired client behavior, written contracts, and a positive relationship between worker and client. Shapiro (1976) found that the same worker handling a case through the first two years and frequent contacts helped move children out of foster care. Improvement in the natural parent was related to frequent contacts in the early phases of treatment, low caseloads, and no worker turnover into the second year.

Stein, Gambrill, and Wiltse (1978) suggest that children entering long-term foster care be assigned to special units and in larger caseloads since their cases require less coordination. Caseloads of other staff can then be reduced, thus facilitating the provision of intensive services. These authors state that the optimal size of caseloads cannot be determined until worker activities are identified. The basic factor in deciding caseload size should be facilitating frequency of contact between the client and the worker, especially in the first year of placement and in working with an intact family to prevent placement.

Case management is tied to the social work process and is most easily thought of as pertaining to direct service or to administrative functions. The emphasis is on immediate intake, assessment, and treatment with decision making and goal planning as critical factors. Some models in case management in child welfare include decision trees to facilitate decision making (Emlen, 1978). Goal planning and contracting with the client require written observable indicators of progress and standardized recording of plans, interventions, and progress (Emlen, 1978; Stein, Gambrill, and Wiltse, 1978).

Time limitations are crucial to child welfare case management, especially in efforts to reunite a child in placement with his or her family. Yet the intervention process itself requires the use of outreach; development of a professional relationship with parents; natural helpers, such as family and friends; or lay services, such as church groups; frequent contacts, usually a minimum of six months in service; and follow-up after termination.

Stein, Gambrill, and Wiltse (1978) elaborate on how behavioral technologies can be used to facilitate the process of reunification of a child with his or her parents, while Helfer and Kempe (1976) focus on the relationship between parent and child and

parent and worker. Although these two approaches differ in emphasis, they are not mutually exclusive. Evaluation of progress and
reassessment occur continually. Case review, one tool for evaluation, consists of reviewing the cases of children in placement at
specified time intervals. Case review may be done within the agency,
by juvenile court, by a professional board, or by a citizen's review
team. The case review is usually done within three months after the
initial placement and every three to six months thereafter. Cases
determined to require long-term foster care may be reviewed less
often. Public Law 96-272 is one example of legislation that mandates periodic reviews.

     Administrative practices and technologies include informa-
tion systems of various sizes and degrees of complexity that assist
in tracking cases and assuring service quality. Case reviews and
interagency coordination are often arranged at the administrative
level. The purchase of service contracts with private agencies are
one way of providing services to child welfare families. San Mateo
County, California, found that these contracts must be carefully
monitored and that payment should be contingent upon evidence
of performance (Ten Broek,1980). Morris, Lesohier, and Wilthorn
(1976) support this with their finding that granting a worker the
power to contract for services was the most effective way to assure
interagency coordination.

Training and Education

     Quality case management practice depends on a high level
of skill and training. Berkeley Planning Associates (1977) found
quality of case management service to be associated with the case
manager's formal education and previous experience in working
with abuse and neglect. Perhaps the key areas for education and
training are skill in working with multiproblem families and skill
in negotiating service systems on behalf of troubled families and
their children (Brown, Finch, Northen, Taylor, and Weil, 1982).
The Alameda and Oregon projects conducted intensive training of
workers in assessment, goal planning, intervention, evaluation, and
working with the court.

     For competent practice in child welfare, specialized education and training are required in the following areas: dynamics and patterns of abuse and neglect, patterns in human bonding separation, loss and deprivation, methods of working with multiproblem families, and principles of child placement and adoption. Equally important are knowledge of social and environmental problems, juvenile court procedures and legislation, police procedures, and community agencies and resources. In addition to this specialized knowledge, case managers in child welfare need a generic base in social work practice and knowledge and skills in monitoring and evaluation required of all case managers.

Rosalie Kane (1975) outlined educational objectives in training for interprofessional teamwork. She suggested that the worker must have knowledge about the group process, evaluation of the group, problem solving in the group, characteristics of the professional group, organizational structure, and teamwork. Skills in writing and speaking and professional attitudes should be developed, and all communications should inspire trust and reflect a respect for others, a tolerance of disagreement, and personal flexibility.

Bertsche and Horejsi (1980) listed the knowledge and skills they find essential for case coordination. This list reinforces Kane's learning objectives and adds a few more. Knowledge of human behavior, particularly behavioral theories and community functioning, form a solid base for developing intervention skills in advocacy, mediating, brokering, crisis intervention, helping the client develop assertiveness, writing behavioral objectives, and using informal resources, such as community or self-help groups. Case coordination also includes negotiating with formal organizations, knowing approaches to organizational management and principles of organizational behavior and change, and maintaining a degree of autonomy within one's own organization. An appropriate use of information requires abilities in record keeping, abstracting and summarizing data, and writing reports. The case coordinator must also understand state and federal regulations, be adept at public relations, and understand community attitudes.

Studies have shown that people with bachelor's degrees and lay helpers are very effective in brokering services and aiding in treatment. However, because of the need for accurate assessments, the importance of making weighty decisions, and the wide variety of intensive services that are required, case managers in child welfare should be highly educated and specifically trained for this complex field of service (Olsen and Holmes, 1981).

Consumer Advocacy

The most significant consumer advocacy issue at present concerns the rights of children. Although permanency planning is a response to the need of the child for a permanent home, there are additional responsibilities in safeguarding children's rights. Representation of the child's point of view in dependency hearings has recently become a major concern. The state and the parents have long had the right to legal counsel, but the child was often unrepresented. The state has the right to intervene on behalf of the child, but this does no˙ mean that the state's desires do not conflict with those of the child. This dilemma has been recognized and addressed by designating a guardian ad litem to speak for the child during court proceedings. The guardian ad litem may be a lawyer or a lay person appointed by the judge to represent the child. Some people feel that a lawyer is best suited for this task because of a lawyer's knowledge of the court system and ability to work within it. Others, believing that a lawyer does not have the time to investigate each case adequately, prefer to use volunteers specifically recruited to represent the child and to have a personal interest in the child. Lay persons serving as guardians ad litem open up the process of dependency proceedings to public scrutiny and may encourage public advocacy for children's rights.

A second advocacy issue concerns the rights of parents who become clients. These parents may not be aware of their rights, may not know how to exercise them, and may not have enough money to hire someone who can intercede for them. If the case manager is also the representative of the state, it is very difficult to protect the child and at the same time act as an advocate for the parents against state intervention. Although case managers in child welfare often begin their work with the client identified as the entire family, the child welfare worker is obligated to safeguard the child if it becomes necessary to recommend placement or the termination of parental rights. As a result, courts have increasingly offered public counsel to parents whose children are being considered for placement. However, such provision may be too late for some parents.

Advocacy in child welfare is the concern of not only the case manager but also the community at large. Advocacy is needed on a case-by-case basis for each child as he or she moves through the child welfare system. Class advocacy asserting the rights of all children subject to dependency hearings or at risk of abuse and neglect is an equal need (Weil, 1979). Volunteers, other professionals, and nationwide organizations such as the Children's Defense Fund are necessary supplements to the case manager's efforts.

Problems in Implementation

There are several barriers to implementing case management in child welfare agencies. Within the agency, worker resistance, administrative inertia, agency policies that inhibit the most effective assignment of personnel, and the lack of consistent monitoring of staff are some of the barriers. Stein, Gambrill, and Wiltse (1978) and Sherman, Neuman, and Shyne (1973) suggest that administrative backing is essential to a successful case management project.

Involvement of the line staff when planning case management systems can help minimize objections to program changes. Additional case management procedures are often resisted by staff because of existing role strains and heavy caseloads. Because helping the client, playing the authority figure, and managing the progression of the case can put conflicting demands on workers, gaining their cooperation in implementing review systems can prove to be very difficult. Stein, Gambrill, and Wiltse (1977) emphasize the importance of change originating within the agency through a cohesive group of people committed to improving the quality of service. At the onset of planned organizational change, it is not necessary that the committed group be administrators, only that they be able to instigate some impetus for the desired organizational change. Stein and others also indicate that the timing of instituting case management and the existence of an outside neutral group pressing for case review and management are helpful.

The implementation of case management in child welfare is

often coupled with the installation of new information and management systems designed to standardize services, maximize productivity, and ensure accountability. In a survey of public welfare workers, Walz (1980) found that management systems did not necessarily reduce caseloads, lower the costs of the program, improve relationships with clients or the public, or improve working conditions. Coler (1980) argues that the failure of a system is rooted in its implementation. If social service managers control the technicians who set up the system and if the professionals who use it are sold on its usefulness, the information gathered is likelier to be pertinent and valid. Instituting a case management system requires the endorsement of policy makers, legislative backing, and a minimalization of paperwork that workers must complete.

Barriers to implementing case management policies may also be external to the agency, such as governmental policies that cause goal confusion at the local level and cultural attitudes about state intervention in family matters (Stein, Gambrill, and Wiltse, 1977). Problems in coordinating the efforts of several agencies arise from a lack of goal congruence, professional territorialism, political constraints, limited technology, and difficulties in coordinating the public and private sectors (Rice, 1977).

Reid (1969) points out that coordinating efforts are not self-perpetuating and must be supported by resources and/or decision making power. These efforts will only succeed when participating agencies perceive a need to exchange resources in order to achieve common or congruent goals. Four basic resources for exchange are money, information, clients, and services (Taylor, 1979). For successful coordination, there must be a relatively formal understanding about who is exchanging what and the conditions for the exchanges. In short, agencies must perceive themselves as being interdependent.

Future Directions

The advent of permanency planning and the increasing use of management systems in the human services have helped spur the implementation of case management practices. Recent indictments of social workers for mismanagement and negligence have also raised the call for more effective systems of accountability (Spearly,

1981). At the same time, however, funding cutbacks are limiting services. The resulting heavier caseloads may be a factor in the decline in quality and deprofessionalization of child welfare services (U.S. Department of Health, Education and Welfare, 1977). Non-social-workers are being hired at both the management and direct service levels. In addition, positions once requiring master's degrees in social work are being opened to holders of bachelor's degrees.

Although quality case management and quality service to the child welfare clientele require workers with high levels of skills and knowledge, policy makers may regard case management as a way to eliminate service delivery from the public sector and cut back on personnel expenses. A more cost-effective solution would be to invest in highly trained workers who can minimize the number of placements and time spent in foster care. These workers could also coordinate intervention teams that include volunteers, staff with bachelor's degrees in social work, and cooperating agencies, as appropriate. Such case managers could coordinate intensive services, supervise line staff and paraprofessionals, oversee lay intervention, and broker other community services. The time spent in any of these activities would vary with the case, the organization, and the community. Intervention and case management in child welfare is a highly complex professional function. The increasing incidence of physical abuse, sexual abuse, and child neglect requires major societal investments and professional services to safeguard children and support American families. Reports to the House Select Committee on Children, Youth, and Families indicate that it is much more cost-effective to provide and monitor preventive and supportive services for children and their families than to stress placement and foster care. Careful service provision and case management in the early stages of family problems can mitigate even serious family problems. As the chairman of the House Select Committee on Children, Youth, and Families has said, the choice is ours: "Do we want to invest in the success of troubled families or do we want to pay for their failure?" (Miller, 1984).

Suggested Readings

Allen, M. L., Golubock, C., and Olsen, L., *A Guide to the Adoption Assistance and Child Welfare Act of 1980*. Washington, D.C.:

Children's Defense Fund, 1983. Also in M. Hardin and D. Dodson (Eds.), *Foster Children in the Courts*. Boston: Butterworth Legal Publishers, 1983.

Brown, J. H., Finch, W. A., Jr., Northen, H., Taylor, S. H., and Weil, M. *Child, Family, Neighborhood: A Master Plan for Social Service Delivery*. New York: Child Welfare League of America, 1982.

Children's Bureau, U.S. Department of Health, Education and Welfare. *Child Abuse and Neglect Information Management Systems: A Report from the 2nd National Conference on Data Aspects of Child Protective Services*. Washington, D.C.: U.S. Government Printing Office, 1978.

Children's Bureau, U.S. Department of Health, Education and Welfare. *Local Welfare Services Assessment Manual*. Part 2. *Resources*. Washington, D.C.: U.S. Government Printing Office, 1979.

Children's Bureau, U.S. Department of Health, Education and Welfare. *Permanent Planning for Children in Foster Care: A Handbook for Social Workers*. Washington, D.C.: U.S. Government Printing Office, 1980.

Compher, J. V. "Home Services to Families to Prevent Child Placement." *Social Work*, 1983, *28* (5), 360–364.

Gambrill, E. D. "Guidelines for Evaluating Services Offered by Social Workers." In M. Hardin and D. Dodson (Eds.), *Foster Children in the Courts*. Boston: Butterworth Legal Publishers, 1983.

Nagi, S. *Child Maltreatment in the United States*. New York: Columbia University Press, 1977.

Stein, T. J., and Rzetnicki, T. L., *Decision Making in Child Welfare Services: Intake and Planning*. Boston: Kluwer-Nijhoff, 1984.

References

Allen, M. L., Golubock, C., and Olsen, L., *A Guide to the Adoption Assistance and Child Welfare Act of 1980*. Washington, D.C.: Children's Defense Fund, 1983. Also in M. Hardin and D. Dodson (Eds.), *Foster Children in the Courts*. Boston: Butterworth Legal Publishers, 1983.

Alston, F. K. *Caring for Other People's Children.* Baltimore: University Park Press, 1984.

Berkeley Planning Associates. *Evaluation of Child Abuse and Neglect Demonstration Projects, 1974-1977.* Vol. 6. *Quality of the Case Management Process.* Springfield, Va.: U.S. Department of Commerce, 1977.

Bertsche, A. V., and Horejsi, C. R. "Coordination of Client Services." *Social Work,* March 1980, pp. 94-98.

Blakeley, S. "The MSW—Is It Obsolete?" Paper presented at the regional conference of the Child Welfare League of America, Pasadena, Calif., April 11, 1984.

Boserup, D. G. *Case Management for Children's Protective Services.* Athens, Ga.: Regional Institute of Social Welfare Research, February 1978.

Brown, J. H. "The MSW and SB-14." Paper presented at the regional conference of the Child Welfare League of America, Pasadena, Calif., April 11, 1984.

Brown, J. H., Finch, W. A., Jr., Northen, H., Taylor, S. H., and Weil, M. *Child, Family, Neighborhood: A Master Plan for Social Service Delivery.* New York: Child Welfare League of America, 1982.

California Department of Social Services. *California Family Protection Report.* Sacramento: State of California, 1981.

"Californians Tell House Panel Foster Care Is Not Last Resort." *Child Welfare Planning Notes,* 1984, *9* (4), 1-3.

Chappel, B. "Organizing Periodic Review in Foster Care: The South Carolina Story." *Child Welfare,* 1975, *54*, 477-486.

Children's Bureau, U.S. Department of Health, Education and Welfare. *Local Welfare Services Assessment Manual.* 2 vols. Washington, D.C.: U.S. Government Printing Office, 1979.

Children's Services Task Force. *Report to the Board of Supervisors, County of Los Angeles, concerning recommendations to improve the delivery of services to abused and neglected children in Los Angeles County,* March 30, 1984.

Coler, G. "But Maybe It Might Have." *Children, Youth, and Family News,* October 1980, pp. 6-9.

Downing, R. "An Exploration of Case Manager Roles: Coordinator, Advocate, and Counselor." In *Three Working Papers.* Los

Angeles Social Policy Laboratory, Percy Andrus Gerontology Center, University of Southern California, 1979.

Emlen, A., and others. *Overcoming Barriers to Planning for Foster Care.* Washington, D.C.: U.S. Government Printing Office, 1978.

Festinger, T. B. "The Impact of the New York Court Review of Children in Foster Care: A Follow-Up Report." *Child Welfare,* 1976, *55,* 515–544.

Fox, S. "Current Child Welfare Legislation in California." Paper presented at the Los Angeles Roundtable for Children Symposium, May 19, 1984.

Goldstein, J., Freud, A., and Solnit, A. *Beyond the Best Interests of the Child.* New York: Free Press, 1973.

Helfer, R. E. *Self Instructional Program in Child Abuse and Neglect: Unit 5.* An audiotape and manual prepared in cooperation with the American Academy of Pediatrics and the National Center for the Prevention of Child Abuse and Neglect, Denver, 1974.

Helfer, R. E., and Kempe, H. C. (Eds.). *Child Abuse and Neglect: The Family and the Community.* Cambridge, Mass.: Ballinger, 1976.

Jenkins, S., and Schroeder, A. G., *Intake: The Discriminant Function: A Report on the National Study on Social Services Intake for Children and Their Families.* Washington, D.C.: U.S. Government Printing Office, 1980.

Jurkiewicz, V. "An Exploratory Descriptive Study of Interorganizational and Case Coordination Programs for the Multiproblem, Frail and Minority Elderly." Unpublished doctoral dissertation, School of Social Welfare, University of California, Los Angeles, 1980.

Kane, R. *Interprofessional Teamwork.* Syracuse, N.Y.: Syracuse University School of Social Work, 1975.

Maluccio, A., and Sinanoglu, P. (Eds.). *The Challenge of Partnership.* New York: Child Welfare League of America, 1981.

Miller, G. "Our Country's Children and Their Needs." Keynote address at the Los Angeles Roundtable for Children Symposium, Los Angeles, May 19, 1984.

Morris, R., Lesohier, I., and Wilthorn, A., "Social Service Delivery Systems: Attempts to Alter Local Patterns, 1970–1974—An Exploratory National Survey at Midstream." Brandeis University, Waltham, Mass., 1976.

National Center of Child Abuse and Neglect, U.S. Department of Health, Education and Welfare. *Specialized Training for Child Protective Services Workers: A Curriculum on Child Abuse and Neglect.* Washington, D.C.: U.S. Government Printing Office, 1979.

Olsen, L., and Holmes, W. M., "The Education of Child Welfare Workers: Differences in Service Delivery." Paper presented at the Council on Social Work Education annual program meeting, Louisville, Ky., March 10, 1981.

Public Law 96-272, U.S. Congress, June 17, 1980. "Adoption Assistance and Child Welfare Act of 1980."

Regional Institute of Social Welfare Research. *The Case Management Model.* Athens, Ga.: Regional Institute of Social Welfare Research, 1977.

Reid, W. J. "Interorganizational Coordination in Social Welfare: A Theoretical Approach to Analysis and Intervention." In R. M. Kramer and H. Specht (Eds.), *Readings in Community Organization Practice.* Englewood Cliffs, N.J.: Prentice-Hall, 1969.

Rice, R. M. "A Cautionary View of Allied Service Delivery." *Social Casework,* 1977, *58,* 229-235.

Senate Bill 14, California Legislature, September 13, 1982.

Shapiro, D. *Agencies and Foster Children.* New York: Columbia University Press, 1976.

Sherman, E., Neuman, R., and Shyne, A., *Children Adrift in Foster Care.* New York: Child Welfare League of America, 1973.

Spearly, J. L. "Caseworker Indictments, A Closer Look." *National Child Protective Services Newsletter,* Winter 1981, *3.*

Stein, T. J., Gambrill, E. D., and Wiltse, K. T., "Dividing Case Management in Foster Care Family Cases." *Child Welfare,* 1977, *56,* 321-331.

Stein, T. J., Gambrill, E. D., and Wiltse, K. T., *Children in Foster Homes: Achieving Continuity of Care.* New York: Praeger, 1978.

Steinberg, R. "Case Coordination: Lessons from the Past for Future Program Models." Paper presented at the 105th annual forum of the National Conference on Social Welfare, Los Angeles, 1978.

Taylor, S. Author's notes from doctoral seminar in community organization, School of Social Work, University of Southern California, Los Angeles, 1979.

Ten Broek, E. "The Family Protection Act—It Can Work." Paper presented at the 25th Child Welfare League of America, Western Region Training Conference, Pasadena, Calif., April 21, 1980.

U.S. Department of Health, Education and Welfare. *Child Welfare in 25 States—An Overview.* Washington, D.C.: U.S. Government Printing Office, 1977.

U.S. Department of Health, Education and Welfare. *System of Social Services for Children and Their Families: Detailed Design and an Overview.* 2 vols. Washington, D.C.: U.S. Government Printing Office, 1978.

Walz, T. "An Opinion: It Didn't Work." *Children, Youth, and Family News,* October 1980, pp. 2-5.

Weil, M. "Interprofessional Work in Adoptions—Collaboration and Beyond." *Social Work Papers,* Fall 1979, *15,* pp. 46-54.

Weil, M. "Research on Issues in Collaboration Between Social Workers and Lawyers." *Social Service Review,* Sept. 1982, *56,* pp. 393-405.

Williams, K. Lawndale California YWCA Program for High-Risk Mothers and Infants, Personal Communication, May 9, 1984.

6

The Elderly
and Their Families

Rachel Downing

Case management with the elderly in community settings is defined in this chapter. Key concepts drawn from organization theory, practice theory, and gerontology are identified. Relevant public policy is reviewed and case management models are described. An approach to analyzing programs from five aspects—organization base, authority base, fiscal base, professional reference group, and practice structure—is given, along with examples of effective programs. Programs discussed include Access, Triage, Alternate Health Services, The Alternative Program, Multipurpose Senior Services Project, and the Senior Health Services Project. In addition, case management practice is examined, utilizing the concepts of client pathway and assessment, and issues in the training, profession, and deployment of case managers are explored. These issues include professional versus paraprofessional, teams versus individual, and task assignment. Current problems in the field, such as lack of consensus on goals and objectives, funding and public policy, and distribution of services, are analyzed. Consumer advocacy issues are raised, from the rights of clients to refuse case management to the clients' right to be adequately informed. The chapter concludes with comments on the rise of clients and family as case managers and a highlight of future direction issues involving long-term care, cost containment, computerization of management systems, and the role of the family in case management.

Case management with the elderly consists of assessing the service needs of older individuals and their families and coordinating the delivery of these services. It differs from other interventions or helping services in both focus and purpose. The focus of case management is on the client's needs in a variety of areas identified in the assessment. The purpose of case management is to ensure the delivery of all services needed to reduce or stabilize the client's problem.

In contrast to the case manager's focus, the service provider's concentration is on the client's need for the particular intervention or service they provide; their objective is to provide that service. For example, in a nursing assessment, the nurse may discover other needs, but since the primary purpose of the assessment is to determine whether or not a nursing service is needed, these other needs would be deferred or referred to other service providers.

Theoretical Basis

Several concepts are valuable in understanding case management systems, goals, and practice. The key concepts are borrowed from theoretical knowledge in the fields of organization, human services practice, and gerontology.

Organizational Concepts. There are three levels of organization: interorganizational, intraorganizational, and client-worker. At the interorganizational level is the relationship between the case management organization and other agencies and systems. This level often includes interorganizational agreements and formal contracts, relationships with welfare and health care systems, and other formal and informal contacts with other agencies. The intraorganizational level consists of the structure of the case management agency itself including staffing (administrative and service staff), fiscal management, personnel policies, and paperwork. The third level includes the client-worker (case manager) relationship. This includes all the interactions between the worker and the client from assessment to termination. Case management programs must be designed with all three organizational levels in mind.

One of the problems in developing and operating case management programs is how to be effective at all three levels. Developing a good system of client-worker intervention is different from developing purchase-of-service agreements between agencies, yet being effective on both levels is critical to a quality case management program. It is difficult to find staff able to handle both client-worker needs and manage complicated interagency relationships. If a project staff spends extensive time developing interagency relationships, it might ignore developing systems for individual clients. But if it only develops systems for individual clients, then the lack of coordination between agencies may cause tremendous pressure and worker burnout.

Another area of organizational theory important to case management with the elderly is that of multiple organizational goals. Case management programs have a diverse range of goals such as providing greater client access to services, ensuring appropriate use of services, improving the quality of services, identifying gaps in services, ensuring continuity of services, and containing cost.

Practice Concepts. The major concept coming to case management from the field of practice with clients is that of the case manager. Often this concept of the case manager is difficult to understand, especially because the role is so similar to that in other professions and disciplines, such as social work, public health nursing, and human services. Essentially the case manager has three primary roles.

The first role is that of service coordinator. Since the emphasis is on managing the service system in the client's behalf, this task is sometimes called service management. The service coordinator compensates for a lack of information, bureaucratic barriers, and a lack of services. This is considered to be the highest form of case management since the case manager does not directly service the client but identifies needed services and arranges for the delivery of those services usually with the power to authorize or control the provision of service.

The second role of the case manager is that of counselor. In this role, the case manager usually functions as a coordinator as well. This role addresses client attitudes and problems. In the counseling role, the case manager is to enable the client to accept and use services. In some cases, the counseling role includes casework or psychotherapy. In such cases, the case manager takes on the dual role of service manager and direct service provider.

The third role of the case manager is that of advocate. The case manager may function as an advocate for the client in relation to the service system, either to enable the client to receive existing services or to advocate the establishment of needed services. This particular role in the case management system focuses on bureaucratic barriers and the lack of services. However, the advocacy function of the case manager might be referred to a separate advocacy system. This might be to a legal aid agency that has the primary task of advocacy in the community, or a planning council such as an area agency on aging.

Gerontology Concepts. The primary concept from the field of gerontology is that of the frail elderly. Because of the multiple effects of aging (changes in social, health, and economic status), the frail older person requires assistance in order to be maintained in the community. Such a person is generally considered to be the primary target for case management. There has been an increasing emphasis in the field of aging on the needs of the frail elderly for several reasons: a desire to prevent inappropriate institutionalization in nursing homes, an interest in community-based services to meet the long-term care needs of the disabled elderly, and a focus on prevention of deterioration of the elderly. Sometimes this population is referred to as the "at-risk" elderly, because they are at risk of being institutionalized. However, these two groups do not necessarily overlap. A person may be frail but not at risk of institutionalization, and a person may change from being well to being frail very rapidly because of an acute health crisis. A more practical definition of elderly people who need case management is elderly people with multiple problems who need assistance to coordinate services that address those problems.

Policy

Official case management policies and legislation at both the federal and state levels are usually connected to legislation for financing health and social services. A brief discussion of the demographics and financing relating to the long-term care and case management needs of older persons will put policy issues in a broader perspective.

In 1980, 25.5 million people in the United States (11 percent of the population) were sixty-five or over. By the year 2030, 64 million people will be over the age of sixty-five (25 percent). Even though the elderly comprise only 11 percent of the population, they use 29 percent of the health care dollars. In 1978 public funds paid for 63 percent of the elderly's health care. This contrasts to 30 percent in 1956. In 1980, 25 percent of the federal budget was spent on programs for the aging. If present policies and trends continue, spending for the elderly will increase to 40 percent of the budget (American Health Planning Association, 1982).

At the federal level, case management projects have been funded through Section 222(b) of the Social Security Act, Amendments of 1972; and the Older Americans Act, Revisions of 1978. These projects were demonstration and research projects, not permanent policy or funding options for case management programs. In addition to these means of directly funding case management projects, sometimes federal policies funding Medicare or Medicaid are waived so that case management programs can directly control expenditures and reimbursements. For example, the Federal Council on the Aging, in the book *Public Policy and the Frail Elderly* (1978), recommends that the frail elderly—which they define as persons over seventy-five—receive case management services as a regular benefit.

Several states have passed legislation to conduct case management research and demonstration projects or to establish statewide systems of case management. For example, in 1982 California passed Assembly Bill 2860, which created a State Department of Aging and Long-Term Care. This department is to set up a new organizational structure that will provide community-based health and social services, including in-home supportive services and case management, to all persons receiving public funds who are eligible for placement in a skilled nursing or intermediate-care facility. Other states with statewide case management programs are Utah, Pennsylvania, Arkansas, and Washington.

At all governmental levels, the development of case management programs for the older person is affected by the increasing concern to minimize public cost. This concern gives rise to several issues: (1) cost containment, or how to reduce the total public cost for services, including the "extra cost" of case management; (2) preventing inappropriate institutionalization (an estimated 10 to 40 percent of all nursing home admissions could remain in the community if there was a coordinated system of community services); (3) the right of clients to be in the least restrictive setting; and (4) control of expenditures through purchase-of-service money or through waivers that enable case management programs to prescribe services that are paid for by public funds.

Case Management Models

There are many different models of case management for the elderly. Models range from the single individual providing informal case management to a statewide, multimillion-dollar research project based on special legislation. Unfortunately, it is not possible to say that any one model is best or correct in all situations. Past attempts to implement a single model in a multi-agency system have met with resistance and problems. In order to understand the various types of models, case management organizations can be analyzed in five ways: organization base, authority base, fiscal base, professional reference group, and practice structure.

Organization Base. The organization base of a case management system can take several different forms. It can be a freestanding agency, meaning its sole function is case management. In addition, case management can be a function of a planning agency, such as an agency on aging or an information and referral (I&R) center, or case management can be set up within a direct service agency, such as a counseling service or a senior center. A major issue in case management conducted by service providers is to make sure that the services given are based on client needs rather than on what the agency has to provide. As a result, there has been an increasing emphasis in the field on making case management independent of service agencies.

Each type of organization base presents its own problems. Freestanding agencies may be in conflict with other agencies in the community. The domain of a planning agency or an I&R agency may overlap the domains of direct service agencies, causing battles within the community and competition for clients. Finally, a direct service agency has its own biases and approach, which tend to undermine the basic case management concept.

Authority Base. Another aspect to consider in establishing a case management program is its authority base—the source and strength of its sanction to order or control services and clients. The least-structured example is an informal agreement among agencies serving elderly within the community that a certain agency is responsible for case management. The next step up in formality is case management on a temporary basis, such as a demonstration project, which may be established by federal or state law. On the far end of the formal authority scale, the state delegates its responsibilities for protecting its citizens to a case management agency either through legislation or by contract. Authority generally includes the right to intervene in a client's life situation and to manage funds. Examples of this formal authority base can be found in conservatorship, guardian, and adult protective service programs existing in most jurisdictions in the country.

Fiscal Base. A third approach to analyzing case management projects is from their funding source or their fiscal base. This involves clarifying the funding base and the ability of the case management project to control the purchase of services needed by clients. Case management programs are funded through a variety of sources. The 1980 National Survey of Case Coordination Programs for the Elderly lists the major funding sources as (1) Title III of the Older Americans Act (67 percent of all programs), (2) county and city funds (45 percent), (3) Title XX of the Social Security Act (44 percent), (4) Comprehensive Employment Training Act (CETA) (41 percent), and (5) state funds (37 percent). In addition, 25 percent of all programs have a mechanism whereby some clients pay for services. Of these programs, approximately 59 percent use a sliding fee scale.

The funding base (and the permanence of the funding) affects the organization and goals of case management programs. A secure funding base allows for a greater emphasis on program development rather than on proposal development and finding additional funds.

Purchase of service is the mechanism whereby a case management project pays for services needed by clients. This ability to pay may be in the form of waivers (for example, a project may be given special permission to distribute or monitor Medicaid funds for their clients) or a sum of money that the project can spend to purchase any needed services for clients. Based on the 1980 National Survey, approximately 39 percent of case management projects have purchase-of-service agreements. Purchase-of-service power is a mixed blessing. On one hand, it increases the ability of projects to guarantee that clients get needed services; on the other hand, the case management agency must monitor the activities of another agency and possibly threaten its funding.

Professional Reference. The professional orientation or reference of the case management staff greatly influences the design and implementation of the case management model. Professional reference does not refer to the profession of the case manager, but rather to the theoretical model of practice used in the case management project. These models vary considerably. Some projects use a medical model of diagnosis and treatment, emphasizing health care needs and medical personnel. Other projects have a mental health emphasis, focusing on psychological needs and a staff with extensive psychiatric training. Another type of project, often based in a welfare department, focuses on low-income elderly and coordinating public-funded services. Yet another type of project takes a multidisciplinary gerontology approach that emphasizes the diagnosis and treatment of conditions related to aging.

Practice Structure. There are two models of case management practice with the elderly: a formal, structured approach and an informal, unstructured approach. Structured programs have standardized assessment instruments and a standardized approach to working with the client and the service system. Informal projects have an ad hoc approach to case management, using staff for case management as needed.

Examples of Effective Programs

A 1979 national survey listed 333 case management programs for the elderly throughout the United States. These ranged from small programs staffed by one person in a senior center to large, statewide programs staffed by hundreds of workers. This section briefly reports on a few programs that have research components and are widely known. The program descriptions are drawn primarily from the working paper *Long-Term Care Demonstration Projects: A Review of Recent Evaluations* (Stassen and Holahan, 1981).

Access. This case management program, located in Rochester, New York (Monroe County), has been in operation since 1977. This single-entry system of case management attempts to reduce the institutionalization of clients. All individuals who are over eighteen years of age, live in the county, and have long-term care needs are eligible. Access can provide a service plan as long as the package of home care services does not exceed 75 percent of the allowable institutional Medicare rate for an equivalent level of care. Medicare waivers provide a greater range of reimbursable services. The assessment includes medical, nursing, and psychosocial services. During the first twenty-eight months of operation, 7,090 unduplicated clients were assessed by the program. As a result of this program Medicaid hospital backup days increased, Medicaid skilled nursing and health-facility days declined.

Triage. Triage, located in a seven-town region of central Connecticut, was begun in 1974. As described by Quinn (1979) it was targeted to serve all elderly through a process of assessment (by a nurse and social worker team) and coordination of health and social services resources. Services were funded by Section 222 of Medicare, and waivers obtained to provide nontraditional services such as dental, mental health, homemaker, and daycare. The project served over 2,000 persons, about 7 percent of the area's elderly population. The project evaluation consisted of a quasi-experimental design in which an experimental group of 307 Triage clients were compared with 195 elderly from another part of the state. Because of differences in the two samples, it was difficult to draw clear comparisons. A greater use of services make the per capita costs for Triage higher than those of the comparison health care system. However, fewer Triage clients experienced increases in functional dependence than control group clients.

Alternative Health Services Project (AHS). This program in Georgia was begun in July 1976 to test the cost-effectiveness of comprehensive, Medicaid-funded, community-based services as an alternative to nursing home care for the elderly. In the project evaluation, published by the Georgia Department of Medical Assistance (1978), subjects were randomly referred to providers (75 percent) or to the control group (25 percent). A preliminary analysis of costs and service utilization of individuals enrolled in at least one year of the program revealed that "AHS served as a potential substitute for nursing home care for 20 percent of the control group" (Stassen and Holahan, 1981, p. 43), even though all AHS participants were certified as eligible for nursing home care. A most striking finding was that community-based services had a statistically significant impact on mortality. The mortality rate for the service group was 13 percent compared with 25 percent for the control group.

The Alternatives Program (TAP). This case management project is a statewide program in Utah. It is administered by the Utah Division of Aging under state legislative authority designed to reduce unnecessary nursing home placements. In the program, which became operational in July 1978, a case manager and a registered nurse assess clients, focusing on strengthening informal supports, providing formal support, or, as a last resort, paying for services with TAP funds. The budget for the project represents 5 percent of the Utah Division of Aging operating budget of $200,000. It serves only those at risk of nursing home placement. An initial evaluation of the first nine months of program operation showed a reduction in the number of inappropriate or premature admissions of elderly in nursing homes by twelve persons per month. Because of these initial results, the program has been expanded through additional funding from the state.

Multipurpose Senior Services Project (MSSP). This statewide California project was authorized by the legislature in 1977 as a research and demonstration program with eight local sites throughout the state. The project, financed through Medi-Cal waivers from the

Health Care Financing Administration, includes a wide range of in-home and community-based services, some not available through Medi-Cal. The assessment is done by a social worker (M.S.W.) case manager and a nurse practitioner. "Preliminary findings after two years of operation show that the total average cost (including administration) per frail elderly client for MSSP services is $566 per month (not including housing). This is substantially less than the $1,500 per month cost of nursing home care which these clients would have faced if not for MSSP services" (Senior Care Action Network, 1982, p. 47).

Senior Health Service Project/Case Management Component. The Senior Day Health Program in Palo Alto, California, provides adult daycare services to frail elderly. During the three-year study of the project, five case managers of various professions served seventy-six participants. These managers served as members of an interdisciplinary team coordinating both services at the site and services in the community.

Case Management Practice

Case management practice with elderly clients is based upon two related concepts. First is the client pathway, which is the process of serving the client from the first meeting to termination. Second is the assessment of the elderly person's functioning and service needs. A standard practice in these two areas is rapidly developing in case management with the elderly.

The Client Pathway. A primary goal of case management is to ensure that clients receive the range of services appropriate to their needs over a period of time. In order to make certain that clients are assessed and followed up in a consistent manner, most projects develop a standard pathway consisting of the following components: (1) engagement and assessment, (2) setting goals and developing a service plan, (3) reassessment and follow-up, and (4) termination and client feedback.

Assessment. What makes case management assessment unique is that it is not an assessment followed by direct treatment but rather an assessment to coordinate and refer to services. There has been an increasing emphasis on functional assessment as opposed to medical diagnosis. This is because a medical diagnosis, such as arthritis, a stroke, or a mental health condition such as depression, does not indicate how functional the person is. There is also considerable debate about whether case management assessment must be done by a professional. There is support for the idea that if the assessment instrument is very good, a professional is not required to administer it. On the other hand, another view is that, even with a good assessment instrument, there is still a need for a professional's subjective judgment. However, there is a consensus that there is a need to standardize the assessment instrument used and that there must be a formal assessment approach.

Most projects begin service with a thorough assessment using an instrument, then develop a plan to determine what services a person needs. Unfortunately, there has been more emphasis on assessment than on the development of a plan and the follow-up documentation of the work done by the case manager. Areas that are commonly considered important are physical health, activities of daily living, independence, social support, social participation, economic status, and mental status, including emotions and cognitive (or intellectual) functioning.

There is an increasing awareness that to coordinate services for the elderly requires a very broad-based assessment of each client's functioning. A common mistake made by case managers is to want to assess a client only once. However, in practice, once an assessment is done by which an older person is referred to a service, the service providers must then do their own assessment. For example, if a case manager determines that an older person needs homemaker service, then the homemaker has to do a homemaker assessment to determine how many hours are needed. Attempts in case management projects to develop a single assessment tool have not succeeded.

There are several well-known assessment instruments currently in use. One is the Older Americans Resource Survey (OARS), developed at Duke University; Philadelphia Geriatric Center has also developed a very effective instrument described by MacBride, Schneider, Ishizaki, and Gottesman (1979). In addition, there are instruments developed by Access and Triage.

After Assessment. Case managers carry out a wide range of activities in addition to assessing a client and planning a package of services. They may provide supportive counseling to enable the client to use services. They may also coordinate the service package, purchase services if funds are available, monitor fiscal aspects of the case, and provide direct service such as money management education. The case manager may also develop new resources from the informal support network of the client, encourage and educate service providers on behalf of the client, advocate on behalf of the client with landlords and service providers, and consult with specialists providing service to the client. In their role as coordinators, case managers deal with a wide range of individuals, including the family of the older person, social services providers, physicians, bureaucrats, and coworkers.

Professional Roles and Collaboration

There is a lack of agreement about the education and professional background needed by staff in case management programs for the elderly. At present, case managers range from housewife volunteers to case management teams comprised of social workers, nurses, and other health professionals.

There are three major issues in staffing case coordination programs: professional versus paraprofessional case managers, teams versus individual case managers, and the division of labor in the client pathway. Of course, these terms are used loosely. Rarely do projects define *professional* or *paraprofessional*. However, it is valuable to review the trends in current projects.

Professionals. The need for professionals as case coordinators usually arises in discussions of the importance of assessment. The central benefit seems to be the ability of the professional to recognize and respond to more than superficial needs. This is especially important in dealing with the frail elderly. Another area where the case coordinator's professional training and skills are valuable is consulting with other professionals about a client, understanding the service system, and negotiating with providers of supporting services. Also, professional preparation can reduce the problem of role strain caused by varied, complex tasks. The disadvantages of professionals as case coordinators have not been comprehensively discussed. A few project reports, however, indicate the following areas of difficulty when professionals are case managers:

1. Professionals from outside the local community can cause conflict.
2. Professionals may be less interested in working with multi-problem clients in whom success is not clear or easily obtainable.
3. Professionals, especially in teams, are costlier than non-professionals.
4. Professionals norms and ideologies may override the task of case management.

Paraprofessionals, Volunteers, and Case Aides. Project experience with paraprofessionals, volunteers, and case aides as case managers has yielded the following observations and recommendations:

1. Paraprofessionals and volunteers need professional supervision.
2. Professional supervision increases costs, and the number of volunteers and paraprofessionals used is limited by the amount of supervision that can be provided.
3. Volunteers and paraprofessionals need to be carefully selected and assigned appropriate tasks.
4. Volunteers, paraprofessionals, and aides are valuable as extensions into the community of the professional staff who find and provide new or extra services for the frail elderly.
5. The major limits on the use of volunteers and paraprofessionals are the following:
    a. Volunteers and paraprofessionals may deal poorly with interagency policy problems.
    b. They may not be seen as competent by other people in the community.
    c. They cannot transport nonambulatory clients.
    d. They may have problems with the agency's eligibility requirements especially if they require turning down the requests of friends and neighbors for needed help.

e.   They may need extra training and supervision to handle case conferences and prepare written reports that are read by professionals.

Teams or Individuals as Case Managers. The major value of the team approach lies in its comprehensiveness and quality. A team model of case coordination usually implies that the assessment and case coordination will be done by professionals. The most common team is a nurse and a social worker; however, team members may include physicians, psychiatrists, and other specialists.

The main problem with a team model is cost. Teams are obviously more expensive than a single individual. In addition, some project reports caution that having a team does not guarantee coordination. Quality of assessments and their accuracy are, however, greater with a team. The consensus in the field is to utilize a team model if funds and trained personnel are available.

Labor in the Client Pathway. The client in case coordination service is usually helped in a series of overlapping steps called the client pathway. These steps are eligibility, assessment, case planning, follow-up, monitoring, reassessment, and termination. There are various ways to handle the division of labor in this pathway. The main options are as follows:

1. The same staff individual carries out all the tasks in the pathway.
2. The intake assessment is handled by one individual; the rest of the tasks are carried out under another individual.
3. The task of follow-up monitoring is assigned to a specific individual.
4. A specific person is responsible for developing new resources for clients based on shortage areas extracted from the caseloads of many case managers.
5. Where a management information system is used, supervisors or control clerks are responsible for data management.
6. Volunteers provide direct services (such as escorting and friendly visiting) to clients.

Other issues that arise in the client pathway are caseload size and skill levels needed to do the various tasks. These issues were discussed earlier, but it is important to note that the division of labor affects the caseload size. When various tasks are assigned to different people, the case manager can handle a larger caseload. However, such an arrangement may fragment the relationship between the client and the case manager.

Another aspect of this issue is the problem of follow-up in case coordination projects. As noted, too often the emphasis has been on assessment and the service plan, and little thought has been given to the follow-up. In each project, it must be decided whether a separate worker should handle follow-up or whether a worker has time for follow-up because he or she has a reasonable caseload. There is no best way to handle this issue. What is important is that the issue be recognized and addressed.

Training and Education Needs of Case Managers

The type and amount of training needed by case managers depend on their professional background and previous training. Training must be an ongoing part of case management programs and involves both content and process. However, training cannot make up for staff problems or a lack of supervision.

Most important is that case managers be trained in assessment, developing case plans, doing follow-up, working with other agencies, and terminating clients. Setting goals, measuring goal attainment, and handling conflicts that arise in setting goals are problem areas for many managers. Some case managers need training so that they can help clients set goals; others need to learn how to write goals that can be measured and understood.

Case coordination is not simply a matter of applying knowledge in an objective, computerlike fashion. The case coordinator needs to communicate effectively with many people. The particular need for training in working with clients was stressed in the results of the National Survey of Case Coordination Projects. When respondents were asked which subject was the top priority for training and technical assistance, 52 percent indicated "working with clients." Other areas in which training is needed are (1) assessing the emotionally disturbed client, (2) assisting the family of the client, (3) dealing with the client who chooses social isolation, the alcoholic, the person with an unorthodox life-style, and (4) ethical issues in case management.

Case managers also need training to know all available community services and how to use them so that a few resources are not overused when others are available. This training should include information on the types of agreements (formal and informal) between agencies and how to foster relationships with agencies. Training in record keeping and using forms is also important. Unless records are carefully kept every day, a project will be poorly documented. Poor record keeping may also cause unmet needs to be underreported. Training in this area is especially important if there is to be a computer-based management information system. Staff education is needed on how to use such a system and why it is needed. This may be time consuming, but an effective management information system requires a well-trained staff.

Current Problems

Among the array of problems in the field of case management, there are three related to working with the elderly that are currently prominent. First is the difficulty in getting a consensus on goals and objectives for case management programs. Second is the social and political climate, as it affects funding and public policy. The third is the uneven distribution of services, resources, and needs in different communities.

Program Goals and Objectives. The most pressing current problem seems to be the lack of consensus on the purpose and objectives of case management programs. Simply put, shall the overall goal of case management be creating a full range of services or that of monitoring and controlling the appropriate use of existing services? Goals often conflict with each other. For example, it is costlier in the short term to provide homemaker, adult daycare, transportation, and counseling services than to provide only those services needed for minimum maintenance in the community. The long-term cost benefit of providing a full complement of service has not been fully documented. Some programs have limits on the amount of money that can be spent to maintain a client in the community. Programs trying to increase services must eventually deal with the conflict between the number and range of services needed and their cost.

Another problem is determining the target population to be served and how to locate this population. Shall the target population be defined as the frail elderly, the elderly over the age of seventy-five, the elderly at risk of being institutionalized, the elderly with multiple service needs, the elderly with functional impairments, or the elderly with specific chronic illnesses?

After the target population is identified, other decisions to be made become more apparent. The issue of how long to serve the client raises the question of whether the goal of service is rehabilitation or maintenance. Which type of program is better cannot be decided without determining the overall purpose of the case management program. The issue of the cost-effectiveness of either goal must be resolved.

Funding and Policy. A second pressing problem in planning and implementing case management programs is funding and the public policy base. Unless there is ongoing funding for case management programs, projects must constantly seek grants and lobby for special legislation to support their programs. The lack of secure funding hampers the development of permanent case management services. This problem becomes more and more critical as funding for social services programs diminishes and case management agencies compete with direct services agencies for a shrinking pool of money. The other side of the funding problem is the issue of public policy regarding case management. Should a case management program be a "superagency"? In which health or social services organization should the case management agency be based? The lack of a secure financial base and the lack of agreement about the policy base for case management makes the delivery of case management services a complicated task of juggling different priorities and needs.

Distribution of Services. The third problem area for case management programs is the uneven distributions of services and resources in different communities. The range, type, and number of services provided for the elderly differ greatly from area to area. One community may have an extensive range of in-home services, including visiting nurses, an at-home hospice program, meals-on-wheels, homemaker and home repair services, and reassurance calling. Another community may have none of these services. In communities lacking services, case management may become a funnel for institutionalizing older people because the only good service plan not involving community resources may be institution-alization. Because of a lack of services, the case management agency may assume the roles of advocate and developer of services rather than of coordinator of existing resources and services.

Consumer Advocacy Issues

Consumer advocacy issues in case management with the elderly have rarely been addressed. For example, the right of clients to choose their own services or to challenge the case management assessment and plan of services has not been legally challenged. Moreover, the right of the case manager to be a "gatekeeper" and to determine what services a client shall receive has not been challenged in the legal process, and the protection of the rights of clients with cognitive impairment in a case management system remains unexplored. In addition, issues of clients as informed consumers have been neglected. Two examples are enabling clients to be their own case managers and educating clients to evaluate and provide feedback on the quality of case management services.

There are three primary issues concerning clients' rights in case management programs: (1) the clients' right to refuse case management and still receive services, (2) the clients' right to challenge an assessment or a plan of prescribed services, and (3) the clients' right to refuse services in a case management plan. In general, clients are not informed of their rights in these areas, and few (if any) projects have a standard review-of-appeal process. Clients are usually not told whether they can receive services without a case manager nor given an option of using case management or coordinating their own services.

In some case management projects, the case manager decides which services an older person can receive. Thus, the case manager controls the purchasing or prescribing of services. In most cases, the case manager and older person agree on the services that are needed; however, sometimes they disagree. For example, an older person may want twenty hours of homemaker service, but the case manager may decide on the basis of a full assessment that this is not necessary. This raises many questions about the legal and social power of the case manager. This is especially an issue if some clients are case-managed and others are not. In this type of system, some older people would have full access to services, and others would have access controlled by a case management system.

Particularly distressing is the problem of serving clients with cognitive impairment, who may need services and refuse them. These clients cannot evaluate the quality of the case management service, and when these clients become part of the public guardian system, the role of the case manager is undefined.

The relationship between the public guardian and adult protective services and case management has not been carefully examined. Various questions arise: Who should be the case manager, the public guardian or a separate case manager? Who should have the final authority over case plans? Should there be a goal of placing the older person in the least restrictive environment? Should there be two case management systems: one for most elderly and one for protective service clients? Thus far there has been little discussion of these issues, and there is no general agreement in the field about how to handle them.

Clients and Family as Case Managers. In the field of aging, there has been practically no attempt to teach older people and their families to be their own case managers. In contrast, in the field of mental retardation, there has been a movement to train families to be case managers for their mentally retarded children. In fact, as case management for the elderly focuses on professional assessment and control of the service dollar, the idea of clients or family as case managers seems less feasible. However, over time projects may begin to teach consumers to be their own case managers in order to diminish caseloads and reduce costs.

Clients as Evaluators of Case Management Service. It has been difficult to get clients to evaluate the quality of services in programs for the elderly because older people are generally glad to receive any service and do not want to jeopardize such help by saying negative things. It is even more difficult to get good client feedback about case management programs, because evaluating the coordinator role is inherently difficult. The client cannot know many of the areas of program evaluation, such as whether the assessment is broad and thorough or whether the case manager documents the follow-up. Most people have had the experience of seeing more than one physician. Thus, they can compare what one physician did with what another one did or did not do, because there is some expectation of what the physician should do. But most clients do not have previous experience with case coordination programs so they cannot compare. Thus, the average client has no good way of evaluating a program other than by judging how he or she was treated by the worker. For older persons to evaluate case management or other services they will need more education about clients' rights, types of services, and what to expect from services.

Future Directions

The future role of case management in the health and social services network must be examined from social, political, and technological perspectives. Four areas need to be addressed: the role of case management in the long-term care system, the role of case management in reducing or controlling the costs of social and health programs in this country, the role of management information systems (computer technology) in case management systems, and the role of the family and social supports in case management systems.

The Long-Term Care System. The future role of case management in the long-term care system of social and health services is unclear. The role of case management as a coordinating agency for individuals receiving services from a variety of service providers would be radically different if social health maintenance organizations were reorganized. The role would also be altered if frail older people received a full range of services from one agency such as an adult daycare center. It is also unclear how the current emphasis on long-term care for individuals with chronic health conditions (mental health problems, disabilities, and limited functional abilities) will affect case management services for the elderly. Any advances in medical research that would decrease or eliminate any of these conditions in the elderly would sharply reduce the long-term care needs and case management needs of the elderly. An increase in environmental supports such as varied housing options and computer technology to monitor the functioning of older persons on a daily basis would also reduce the needs of the elderly for case management.

Reducing Costs. The future of case management also depends on the role of case management in reducing or controlling health and social services costs. Case management could be the gatekeeper of the resources. The case management assessment could determine the services needed by the older person and the cost of those services. Access to services could be controlled by the case management process. This could reduce the inappropriate or excessive use of particular services; for example, an older person applying for nursing home placement may need only a group of in-home services that are cheaper to provide than nursing home placement. On the other hand, an individual or family member may want to keep an older person at home whom case management assessment indicates should be placed in a nursing home. In both of these cases, values, consumer preferences, and clients' rights must be taken into account. If case management is to take a primary role in controlling expenditures, then standards (the quality of assessment procedures and scientific basis for decision making) and values will become more critical.

Management Information Systems. The role of management information systems in case management projects involves several areas: providing a common data base on clients, confidentiality and client access to records, evaluation of programs, research on other case management models, and problems in current computer technology. Computers could provide an efficient system of keeping track of clients and expenditures. The most immediate problem facing case management systems wanting to use computer technology is the task of developing programs that meet the needs of the agency and that provide efficient access to data that are usable by staff.

Confidentiality of computer-stored data and the exchange of data between organizations are issues facing all case management programs. The client access to data is another issue when computers are a part of the data management system. The use of computers in evaluation and in the research of programs raises the obvious questions of what data to collect and how to use and analyze them.

Family and Social Supports. Another area of concern facing case management systems is the role of the family and social supports in the case management system. The family plays a vital role in maintaining the elderly person in the community. It has been noted that the family and social supports provide 80 percent of all services to the elderly. The potential role of the family affects all aspects of case management programs. Pertinent issues include the following: How should family needs be assessed? How broad should a family assessment be? Should family members be paid for providing services to their elderly relatives? Can family members be trained to be case managers? Is professional case management needed? How should the services provided by families be figured in cost-effectiveness studies? How should differences between older persons and family members about service needs of older persons be handled? How do ethnic and cultural factors affect family involvement in the care of the elderly? How can the support provided by families be decreased? When should such support be decreased and agency services offered instead? How will changing demographic and work patterns affect the role of the family in the future? The role and importance of the family in the care of the elderly must be taken into account in planning the future of case management programs, policies, and practices.

Suggested Readings

American Health Planning Association. *A Guide for Planning Long-Term Care Health Services for the Elderly.* Washington, D.C.: American Health Planning Association, 1982.

Carter, G. W., Downing, R., Hutson, D. O., and Ishizaki, B. S. *Case Coordination with the Elderly: The Experiences of Front-Line Practitioners.* Proceedings and summary of findings from the symposium on Geriatric Practice, Andrus Gerontology Center, University of Southern California, Los Angeles, January 20–22, 1979.

Frankfather, D. L., Smith, M. J., and Caro, F. G. *Family Care of the Elderly*. Lexington, Mass.: Heath, Lexington Books, 1981.

Gottesman, L., and Schneider, B. "Case Management: Variations on a Theme." In *Final Report, Community Care Systems Project*. Philadelphia: Temple University, 1983.

MacBride, S. M., Schneider, B., Ishizaki, I., and Gottesman, L. E. *A Service Management Manual: A Guide to the Development of a Client-Oriented Approach to Coordinated Service Delivery*. Second working draft. Philadelphia: Philadelphia Geriatric Center, November 1979.

Steinberg, R. M., and Carter, G. W. *Case Management and the Elderly*. Lexington, Mass.: Heath, Lexington Books, 1983.

Wan, T. T. H. *Stressful Life Events, Social-Support Networks, and Gerontological Health*. Lexington, Mass.: Heath, Lexington Books, 1982.

Wasser, E. *Creative Approaches in Casework with the Aging*. New York: Family Service Association of America, 1966.

Zimmer, A. H., and Mellor, M. J. *Caregivers Make the Difference: Group Services for Those Caring for Older Persons in the Community*. New York: Community Service Society of New York, 1981.

References

American Health Planning Association. *A Guide for Planning Long-Term Care Health Services for the Elderly*. Washington, D.C.: American Health Planning Association, 1982.

Assistance Group for Human Resources Development. *Service Systems for Older People in Four State Aging Networks: Arkansas, Pennsylvania, Utah, and Washington State*. Kensington, Md.: Assistance Group for Human Resources Development, 1982.

Downing, R. *Three Working Papers*. Los Angeles: Social Policy Laboratory, Andrus Gerontology Center, University of Southern California, March 1979.

Federal Council on the Aging. *Public Policy and the Frail Elderly: A Staff Report*. Department of Health, Education and Welfare Publication no. (OHDS) 79-20959. Washington, D.C.: U.S. Government Printing Office, December 1978.

Georgia Department of Medical Assistance. *Alternative Health Services, Annual Report 1977–1978.* Atlanta: Georgia Department of Medical Assistance, June 1978.

MacBride, S. M., Schneider, B., Ishizaki, I., and Gottesman, L. E. *A Service Management Manual: A Guide to the Development of a Client-Oriented Approach to Coordinated Service Delivery.* Second working draft. Philadelphia: Philadelphia Geriatric Center, November 1979.

Midpeninsula Health Services, Inc., and the Senior Day Health Program of the Senior Coordinating Council of Palo Alto. *A Better Way: Final Report of the Senior Health Services Project.* Palo Alto, Calif.: Midpeninsula Health Service, 1981.

Quinn, J. L. *Triage, Inc.: An Alternative Approach to Care for the Elderly, 1974–1979.* Hartford: Connecticut Department on Aging, 1979.

Senior Care Action Network. *Developing Long-Term Care: A Framework for the Los Angeles County Area Agency on Aging.* Los Angeles: UCLA/USC Long-Term Care Gerontology Center, Andrus Gerontology Center, University of Southern California, 1982.

Stassen, M., and Holahan, J. *Long-Term Care Demonstration Projects: A Review of Recent Evaluations.* Working paper. Washington, D.C.: Urban Institute, 1981.

7

%%%%%%%%%%%%%%%%%%%%%%%%%%%%%%%%%%%%%%

Case Management
in Health Care
Settings

Rosalie A. Kane

Case management, as practiced in health care settings, is described and defined in this chapter. Client-centered and system-centered approaches are discussed in the context of recent literature and research on interdisciplinary teamwork, health behavior, and inter-organizational theories. Public policy affecting case management development, ranging from the Health Maintenance Organization Act of 1973 through relevant sections of the Social Security Act to the Section 1115 waivers by the Health Care Financing Administration, is reviewed as well.

A proposed new model for case management, the social/health maintenance organization, is described along with several model programs in the United States, England, and Canada. Case management practices are identified: these include screening and targeting, assessment, decision algorithms, and management information systems. The most critical consumer issue is achieving both the lowest level of cost and the highest level of care. Determining the effectiveness of case management is seen as an unresolved problem attributable to the difficulty of conducting evaluative research in public programs. Despite problems, client-centered case management appears successful in coordinating services.

In health care, case management may be a role self-selected by a professional or assigned by the eye of the beholder. Primary care physicians may define themselves as case managers when they advise patients about their need for more specialized health and health-related services and arrange for them to take place. In a health maintenance organization (HMO), a referral by a primary care physician might be the enrollee's only access to other services offered under the plan. A social worker in a hospital or in outpatient services may also be a case manager who consciously seeks to bridge the gap between health and social services inside and outside the employing organization. Such a worker makes referrals, conducts case conferences, coordinates activities, tries to ensure that everyone involved with the patient understands each other's roles, and includes the patient in the complicated, multidirectional communication. Sometimes this case management role is assumed by the social worker, but sometimes it is explicitly incorporated in the job description.

Hospital discharge planners, many of whom are social workers, may also perceive themselves as case managers. They coordinate information and services to foster a timely, smooth, and appropriate continuation or introduction of care after acute hospital care is no longer needed. In large, complex organizations, case managers are sometimes appointed to ensure that someone on an unwieldly, complex, multidisciplinary team or program staff knows each patient's problems, needs, preferences, and progress over time and can bring this information to the attention of others as required. Thus each patient might be assigned a "primary care nurse," who has a role over and above regular nursing duties. Similarly, one member of a rehabilitation team, regardless of discipline, may become a case manager for a particular group of patients. This sort of manager-cum-advocate role is sometimes, but not always, made explicit to the patient. Paraprofessionals may also serve as case managers for a health care team. For example, some nursing homes assign a small number of residents to each nurse's aide, who is expected to plan with and for her "own" patients.

In the last decade, case management in health care has taken on a more precise meaning linked to reimbursement under Medicare and Medicaid. Particularly in long-term care, case management allocates resources to beneficiaries and monitors their use to promote equitable, appropriate, and cost-effective decisions. Case management of this type has been integral to federal and state demonstration projects that provide alternatives to nursing home care (especially for Medicaid recipients). The case manager's role in such programs may involve any or all of the following: case finding or screening, multidimensional assessment, care planning, authorizing services, and monitoring or follow-up.

A definition of case management that fits all the above examples must be rather elastic. Such a definition is contained in Section 2176 of the 1981 Omnibus Budget Reconciliation Act (PL 7970-35). This provision permits states to waive Medicaid regulations to offer a range of health and personal care services to persons eligible for nursing home care provided that the costs of the services do not exceed the costs of the nursing home itself (U.S. Congress, 1982). Another condition is that the waiver and services must be provided under an individual care plan. Not surprisingly, therefore, case management headed the list of services permitted under 2176 waivers. Case management was defined as "a system under which responsibility for locating, coordinating, and monitoring a group of services rests with a defined person or group" (p. 373).

That general definition will be used in this chapter. It has the advantage of applying to a wide range of examples. The primary care physician, the discharge planner, the patient advocate on the team, and the social worker as case coordinator are all involved in locating, coordinating, and monitoring a group of services. The boundaries of the services coordinated may be within a single institution such as a hospital. On the other hand, the boundaries may be indeterminate; for example, a case manager for a cancer rehabilitation program or a crippled children's program may be responsible for coordinating resources that cross health care, social services, employment services, recreational, and educational system boundaries.

Sometimes the case manager has purchasing power, as is typical in some crippled children's programs. Similarly, the rehabilitation counselor is a case manager with extensive discretionary purchasing power on behalf of clients. In long-term care demonstrations, some case managers have had considerable authority. For the particular target population and for the specified group of services, the case manager authorizes reimbursement for an array of community health services. This control of purse strings goes well beyond the power of case managers within a single-care institution, who control access to a much narrower range of services and privileges.

An unidentified pundit remarked that coordination means that *you* want to do something with *my* resources. This notion encapsulates practical problems that arise when practitioners in health care agencies act in the capacity of case manager, especially when their service expands beyond a single organization. Therein lies some of the reluctance of health care organizations to cooperate with community-based case managers who are authorized to control reimbursement. Case management is most effective when it operates within an identifiable system of service, but this, too, creates operational problems when applying the concept to the unruly health care field.

Theoretical Basis

Case management in health contexts has two distinct rationales—client centered and system centered. The client-centered rationale recognizes the complexity of the health care delivery system in all its multidisciplinary glory, the vulnerability of the client (who is too often the passive recipient of care), and the bewildering effects of high technology on the health care consumer. Physical, mental, and social factors are further intertwined in the presentation of many health problems and in the course of recovery. Therefore, case management is suggested as an antidote to a complex and inhumane system that consumers cannot readily manipulate on their own behalf. Theoretical justification for the client-centered side of case management can be found in the multidisciplinary teamwork literature, the behavioral science literature on health-related behaviors, and a body of theory about organizational and professional behavior.

The system-centered rationale for case management recognizes that health care resources are finite. Equity and cost-effectiveness require some management of the allocation of these resources in a community, city, or state or even in a particular patient population such as all patients with cerebral palsy in a given area. Case management serves a rationing and priority-setting function by husbanding resources or, more positively, by targeting those persons in a large population who could most benefit from specific services. Theoretical underpinnings for the system-centered side of case management come from health economics and organizational theory.

Case management as it has evolved in health care settings, however, is more pragmatic than theoretical. In all its guises, it has usually been designed as a practical solution to a confusing situation in which some patients or beneficiaries receive too little, too much, inappropriate, fragmented, or dehumanized service. Poor distribution and poor quality of services affect more than the well-being of the individuals concerned. The efficiency and effectiveness of programs and the solvency of agencies, institutions, and funding sources are also at stake.

Interdisciplinary Teamwork. The literature supporting various forms of interdisciplinary teamwork in health care settings is contradictory and, for the most part, based on belief rather than empirical study. Over the years, however, it has been documented that health care providers are uninformed or misinformed about each other's roles and that the patient may often be caught in the middle. Services may be duplicated or not delivered at all. Worse still, sometimes nobody takes responsibility for maintaining a continuous relationship with a patient and the patient's family.

A multidisciplinary health care team may be defined as a work group with a common purpose, separate roles for achieving that purpose, and a process of communication. A review of programs completed in the mid 1970s shows that teams were not living up to these definitions. On the whole, their purposes were vague or unarticulated, roles were blurred, and communication was haphazard (Kane, 1975). In the last decade, the pendulum has swung toward preoccupation with improving teamwork through efforts to make each health professional more open to colleagues' suggestions, to reduce the automatic authority of the physician, and to introduce democratic decision making (for example, Wise and others, 1974; Brill, 1976). This attention to process may have gone too far. Although cumulative evidence suggests that team training can increase the satisfaction of team members, a positive effect on patient outcomes has not been demonstrated (Kane, 1980). The more recent emphasis on case management has, at the least, suggested that the concept of the "core team" and clear channels for multidisciplinary communication might replace the model of the large, highly interactive team (Kane, 1981).

Teamwork may not boast a large empirical literature, but the desirable characteristics of teamwork have at least received some attention. In contrast, the process of making effective referrals to persons in other disciplines or other organizations, which also requires clearly defined purposes and roles and good communication, has barely been conceptualized. It is known, however, that patients do not always act upon referrals. This may happen because the referral is not explained to the patient or because the patient lacks the motivation or ability to do so. Case management attempts to assist an individual in wending his or her way through the health care maze and getting linked to necessary services.

Health Behavior. Case management receives some impetus from the view that patient compliance increases when the patient is satisfied with the care giver. Satisfaction, in turn, is likelier when patients perceive that care givers are personally interested in them (Vida, Korsch, and Morris, 1969; Sackett and Haynes, 1976; Starfield and others, 1976) and go beyond a particular symptom or organ system to take a general interest in the client's well-being.

The hallmark of family practice as a medical specialty is a continuous, coordinated, comprehensive approach to medical care. Although family practice as a vehicle for continuous, coordinated, comprehensive care has probably been oversold (Holmes and others, 1978), it is indisputable that the medical care system, be it physician or emergency room, is the place where people go with a variety of social as well as physical problems. The presenting medical symptoms may not even be the problem most worrying the patient (Gallagher, 1978). The relationship between stress and physical illness is also becoming well recognized (Dohrenwend and

Dohrenwend, 1974; Pearlin and others, 1981). For all these reasons, a case manager who can interact responsibly with the patient, assess a broad variety of social as well as health care needs, and make necessary referrals will enhance overall patient well-being.

Interorganizational Theory. Several streams of thought are germane to case management in health care settings. Representatives of care-giving institutions are likely to shape a client's needs to fit the services that they offer (Hasenfeld and English, 1974), and some independent assessment of those needs is useful. Furthermore, many health care settings are total institutions (such as hospitals and nursing homes) that engender dependency. Some countervailing force is needed to help the individual assert his or her autonomy.

Interorganizational relationships may be described as a series of exchanges (Levine and White, 1974). In health care, the exchanges involve patients, expertise, and resources. A skillful case manager might mediate those exchanges to encourage desired changes in the delivery system itself (Austin, 1981, 1983). The case manager can not only help bring about good care for a particular individual but also influence the quality of care throughout the system by his or her recommendations and decisions. The power of the case manager to alter interorganizational relationships is increased when he or she also has authority over expenditures. Even without that buying power, the case manager has considerable potential to improve services in a system. For example, hospital discharge planners can theoretically influence the quality and supply of institutional and home-based services by their recommendations.

Health Economics. Health care expenditures seem resistant to the usual laws of supply and demand. Physicians generate costs by recommending additional treatments (including medical consultations, drugs, laboratory tests, surgery, and nursing home placements). It seems that the greater the supply of physicians, the greater the costs of health services (Knowles, 1977; Enthoven, 1980). A similar principle seems to hold true for hospital and nursing home beds—if they are available, they are likely to be full. Many commentators have pointed out that our present payment systems, private insurance and Medicare, diffuse the responsibility for expenses in the system. Treatments are ordered by a first party, received by a second, and paid for by the third-party payer.

Consumers have few incentives to economize at the point of illness. Providers, be they physicians, hospitals, or nursing homes, have positive disincentives to streamline treatments. By and large, reimbursement formulas have been keyed to the number of services delivered. Until the recent advent of diagnosis-related groups (DRGs), Medicare has reimbursed hospitals on a cost-plus basis. Doctors are paid by the procedure. Nursing home reimbursement formulas vary by state, but for the most part, the incentives encourage disability. The bifurcation between care in skilled nursing home facilities (SNFs) and intermediate care facilities (ICFs) is an example of a perverse incentive. It is actually against the interest of the nursing home to rehabilitate SNF patients to the ICF level of independence. Case-mix reimbursement for nursing homes, which has been introduced in several states, similarly pays the home more for residents who function poorly and are deemed to require more nursing time.

Various methods have been suggested to correct such marketplace problems. They include limiting the supply of services, changing the incentives of either the providers or the consumers to use those services, or limiting access on the basis of some predetermined criteria. Case management is one method of limiting access and controlling the amount of service that a given client receives. Through case management, it is possible to direct clients to a less expensive service or to a type of service theoretically more appropriate.

Policy

Federal and state policies directly support the current interest in case management for health care delivery. Concern for the high costs of hospital care predates Medicare and Medicaid. The Health Maintenance Organization Act of 1973 promoted the concept of prepaid comprehensive services as an alternative to fee-for-service arrangements with the goal of encouraging preventive and outpatient services instead of more expensive inpatient care. In theory at least, some sort of case management was built into HMOs, which are expected to offer each enrollee the appropriate mix of services.

The major health policies that create the need for case management in health care, however, are Medicare and Medicaid (Titles XVIII and XIX of the Social Security Act). Almost immediately after their passage in 1967, concerns about the cost, appropriateness, and quality of the care reimbursed under those new programs emerged. Case management must be understood against the backdrop of the high public costs of health care (especially in hospitals and nursing homes) and the particular nature of Medicare and Medicaid, both of which purchase services rather than provide them directly.

Medicare is a health insurance entitlement for most persons over age 65 or those drawing Social Security disability payments. In 1972, end-stage renal disease patients were added, and in 1982, terminally ill hospice patients. Medicare pays for substantial portions of hospital care and physician services for program beneficiaries. Coverage of skilled nursing home care and home health care is extremely limited, and the home care is further circumscribed by numerous rules.

Medicaid is a means-tested program providing health care for the poor, which includes a wide range of mandatory services. Federal guidelines require that, at a minimum, people on categorical income maintenance programs such as Aid to Families with Dependent Children and Supplemental Security Income be eligible. Benefits include certain specified items, such as physician services, hospital care, and skilled nursing home services, and others at state options. Federal and state governments share the cost of Medicaid, each state being responsible for administering its program and, within federal guidelines, defining the benefit packages and establishing the eligibility criteria.

Both programs suffer from uncontrolled, accelerating costs. Medicare's provisions encourage the use of expensive hospital care over outpatient service and nursing home care over home care. In 1972, the Social Security Act was amended to curb abuses of the new benefit. The Professional Standards Review Organization (PSRO) was established as a mechanism for monitoring the appropriateness and quality of care. Hospital services received the greatest attention; vigorous discharge-planning efforts were introduced to ensure that patients did not remain in the hospital beyond the requirements of "medical necessity." In a later development, the review technology spread to the nursing home. Reviews of nursing home residents, however, showed that even if institutionalization was medically required, social circumstances militated against discharge. Therefore, preadmission review programs sprang up to prevent inappropriate nursing home placements in the first place, and these necessarily had elements of case management in locating alternative community resources (Kane and others, 1979).

The 1972 amendments also permitted demonstrations to assess the cost-effectiveness of alternatives to institutionalization. Under this authority, known as Section 222 waivers, Medicare rules could be waived to demonstrate the effects of broader services on institutionalization and total costs. Case management has been a feature of most 222 demonstrations.

Medicaid similarly has experienced high costs, especially for nursing home care. Nursing homes constitute a catastrophic expense not covered by Medicare, and many nursing home residents exhaust their private funds soon after their admission. Once residents "spend down" to Medicaid, the state Medicaid program is left with the burden. Nursing home costs now amount to over 40 percent of total Medicaid payments.

In searching for better and less expensive ways of delivering care under Medicaid, the Health Care Financing Administration (HCFA) has allowed states to apply for Section 1115 waivers, which permit changes in Medicaid rules for demonstration purposes. Over the years, well-known community care projects have been developed with Medicaid waivers, and most of these have had a case management component. Although Medicaid is a health program, needs for shelter, homemaking, protection, and other social services seem to account for many Medicaid-covered nursing home placements. For each person in a nursing home, it is estimated that two or three people with the same degree of functional impairment reside in the community, and social factors more than health status determine that outcome (U.S. Comptroller General, 1979). Therefore, the challenge of the demonstrations has been to develop and coordinate both health and social services so that (1) individuals are likelier to remain in the community longer and (2) the overall costs under Medicaid are contained.

The various demonstrations under Section 1115 Medicaid waivers culminated in a special congressional authorization in 1980 for the National Long-Term Care Channeling Demonstration. Ten projects in ten states have been mounted to test the effectiveness of different organizational structures on the costs and outcomes of long-term care using a relatively rigorous research design. Again, case management is an integral component of each channeling project (Baxter and others, 1983). Finally, as already noted, Section 2176 of the 1981 Omnibus Budget Reconciliation Act permits all states to waive Medicaid regulations to offer a range of services to persons otherwise needing nursing home care provided that the costs of the care are no more than 75 percent of the predicted nursing home costs and provided that the waivered services conform to a management plan. Of the first twenty-nine waivers approved, case management was a feature of all but two applications (Greenberg, Schmitz, and Lakin, 1983).

At the state level, many legislatures have produced their own case management programs. For example, in 1973 Massachusetts created its Department of Elder Affairs, which began developing a statewide network of twenty-three home care corporations. Each of these agencies provides case management and purchases a variety of personal care and in-home services for its clients. The Massachusetts program has no means test, and the key to the service distribution is the assessment of the case manager. Case management was deliberately vested in a network apart from the established welfare system. By 1982, the system was serving more than 40,000 elderly clients. Pennsylvania has a similar, well-established program (Gottesman, Ishizaki, and MacBride, 1979), and many other states have developed a community-based case management capacity of some kind.

Various states have also mandated demonstrations. In 1977, California passed Assembly Bill 998, which required the state to establish multipurpose senior services projects (MSSPs) at various sites. The projects were to test the effects of single-entry access to health and social services for Medicaid-eligible populations. By 1980, eight such projects were operating. Case management is the vehicle through which reimbursements under 1115 waivers for an array of health and social services (for example, social daycare, housing assistance, in-home support services, nonmedical transportation, legal services, and nonmedical respite care) are coordinated with regular Medicaid services and with services available under Title III and Title XX of the Older Americans Act (pertaining to multipurpose senior centers and nutrition programs). In August 1982, California enacted Assembly Bill 2860, which would implement statewide county-based long-term care programs featuring case management and a pooling of funds from Medicaid, Title XX, and the Older Americans Act. (As of 1984, Assembly Bill 2860 has been superseded by a less dramatic approach without the pooling of funds.) Many other states have introduced or are working on similar legislation supporting coordinated case management efforts (Toff, 1981).

Case Management Models

Case management in its most developed form is comprised of a sequence of repetitive activities: case finding or screening, assessment, care planning, service authorization, monitoring, and reassessment. Case management programs vary in the construction of these core activities. For example, case finding may be an active process of repeated screening of a population at risk for care or may be a more passive screening of people referred for service. Assessment may be an in-depth, multidisciplinary process that seeks to depict the interaction of physical, mental, social, and environmental factors in creating need, or it may be a more perfunctory eligibility determination. At the least intensive end of the spectrum, the case manager's assessment may even be done without face-to-face contact with the client. Monitoring of service varies in intensity, and reassessment varies in frequency. Sometimes monitoring of service includes an oversight function to ensure that the patient actually receives all the services ordered. Sometimes monitoring includes surveillance of the quality of a wide range of community services used by program participants.

Other elements in the case management scheme may also vary considerably. For example, case management programs differ in the amount of authority that the program has over benefits, the scope of the services being managed, the entry point into the case management system, and the case management program's relation-ship to existing services.

Authority over resources and reimbursement may be the most important variable of all. In some models of case management, the case manager can only make recommendations. In other instances, the case manager can deny payment for a variety of health-related benefits or authorize payment for innovative services not ordinarily covered under Medicare or Medicaid. Most often in the United States, the case manager has real authority over Medicaid recipients only. The case manager may determine that nursing home care is inappropriate and recommend community-based alternatives for a particular patient; however, that recommendation ordinarily can-not prevent affluent clients from using their own funds to enter a nursing home.

The scope of services managed is another important dimen-sion. In a single agency, the case manager may deal only with those services contained under its organizational umbrella. More com-monly, case managers (with or without authority) coordinate a broader array of services. The extent to which a range of social and health services are available to the case manager varies, as does the case manager's ability to fund unconventional services. For exam-ple, some case managers are bound by rules that home care may be purchased only from certain types of licensed agencies, whereas others can authorize innovative arrangements. In the latter case, college students might be paid to do intermittent services, meals could be purchased from nearby restaurants, or family members could be paid to do extra services. Presently there are few models of case management wherein the manager has any authority at all over expensive acute hospital and medical services. The On Lok pro-gram in San Francisco, discussed below, is an exception.

Some case management programs have a single agency as an entry point to case management, and others have multiple entry points. In the former type of organization, one agency, perhaps with decentralized regional branches, is the only access point for case management services. In the second type of organization, various providers are authorized, sometimes under contract, to do case management; typically, a hospitalized patient may receive case management from a social worker or discharge planner employed by the hospital who is designated for this role. The authority presiding over the case management agency can also differ. Examples include public social services departments, health departments, aging departments, and nonprofit agencies such as hospitals and family service associations. Area Agencies on Aging (which themselves are under different authorities) may do case management. Sometimes an independent case management agency is created.

Finally, the relationship between case management and service provision varies. At one extreme, the agency doing the case management also provides service, but usually services are purchased from other organizations in the community. If case management is in itself a professional function performed, for example, by social workers or nurses, the case manager is likely to establish a supportive relationship with the client and remain a figure in the service delivery. The flexibility that case managers have to authorize service from a specified service provider also varies. For example, some case managers are bound to select a home health agency according to the client's geographical neighborhood rather than any other criterion, and some are obliged to use formulas that distribute business evenly throughout the community.

A new model of case management on the horizon is the social/health maintenance organization (S/HMO) (Diamond and Berman, 1980). In 1980, HCFA awarded Brandeis University a contract to demonstrate the feasibility of a prepaid system of health and social services based on an annual fixed capitation fee. The services to be included in the S/HMO are acute hospital care; ambulatory medical services; nursing homes; home health, home-making, and chore services; emergency psychiatric care; and a wide variety of social services such as meals (home delivered and congregate), counseling, transportation, and information and referral. The S/HMO differs from previously discussed models because it incorporates the gamut of health services under the belief that appropriate and timely provision of social and personal care will decrease the need for acute medical care. The S/HMOs may provide services themselves or contract for them, but the case management responsibility and the decision making about the service mix for any enrollee rests with the S/HMO itself (U.S. Department of Health and Human Services, 1982).

Examples of Programs. Case management demonstrations in health and long-term care are too numerous to discuss in any detail. Some of the best-known demonstration programs are Access in Rochester, New York (Eggert, Bowlyow, and Nichols, 1980); Triage in Plainfield, Connecticut (Quinn and others, 1982); the Wisconsin Community Care Organization (Applebaum, Seidl, and Austin, 1980); Alternative Health Services in Georgia (Skellie, Mobley, and Coan, 1982); and the recently established Long-Term Care Channeling Demonstration Projects. Greenberg, Doth, and Austin (1981) analyzed in considerable detail innovative long-term care demonstrations developed through 1980.

As of September 1981, at least twelve states (Arkansas, Connecticut, California, Florida, Georgia, Illinois, Massachusetts, New York, Oregon, Virginia, Utah, and Washington) had developed coordinated, community-based programs for the elderly (Toff, 1981). Most of these programs use a case management model of service with a central agency located at a local level bearing responsibility for coordinating resources, assessing the client's physical, mental, and social functioning, developing a care plan, negotiating service, monitoring service, and reassessing the client. These projects came about as a result of state legislation and often pooled funds from different programs. For example, Florida passed the Community Care for the Elderly Act in 1973, which authorized demonstration projects, and amended that act in 1980 to authorize a statewide community care service system to prevent unnecessary institutionalization of the frail elderly. Readers are referred to Toff's monograph for details about each state program and early findings on cost savings. Note, too, that case management techniques are widely used in England to integrate local social services with the National Health Service programs and that several Canadian provinces have developed single-entry case management systems to mediate long-term care benefits (Kane and Kane, in press).

The variation of case management programs in health is illustrated below with brief descriptions of four programs. This section draws heavily on Greenberg, Doth, and Austin (1981) and is based on the programs as set up in the mid and late 1970s rather than later, when some programs took different directions. Although each of these programs was a demonstration project with a research design, the emphasis here is on program description, not evaluation.

Triage. Begun in 1974, the Triage program was targeted at the Medicare population in a small, seven-town area in central Connecticut that includes urban, suburban, and rural districts. Triage was a single-entry, service coordination organization that used teams composed of a nurse clinician and social worker to assess clients and arrange for services from a well-established provider network. Section 222 waivers enabled Triage to authorize payment for ancillary services not usually included in Medicare and to waive Medicare copayments, deductibles, and restrictions on home health care. The services available beyond traditional Medicare benefits were home health aides, homemakers, nursing and physician visits, psychological and family counseling, home-delivered meals, chore services, companion services, and dental care.

Triage differed from many other demonstrations because its care was prescribed according to need rather than according to third-party payer restrictions, and it used highly skilled teams for assessment and case management. A team's caseload numbered about 200, and its care plans were monitored carefully. All Medicare beneficiaries over age sixty-five were eligible, and referrals were accepted from any individual or agency. When fully operational, Triage had seven case management teams serving about 1,500 clients. After referral, clients were put on a waiting list, and some clients waited a year to get to the top of the list and be seen by the team.

Access. Operational since 1977, Access is centered in Rochester, New York (Monroe County), with a single-entry model for all long-term care services in the county. A freestanding, nonprofit organization was developed to authorize services under 115 Medicaid waivers; these waivered services include friendly visiting, home maintenance, transportation, and respite care. All persons aged eighteen and over requesting long-term care are eligible, but the leverage over private-pay patients is minimal. In 1981, Access was expanded to offer service to Medicare beneficiaries over age sixty-five (using 222 waivers).

Access uses a preadmission assessment form (PAF) containing medical data, a nursing assessment, and a psychosocial assessment, which form the basis for judgments. Assessments are done by community health nurses from the health department or visiting nurse associations if the client is in the community. A discharge planning nurse and a social worker provide the assessment information on hospitalized clients. The psychosocial assessment is a series of judgments on client status rather than responses to direct questions. If home care is judged feasible, the assessor develops a care plan. The case manager then calculates whether the estimated cost of that plan is less than the costs of a nursing home placement. If those costs are 75 percent or less than those of institutionalization, the plan is implemented. Sometimes a special home assessment is authorized to determine whether architectural barriers need attention. Negotiations are conducted with the client and the family to develop an optimum plan. Access separates the assessment function from the responsibility for authorizing a care plan. All clients are followed up through a formal review system. Waiting periods are minimal for assessment under Access, and case aides handle the details of implementing the service plan. In contrast to Triage, Access is a high-volume program that has saturated an urban area, but the case manager's direct relationship to the client is quite minimal.

On Lok Senior Health Services. On Lok Senior Health Services is a single-entry organization serving about 400 disabled elderly clients in San Francisco's Chinatown. The project evolved from a day health program funded by the Administration on Aging to an HCFA demonstration of the feasibility of a capitation system of reimbursement under 222 waivers. Unlike the previous examples, On Lok delivers many services directly, including physician, nursing, pharmaceutical, occupational, speech, and recreational services; social work services; transportation; personal care; escort and interpreting services; meals; home health care; and homemaker services. Much of the direct service is organized around two day health centers and one social center. In addition, On Lok may purchase or otherwise arrange additional services, including acute hospital care; skilled and intermediate nursing home care; dental, optometric, and prosthetic services; ambulance, medication, podiatry, and laboratory services; psychiatry; medical equipment; and attendant care. Presently all services are provided on a cost basis under Medicare waivers, but data are being gathered to predict costs and set capitation fees.

Assessments and case management are done by a team that includes a staff physician, a social worker, a nurse, physical and occupational therapists, and a dietitian. Each team member sees all patients, and the team meets weekly to discuss its findings and to refine its treatment plans. When a plan for a client is first developed, the social worker reviews it with the client and his or her family and incorporates any changes. The final care plan is written up as an agreement, signed by the client and On Lok, and a copy is sent to the client's personal physician. Clients are reevaluated at predetermined intervals, and the plan is updated as needed.

Alternative Health Services. The Alternative Health Services (AHS) was initiated in 1976 as a research and demonstration project serving the seven-county metropolitan Atlanta area and ten rural counties around Athens, Georgia. In 1980, the Georgia legislature began implementing the service statewide as part of the Medicaid plan. Persons over fifty years of age who are eligible for Medicaid and need long-term care are the target population. Under 1115 waivers, three distinct programs are available: adult day rehabilitation (including ambulatory health care and health-related supportive services at an adult daycare center); home-delivered services (including meals and medical equipment as well as homemaking and personal care); and alternative living services such as adult foster care, boarding care, or congregate housing. A dollar cap was established on the amount of money that could be spent on each client, and fixed-rate contracts were made with local providers.

The program operates from the county department of medical assistance, with county caseworkers taking the initial referrals, completing a standard assessment, and seeking medical information from each client's physician. An AHS team of a nurse and social worker with an M.S.W. along with the county caseworker reviews those data, designates the client to one or more service streams, and makes referrals to AHS providers. Upon referral, the provider organization does its own assessment and suggests a level of necessary service. One member of the AHS team is designated case manager to interact with the providers, to approve service levels, to monitor the quality of service received by the client, and to coordinate planning in case admission to a hospital or long-term care facility becomes necessary.

In this program, caseworkers with neither nursing nor social work training do the initial assessments, but these personnel receive training from the AHS assessment team. Initial resistance to this staffing pattern had to be overcome. Another serious initial problem was to arrange start-up service quickly for persons discharged from the hospital. Coan, Stodgill, and Neughroschel (1981) report that hospital discharge planners were reluctant to use the community-based services because they were not confident that they could be provided immediately upon hospital discharge. Earlier discharge planning by hospital staffs and better communication between AHS and the hospital were required to solve these problems.

Update. Although these program descriptions have become dated since they were originally written in early 1982, the salient issues remain constant. If anything, the last few years have heightened interest in case management in the health field and renewed discussion about the potential of various models. The following points are offered to update this section.

1. The results of the major demonstrations in case management are still unavailable. The National Long-Term Care Channeling Demonstration findings will shed light on the subject, but so far only a preliminary report (Baxter and others, 1983) is available. It attests to the difficulty of starting up projects. The S/HMO demonstration was delayed and just entered the field in the fall of 1984.

2. Medicare phased in a new method of reimbursing hospitals for the care of Medicare beneficiaries in 1983. Essentially, the hospital is paid a fixed sum for each admission based on the assignment of the patient to one of 468 diagnosis-related groups (DRGs). This reimbursement system gives hospitals the incentive to keep hospital stays as short as possible and discourages a rich mix of comprehensive inpatient services that are unrelated to the admitting diagnosis. This environment has increased the interest in a form of case management that focuses on posthospital planning and has encouraged the trend of

hospitals diversifying into delivering a range of community services (which themselves require case management).

3. Partly stimulated by 2176 waivers, there has been a marked increase in community-based case management efforts as well as statewide programs of preadmission screening for nursing homes. These developments are often led by Area Agencies on Aging and social services departments. This has meant that case managers from the community come into the hospital. It has also intensified the debate about the relative roles of health departments, hospital personnel, home health agencies, and social agencies in the case management of health-related services.

4. The Robert Wood Johnson Foundation began a program of grants to nonprofit hospitals with more than 200 beds to stimulate their community-based long-term care efforts. Case management is an integral component of the Johnson projects. The high level of interest in the initiative is evidenced by the 480 written inquiries and the 240 completed applications for the three-year awards. In 1984, twenty-five grants were made. This program has lent legitimacy, visibility, and encouragement to the interests of hospitals in case management.

Case Management Practices and Tools

The technology required for case management in the health field can be deduced from the description of models and exemplary programs. Screening and targeting procedures, assessment tools, decision-making formulas, and management information systems are all being developed and refined.

Screening and Targeting. Many case management programs aim to offer persons with chronic health problems and the frail elderly alternatives that are more humane and less expensive than nursing home care. To keep costs down, programs must be targeted at a clientele genuinely at risk of being placed in a nursing home. For every person in a nursing home, there are several counterparts in the community who are cared for by family and friends or who go without care. If new programs merely replace that unpaid care rather than prevent nursing home placement, they become expensive add-ons (Kane and Kane, 1980). Therefore targeting the correct population becomes an important task for a case management program.

Assessment. Case management has come to depend on formal, standardized assessment procedures and instruments. Such instruments typically assess functional abilities, cognitive capacity, emotional and social well-being, and the strength of social support systems. Sometimes these instruments yield a score. Assessment tools have proliferated in the last decade, and many are of dubious reliability and validity (Kane and Kane, 1981). Yet a routine assessment approach is needed for many reasons: (1) to compare the needs of clients, (2) to monitor change over time, (3) to determine eligibility for various services, and (4) to judge the adequacy of existing informal supports and determine when they need to be shored up by formal assistance.

Decision Algorithms. The road from the assessment instrument to the care plan is still paved by clinical judgment. The step from assessment to the care plan is the most poorly specified part of the case management process. Sometimes, of course, the range of services available in the community is so narrow that the case manager's choices are limited. Even then, however, questions arise about how much of a particular type of service is needed. Some researchers have done computer modeling to replicate clinical decision making and thereby derive decision rules (Falcone, 1979). However, this procedure tends to preserve the status quo rather than to accentuate decisions that lead to good outcomes.

If decision making can be systematized and empirically linked to the assessment data through decision rules, then less highly trained personnel can make case management decisions.

Management Information Systems. Case management programs require focus on the system of care in the community. The case management unit must know all the community resources and their use at any given time (for example, nursing home waiting lists or backup in the hospital). Similarly, tracking individual clients through the system is necessary. At the very least, clients must be reassessed periodically and when their status changes (for example, upon hospitalization), and a triggering system is needed to ensure this follow-up. Beyond that, the effectiveness of programs (in maintaining functional abilities and preventing institutionalization) and their cost-effectiveness cannot be determined without a management information system that identifies specific expenditures and links them to particular characteristics of the client group.

Management information systems are difficult to develop, partly because information on Medicare, Medicaid, and Title XX expenditures are often incompatible and partly because some programs, most notably Older Americans Act programs at nutritional sites or multipurpose centers, rarely keep client-specific information. Most models of case management in health in the United States began as research and demonstration projects—sometimes with control groups so that the effect of the new procedures could be more accurately gauged. Considerable energy has been expended to develop management information systems capable of facilitating ongoing program activities and yielding information about cost-effectiveness. However, program staff complain that they are inundated with paperwork and that they rarely receive timely and useful displays of data from the system.

Consumer Issues

Case management approaches should benefit health consumers by enhancing their access to an array of appropriate services to meet specific needs. But a number of nagging problems remain. First, it is rarely possible to maximize the attainment of several goals simultaneously. Finding the mix of service that brings the greatest functional ability at the cheapest price is, therefore, impossible. If cost considerations become paramount, other client-centered goals are jeopardized. Second, the perhaps more difficult, laudable patient-centered goals may be in conflict. For example, autonomy may come at the expense of security; relief from pain and discomfort may come at the price of reduced cognitive awareness; optimal physiological balance may be achieved at a social cost. When case management programs focus on minimizing a single concrete outcome—such as admission to nursing homes—the complexities of defining desirable program outcomes are masked. But regardless of the place of treatment, be it community, nursing homes as we know them today, or some other congregate arrangement, sooner or later case management programs need to face the value issues inherent in their function. Case management to what end? Who decides what the desirable goals of the plan are? Do the goals change according to the preferences of the primary patient, the patient's family, or the current crop of taxpayers (Kane and Kane, 1982)?

On a small scale, investigators have shown that hospital discharge planning too often takes place without the informed consent of patients or careful appraisal of the alternatives (Coulton and others, 1982). Prospective nursing home patients are often not even asked about what risks they are willing to take or what results they seek. In a more coordinated and elaborate case management system, more dangers lurk. To what extent does the client have the right to choose among service packages? How much explanation should each client receive?

A case management project run by the Community Service Society of New York illustrates the problems of incorporating client preferences into service packages. Despite all good intentions, case managers tended to use their own preferences and values for counseling and tended not to order a range of innovative services. Moreover, clients were often unaware that they had entered into a contract for specific services, choosing counseling over other possibilities for spending the same amount of money (Frankfather, Smith, and Caro, 1981). At the very least, the program evaluators suggest that a major commitment to sharing information is needed, complete with "a standardized display of service options with detailed descriptions of housekeeping, personal care, companion, heavy-duty housecleaning, home maintenance, counseling, escort, household modification, prosthetic equipment, transportation financial aid, and assistance in securing specialty (medical and legal, for example) services" (Frankfather, Smith, and Caro, p. 85). This would have encouraged cost comparisons and allowed the consumer to realize that the case manager's counseling and friendly visiting were assigned as a benefit and assigned a cost. Taking the argument a step further, the same authors suggest that a "service claim model" of case management would more truly incorporate client preferences. For example, in a client-driven system, a client would be assessed for need and assigned a benefit level. The mentally able client could then purchase services against his or her account with a "case accountant" tabulating the ledger and offering advice rather than a case manager authorizing service.

Case managers presently tread an uneasy path with few explicit roadmarks. The very concept of allocating benefits cost-effectively according to assessed needs requires equitable decision rules. It would be unreasonable to authorize any service mix preferred by the client, and given the litigious nature of American society, criteria for program eligibility need to be clear and uniformly applied. Furthermore, community providers are quick to cry "constraint of trade" if the case managers vigorously recommend particular organizations above others, and this is a further barrier to an open discussion of alternatives.

At the same time, the client should be free to refuse service of a particular kind and perhaps make do with less service than the assessment suggests is required, providing that such action poses no danger to society. Issues about the risks that individuals should be allowed to accept for themselves and the risks the case managers should accept on behalf of a client have barely been discussed. The more efficient case management becomes and the more real authority the programs hold, the more the value questions surface. Preliminary evidence suggests that clients can be involved in forging a personal care plan without risk of grandiose and expensive plans. In the Massachusetts statewide program, clients tended to suggest less service for themselves than did the professional case managers (Piktialis and Callahan, 1983).

Another consumer issue arises when case managers allocate service to fill gaps in a patient's resources. The question arises about the proper expectations to hold for adult children or other relatives of the primary patient. Legal responsibilities of spouses for each other and adults for minor children can be used as a guideline. No such legalities govern other relationships, and equity issues abound. Is it fair to provide amply for the person with no adult children while expecting others to rely on their offspring? Is geographical proximity of the adult child a fair determinant? Should the assessment and judgment take into account the total burden on that adult child's time and pocketbook? If case managers see adult children voluntarily struggling with a heavy care burden, should they offer assistance unasked?

Turf Issues

Case management in health care settings is rife with territorial battles among professional disciplines and among agencies. No single best training for case management roles has emerged, but the social worker and the nurse are most often suggested for health settings. In some programs, social workers and nurses are used interchangeably, and in others they act as teams. However, the team model is expensive. If a highly professionalized team is advocated for case management in health care, the system may topple of its own weight. The challenge is to develop a system that permits input from appropriate professional disciplines when needed but streamlines case management itself.

Physician involvement with case management in health is a nagging issue. On the one hand, the status quo arrangement, whereby the primary care physician is a de facto case manager, is clearly faulty. Physicians have neither the knowledge of community resources nor the human relations training to make them ideal for the role of brokering service. For example, physicians are unlikely to make referrals to community-based home health agencies despite efforts to publicize the availability of that care (Trager, 1980). Using the physician's order as an open sesame to an array of social services seems an archaic custom. On the other hand, case management devoid of medical participation is incomplete. Establishing viable working relationships between community case managers and practicing physicians is critical. The danger that physicians, once relieved of the responsibility for sole authorization of nursing home and other health-related services, will withdraw is an outcome that the most enthusiastic advocate of "social models" of health care would hardly desire.

Other turf issues arise at an organizational level. A tension exists between hospital and community-based case management programs, fueled by poor communication and different role perspectives (Kane, 1984). (The entire Fall 1981 issue of *Discharge Planning Update* depicts this uneasy relationship.) Hospital discharge planners and social workers sometimes perceive case management as an unnecessary add-on, offering services that duplicate existing hospital-based services. Community case managers typically complain that when their clients enter hospitals, all the carefully laid groundwork is lost, the patient deteriorates, and discharge planners set nursing home placements in motion without involving the original case manager. Part of the problem is that hospitals with high occupancy levels have an immediate, compelling incentive to discharge promptly those patients who are no longer eligible for payment, whereas the success of the case management program can be measured in cost savings over a much longer period of time. The DRG system of Medicare reimbursement (in which the hospital is paid a fixed sum for each patient depending on the admitting diagnosis) exacerbates the hospital's incentive for early discharge. Another aspect of the problem is the inevitable jostling for power that occurs when the duties of different positions substantially overlap. In some instances, the hospital-based personnel represent a higher level of training than the community case managers. A possible "system solution" is to designate hospital personnel responsible for case management when an individual is in the hospital, but the orderly transfer of information continues to be a problem.

Finally, turf issues arise about which agencies in the community should actually be doing the case management. Any designation of a lead agency disrupts the balance of organizational power in the region. As proposals are advanced that would pool funds of county Medicaid agencies, county social services, health departments, and Area Agencies on Aging, the question of who controls the purse strings takes on added importance. In some instances, statutory responsibilities also enter into the jostling for position.

Training

Schools of social work and schools of nursing hardly address case management in their standard curricula. Considerable education and socialization are needed before professionals from these schools will be comfortable with case management. More education is needed about the specific associated technologies. The latter include screening, targeting, assessment, and care planning. In general, some quantitative and measurement skills are required that are not usually taught in core social work and nursing programs.

On-the-job training is particularly important in early phases of program development. Too often it is taken for granted that case managers are using an assessment tool reliably and have consistent approaches to care planning.

Unresolved Issues

Many case management efforts have vigorous evaluation components. At times, the evaluation has seemed to drive practitioners into adopting lengthier or more standardized assessment procedures than they would otherwise use. The ongoing tensions between research and practical uses of information may abate somewhat as programs become operational. Unresolved questions will still remain, however, about how much information is needed on what dimensions and how frequently. Case management programs should be able to generate systemwide information that will assist in community planning. But any information system depends on uniform, consistent data collection that may interfere with the clinical relationship. Conversely, data managers worry about the quality of data that are begrudgingly collected by a clinically oriented group.

The demonstration status of many case management projects influences the kind of information available about their effects. Critics state that the long-term care demonstrations failed to prove that the programs reduce nursing home use (Greenberg, Doth, and Austin, 1980). Some of the problem lies in faulty research design and the absence of control groups. Another problem more integral to the programs themselves concerns targeting. If programs did not select a population at substantial risk of nursing home placement, they would be unlikely to show a reduction in nursing home use when the target population was compared with a control group.

An issue unique to demonstration projects is their generalizability. Many of the long-term care demonstrations were slow to develop caseloads and encountered considerable resistance that might not have been the case if the programs had been expressions of public policy. Any demonstration, moreover, has an artificiality that limits extrapolation to an operational context. Often the demonstrations serve predetermined, relatively small numbers of clients in particular geographical areas; consequently, one cannot safely infer the effects on a general delivery system. From the experience of the Massachusetts Home Care Corporation, however, one gets reassurance that, after an initial start-up period, the demand for additional health-related social services and personal care stabilizes at an affordable level (Piktialis and Callahan, 1983).

A discussion of the effectiveness of the various case management projects in either enhancing patient outcomes or forestalling costs is beyond the scope of this chapter. In addition to the multiple research design problems in choosing control groups and measuring outcomes, problems of multiple funding jurisdictions confuse the question of cost savings. Because Medicare and Medicaid are separate programs, costs are sometimes viewed in too narrow a programmatic sense rather than as the sum of public expenditures per client. Similarly, Greenberg, Doth, and Austin (1980) assert that when certain home care services became covered under Medicaid waivers, states sometimes served additional clients, raising their Title XX allocation.

In practice, the term *case management* means different things to different health professionals. Practitioners from various vantage points seem to believe that they are acting as case managers. This is true, for example, of the public health nurse who integrates an educational, treatment, and referral function into her role. It is also true of the hospital discharge planner. Information and referral specialists in Area Agencies on Aging may perceive themselves as doing case management, and if health resources are part of the resource bank, they, too, will see themselves as doing health-related case management. Gaining community acceptance for a genuine case management function in health care is difficult indeed. Hours of painstaking coalition building are needed, and considerable compromise usually weakens case management as a system-centered intervention.

The major unresolved problems relate to the authority of the case managers and the incentives that can be introduced for both efficiency and quality control. Few case management programs have the authority to make a major difference in health delivery, although, on a client-by-client basis, they may improve care.

Conclusion

In some ways, the title for this chapter is misleading. If the chapter had dealt strictly with case management in health care, it would have been limited to the various team and case coordination arrangements through which health professionals in various health care delivery settings channel their work. But the more vigorous case management efforts seek to bridge health services of various kinds with other human service needs that coexist with and are exacerbated by the health problem. Oddly enough, the core medical services themselves—hospital care and physician services—are often out of the practical jurisdiction of case management as it has thus far evolved.

An early point merits reiterating: Case management in relation to health care has a client-centered and a system-centered rationale. To date, case management programs have had considerable success in coordinating an array of services to meet the assessed needs of given individuals. Although technology for every part of the operation—assessment, care planning, and monitoring—must be refined, many practitioners and researchers are working on the problems. A truly client-centered program would perhaps allow more client preferences to be incorporated into the plans than is presently common, but such reforms are certainly possible.

The system-centered goals, in contrast, have had less application. A well-established and well-accepted case management program should be able to make services in the community more efficient and encourage high-quality care. But even when existing programs have had the authority to purchase services and a mandate to reduce the use of expensive nursing home care, they have not generally been seen as agents of community change. The more authority a case management system holds, the more both consumers' preferences and the vested interests of providers may be jeopardized. The possibility of modifying the health care delivery system through case management is implicit but rarely openly espoused. Until that time, some case management programs in health confront an anomalous situation: The management team is ready, but the services to be managed are sadly wanting.

Suggested Readings

Austin, C. D. "Case Management in Long-Term Care: Options and Opportunities." *Health and Social Work,* 1983, *8,* 16–30.

Greenberg, J. J., Doth, D. S., and Austin, C. D. *Comparative Study of Long-Term Care Demonstrations: Project Summaries.* Rockville, Md.: Aspen Systems Corporation, 1981.

Kane, R. A.. *Case Management in Long-Term Care: Background Analysis for Social Work.* Chicago: Society for Hospital Social Work Directors, American Hospital Association, 1984.

Knowles, J. (Ed.). *Doing Better and Feeling Worse: Health in the United States.* New York: Norton, 1977.

Starfield, B., and others. "Continuity and Coordination in Primary Care: Their Achievement and Utility." *Medical Care,* 1976, *14,* 625–632.

Trager, B. *Home Health Care and National Health Policy.* New York: Haworth Press, 1980.

Wise, H., and others. *Making Health Teams Work.* Cambridge, Mass.: Ballinger, 1974.

References

Applebaum, R., Seidl, F. W., and Austin, C. D. "The Wisconsin Community Care Organization: Preliminary Findings from the Milwaukee Experiment." *Gerontologist,* 1980, *20,* 350–355.

Austin, C. D. "Client Assessment in Context." *Social Work Research and Abstracts,* 1981, *17,* 4–12.

Austin, C. D. "Case Management in Long-Term Care: Options and Opportunities." *Health and Social Work,* 1983, *8,* 16–30.

Baxter, R. J., and others. *The Planning and Implementation of Channeling: Early Experiences of the National Long-Term Care Demonstration.* Princeton, N.J.: Mathematica Policy Research, 1983.

Brill, N. I. *Teamwork: Working Together in the Human Services.* Philadelphia: Lippincott, 1976.

Coan, R. E., Stodgill, J. D., and Neughroschel, W. "Case Management in the Georgia Alternative Health Services Program." *Discharge Planning Update,* Fall 1981, pp. 4–8.

Coulton, C. J., and others. "Discharge Planning and Decision Making." *Health and Social Work,* 1982, *7,* 253–261.

Diamond, L., and Berman, D. "The Social/Health Maintenance Organization: A Single Entry, Prepaid Long-Term Care Delivery System." In J. J. Callahan, Jr., and S. Wallack (Eds.), *Reforming the Long-Term Care System: Financial and Organizational Options.* Lexington, Mass.: Heath, Lexington Books, 1980.

Dohrenwend, B. S., and Dohrenwend, B. P. (Eds.). *Stressful Life Events: Their Nature and Effects.* New York: Wiley, 1974.

Eggert, G. M., Bowlyow, J. E., and Nichols, C. W. "Gaining Control of the Long-Term Care Systems: First Returns from the Access Experiment." *Gerontologist,* 1980, *20,* 356–363.

Enthoven, A. C. *Health Plan: The Only Practical Solution to the Soaring Cost of Medical Care.* Reading, Mass.: Addison-Wesley, 1980.

Falcone, A. R. *Development of a Long-Term Care Information System: Final Report.* Lansing: Michigan Office of Services to the Aging, 1979.

Frankfather, D. L., Smith, M. J., and Caro, R. G. *Family Care of the Elderly: Public Initiative and Private Obligations.* Lexington, Mass.: Heath, Lexington Books, 1981.

Gallagher, E. G. (Ed.). *The Doctor-Patient Relationship in the Changing Health Scene.* DHEW Publication no. NIH 78-183. Washington, D.C.: International Center for Advanced Study in the Health Sciences, 1978.

Gottesman, L. E., Ishizaki, B., and MacBride, S. M. "Service Management—Plan and Concept in Pennsylvania." *The Gerontologist,* 1979, *19,* 379–385.

Greenberg, J. J., Doth, D. S., and Austin, C. D. "Comparative Study of Long-Term Care Demonstration Projects: Lessons for Future Inquiry." Mimeograph. Minneapolis: University of Minnesota Center for Health Services Research, 1980.

Greenberg, J. J., Doth, D. S., and Austin, C. D. *Comparative Study of Long-Term Care Demonstrations: Project Summaries.* Rockville, Md.: Aspen Systems Corporation, 1981.

Greenberg, J. N., Schmitz, M. P., and Lakin, K. C. *An Analysis of Responses to the Medicaid Home- and Community-Based Long-Term Care Waiver Program (Section 2176 of PL 97-35)*. Washington, D.C.: State Medicaid Information Center, National Governors Association, 1983.

Hasenfeld, Y., and English, R. A. "Human Service Organizations: A Conceptual Overview." In Y. Hasenfeld and R. A. English (Eds.), *Human Service Organizations*. Ann Arbor: University of Michigan Press, 1974.

Holmes, C., and others. "Toward the Measurement of Primary Care." *Health and Society*, 1978, *56*, 231-252.

Kane, R. A. *Interprofessional Teamwork*. Syracuse, N.Y.: School of Social Work, University of Syracuse, 1975.

Kane, R. A. "Multidisciplinary Teamwork in the United States: Trends, Issues, and Implications for Social Work." In S. Lonsdale, A. Webb, and T. L. Briggs (Eds.), *Teamwork in the Personal Social Services and Health Care: British and American Perspectives*. London: Croom Helm, 1980.

Kane, R. A. "Education for Team Work Revisited: Caveats and Cautions." In J. A. Browne, B. A. Kirlin, and S. Watt (Eds.), *Rehabilitation Services and the Social Work Role: Challenge for Change*. Baltimore, Md.: Williams & Wilkins, 1981.

Kane, R. A. *Case Management in Long-Term Care: Background Analysis for Social Work*. Chicago: Society for Hospital Social Work Directors, American Hospital Association, 1984.

Kane, R. A., and Kane, R. L. *Assessing the Elderly: A Practical Guide to Measurement*. Lexington, Mass.: Heath, 1981.

Kane, R. A., and others. *The PSRO and the Nursing Home*. Vol. I. *An Assessment of PSRO Long-Term Care Review*. R-2459/1-HCFA. Santa Monica, Calif.: Rand Corporation, 1979.

Kane, R. L., and Kane, R. A. "Alternatives to Institutional Care of the Elderly: Beyond the Dichotomy." *The Gerontologist*, 1980, *20*, 245-259.

Kane, R. L., and Kane, R. A. (Eds.). *Value Preferences and Long-Term Care*. Lexington, Mass.: Heath, 1982.

Kane, R. L., and Kane, R. A. *A Will and a Way: What the United States Can Learn About Care of the Elderly from Canada*. New York: Columbia University Press, in press.

Knowles, J. (Ed.). *Doing Better and Feeling Worse: Health in the United States.* New York: Norton, 1977.

Levine, S., and White, P. "Exchange as a Conceptual Framework for the Study of Interorganizational Relations." In Y. Hasenfeld and R. A. English (Eds.), *Human Service Organizations.* Ann Arbor: University of Michigan Press, 1974.

Pearlin, L. I., and others. "The Stress Process." *Journal of Health and Social Behavior,* 1981, *22,* 337-356.

Piktialis, D. S., and Callahan, J. J., Jr. "Organization of Long-Term Care: Should There Be a Single or Multiple Focal Points for Long-Term Care Coordination?" Paper presented at the Conference on the Impact of Technology on Aging in America, Millwood, Va., February 16, 1983.

Quinn, J., and others. *Coordinating Community Services for the Elderly.* New York: Springer, 1982.

Sackett, D., and Haynes, R. B. (Eds.). *Compliance with Therapeutic Regimens.* Baltimore, Md.: Johns Hopkins University Press, 1976.

Skellie, F. A., Mobley, G. M., and Coan, R. E. "Cost-Effectiveness of Community-Based Long-Term Care: Current Findings of Georgia's Alternative Health Services Project." *American Journal of Public Health,* 1982, *72,* 353-358.

Starfield, B., and others. "Continuity and Coordination in Primary Care: Their Achievement and Utility." *Medical Care,* 1976, *14,* 625-632.

Toff, G. E. *Alternatives to Institutional Care for the Elderly: An Analysis of State Initiatives.* Washington, D.C.: Intergovernmental Health Policy Project, George Washington University, 1981.

Trager, B. *Home Health Care and National Health Policy.* New York: Haworth Press, 1980.

U.S. Comptroller General. *Entering a Nursing Home—Costly Implications for Medicaid and the Elderly.* PAD 80-12. Washington, D.C.: Government Accounting Office, 1979.

U.S. Congress. Senate. *Developments in Aging: 1981.* Washington, D.C.: U.S. Government Printing Office, 1982.

U.S. Department of Health and Human Services. Health Care Financing Administration. *Research and Demonstrations in*

Health Care Financing: 1980–81. HCFA 03144. Washington, D.C.: U.S. Department of Health and Human Services, 1982.

Vida, F., Korsch, B., and Morris, M. "Gaps in Doctor-Patient Communication: Patients' Response to Medical Advice." *New England Journal of Medicine,* 1969, *280,* 535–540.

Wise, H., and others. *Making Health Teams Work.* Cambridge, Mass.: Ballinger, 1974.

8

~~~~~~

The Chronically
Mentally Ill
in the Community

Ron Honnard

This chapter describes the application of case management when
treating the chronically mentally disabled through community
mental health services. Because case management can take a variety
of forms, it is important to understand the focus of a particular
program and to note the variables that affect the process. Issues associated with the service delivery system, agency organization and
structure, personnel and manpower, and the political environment
are discussed. A conceptual approach to the development of case
management models, roles, functions, and authorities is also presented. The principles developed from examining these issues can
be applied to all the human services.

A Definition of Case Management

Case management has been proposed as a method for integrating human services. It has been implemented in various human
services fields including child welfare (Bedford and Hybertson,

1975), developmental disabilities (Fitz, 1978), gerontology (Ross, 1979), care of medically ill patients (Beatrice, 1979), and mental health (Ozarin, 1977; Altschuler and Forward, 1978; Talbott, 1978; Turner and TenHoor, 1978). Case management is being recommended with increasing frequency and fervor within the mental health field as an approach to caring for the needs of chronically mentally ill persons. To be effective in this area, case management should be perceived as a component of the larger service system, a component that attempts to alleviate some, not all, of the imperfections inherent in the system. Thus, certain systemwide functions need to be performed for case management to be successful. These functions can be viewed on two levels, the client or direct service level and the agency or administrative level (Benjamin and Ben-Dashan, 1979).

On the client level, case management should be narrowly defined. It should link the necessary basic services, namely, intake, assessment, planning, referral, follow-up, and monitoring. These functions should be focused on clients and their needs and should have fairly direct and immediate results. Functions at the agency level should integrate service agencies and providers as well as enable the case manager to cross agency boundaries. The process of developing linkages involves resource and program development, joint programming and planning, and interagency agreements. Case management will not be effective if the case manager is charged with both meeting the client's direct service needs and filling the gaps in the service delivery system. For example, case managers ought to be accountable for coordinating services for their clients even when there are difficulties or gaps in the service system; they also ought to be responsible for reporting such gaps to program administrators. However, the direct service case manager should not be expected to develop resources or deal with the system's difficulties single-handedly.

Resource planning, program development, and community advocacy at the systems level are complex, time-consuming activities. If they are to be dealt with effectively, they should be performed by staff with the power, mandate, and funding to do so. That is not to say that the case manager should not be responsible for advocacy on a client-by-client basis. Case managers should carry out client advocacy and be responsible for creatively utilizing existing resources to meet the needs of the client. In short, administrative and client level functions must be realistic and clearly delineated and must be performed together if case management is to benefit the client.

Theoretical Basis for Case Management
in Mental Health Services

The major reason for the emerging prominence of case management in the mental health field has been the process of deinstitutionalization, that is, the transfer of mentally ill persons from state hospitals and other institutions into community settings such as board and care facilities or the placement of these patients with families. The basic goal of deinstitutionalization is to humanize the care of victims of chronic mental illness (Bachrach and Lamb, 1982). The philosophical basis for deinstitutionalization has been articulated by Lamb (1976) and others in a series of articles. The assumptions of this philosophy pertain to planned changes in the scope and pattern of service for chronic mental patients. The major factors that made deinstitutionalization feasible were clinical (the introduction of psychotropic drugs) and fiscal (the imposition of fiscal constraints on the states and federal funding allocations for the room and board of chronic mental patients in community facilities). The guiding principle behind the political and programmatic processes of deinstitutionalization was the desire that persons afflicted with chronic mental disabilities live in environments with as few restrictions as possible.

As attempts have been made to integrate deinstitutionalized, chronically mentally disabled individuals into less restrictive community settings, their needs and the obstacles they may encounter have been identified by writers concerned with human service delivery systems, by service providers in the field, and by the clients themselves. To meet these needs and overcome these barriers, case management has been widely promoted as a suitable mechanism to link and integrate services.

The mentally disabled, specifically those with severe or persistent mental or emotional disorders that seriously limit their functional capacities, have a number of significant characteristics in addition to their basic psychiatric problem. These range from factors such as an impaired ability to perform the basic activities of daily living to a variety of interpersonal difficulties (Talbott, 1978). Frequently such persons lack motivation and the ability to seek help from or sustain rapport with human services workers, who frequently avoid or prefer not to work therapeutically with the chronically mentally ill.

Mentally disturbed adults, like the general population, need food, shelter, clothing, medical and dental care, transportation, recreation, education, and money (Turner, 1977). In addition to these basic needs, the chronically mentally disabled have critical needs of their own. These include assistance in applying for income, medical, and other benefits; twenty-four-hour crisis assistance; psychosocial rehabilitation; long-term supportive services such as sheltered work opportunities and supportive living arrangements, as well as medical and mental health care (Turner, 1977; Turner and TenHoor, 1978; Turner and Shifren, 1979).

Given this broad spectrum of needs and given the fact of deinstitutionalization, a number of significant problems in meeting clients' needs have emerged both within the service delivery system and the community (Benjamin and Ben-Dashan, 1979). These problems result from the demands placed on agencies, service providers, and the community by the chronically mentally disabled and include the lack of accountability and continuity in services and the fragmentation and lack of quality care within the service delivery system itself. A common problem is the absence of needed services in the community setting. In addition, communities have resisted and opposed housing the mentally disabled.

Policy Parameters

Mental health programs, like other public sector services, have been both beneficiaries and victims of congressional and administrative policies since the 1946 National Mental Health Act, which was the first national response to mental health problems (Andrulis and Mazade, 1983). With the presidential reports and commissions of the 1950s and early 1960s providing a foundation for mental health legislation, mental health professionals tried to show that many individuals, including people with problems in daily living and people under stress, in crisis, or with severe disturbances could benefit from mental health services as they could from other health and social services (Andrulis and Mazade, 1983). Since that time, mental health professionals have adopted a variety of strategies to survive in a time marked by austerity and increased state control over health care.

According to Andrulis and Mazade (1983), the mental health programs initiated under the 1963 Community Mental Health Centers Act were developed to provide a range of mental health services for the nation's population. This act also emphasized comprehensive care in a community setting. This care included not only psychotherapy and crisis intervention but also preventive and other indirect services available to communities and organizations through mental health education programs and consultation from community mental health center staff. Public Law 94-63, passed in the mid 1970s, required community mental health centers (CMHCs) to assume more responsibilities by expanding "essential services." This resulted from policymakers more fully identifying and documenting the plight of the chronic mentally disabled in the community and attempting to improve service delivery. Consequently, access to available services improved, and more effective and efficient methods of delivering a broad range of services were developed. In addition, rehabilitation and social supports were emphasized in service delivery systems that were developed during this period. A number of these approaches identified case management as a necessary component in a coordinated service structure.

The President's Commission on Mental Health, formed during the Carter administration, intensified federal interest in mental health. This interest included an examination of the overall mental health delivery system and, in particular, the effectiveness of the federally funded CMHC program. The commission recognized that, even with modifications, the CMHCs were not significantly improving care for the neediest populations or making progress in preventing mental disorders.

Specific problems of the CMHC service system included the inability of many poorer communities to

> develop a comprehensive program with twelve servi-
> ces as required under the CMHC Act; failure to
> involve state mental health authorities in developing,
> administering, and coordinating community mental
> health services; inadequate assistance to individuals
> with mental disorders who were patients in general
> health care settings; and ineffective targeting of servi-
> ces for the chronically mentally ill who were released
> from state hospitals. The lack of community pro-
> grams precluded many of these patients from living in
> the least restrictive setting possible [Andrulis and
> Mazade, 1983, p. 602].

Interest in case management developed as one response to the problems identified in service delivery systems. Case management, however, is by no means a new concept in service provision. Aspects of case management have been performed continually in traditional casework practice in most human services agencies. The history and assessment of the "services integration" movement of the 1960s and early 1970s indicate that case management was one of a number of linkage mechanisms used to integrate human services (Ben-Dashan, 1979).

Because of the above trends, case management has received increased attention. The Rehabilitation Act, Social Securities Act Title XX, and the Developmentally Disabled Assistance Act have shaped policies and programs at the federal level and have influenced service priorities and mechanisms at state and local levels. Each of these pieces of major public policy have affected the development and implementation of plans for case management activities by either requiring case management or implying its need. In addition, the development of conceptual frameworks such as the Community Support Program and the Balanced Service System coupled with various legislative mandates have heightened the emphasis on, concern for, and to some extent the confusion over case management (Ben-Dashan, 1979).

States have cited case management in statutes pertaining to continuing care, protective services, and precare and aftercare services. Thus, in some states case management is seen as but one component in a continuum of care provided for the mentally disabled in order to facilitate their functioning in the least restrictive setting. These policies are intended to provide mental health social services with the available resources at the local level, to use all appropriate community resources, and to make services available and accessible for all mentally disabled individuals in need of them.

In California, efforts to attain the above goals include Section 5001 of the Community Mental Health Services Act; requirements for precare and aftercare as established in law and regulations under the Welfare and Institutions Code (Section 5661.5); the need for an aftercare plan as established in the Welfare and Institutions Code (Sections 4318 and 5622) and Health and Safety Code (Section 1284); the provision of protective social services as established under Welfare and Institutions Code (Section 4012.6); and the establishment of a case management system within the Welfare and Institutions Code (Section 5675). In addition, the Bates Act and the Petris Act supplemented federal legislation and indicated the need for and mandated the implementation of case management services.

At the present time, state mental health agencies are hampered by interorganizational conflict. States will continue to attempt to influence the distribution of federal funds, and case management will be only one of a number of priorities. Within individual states, various state-supported agencies, programs, and projects will compete for a limited amount of funds. Mental health programs, particularly community-based services receiving federal support, will compete with other agencies for state funds whose purchasing power is shrinking because of inflation and a limited capacity to generate revenues (Andrulis and Mazade, 1983).

Compounding the above problems is the fact that most public jurisdictions have not incorporated the various mandates for case management into a comprehensive and definitive policy applicable within the mental health service delivery system. In addition, despite the rapid development of policy mandates, rarely has the operation of case management been specified. As a matter of fact, the existence of various mandates has maintained the confusion and ambiguity about case management procedures. Numerous questions arise: Which agencies should take the lead role and be held accountable for case management operations? How should responsibilities for tasks be allocated within and among various mental health agencies? How should involved agencies interact with each other? Each of these questions identifies a problem that needs to be resolved.

It is clear from this discussion that legislative policies and mandates for case management vary from state to state, from community to community, and from agency to agency. It is also evident that prevailing attitudes, values, and ideologies affect treatment approaches and services. Needless to say, the effect of these factors on the development of case management needs to be taken into account.

Case Management Models

Although there is no universally accepted model or framework for case management in community mental health programs, there is considerable agreement about the program elements necessary to perform the tasks. These elements can be organized in different ways to create a useful model. It is important to note that the choice of a case management model largely dictates the type of evaluative or monitoring strategy that can be used. In general, case management approaches and models can be characterized by their major focus. In the mental health services, the major foci for case management models are the provider, the role, the service, the client, the goal, and combinations of these.

The predominant concern for the provider model is who provides the case management services. The major issue is whether to designate the primary therapist as the case manager or someone else. When there is a separate case manager, it must be decided whether the case manager should be a professional or a paraprofessional. There are advocates for each position. Lamb (1980) strongly argues for the primary therapist as the case manager, citing advantages in working with clients and agencies. In contrast, Ozarin (1977) and others argue that having a case manager who is not the primary therapist creates administrative and monitoring advantages.

Role-focused models of case management have been used extensively and are concerned with the primary role taken by the case manager. In these models, the case manager can be any of the following: (1) a supervisor who assigns cases to other workers and monitors their activities; (2) an intake worker who performs an initial assessment and links the client to the appropriate service unit; (3) a client programmer or diagnostician who develops the treatment plan and monitors compliance; (4) a service manager or broker who identifies client needs, uses agency resources and services for the client's benefit, refers clients to appropriate service units, and continually updates the service plan; (5) a generalist who does whatever is needed whenever the client needs it; (6) a service provider; (7) a case coordinator; or (8) a client advocate. The definitions of these roles then determine the functions, activities, and accountability procedures for the case manager.

In contrast, service-focused models are oriented toward the types of services provided for the client by the case manager. This includes activities identified as components of the Balanced Service System (Melville, Kiber, and Haddle, 1977), which include identification, assessment, planning, linking and coordinating, monitoring and evaluation, and advocacy. Also included as options in service-focused models are education (counseling services for at-risk individuals and their families about noninstitutional support services); identification and documentation of gaps in service; documentation of a lack of capacity to provide services and resistances within the service system; training suppliers of long-term care; and resource location and development (Benjamin and Ben-Dashan, 1979).

Client-focused models emphasize characteristics of the case management system's target population. Within community mental health, the emphasis might be on patients who have recently been discharged from mental hospitals; young adult clients who have chronic mental disabilities; persons who are involved only in therapeutic treatments such as group therapy, socialization group therapy, or day treatment; or persons who are at risk of being rehospitalized because of deteriorating mental functioning (Schwartz, Goldman, and Churgin, 1982).

In goal-focused models, the agency or case manager is concerned with the attainment of stated objectives for each client and for the system. These goals might pertain to the individual client, to program goals for type of treatment, or to program management and system efficiency. A goal for individual clients might relate to progress in treatment and functioning; an agency goal might be concerned with maintaining a particular staff-to-client ratio.

Each model described earlier specifies the particular interest of agencies or case managers. Of course, these foci are organizing principles for service delivery and are not usually found in a pure form in practice. Indeed, a given agency might highlight some elements of a model or utilize aspects of several of the models according to its needs. In analyzing case management procedures in any agency, a "model profile" comparing the procedures with identified models can be useful. Defining an agency's model for case management is an important step in planning the coordination of services within a specific agency or agency network. It is also helpful in clarifying and identifying criteria for program evaluations.

In applying any of these models, the authority of the case manager within the service network and the interactions between the agencies in the service network must be considered. The ability to integrate services depends on the power of an agency or its case managers to coordinate activities—a power that derives from administrative control and authority or funding. The success of case managers is related directly to their ability to integrate the system of services to benefit the severely mentally disordered client.

One factor that affects the case manager's control over resources is the organizational distance of the case manager from the direct service providers (Schwartz, Goldman, and Churgin, 1982). When case management is a function of the local mental health authority, case managers can be given the authority to mandate and monitor service delivery by other agency personnel. A similar procedure may be used where several small agencies are gathered under a single human resources agency and the case management function is clearly authorized to operate within that set of agencies. When there is no single umbrella agency, interagency agreements should be developed that specify the authority of the case manager. If case managers are not part of clinical service units, they may be unable to affect how clinical service staffs treat clients. Such a separation is often caused by a lack of credibility within the system of services, which is often related to the case manager's lack of professional affiliation and credentials. Clinicians in particular may resent the intrusion of persons whom they consider to be nonclinicians (Schwartz, Goldman, and Churgin, 1982).

Whatever model for case management is chosen, specifying the case manager's authority and range of responsibilities is crucial to the success of monitoring procedures. Schwartz, Goldman, and Churgin (1982) have summarized the different kinds of authority that are necessary for successful case management. They include the following:

1. *Administrative authority.* The existence of clear policies and formal agreements within and between agencies that help the case manager to integrate the decentralized network of service providers.
2. *Legal authority.* A clear mandate, granted through legislation, that specifies which organization is responsible for providing case management services for the chronically mentally ill.
3. *Fiscal authority.* Control over specific funds for purchasing services needed in case management to ensure that clients receive the services when required and from providers who are strictly accountable.
4. *Clinical authority.* An understanding of the clinical issues a given client must face and an ability to interact as a peer with clinical service providers.

Ideally, all four of these sources of authority should be used in a balanced fashion. The development of legal, administrative, and informal relationships among case managers, providers of service, community groups, and local governments will facilitate this practice.

Case Management Practices and Professional Roles

Case management has been central in efforts to integrate services at the state, federal, and local levels (Johnson and Rubin,

1983). At the state level, case managers have not been viewed as service providers themselves but as case coordinators and personal service brokers who guide consumers through the many services to which they are entitled.

Under the Balanced Service System approach recommended by the National Institute of Mental Health, the case manager assumes a variety of functions, including assessment, planning, linking, monitoring, and advocacy. In addition, the case manager may assume various specialized roles depending on the service unit, the caseload, and the current needs of each client. Case managers in this type of system have acted as primary therapists, patient advocates, and case aides among other roles. The professional discipline and title of the case manager is considered secondary to the function performed.

Comparing case management operations in mental health settings with those in other settings leads to the conclusion that many mental health case management programs employ a mixed model of case management. These programs stress both extensive client contact with therapeutic counseling and extensive evaluation of client status, but there is little emphasis on follow-up (Johnson and Rubin, 1983). Case managers in these settings report confusion about their roles and expected tasks and activities. Their work environments are least supportive of the case management job. This research suggests that emphasis on psychotherapy blocks the development of case management systems (Johnson and Rubin, 1983).

Case management has been mixed with conventional clinical activities in mental health facilities for several reasons. One involves fiscal support. Currently, "indirect services" in mental health settings receive only marginal support from public funds. As client fees and third-party reimbursements become more important, agencies have had to shift to office-based psychotherapy in order to survive. In addition, although case management plays a key role in the proposed National Plan for the Chronically Mentally Ill and in the Mental Health Systems Act, the federal administration's proposed block grant system would repeal the act and give state and local agencies control of federal funding. Under this plan, the mental health planning office of each state would interpret case management.

Another factor in the mixed approach to case management is the traditional emphasis in mental health settings on psychotherapy and psychodynamics in treating clients' problems. Clinicians may view as superficial service activities concerned with provision of resources because these services do not deal with the clients' underlying pathology (Johnson and Rubin, 1983). In many instances, organizations and administrators reward (with status or promotion) those mental health practitioners who include traditional diagnostic and treatment functions in their case management roles. This process of role creation, whether intentional or unintentional, is often supported by the absence of clearly defined case management roles and functions. In general, practitioners tend to interpret case management roles in terms of prior interests, commitments, and career goals. Compounding this problem is the uncertainty in much of the mental health system about whether the case manager is a professional or a paraprofessional role. To the extent that the case management role does not involve direct clinical treatment, case managers in mental health may not be perceived as professionals.

There is, however, another interpretation of the combination of case management and clinical roles in mental health settings. Diagnostic and therapeutic functions may be incorporated out of concern for client welfare, particularly the unique needs of the chronically mentally disabled. Proponents of this view maintain that the chronically mentally disabled are unlike other target populations receiving case management services—they need ongoing psychological assessment, including monitoring of their medication, and a supportive therapeutic relationship with their case manager. In addition to diagnostic and therapeutic functions, the functions of the case manager as conceived here also include (Johnson and Rubin, 1983):

1. ensuring that the case manager recognizes early signs of decompensation, unmanageable stress, or environmental circumstances likely to affect a client's illness;
2. ensuring that the case manager motivates and secures patient compliance with aftercare plans, including service utilization; and

3. providing the client with a stable, dependable relationship as he or she crosses institutional, community, and agency boundaries.

Lamb (1980) endorses this approach, arguing that good therapists are also good case managers and that the two functions cannot be separated.

Differing conceptions of the case manager's role (as primary therapist or generalist) create doubt about which professional background is most suitable for a person assuming this role in mental health settings. At present, several professions are favored, including social work, nursing, and vocational rehabilitation. Many people within the mental health services sector believe that no one profession is best suited to the case management function. In fact, some experts argue that a case manager does not need professional training and can be part of the paraprofessional staff. Some authors argue that "the case management function may be carried out by a variety of disciplines and agencies. However, the case managers should have the minimum level of skills so that higher-skilled staff are not underutilized and so that costs are contained. A new discipline does not seem to be needed. However, training for case managers through in-service or other methods is needed" (Ozarin, 1977).

People endorsing the most comprehensive conception of case management in mental health envision a higher and more diverse level of professional skills, such as combining clinical functions with the basic functions of case management. This approach would require case managers to be competent in several areas, including service brokerage, client motivation, community intervention, clinical treatment, and rehabilitation methods.

Some authors and practitioners hold that the social work practice framework that focuses on the person-in-environment offers the best opportunity for improving methods of case management practice. The argument for social workers assuming leadership in case management and service coordination for the chronically mentally ill is supported by the fact that social work is the most common profession among workers in community mental health. The major problem with this argument lies with the social workers themselves. Many social workers in community mental health appear indifferent to case management. One explanation for this attitude may be social workers' orientation toward psychodynamic theory and psychotherapeutic intervention. Their estimation of monitoring, coordinating, linking, and advocacy seems to be inversely related to their estimation of psychodynamics and their experience in practicing psychotherapy.

Another approach to staffing in case management is the establishment of two new professional classes. One would result from training paraprofessionals, including psychiatric technicians and community health workers, to become "clinical resource managers"; the other would result from creating new mid-level professional case manager positions occupied by nurse practitioners and physicians' assistants with special training in psychiatry, as well as social workers interested in community casework rather than therapy (Schwartz, Goldman, and Churgin, 1980).

Regardless of the approach, further analysis and planning of the selection of trainees, approaches to training, relationships of case managers with existing professionals, and cost-effectiveness is needed. One or more experimental projects are required to evaluate the various approaches to this difficult and complex problem of determining the most appropriate level and training for case managers. According to Benjamin and Ben-Dashan (1979), the following questions should always be considered:

1. What are the case management activities?
2. What skills, knowledge, and abilities are particularly important?
3. Under the case management model being used are there conflicting demands for (a) provision of services to clients, (b) accountability to the agency, or (c) mandates for providing linking, coordinating, and advocacy functions?
4. What discipline or background is most appropriate for the case manager?
5. How can the existing manpower be best used?

Consumer Advocacy

One of the objectives of case management is to ensure that members of the target population receive the services they need in order to function adequately in the least restrictive setting possible. One of the objectives of the consumer advocacy movement in mental health has been to provide consumers with a voice independent of the medical or treatment community and to increase the accountability of service providers through legal means. Legal decisions that mandate and require the right to treatment, the right to the least restrictive alternative in treatment, and the right to compensation in cases of malpractice have led to requirements for specified treatment plans with goals and objectives that can be tracked and measured. These decisions coupled with increased consumer awareness about their rights in treatment have also created a demand for auditing and coordinating services. Inevitably, case managers must protect clients' rights when problems arise.

In the National Plan for the Chronically Mentally Ill, legal advocacy and service advocacy are distinguished. Legal advocacy for patients' rights is often depicted as adversarial and focused on clients' freedom rather than their care. Many clinicians feel this position harms programs for the chronically mentally ill. In contrast, service advocacy in case management is an attempt to provide the mentally ill with better, more comprehensive, and more accessible treatment and care.

The National Plan recommended funding for service advocacy programs and technical assistance to encourage advocacy. It proposed having the National Institute of Mental Health assume an advocacy role with several functions: (1) to act as a clearinghouse for advocacy efforts and for investigations of public understanding of advocacy, (2) to conduct research and evaluation of self-help and client-controlled service alternatives, (3) to encourage advocacy efforts in community mental health centers, and (4) to convene a meeting of all people engaged in advocacy efforts.

From the state level, advocacy as part of case management has generally been viewed as interceding on behalf of an individual to assure equal treatment for all clients. There are two essential types of advocacy: (1) case-specific advocacy, the process of influencing human services systems and family support systems to respond to individual client needs, and (2) class-specific advocacy, the process of influencing human services systems and family support systems to change in response to documented deficiencies in their capacity to serve and nurture people who are chronically mentally disabled. In carrying out case-specific advocacy, the case manager should do the following:

1. coordinate the various elements of the system and be an active advocate for clients in the system;
2. assure that clients receive the appropriate type of service under an administrative structure where the case manager shall, upon request, be able to secure appropriate and timely services for case management clients;
3. meet regularly with clients and work closely with program staff;
4. develop a plan for each client, the elements of which include the appropriate assessment of mental status, economic need, vocational potential, physical health, need for resocialization, appropriate living environment, and appropriate individual treatment;
5. involve clients in their own treatment and service plans, preferably through a contractlike agreement; and
6. ensure the safeguarding of clients' property and their legal and civil rights.

Other arrangements for the provision of case management outside the public sector have been proposed. Although the public sector currently provides case management for the chronically mentally ill, a variety of financing and administrative mechanisms have been developed to purchase services for this population in the private sector using public funds. These mechanisms include the fee for service by public, third-party payers such as Medicare and Medicaid; CHAMPUS and CHAMPVA; purchase-of-service agreements between state and local governments that permit a client in consultation with a case manager or counselor to obtain services from private providers; and formal contracting for a given amount of service over a specified period of time (Schwartz, Goldman, and Churgin, 1980). Each of these mechanisms has its appropriate use.

In general, past experience indicates that these mechanisms do not constitute the answer for the care of the chronically mentally ill. Furthermore, contracts with the private sector cannot and should not eliminate the provision of direct services by the public sector or eliminate the ability of the public sector worker to maintain control over and accountability for the use of public resources. Case management services are probably best provided by the public sector, especially where case managers have the authority to purchase services for their clients. The appropriate mechanisms must be selected with the knowledge that the final test is the availability of and access to quality services.

Training and Education of Case Managers

Although case managers need not have any specific professional background, they should be generalists with some technical knowledge and should be able to negotiate the entire range of human services. Whatever their background, case managers must understand that their major functions are assessment, planning, linking, monitoring, advocacy, and service. In developing curriculum and training programs for case managers, special attention should be given to the need to provide case managers with the skills and knowledge required to assist clients in managing the activities of daily living on the one hand and to manage the more complex requirements of becoming independent in a complex society on the other. Case managers from different professional levels of training may be required. Some clients may need the support of a paraprofessional case manager who is willing to accompany them on a first bus trip after discharge from a hospital. Others require the kind of case management intervention that only highly trained case managers can provide—such as being able to detect a deteriorating psychological condition and having the skills to ensure that adequate and timely psychiatric care can be obtained.

The substantial disagreement that exists over the best way to establish case management with the chronically mentally ill prevents identification of a particular discipline or professional level as most appropriate for case managers. At this stage there is not even conclusive evidence that case management significantly improves care for the chronically mentally ill. Without such evidence, it is difficult to refute arguments that case management is a bureaucratic creation that simply generates more red tape by adding unnecessary services and communications (Johnson and Rubin, 1983).

If this conclusion is to be avoided, the effectiveness of the various conceptions of the case management role must be compared. Which approaches provide the most effective service delivery? What approaches best assist the different types of chronically mentally disabled clients in adapting to community life? Perhaps each of the current conceptions of case management should be used for different clienteles. For example, Lamb's therapist–case manager aproach might prove most effective for clients with minor impairments or those who return to their families at discharge, whereas the brokerage approach might work best with clients who need a number of community resources.

The most appropriate personnel for case management positions should be determined after enough outcome data are available and confusion over the case management role has subsided. At that point, research will be needed to evaluate the skills relevant to each approach and the effectiveness of staff from different disciplines and professional levels. According to proponents of the various approaches, the professional skills needed in the broader therapist–case manager approach might be higher than those needed in the narrower, service expeditor approach. However, research may show that this is not the case.

For example, to be effective in obtaining entitlements and expediting care for clients, even an approach that relied purely on expediting services would require political acumen and access to administrators in various organizations. Although service expediting may require a narrower range of skills than approaches where case managers are therapists as well, it does not necessarily follow that a lower level of professional skill is warranted. Indeed, overcoming bureaucratic rigidity may be the hardest part of the case management task.

Johnson and Rubin (1983) have proposed one solution to the confusion over the training and education of case managers. They state that irrespective of the ultimate form of case management or which case management model is chosen, social work can claim case management as being under its domain. No other professional discipline has an underlying philosophy and practice framework that is more compatible with case management. Because of its history and commitments, social work has every reason to assume a leadership role in this area. It remains to be seen whether social work practitioners will do so.

Effectiveness of Programs

The assessment of program effectiveness in mental health largely depends on clearly defined program elements and operations. A review of existing case management programs throughout the country reveals that there is no common conceptual and operational framework for case managers involved in mental health (Benjamin and Ben-Dashan, 1979). Contrasts among the conceptual models and the diffuse descriptions of the needs of chronic mental health clients in community settings, such as the Balanced Service System and the Community Support System developed by the National Institute of Mental Health Community Support Program, are partially responsible for this state of affairs.

There is general agreement that case management of the chronically mentally ill in the community requires several general functions, including client assessment, the identification of service needs, planning, linking, service monitoring, and advocacy to ensure that individual clients receive the range of services that they need. There is also agreement that case management is essential to ensuring access to all services required by individual clients and that case management can serve as a point of accountability for examining the performance of system elements (Johnson and Rubin, 1983).

Definitions of case management have been quite broad despite the acceptance of case management as an important mechanism for integrating and coordinating services. Many state agencies claim that they have been doing case management for years. Some programs see case management as an "intensive involvement with clients" (Benjamin, 1979). Vaughn (1978, p. 2) defines case management as a process "ensuring that clients are evaluated and matched with available agencies, providing a point of information, coordination, and accountability regarding the client's progress and acting as a resource and advocate for the development of services required to meet the client's needs."

In some mental health programs, case management is viewed as providing specialized assistance to each individual deserving and needing assistance in accordance with the individual's overall plan of service. Other programs define case management as the management of services across agencies and professional boundaries in order to develop and attain individual goals and objectives with optimum participation by the client and family. Still other programs recommend that a case management team assure that members of the target population are made aware of, are given the opportunity to participate in, and have transportation to all appropriate human services.

What is needed in the mental health system is a translation of the abstract definitions of case management into concrete operational definitions that can then be applied to staffing patterns, organizational structure, appropriate authority and accountability structures, specified relationships with other agencies, and clearly described agency functions and leadership styles. Additionally, to develop an effective case management system, who determines what services will be provided and who determines when a client's needs are met must be decided. Until these points are specified, the effectiveness of programs cannot be satisfactorily determined. According to these criteria, very few, if any, case management programs for the chronically mentally ill can be described as effective. If case management is defined only as as service function, the issue of overall case management effectiveness may not arise; however, without overall case monitoring, it will be difficult to assess program success adequately.

Where case management is intermingled in the provision of services, determining the effectiveness of the case management components becomes less important. Case management then becomes confounded with all the services with which it is involved. Thus, measuring the effectiveness of case management becomes moot. Because most publicized case management programs approach case management from this vantage point, currently it is common to find programs that are effective only in a particular situation and to find many case management programs that lack measurable outcomes.

Current Problems

A number of major problems affect case management for the chronically mentally ill. They are related to: (1) legislative policies, (2) the types of clients requiring case management, (3) resistance from the practitioners in carrying out case management functions, (4) a lack of funding and case management as an indirect service, and (5) insufficient resources.

There is evidence of a swing from supporting the chronically mentally ill in the community to institutionalizing certain classes of clients in state psychiatric hospitals. There is also less emphasis on treating clients in the least restrictive setting and more on treating them in a more therapeutically beneficial environment. Such thinking tends to clear the way for reinstitutionalizing some clients.

An additional problem that arises is the emergence of the "new chronic" client in the urban setting (Pepper, Kirshner, and Ryglewicz, 1981; Schwartz and Goldfinger, 1981; Schwartz, Goldman, and Churgin, 1982). These patients tend to overuse acute and crisis-oriented services in the community, including inpatient services. Such clients pose serious problems for agencies attempting to provide effective community support systems and to reduce the amount of hospitalization. The challenge for the case manager is to prevent unnecessary hospitalization of the "new" chronic clients and to provide alternative forms of treatment within the community to prevent the misuse of emergency and twenty-four-hour care services.

For social work in particular, the evidence indicates a substantial gap between ecologically based person-in-environment models of social work practice and the orientation of many social workers working in mental health settings. This gap defines an underlying issue: the difficulty encountered by social work practitioners in mental health of combining the psychotherapeutic aspects of service and aspects relating to providing and coordinating resources. Although consideration of the person-in-environment is a time-honored maxim in social work, social work clinicians seem to pay little attention to intervening in broader social systems. Many workers seem to have abandoned the distinctive dual focus of social work (person and environment) in favor of a psychological focus, even though the latter creates an area of intense competition with other professionals. In short, despite the importance that several social work practice models place on brokerage and advocacy and despite the notion of a distinct ecological perspective, the prevailing notion in direct services in mental health is that in-depth therapeutic skills distinguish the more advanced from the less advanced (and thus less prestigious) clinical practitioner (Johnson and Rubin, 1983).

Another major problem facing case management systems in many states is fiscal constraints. Case management services are currently not reimbursable through such third-party payment sources as Medicaid since they are seen as indirect rather than direct or treatment services. As a result, communities have limited options. One is to use the primary-therapist-as-case-manager model, in which instance case management is hidden within the direct delivery of services and is thus reimbursable. The other typical option is to utilize limited state dollars to support the case management function. This approach often leads to more stringent eligibility requirements for clients, since it is impossible to fund full-scale case management for all clients (Schwartz, Goldman, and Churgin, 1980).

Another problem in developing case management strategies and providing case management services is the lack of resources to provide for the needs of clients. Resources are essential for service provision. All too often, it is assumed that sufficient resources exist in the community to meet clients' needs. The case manager is expected to mobilize those resources for which the client is eligible. However, most case managers in the mental health system do not have enough resources at their disposal, and those services that do exist are often inadequately supplied, insufficiently comprehensive, or of poor quality.

A scarcity of resources can affect every aspect of case management. If mental health services are inadequately supplied or are not comprehensive, case managers may be drawn into a direct service role to fill these gaps in service. This may solve one problem, but it creates others. Some authorities feel that case managers are not ideal providers of direct services and the time they spend performing direct service functions prevents critical case management functions from being performed for many clients (Ozarin, 1977). Scarce resources also lead to a narrowing of the target population, such as focusing only on the neediest clients or on clients who are considered to be at greatest risk of rehospitalization. As a result, a class of underserved clients is created whose mental health needs must be met in less acceptable ways.

In addition to a scarcity of mental health services in any community, there may also be waste through the duplication of existing resources. Some communities have several case managers under various program authorities. For example, a single client may ostensibly have two case managers, one who is in the mental health system and another who is a court-appointed public guardian. Unfortunately, the presence of several systems does not constitute a comprehensive, integrated service system. To solve these pressing problems, there must be an interagency agreement that designates which authority is responsible for the case management of clients.

Future Directions

Interagency agreements that designate a case manager to whom the provision of services must be accounted for is a key issue in case management. A necessary step in achieving this goal is to assess the service delivery system. Such analysis is necessary to specify the type and range of interagency agreements needed. These agreements serve a variety of purposes. They heighten the awareness of shared responsibilities and problems through formal, public acknowledgment of the issues. Moreover, they formally recognize that case managers are the appropriate people to cross organizational boundaries and perform these monitoring tasks. Interagency agreements also serve to maintain paths between organizations and provide case managers with backup and redress procedures for resolving problems related either to individual client service or agency interactions.

Some critical organizational questions must be considered before a case management program is implemented. These include the following (Benjamin and Ben-Dashan, 1979):

1. To what extent do gaps in services and duplication, fragmentation, and overlap of services exist? What negative consequences do these deficiencies have for clients?
2. What range of services will be utilized by case managers?
3. What problems have been reported by mental health workers attempting to secure resources for clients in the past?
4. How complex are the negotiating tasks to be performed by case managers?
5. Are highly skilled workers asked to perform tasks far below their level of expertise? Are less skilled workers expected to perform tasks beyond their abilities?
6. What staffing patterns are possible?
7. What case management model is optimal given the available resources and organizational limitations?
8. What level of authority will be given to case managers seeking to obtain resources for clients? What level of authority is needed for case managers to obtain services for specific clients and to resolve problems in interaction between agencies?
9. What tasks do administrators and supervisors think that case managers should perform?
10. To whom should the case manager report and what is the extent of the supervisor's authority?

Although there are many questions about developing a case management system that are unique to each setting, the answers to these questions establish the basic foundation upon which particular case management programs can be built.

In planning any case management program within community mental health, the extent to which the program fulfills the following requirements should be assessed:

1. Is the case management program complete? Are program objectives and assumptions clear and are measures of the objectives agreed upon by the program management?

2. Is the description of the case management program acceptable to policy makers?
3. Does the program description represent the program as it will actually exist?
4. Are the expectations of the program reasonable?
5. Can the evidence of program success required by management be reliably produced?
6. Can the information obtained by the case management program affect performance within the service system?

Most experts will agree that the ways of initiating and operating a case management program will vary depending on the circumstances discussed in this chapter. They will also agree that while fulfillment of the conditions just listed might not ensure program success, it will at least provide clarity about the program's concepts and objectives. This in turn will provide the framework for operating and assessing a case management program for community mental health. In fulfilling these requirements, it should be kept in mind that the nature of the population defined as chronically mentally ill has shifted in significant ways, and case management programs must be adapted to deal with the needs of the changing population.

There is also a need to balance the psychosocial and rehabilitative approaches to the care of the chronic patient with medical and psychiatric approaches. Finally, there is a need to recognize that coordinating and integrating services in the interests of the individual client are enormously difficult tasks, requiring clinical as well as managerial skills.

Suggested Readings

Bachrach, L. L., and Lamb, H. R. "Conceptual Issues in the Evaluation of Deinstitutionalization." In G. J. Stahler and W. R. Tash (Eds.), *Innovative Approaches to Mental Health Evaluation*. New York: Academic Press, 1982.

Lamb, H. R. *Treating the Long-Term Mentally Ill*. San Francisco: Jossey-Bass, 1982.

Talbott, J. A. (Ed.). *The Chronic Mental Patient*. Washington, D.C.: American Psychiatric Association, 1978.

Turner, J. C. *Comprehensive Community Support Systems: Definitions, Components and Guiding Principles.* Rockville, Md.: National Institute of Mental Health, 1977.

References

Altschuler, S. L., and Forward, T. "The Inverted Hierarchy: A Case Manager Approach to Mental Health Services." *Administration in Mental Health,* 1978, *57,* 57–68.

Andrulis, D. P., and Mazade, N. A. "American Mental Health Policy." *Hospital and Community Psychiatry,* 1983, *34* (7), 601–606.

Bachrach, L. L., and Lamb, H. R. "Conceptual Issues in the Evaluations of Deinstitutionalization." In G. J. Stahler and W. R. Tash (Eds.), *Innovative Approaches to Mental Health Evaluation.* New York: Academic Press, 1982.

Beatrice, D. F. *Case Management: A Policy Option for Long-Term Care.* Washington, D.C.: Health Care Financing Administration, Department of Health, Education and Welfare, 1979.

Bedford, L., and Hybertson, L. D. "Emotionally Disturbed Children: A Program of Alternatives to Residential Treatment." *Child Welfare,* 1975, *54,* 109–115.

Ben-Dashan, T. "Case Management: An Annotated Resource Handbook." Paper presented at the 4th Learning Community Conference, Washington, D.C., November 1979.

Benjamin, M. P. "Case Management Services to the Severely Psychiatrically Disabled Adult." Paper presented at the Interdisciplinary Conference on Preparing Future Mental Health Specialists, University of Georgia, Athens, 1979.

Benjamin, M. P., and Ben-Dashan, T. "Case Management: Implications and Issues." Paper presented at the New Hampshire Case Management Conference, Concord, September 1979.

Fitz, J. *Case Management for the Developmentally Disabled: A Feasibility Study Report.* Raleigh: North Carolina Center for Urban Affairs and Community Services, 1978.

Johnson, P. J., and Rubin, A. "Case Management in Mental Health: A Social Work Domain?" *Social Work,* February 1983, pp. 49–54.

Lamb, H. R. "Guiding Principles for Community Survival." In H. R. Lamb and associates, *Community Survival for Long-Term Patients*. San Francisco: Jossey-Bass, 1976.

Lamb, H. R. "Therapist–Case Managers: More Than Brokers of Services." *Hospital and Community Psychiatry*, 1980, *31*, 762–764.

Melville, C., Kiber, J., and Haddle, H. *The Balanced Service System: An Approach to the Delivery of Mental Health Services*. Atlanta: Georgia Mental Health Institute, 1977.

Ozarin, L. "The Pros and Cons of Case Management." In J. A. Talbott (Ed.), *The Chronic Mental Patient*. Washington, D.C.: American Psychiatric Association, 1977.

Pepper, B., Kirshner, M. C., and Ryglewicz, H. "The Young Adult Chronic Patient: Overview of a Population." *Hospital and Community Psychiatry*, 1981, *32* (7), 463–469.

Ross, H. L. *A Volunteer-Operated System to Provide Comprehensive Services to Older Persons*. Proceedings of the Conference on the Evaluation of Case Management Programs, Los Angeles, March 1979.

Schwartz, S. R., and Goldfinger, S. M. "The New Chronic Patient: Clinical Characteristics of an Emerging Subgroup." *Hospital and Community Psychiatry*, 1981, *32* (7), 470–474.

Schwartz, S. R., Goldman, H. H., and Churgin, S. *Manpower Issues in the Care of the Chronically Mentally Ill*. Sacramento: Department of Mental Health, State of California, 1980.

Schwartz, S. R., Goldman, H. H., and Churgin, S. "Case Management for the Chronically Mentally Ill: Models and Dimensions." *Hospital and Community Psychiatry*, 1982, *33* (12), 1006–1009.

Talbott, J. A. (Ed.). *The Chronic Mental Patient*. Washington, D.C.: American Psychiatric Association, 1978.

Turner, J. C. *Comprehensive Community Support Systems: Definitions, Components and Guiding Principles*. Rockville, Md.: National Institute of Mental Health, 1977.

Turner, J. C., and Shifren, I. "Community Support Systems: How Comprehensive?" In L. I. Stein (Ed.), *New Directions for Mental Health Services: Community Support Systems for the Long-Term Patient*, no. 2. San Francisco: Jossey-Bass, 1979.

Turner, J. C., and TenHoor, W. J. "The NIMH Community Support Program: Pilot Approach to a Needed Social Reform." *Schizophrenia Bulletin,* 1978, *4,* 319–348.

Vaughn, R. L. "Client Services Management—Proposed Role Definition." Unpublished report submitted to the Community Support Program, Division of Mental Health Service Programs, National Institute of Mental Health, Rockville, Md., 1978.

9

Developmentally
Disabled Persons
and Their Families

Kathleen Burch Caires, Marie Weil

This chapter focuses on the application of case management in community-based programs serving the developmentally disabled. The term *developmental disability* is defined, and its antecedents, such as idiocy and mental deficiency, are noted in a summary of the history of western care systems. Public policy, ranging from formation of the Children's Bureau in 1912 to the federal legislation of the 1960s and 1970s, is reviewed as well. A description of the case management system of the California Regional Center illustrates an approach based on the concepts of human development and normalization. Family involvement in the care system is addressed, and topics include the use of parents as case managers, parent training, conflicts with professionals, and parental authority to provide services. Other issues considered are as follows: the incompatibility of the traditional disease-oriented medical model of care with the developmental model, lack of comprehension of basic rights by many developmentally disabled persons, and reductions in public funding.

Case management for developmentally disabled persons is a growing area of practice. The political and social status of persons with disabilities in mental functioning has been problematic, and the history of treatment and training for these people is particularly important for understanding current program directions. Developmentally disabled persons are vulnerable: they may have difficulty functioning, making informed decisions, and performing the most basic skills of daily life. Because of this vulnerability, case managers often need to work with family members (parents or adult siblings) as well as with the person who has a developmental disability. The population may be institutionalized, living alone, living with family, or living in one of a variety of supportive residential settings. Within institutions, the case management functions are fairly stable and related to intraorganizational coordination. This chapter will concentrate on the case management issues of developmentally disabled persons living in noninstitutional settings. The California Model, which stresses involving family members in case management, is highlighted as one approach to dealing with the special needs of the developmentally disabled.

Developmental disability is a term applied to a variety of handicapping conditions, including mental retardation, cerebral palsy, epilepsy, autism, and any other condition that impairs intellectual functioning or adaptive behavior in ways similar to that of mentally retarded persons. Whatever the etiology of the handicapping condition, members of the developmentally disabled target population generally require treatment and services that resemble the care needed by mentally retarded persons. Legislative definitions of those eligible for service typically stipulate that the disability must have originated during or before early adulthood and have continued or be expected to continue indefinitely. Any condition defined as a developmental disability constitutes a substantial impediment to the person's ability to function independently and normally in society.

Although persons with conditions of mental retardation have always been a large group needing services, historically care was provided in one of two ways: the person was either cared for by the family or institutionalized. In the past two decades, interest in normalization and community-based care and concerns for civil rights as well as changing models of practice have spurred the creation of a complex service network for children and adults with developmental disabilities and their families. Developmental disability as a category of service has grown as various types of impairment have been included in recent legislation. From state to state, the legal and practice definitions of developmental disability vary, but the definition given above generally indicates who is eligible for services and programs designed for the developmentally disabled.

Historical Perspective

Services for people with developmental disabilities have always been affected by society's changing views, as is illustrated by a survey of the changes in labels applied to people with such conditions.

In the mid-nineteenth century, people sympathetic to the mentally retarded referred to them as did society in general: *Idiot* was the generic term to denote persons with mentally handicapping conditions. Although this term now has pejorative connotations, its adoption co-evolved with the earliest western European efforts to develop humane treatment rather than isolation or incarceration for the mentally handicapped and mentally ill (Zilboorg, 1941). Itard's work with Victor, the "wild boy" of Aveyron, sparked interest in developing sensory and mental stimulation for people considered subnormal (Itard, 1932; Silberstein and Irwin, 1962). In the United States and Europe, the earliest therapeutic work with mentally retarded persons was related to sensory handicaps, where staff at institutes for the deaf and dumb and for the blind became involved in stimulation and development work with multihandicapped children.

Additional theoretical and empirical foundation for work with the intellectually handicapped was provided by Seguin, whose educational experiments with the children placed in the "idiots' sections" of two hospitals for paupers in Paris were also based on earlier work with an "idiot boy" that he had reported to the Academy of Sciences (Talbot, 1964). In a sense, Seguin was the forefather of current concerns for normalization, because he did not look for a cure for mental deficiency but strove to maximize potential.

In the United States, physicians followed the work of Itard and Seguin with great interest. Treatment for "mental defects" was coupled with treatment for sensory handicaps. Hervey Wilbur, director of the first "private school for defective boys" in Barre, Massachusetts, began that endeavor in 1848. He was drawn to his work after reading about Seguin's efforts (Adams, 1971, p. 20).

In 1848, Massachusetts established an experimental program that later became the Massachusetts School for Idiotic and Feeble-minded Youth (Kanner, 1964). This program spawned others; by the end of the century, institutions for training and rehabilitation had been developed in nineteen states. Children who were chosen for the programs were thought to have the ability to improve in functioning with special help (Kanner, 1964). These programs were all institutionally based and followed the notion of creating a safe and stimulating environment with an educational emphasis including clinical and social components.

By 1879 a school in Frankfort, Kentucky, had begun to provide industrial training to prepare the retarded residents for an economically independent life that would culminate in community release (Stewart, 1882). In this program, girls were trained in cooking, laundering, sewing, and kitchen maintenance, while boys worked in carpentry, mattress construction, mop and broom making, and shoemaking (Stewart, 1882). Adams (1971) postulates that the emphasis on vocational training at this time was due to the influence of Jeffersonian theory, which held universal education to be the backbone of a democratic society, and to the prevailing societal belief that youth should contribute to growing national productivity.

The economic upheaval in and rapid industrialization of the United States during the last quarter of the nineteenth century so vastly changed environmental conditions that custodial programs replaced community release. Observers at the time noted with dismay that despite good training, graduates of industrial training programs were not able to sustain themselves in the extremely chaotic and harsh social and economic conditions, and most graduates could not be supported by their families because of economic circumstances or other family problems (Stewart, 1888). A trend to reestablish custodial care developed in several states, but tensions over the selection of target populations developed because the need for institutional care far exceeded available space.

Because of limited state funds, the typical solution was to "devise economical means by which a moderate good [would] be done for the greatest number" (Kerlin, 1888, p. 166). By the turn of the century, progressive states were stressing long-term custodial care in total institutions to protect vulnerable populations from exploitation.

However, the next quarter of a century witnessed a drastic change in social perception. American social thought and public opinion entered a period dubbed in mental health history as the "eugenic scare" (Davies, 1959, chaps. 5–7). Social conditions such as poverty, alcoholism, delinquency, and vagrancy drastically increased. Although these social problems were not related to mental retardation, concern about "moral degeneracy" was rife. Public attitudes shifted to "protecting society from the feared contamination of inferior mental stock" (Adams, 1971, p. 30). Adams notes the impact of the studies of the Juke and Kallikak families and others in which some individuals evidenced high degrees of social pathology as well as low mental functioning ability. These scientific reports, such as Goddard's (1912), produced the belief that low intelligence was the cause of all the other social ills and dysfunctional symptoms.

The ability to measure intelligence as developed by Binet provided the means to screen individuals and protect society. Emphasis then shifted to social control of people judged to be feebleminded. Sterilization laws resulted, the first being passed in 1907, and massive efforts to institutionalize individuals ensued (Davies, 1959). This eugenic scare did not change society as much as it shifted the prevailing attitude from one of moderate compassion to one of fear leading to social control and isolation. Wolfensberger (1969) holds that the physical and psychological isolation of the mentally retarded was equaled in Western medical history only by the quarantining of lepers in the Middle Ages.

However, throughout this period, small, progressive, community-based programs began to appear. Public schools developed special classes, and community clinics provided some care for mentally retarded children. A clinic in Waverly, Massachusetts, can be credited with developing the concept of community-based care; this clinic provided families who had retarded members with counseling, advice, and nursing services (Fernald, 1921-1922). The program had rudimentary aspects of case management, since programs of the clinic, the public schools, and other available services had to be coordinated. This early form of community-based care was accompanied by renewed efforts to provide rehabilitation and training. Some residents of institutions were released to their families; others were placed in "colonies," where they had a protected, group living environment and worked on farms or in urban settings during the day (Bernstein, 1919-1920). Placement of some retarded individuals with foster care families and some educational and group programs conducted in community centers followed (Vaux, 1934-1935).

This history of program efforts indicates, as Adams (1971, p. 43) suggests, "that most of the components of a comprehensive and coordinated service had been conceived and attempted in some place at some time." She concludes that if these various efforts had been joined, made accessible, and continually supported, the nation would have had from the mid 1930s the *"continuum of care* [emphasis in original] which the President's Panel of 1962 projected as the prototype of care for today's retarded population" (Adams, 1971, p. 43; President's Panel on Mental Retardation, 1962). Unfortunately, emphasis on programs and service for this population waned, and for a quarter of a century, service programs did well to hold their own. Innovation was lacking, and the public was largely unconcerned about the needs of the mentally retarded. Mental retardation was considered an isolated, specialized problem; despite the successes of the foster placement and colony programs, institutionalized care remained the norm.

Adams (1971) attributes this societal and to some degree professional disinterest to the societal hardships caused by the Great Depression. Social programs turned their focus from this vulnerable population to the needs of unemployed workers. As women entered the work force in greater numbers to help support their families, more children were placed in institutions and overcrowding became common. The economic productivity generated in World World II did not increase interest in the retarded, although the large number of men rejected for military service on the basis of subnormal intelligence did cause concern.

This brief history brings us to recent developments in federal policy, but it is instructive to note the power of labeling and its stigmatizing force. In the relatively short time discussed above, the labels for this disabled population shifted from *idiot* to *feeble-minded* to *mentally defective* to *mentally deficient* to *mentally retarded* to the current term, *developmentally disabled*.

Public Policy

Improvements in national standards and the coordination of care resulted from policies implemented by the Children's Bureau (established in 1912), which had as part of its mandate the responsibility of investigating mental retardation as well as other problems affecting children. It sponsored several studies of the care of the "mentally defective" that documented inadequate care and the coincidence of mental defects with social conditions such as poverty, neglect, and dependency (Children's Bureau, 1964). The bureau tracked changes in programs and attempted to monitor the care of retarded children. The Social Security Act of 1935 assigned the bureau the task of administering crippled children's grants, and the bureau then conducted basic research and funded demonstration grants for clinics.

A major change in the network of people concerned with mental retardation was the formation in several states of small groups of families who had retarded members. By 1947 the phenomenon received attention through a paper presented at the conference of the American Association of Mental Deficiency (Sampson, 1947). Two years later two parents and a social worker involved with their group addressed the same association (Adams, 1971). A social movement of parents of mentally retarded children developed, and in 1953 the National Association for Retarded Children, now known as the National Association for Retarded Citizens (Scheerenberger, 1976), was chartered. This group and other advocacy groups were one of two primary forces pressing for and influencing the development of legislation governing the care of developmentally disabled persons.

Another major force in the development of social change and service change for the mentally retarded was President John F. Kennedy. He spurred unequaled changes in the treatment, care, and service network for people who were later to be called developmentally disabled. The early 1960s was a watershed period for this population. Parents' frustrations with an inadequate system of care were not new, but parents at this time acted strongly and issued articulate statements, and their presentations attracted public and governmental attention (Segal, 1970). Kennedy's leadership in describing the problems and calling for legislation further galvanized the actions of parents and aroused national and regional interest in the needs of this population. This interest made change possible. President Kennedy had a sister, Rosemary, who was developmentally disabled, and his experience with her care sensitized him to the needs of people with mental disabilities. Kennedy's personal involvement with and concern for the service needs and rights of the mentally retarded was transformed into legislation for social change during and following his administration (Varela, 1983).

In his call for a national plan to combat mental retardation, Kennedy urged that "our goal should be to prevent mental retardation" (Kennedy, 1961, p. 4). He created a President's Panel on Mental Retardation in 1961, which proposed a national program. This panel defined the mentally retarded as "children and adults who, as a result of inadequately developed intelligence, are significantly impaired in their ability to learn and to adapt to the demands of society" (President's Panel on Mental Retardation, 1962, p. 1). Their *A Proposed Program for National Action to Combat Mental Retardation* documented the plight of the retarded in overcrowded institutions. The panel pointed out the woefully inadequate numbers of staff, and calculated that the average for the nation for patient costs per day was $4.55 (President's Panel on Mental Retardation, 1962). Major policy changes and new services were proposed.

In a major address to Congress in February 1963, President Kennedy issued a clarion call for changes in the treatment and care of the mentally retarded and disabled. He urged the following actions:

> to bestow the full benefits of our society on those who suffer from mental disabilities;
>
> to prevent the occurrence of mental illness and mental retardation wherever and whenever possible;
>
> to provide for early diagnosis and continuous and comprehensive care, in the community, of those suffering from these disorders;
>
> to stimulate improvements in the level of care given the mentally disabled in our State and private institutions, and to reorient those programs to a community-centered approach;
>
> to reduce, over a number of years, and by hundreds of thousands, the persons confined to these institutions;
>
> to retain in and return to the community the mentally ill and mentally retarded, and there to restore and revitalize their lives through better health programs and strengthened educational and rehabilitation services; and
>
> to reinforce the will and capacity of our communities to meet these problems, in order that the communities, in turn, can reinforce the will and capacity of individuals and individual families.
>
> We must promote—to the best of our ability and by all possible and appropriate means—the mental and physical health of all our citizens [Kennedy, 1963, pp. 13–14].

In 1963 Kennedy signed into law the Maternal and Child Health and Mental Retardation Planning Amendments Act of 1963 (PL 88-156). This legislation was the beginning of a series of legislative efforts to enact the recommendations of the panel's report. It amended the Social Security Act to provide assistance to states and communities to combat and prevent mental retardation and provided funds to stimulate services for the mentally retarded.

Federal grants were to be provided to help each state assess its current programs and plan for future expansion and coordination of services. A second major piece of federal legislation was also passed in 1963, the Construction of Research Centers and Facilities for the Mentally Retarded (PL 88-164), which dealt with the creation of facilities and the training of professionals. States could receive funds from these two acts only if they had developed a plan for services approved by the federal government. As Varela (1983, p. 38) notes, "These acts encouraged the states to examine the varying needs of a varied population and, whenever feasible, to provide services within the community."

Four other legislative landmarks followed in fairly rapid succession: the Social Security Amendments of 1965 (PL 89-97), the Mental Retardation Facilities and Community Mental Health Centers Construction Act Amendments of 1965 (PL 89-105), the Elementary and Secondary Education Act of 1965 (PL 89-10), and the Vocational Rehabilitation Amendments of 1965 (PL 89-333). Each of these acts significantly affected the services provided for developmentally disabled people and their families. They were developed out of the increasing concern for community-based care and normalization models of treatment and service delivery.

In 1970 President Nixon signed into law the Developmental Disabilities Act (PL 91-517), designed to create the needed continuum of services for persons with developmental disabilities. In addition, there are several more recent federal laws pertaining to the needs of developmentally disabled persons. Public Law 94-142, the Education for All Handicapped Children Act, was passed in 1975 to assure a free and appropriate public education for all children including those handicapped by a developmental disability. The act asserts the unique needs of the handicapped and asserts their rights. Section 504 of the Vocational Rehabilitation Act of 1973 addresses the civil rights of the handicapped of all ages. The 94th Congress also passed the Developmentally Disabled Assistance and Bill of Rights Act (PL 94-103), specifically serving this population.

Both federal and complementary state legislation generally acknowledge that the developmentally disabled population requires various services throughout their lives; that a combination of federal and state funds can be used to encourage the development and coordination of services; and that specialized and generic services available through health, welfare, education, and rehabilitation facilities, both public and private, can be used to promote the well-being of persons with developmental disabilities.

Current federal policy as articulated in the Developmental Disabilities Act of 1970 addressed the service needs of people with developmental disabilities and formally defined a developmental disability as including mental retardation, cerebral palsy, epilepsy, or other substantial neurological handicapping conditions (Public Law 91-517).

Although policies vary among states, the general evolution of state policies and services for the developmentally disabled population can be traced by examining the programs and guidelines in California, which can be considered typical. For a number of years California was in the forefront of the movement to promote services for the developmentally disabled. The guiding state legislation, the Lanterman Developmentally Disabled Services Act of 1976, updated and modified the earlier Lanterman Mental Retardation Services Act, which had been approved in 1969, implemented in 1971 after a planning period, and updated in 1973. The 1976 act defined *developmental disability* as

> a disability which originates before an individual attains age 18, continues, or can be expected to continue, indefinitely, and constitutes a substantial handicap for such individual. As defined by the Director of Developmental Services, in consultation with the Superintendent of Public Instruction, this term shall include mental retardation, cerebral palsy, epilepsy, and autism. This term shall also include handicapping conditions found to be closely related to mental retardation or to requrie treatment similar to that required for mentally retarded individuals, but shall not include other handicapping conditions that are solely physical in nature [State of California Welfare and Institutions Code, Division 4.5, Section 4512(a)].

In 1978, U.S. Public Law 95-602, Section 102(7), amended the federal definition of a developmental disability. The new definition extended the age of onset to twenty-two years of age and defined developmental disabilities in a flexible, functional manner rather than in a categorical or diagnostic one as before. The intention of this change was to avoid later amendments to add specific disability categories (Summers, 1981).

California Model

To illustrate a state service system for persons with developmental disabilities, the program in California will be examined. Before the 1960s, the only service choices for families with developmentally disabled children were institutionalization following a lengthy waiting period or maintaining the child at home with little outside support. Out of the frustration of these parents, as in other states, a social advocacy movement was born that focused public and governmental attention on the plight of the developmentally disabled and their families. During this period, the population was usually referred to as the "mentally retarded," and that was the language employed in the legislation.

Parents and professionals pushed for a more effective service system for the mentally retarded. With the impetus of increased federal support and efforts to establish standards, the California legislature documented the conditions and needs of the mentally retarded population in two studies. The Study Commission on Mental Retardation published *The Undeveloped Resource: A Plan for the Mentally Retarded in California* in January 1965, and the Assembly Subcommittees on Mental Health Services published *A Redefinition of State Responsibility for California's Mentally Retarded* in March of the same year.

In his charge to the study commission, Governor Edmund Brown illustrated the growing concern about the welfare of the mentally retarded:

> No longer is mental retardation a subject to be relegated to the back room, as the retarded child was once kept hidden from society. Today it is recognized that mental retardation, while a tragic occurrence, is no disgrace—that it may occur in any family—and that it

is indeed a *social* rather than merely a personal or family problem [Brown, 1965].

The study commission report, completed two years later, identified the mentally retarded population and assessed service needs, evaluation needs, and funding.

The study commission report, *The Undeveloped Resource: A Plan for the Mentally Retarded in California,* articulated principles for service development and made recommendations for administrative structure and fiscal support. The principles adopted in the report reflected the perspective that all humans have potential for growth, called for a service continuum and community-based services, and asserted support for the self-determination of retarded individuals and their families:

> Services should be planned and provided as part of a continuum, which means that the pattern of facilities and eligibility shall be so complete as to meet the needs of each retarded person, regardless of his age or degree of handicap, and at each stage of his life development. It also means a continuity, including uniform eligibility standards, to insure that no retarded individual is lost in the transition from one service to another.
>
> Because the retarded person is a human being first, and a handicapped individual secondarily, he should have access to all the general community services that he can use in common with others. Only when integrated services fail to meet his needs should there be specialized services.
>
> Services for retarded persons should be close to their homes and families. This applies to state hospitals and other residential facilities as well as to diagnostic, educational, recreational, and other community services. Moreover, no retarded person should remain in an institution who can adjust outside.
>
> Retarded persons, or their families acting in their behalf, should have substantial freedom of

choice among public and private services. This accords with the dignity of the individual and his right of self-determination for his own life [Study Commission on Mental Retardation, 1965, p. 11].

The first three recommendations by the study commission called for the establishment of regional diagnostic and counseling centers as the cornerstone of the service system; the development of various residential alternatives, including residential schools, foster homes, boarding homes, and supervised living arrangements; and the provision of rehabilitation services. Other recommendations dealt with special education programs, child care, professional training, and the encouragement of research.

The second report presented the work of the Mental Health Services Committee, of which Frank Lanterman was a member. It documented the problems of institutional placement and also proposed a service system of regional diagnostic and counseling service centers to develop and coordinate services for the retarded population.

As the process of study and recommendation escalated, parents and their supporters continually pressed for state funds to develop community-based services for the developmentally disabled. Because of these efforts and growing support from professionals and the public, the state legislature directed in 1968, in accordance with federal legislation, that a further study be conducted documenting the use and access to facilities and programs for this population.

The mandated study required examination of seven major areas of concern including the need for a single coordinating agency, funding for services, overuse of the state hospital system and gaps in community services, lack of service coordination, inequitable fees, and failure to use federal funds available for the mentally retarded population (Human Relations Agency, n.d., p. 4).

After the study was completed, its results were analyzed; then legislation effective July 1, 1971, the Lanterman Mental Retardation Services Act, was designed and passed in 1969. Numerous state agencies and the California Association for the Retarded and other citizens advocacy groups collaborated in planning for the implementation of the act. The intent of the legislation was "to meet the needs of each retarded person, regardless of age or degree of handicap, and at each stage of his life's development." Unlike legislation developed in the mid to late 1960s, this act was designed to assist in service integration, to eliminate the duplication of services, and to fill gaps in services for the developmentally disabled.

The resulting legislation mandated the development of regional and diagnostic counseling centers in order to

> provide fixed points of referral in the community for the mentally retarded and their families; establish ongoing points of contact with the mentally retarded and their families so that they may have a place of entry for services and return as the need may appear; provide a link between the mentally retarded and services in the community, including state-operated services, to the end that the mentally retarded and their families may have access to the facilities best suited to them throughout the life of the retarded person; offer alternatives to state hospital placement; and encourage the placement of persons from the state hospital. It is the intent that a network of regional diagnostic, counseling, and service centers for mentally retarded persons and their families, easily accessible to every family, be established throughout the state [Human Relations Agency, n.d., p. 6].

This legislation stressed community-based care and mandated "Area Planning Boards" and periodic program evaluations. The following types of services were urged as part of a comprehensive service program: prevention, information and referral, case finding, diagnosis and evaluation, care and treatment, family counseling, home training, special education, daycare, short-term residential care, long-term residential care, vocational services, recreation, religious training, legal services, and statewide supportive services.

The Lanterman Developmentally Disabled Services Act (1976) alters the language to the less stigmatizing term and mandates each regional center to provide the following services: (1) diagnosis, evaluation (including court-ordered evaluations), counseling, and development of an "Individual Program Plan"; (2) program coordination (case management) on a continuing basis through the purchase or referral of services; (3) utilization and accountability of funds; (4) maintenance of a client registry and individual case records; (5) community education, outreach, resource development, and consultation with service agencies; (6) advocacy for the protection of civil, legal, and service rights; (7) state hospital preadmission and discharge services; and (8) other such services as necessary to carry out the provisions in law, regulation, or contractual obligations. In addition to these mandated responsibilities, each regional center refers its clients to existing services and provides available services that are deemed essential for improved functioning, if funds are available.

Since each regional center contracts with the state of California, it must also operate under a set of operating guidelines contained in the *Regional Center Operations Manual*. This operating manual is updated periodically by the Community Services Division of the State Department of Developmental Services. It "includes state policies where required by statute; references state law, regulations, and so on, pertaining to specific program areas; and provides a framework for the development of specific programs to serve the developmentally disabled tailored to the needs and priorities as expressed by each regional center" (Community Services Division, 1980, p. 1000).

Case Management

Federal legislation and most state codes explicitly identify case management (sometimes referred to as case or service coordination) as a necessary service. The major purpose of case management for developmentally disabled persons is to enable them to participate in the normal processes of life in the least restrictive environment possible. The process of case management begins when a client enters the services system. First, an interdisciplinary team assesses the client. The interdisciplinary team usually consists of an intake worker, most often a social worker, who does a psychosocial assessment; a psychologist, who does testing and psychological evaluations; and a physician, who does a medical evaluation or requests medical records. Other members of the interdisciplinary team may include an educational consultant, a physical therapist, a nurse consultant, a nutritionist, a coordinator for prevention services, a speech consultant, and various other consultants relevant to the particular situation and needs of the client.

If the client is found eligible for services, a program plan, which must be implemented and evaluated each year, is formulated. The Individual Program Plan (IPP) outlines the service needs of the client and sets forth the goals, objectives, and plans for the next year. In addition to developing the annual IPP, the case managers provide the following services: (1) coordination, integration, and direction of appropriate services obtained through referral or purchase and needed to implement the program plan; (2) documentation of the progress and problems of the client in "Interdisciplinary Notes"; (3) identification of any gaps in services in the current program for the client; (4) assessment and documentation of any unmet needs and development of plans to meet them; (5) modification or update of the plans and objectives in the IPP as necessary; (6) measurement and monitoring to ensure that appropriate services are being received and progress is being made; (7) purchase of services and assurance that purchased services are being provided; (8) proper maintenance of all records, including collection of records or reports from other programs or specialists; and (9) advocacy for clients' rights or for appropriate services, so that clients may achieve optimum development in the least restrictive environment.

Theoretical Base. The current ideology underlying services for the developmentally disabled consists of two major concepts, the developmental model and the principle of normalization (Scheerenberger, 1976; Lensink, 1980). This ideology provides a conceptual framework for staff that promotes creativity and lends stability in times of organizational strain (Lensink, 1980). Lensink states that the normalization of services for the developmentally disabled has the following components: "developmental model, specialization of services, statewide dispersal, community integration, and continuity of services" (1980, p. 50).

The developmental model sets the tone and direction of services and is tied to the uniqueness of each individual. It proposes that life is change, that all human beings develop throughout their life span, and that human development progresses in an orderly and predictable manner. Systematic training and services can influence the rate and direction of development, but if training is to be effective, physical, psychological, social, and economic conditions must be considered.

According to the developmental model, "retarded children and adults are considered capable of growth, learning, and development. Each individual has potential for some progress, no matter how severely impaired he might be. The basic goal of programming for retarded individuals consists of maximizing their human qualities" (International League of Societies for the Mentally Handicapped, 1971, p. 2). The uniqueness of each client should be considered, and each should be assisted in learning skills that give him or her the greatest degree of independence possible. The more impaired or dependent the child or adult may be, the more professional concentration should be on providing services, creating access to services, and case management to coordinate the various services and opportunities available to the individual. However, the main virtue of the model is its emphasis on developing independent living skills and self-direction to the maximum degree possible.

The developmental model is also based on respect for the individual and concern with maximizing human potential. Most agencies and organizations serving the developmentally disabled population have adopted this approach to service. In a pamphlet, *Residential Programming for Mentally Retarded Persons,* the National Association for Retarded Citizens (1972) endorses and explicates the model. In addition, Lensink (1980, p. 50) notes that programs based on the developmental model are geared toward growth and learning: "The system therefore accommodates growth and development by offering (or by securing within the community) program options that take into account the individual's development by providing less structure, more integration into the community, and more normalized conditions in which to learn, work, and live." This conceptual model has become the foundation of an evolving theory for work with the developmentally disabled. Components of social and behavioral science theories that fit with the aims of the developmental model have been incorporated to create a model of practice that reflects the value of self-determination and rejects pathology as a guiding concept.

A hallmark of the developmental approach is its rejection of the medical model, which had prevailed in inpatient care and residental treatment of the mentally ill. The major points of disagreement between the two models, cited by Wolfensberger (1969) and Ross (1971), are whether mental retardation is an illness and whether it is appropriate to treat developmentally delayed persons as though they are sick. The medical model, based on diagnosis, treatment, and cure, is not applicable to this population because at present there is no cure for mental retardation, cerebral palsy, epilepsy, or autism. The medical model has also been criticized for emphasizing pathology, increasing dependence, and relying on custodial care in institutions rather than community-based care (Wolfensberger, 1969).

Although medical personnel are expected to provide treatment in the developmental model, greater emphasis is placed on an interdisciplinary team approach to service delivery. According to the model, it is important that staff recognize that each individual has her or his own rate of development. Service objectives and goals should reflect existing developmental skills and specific developmental needs. Therefore, developmental programming and services must always be individualized. Standardized group goals and objectives are not acceptable. Persons cannot be made to fit programs; programs must be tailored to meet individual needs. The "majority rules" approach is not acceptable in services for developmentally disabled people (Chapman, 1979). The developmental model acknowledges each person's capacity for learning, growing, and doing regardless of how severely disabled he or she may be. It acknowledges that "as a retarded citizen grows and develops, the system must allow more independence and less structured program alternatives" (Lensink, 1980, p. 50).

The corollary to the developmental model is the concept of normalization as discussed by Nirje (1969). He defined *normalization* as "making available to the mentally retarded patterns and conditions of everyday life which are as close as possible to the norms and patterns of the mainstream of society." The thrust of this concept is to assist the individual to lead as normal and independent a life as possible. Although there has been considerable debate about exactly what normalization constitutes and how it can best be carried out, the concept has generally been accepted. This statement from the American Academy of Pediatrics, Committee for the Handicapped Child (1973, p. 2) indicates the adoption of this principle:

> All children, regardless of the severity and nature of their handicaps, have the right and should have the opportunity to receive services in educational, recreational, social, and medical settings equal to those available to their nonhandicapped peers. Such services should be in the same or specialized facilities as their peers and manned by staff with special skills. To these ends the pediatrician should support the human management practice which enables a mentally or physically handicapped child to function in ways considered to be within acceptable norms for his society and advocate the mandating of resources which will provide families with the necessary support for the maintaining of their children within the community.

Concepts used in conjunction with the developmental model and developmental theory have been drawn from theories of crisis intervention (Parad, 1963, 1965, 1971; Golan, 1978), systems theory (von Bertalanffy, 1967; Boulding, 1968), behavioral theory (Bandura, 1969, 1971), the process of grief and mourning (Kübler-Ross, 1969), problem-solving casework (Perlman, 1957), the ecological model (Meyer, 1976; Germain, 1979; Germain and Gitterman, 1980), and family therapy and family systems theory (Minuchin, 1967, 1974; Bowen, 1978; Satir, 1964, 1972). None of these theories focus on pathology, and together they form a workable armamentarium from which the practitioner can select an appropriate method for working with developmentally disabled individuals and their families.

Let us consider an illustration of how one of these theories is incorporated into practice. Families with a developmentally disabled member often suffer from chronic sorrow or grief similar to the mourning process outlined by Kübler-Ross (1969). Although such families may experience predictable emotional stages in coping with the loss of expectations and hopes that results from the birth of an afflicted child, setbacks or crises do occur at various times throughout the life span of the disabled person. Mary Leydorf (1978), after working with parents of disabled children, outlined seven stages of the parents' reactions: confusion, denial, anger-guilt, hope, depression, acceptance, and understanding. Counseling can greatly help parents work through the negative reactions to having a child with a developmental disability, and the case manager needs to understand the theory and methods of work in counseling at each stage.

At the acceptance level of coping, a parent is an important working member of a team that may consist of staff persons involved in medical care, educational therapy, physical therapy, speech therapy, and psychological management. If there is a disruption in services, a medical crisis, or even a developmental change within the disabled person, parents may regress in their emotional coping to a previous level, such as depression or even anger-guilt. Of course, none of these stages have clear boundaries in reality, and there may be considerable overlap between stages or even a mixture of feelings from several stages at one time. A case manager should know about these seven stages and determine how each family member is functioning individually and then consider the total family from an interaction approach of systems theory in order to intervene as effectively as possible.

Adjusting to the special problems and hardships created by the developmentally disabled child or children involves utilization of problem-solving models such as Perlman's (1957), in which alternatives are "jointly explored with the developmentally disabled person/family to find resolutions to situational stresses at the various developmental stages of life" (Community Services Division, 1980). Another relevant practice model is the ecological model proposed by Germain (1979), Germain and Gitterman (1980), and Meyer (1976). This model stresses the interaction of the individual, the family, the supportive environment, and the service system.

In combination, the systems and ecological models provide a framework for dealing with the developmentally disabled person and his family throughout his life. As the disabled person grows older, new situations arise and new skills or behaviors need to be acquired. The family, with the aid of the case manager, must address these needs. This is not the same as viewing the client as a set of problems or pathologies, as is done when following the diagnostic or pathology-oriented model. Problem-solving casework and family systems intervention is much more positive and dynamic, and the family and client are active participants in problem solving.

Case Management Process and the California Model. The case management model and process presented here was developed under the California regional center program. It consists of (1) the use of the developmental model as described; (2) an interdisciplinary approach to individual evaluation, service planning, and service implementation; (3) an ongoing assessment of the client's developmental needs throughout the various stages of life; (4) an individualized plan for programs and services; (5) an emphasis on the principles of normalization in providing services and interventions; (6) coordination of services for the developmentally disabled individual; (7) inclusion of the client and/or his or her family in the planning process as well as various service providers; and (8) recognition and protection of the client's basic human and legal rights (Chapman, 1979; Community Service Division, 1980, appendix 3).

The core of this case management model is the IPP. This is the plan of intervention and action for the ongoing development of the individual that is written at the time of the initial assessment and updated annually. It is a developmental guide based on a comprehensive assessment of the client's developmental status, potential, and needs and it is formulated through a collaborative interdisciplinary process with the participation of the client (when possible), the client's family, relevant staff of agencies serving the client, and other persons who may be significantly involved in the client's development.

Team meetings are the major format of collaboration, and they are supported by communication, service provision, and team follow-up in smaller groups. The family is included when possible because of the belief that the family knows the client better than anyone else. Even though professionals have their areas of expertise, the family members live with the client daily and have a direct knowledge of parenting. The family, therefore, is an important component in interdisciplinary planning and coordinating. The participants share all information and recommendations and as a team develop a single, integrated plan designed to meet the individual's identified needs (Chapman, 1979). This plan becomes the focal point in assisting the client to achieve individualized goals in accordance with the developmental model and with the belief that all individuals are capable of continuous growth and development throughout their lives (Community Services Division, 1980).

Certain specific domains, or areas of function, are looked at when identifying client needs: sensorimotor, communicative, social, affective-emotional, cognitive, health, medical, vocational, and independent living skills (such as toilet skills, self-help skills, travel skills, money management, and so forth).

The IPP specifies developmental objectives intended to help the client reach the goal of functioning as normally as possible. These developmental objectives describe specific behaviors or skills to be learned. They are therefore written in behavioral terms ("will do . . ." or "will accomplish . . ."), which are time limited (to be completed by a certain time) and provide measurable indexes of developmental progress so that the effectiveness of services and programming can be monitored and evaluated. For each developmental objective entered in the individual's program plan, at least one plan must be written that lists strategies for achieving the objectives, including the names of individuals and agencies and their specific responsibilities (Chapman, 1979). When a developmental objective is achieved, the next step would be addressed on a subsequent annual IPP. An example of a developmental objective is: "Client will be able to tie his shoes in three out of five attempts, with assistance, by December 1985." The plan for such an objective might be: "Parent and teacher at Corner School will teach and assist client to tie his shoes."

In addition to developmental objectives that are written in behavioral terms, there are maintenance objectives and event objectives. A maintenance objective is written when a concern is to maintain the status quo; for instance, to control seizures. An event objective is written to describe a particular event that will occur; for instance, that the client will receive a speech evaluation or obtain a wheelchair. At least one plan would be written for each maintenance or event objective. The IPP, of course, can be modified at any time when gaps in services are noted or additional resources are needed.

The case manager monitors progress on each item through quarterly checks on each IPP. Because the objectives are measurable, the case manager can readily determine whether progress is being made. This can be done by visiting the client at home, school, or workshop and by talking to the people involved with the client in the client's different environments.

Besides the IPP, a section in the client's record called Interdisciplinary (ID) Notes is kept as a running log of what happens in the daily life of the client. It is in this section that the case manager records the client's progress. If progress is not being made on a particular objective, the case manager records the probable reason, such as an unrealistic objective, interference by something, lack of follow-through, and so forth. These ID Notes then serve as a guide in developing and evaluating the annual individual program plan.

In addition to gathering reports and information from the various service providers, the case manager evaluates the client's functional development level using an instrument called the Client Development Evaluation Report (CDER). This instrument is essentially a list of areas of function referred to as domains and consists of a checklist of abilities in each such domain. An example in the independent living domain is: "Bathing: 1 = does not bathe or shower self, 2 = performs some bathing or showering tasks, but not all, 3 = bathes or showers self independently." By checking off the client's present abilities in each domain, the case manager can get a fairly accurate analysis of the client's functional level. This information is then utilized, along with other documentation, to formulate the IPP.

Underlying this operating framework is the philosophical concept of normalization: "the utilization of means which are as culturally normative as possible, to establish or maintain personal behavior and characteristics which are as culturally normative as possible," taking into account local and cultural values (Wolfensberger, 1972, p. 28). Normalization does not mean that a disabled person will become normal but that he or she will learn to function as normally as possible. By changing the focus from being different from other people to being similar, a developmentally disabled person can become a member of the community rather than being stigmatized or ostracized.

Case Management Practice. The major function of the case manager is to implement the IPP. Since developmentally disabled individuals have a variety of special needs, a single agency cannot provide all the needed services (medical, educational, vocational, recreational, and so forth). Therefore, the service delivery system is the network of specialized and generic services provided by various agencies intended to meet the needs of developmentally disabled people. The regional centers serve as the coordinators of these agencies; regional center case managers have the primary responsibility for conducting interdisciplinary team meetings, gathering and disseminating the data needed, writing the individual program plan, monitoring the implementation of the plan and the progress of the client, providing support, and obtaining and coordinating direct services for the client.

During the planning meeting of the interdisciplinary team, programs to meet the needs of the particular client are developed. The case manager is then responsible for investigating a number of specific programs with the client and/or his or her family to determine which programs can best serve those needs. For example, if the need is for a community living placement, the interdisciplinary team would first determine whether a small family care home, a group home, a large residential facility with specialized services, a skilled nursing facility, or independent living would be most appropriate for the client. If a small family care home is selected, then the case manager and the family would look at location, entry criteria such as sex, age range, and type of disability served, openings, ethnic and cultural factors, language, other services that are available nearby, and so forth. Once the living placement is determined, the case manager would need to prepare the appropriate documentation, provide for funding arrangements, and do whatever else is needed to transfer the client to the new living arrangement (including counseling the client and/or his or her family and providing ongoing emotional support). The case manager must also ensure that the client's rights are not violated by informing the client, the client's family, and the care provider of these rights and then periodically monitoring the program.

If there is need for schooling, the team develops the educational or training program with the client. The case manager then sees that the client is enrolled in an appropriate day program (school, vocational workshop, activity center, or on-the-job training program) and receives any other services that may be needed to address the client's particular needs (such as speech therapy, physical therapy, respite care, and so forth). The case manager then acts as a coordinator, linking all the service providers with the client and his or her family. Coordination involves initiating and sustaining relationshps with the various parts of the service delivery system. A great deal of communication and cooperation is also required to ensure the continued growth and development of the client (Accreditation Council for Services for Mentally Retarded and Other Developmentally Disabled Persons, 1977).

If any conflict occurs between service providers, the case manager must act as mediator. If a conflict occurs between the client and a service agency or if an agency does not live up to its service agreement, then the case manager must act as an advocate for the client. A major, ongoing aspect of individual and class advocacy for the developmentally disabled is to identify gaps in services and to encourage innovative programs. When client needs are not met by the service system, the case manager has the responsibility of speaking for the client—advocating his needs, assisting the client and the client's family in obtaining service, and protecting the client's rights.

As changes occur and progress is made by the client, changes must also be made in the individual program plan and the methods for providing services to the client. Case management is therefore a process that continues throughout the life of the developmentally disabled individual.

Counseling is an important function of the case manager. Ways to resolve periods of stress caused by the various developmental stages of life are jointly explored with the developmentally disabled person and/or the person's family. Counseling may also be needed to enhance social functioning and to develop potential abilities and coping behaviors (Community Services Division, 1980).

In order to practice case management as outlined above, a case manager must understand guiding philosophical concepts such as normalization, the developmental model, and client advocacy as well as be trained in the structured methods and the technical development of program planning. These concepts are not as simple as they may seem. For example, normalization should include: (1) integration of the client into the community rather than segregation away from the community; (2) avoidance of congregating groups of people with special needs in numbers large enough to attract excessive attention; and (3) adoption of positive images, symbols, and language (including matters pertaining to personal appearance and age-appropriate and culture-appropriate dress and activities), to counter social stereotypes and attitudes (Wolfensberger, 1978). Disabled persons should be allowed to take risks by trying new experiences rather than being overprotected out of fear of failure. They should be allowed "to take full advantage of their culture, to have access to the same privileges and amenities as other citizens, to play valued roles, and to lead valued lives" (Wolfensberger, 1978, p. 17).

Family Involvement. In California, parent, family, and client involvement is a significant component in helping developmentally disabled individuals attain their maximum potential. One of the goals in promoting extensive involvement is to help parents and clients become more self-sufficient and more capable of acting as advocates. The California Lanterman legislation addresses the issue of program coordination by clients or family members:

> Nothing shall prevent a person with developmental
> disabilities or such person's parent, legal guardian, or
> conservator, from being the program coordinator of
> the person's individual program plan, if the regional
> center director agrees that such an arrangement is
> feasible and in the best interest of the person with the
> developmental disabilities. If any person listed above
> is designated as the program coordinator, such person
> shall not deviate from the agreed-upon program plan
> and shall provide any information and reports as may
> be required by the regional center director [California
> Welfare and Institutions Code, Section 4648(a), Chap-
> ters 1–11, Division 4.5].

Accordingly, several of the twenty-one regional centers in
California provide training for parents to become program coordinators (case managers) for their own children. These regional
centers are encouraging parents of clients to become equal partners
in obtaining and delivering services to individuals with special
needs. Many parents can function well as case managers since they
know their child best, they know what will work for their child and
their family, and they can provide continuity in planning to
maximize their child's potential. They also have more at stake in
their child's progress and have more time to devote to their child's
programs. The fact that an agency case manager may have seventy
or eighty clients while a parent usually has only one developmentally disabled child is a point not to be overlooked. In addition,
parents trained in case management are better able to obtain
appropriate services and to become stronger advocates for their
children than those parents without training.

The length and content of training may vary, but training
usually consists of two to three hours per week for approximately
ten weeks. One staff member is responsible for the training, but
there may be a series of speakers on different topics ranging from
philosophical concepts, to how to become more assertive with
service providers and governmental agencies, to how to perform
case management duties. The training is also designed to develop
the parents' confidence to advocate for their children by teaching

them their rights, the rights of their children, and what community resources are available.

Upon successful completion of the training, a parent, guardian, conservator, or client may apply to the regional center director to be designated as the official program coordinator (case manager). He or she then has access to all material, supervision, and other resources needed in case management and assumes all of the responsibilities of case management.

The Case Management System for the Developmentally Disabled

The previous discussion illustrated the processes and general tasks involved in a typical case management model in the field of developmental disability. Essentially, the case manager is responsible for developing an appropriate plan with the client and his or her family, assists in securing and making linkages with services, monitors service provision, troubleshoots and provides advocacy and assistance where needed (especially if the developmentally disabled individual is becoming increasingly independent), coordinates services, and evaluates their outcomes for and with the client. The population in need of developmental disability services is quite diverse, ranging widely not only in age but also in degree of impairment. The many developmentally disabled individuals with multiple handicaps also require complex arrangements for services. Together the nature of community-based care and the variety of service needs form another important reason to involve the client and, if feasible, the client's family in case management. The complexity of the case manager's responsibilities is illustrated in Figure 1, which was developed by Lensink (1980, p. 55). The figure illustrates four major types of service and indicates some of the needs in service coordination and case management that a developmentally disabled individual might have.

When the case manager knows what services an individual will need, the central task becomes implementation of the individual plan. This requires management of the three major components of the service delivery system. Figure 2 (Lensink, 1980, p. 61) illustrates the interactions between these major components.

Figure 1. Individual Services for the Mentally Retarded.

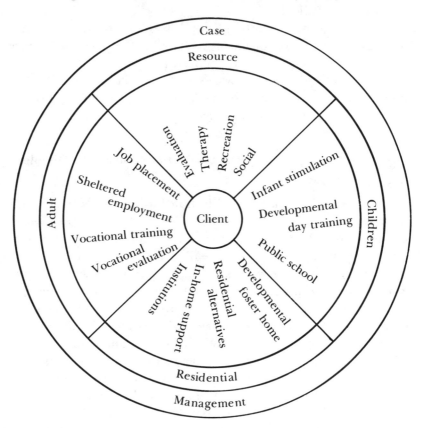

Source: Lensink, 1980, p. 55.

Identifying needs is critical, and priorities of needs must often be established. The thorough assessment of needs involves the collaboration of service providers, clients, parents, and sanctioning and funding sources. Feedback from parents, clients, and advocacy groups is of considerable importance in making the planning process accountable and productive.

Service development and implementation entail carrying out the plan and seeing that the client receives needed services. Since so many services for people with developmental disabilities are provided through purchase-of-service arrangements, it is critical that

Figure 2. The Major Delivery Components.

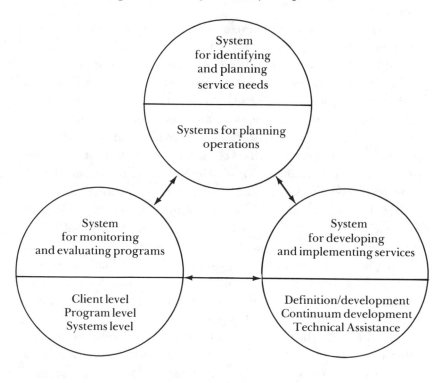

Source: Adapted from Lensink, 1980, p. 61.

the case manager be very specific in service requests and that the client and/or family be well prepared to explain their needs. Agencies having contracts with regional centers are usually committed to specific, behavioral service goals that can be measured and evaluated. When there are purchase-of-service arrangements, it is very important that staff receive training in developing agreements that specify services and in service monitoring. The service is likely to be only as good as the contract that governs it.

Case management also involves collaboration with a variety of agencies and programs. Case management team meetings can be very effective in building cooperation and improving the coordination of services. A responsive service network can also identify gaps in services, note new technology that might be of assistance to developmentally disabled persons, and create new and appropriate services.

Data from various sources are often required to evaluate a program accurately. Attkisson (1978) and others advocate the use of multiple data sources and multiple measures of program results and effectiveness. It is necessary to evaluate services and coordination within the regional center or primary service agency as well as the interaction of agencies and programs that comprise the service network. Clients and parents should be involved in the evaluation process. The standards of the Accreditation Council for Facilities for Mentally Retarded and Other Developmentally Disabled Persons developed in 1978 provide useful guidelines for monitoring and evaluating programs. Lensink (1980) presents an analysis of approaches and data sources needed in evaluations. Any evaluation must include client outcomes, program outcomes and program effectiveness, and program costs and benefits. Evaluation both of individual services and of the total service system is also necessary to provide information and feedback for improving the service system for the developmentally disabled.

Although the working models of case management will differ depending on the scope and responsibilities of organizations and the degree of parental and client involvement, case management has a primary role in providing services to the developmentally disabled.

Least Restrictive Environment and Independent Living. One of the interesting effects of the developmental model and its concept of normalization has been in the area of housing. In the not-too-distant past, developmentally disabled people were either institutionalized or lived with their families throughout their lifetime. Under the concept of normalization, it became acceptable for a developmentally disabled person to leave home during adulthood, as any siblings would, and move into the least restrictive environment feasible in the community.

Programs have been developed to train developmentally disabled individuals for independent or semi-independent living in the community. Living independently enables these people to make choices about their own lives without depending on their families or society. To avoid conspicuousness by grouping together, clients are placed in their own apartments scattered throughout large apartment complexes during the training period (usually about two years). Two or more clients share an apartment and a resident instructor lives nearby.

While in their own apartments, these clients are taught basic living skills such as cooking, menu planning, shopping, budgeting, housecleaning, clothes washing, and personal hygiene, as well as social skills and age-appropriate activities and hobbies. In addition, they are involved in prevocational skills development, career exploration, vocational education, and specific job skills training, ranging from custodial work to restaurant work to nurse's aide work. After graduating from a training program in independent living skills, most clients can seek employment and live together more independently in the community with only periodic follow-up by professional case managers.

Professional Roles and Collaboration

Professional roles and status are important issues to the case manager. A professional case manager in the field of developmental disabilities must have a strong educational grounding in social, behavioral, or life science. Since social work includes training in social policy and community organization as well as in the dynamics of the person in his or her environment, social workers seem particularly suited for case management with the developmentally disabled. It is therefore not surprising that most case managers in California's regional center network have degrees in social work. In addition, social work traditionally includes the concepts of client participation and self-determination, which are also embodied in federal and state law.

As stated previously, case management requires an ability to collaborate with other professionals as part of an interdisciplinary team because developmentally disabled clients require the services of many professionals throughout their lives. These other team members may evaluate the client according to their own professional discipline and expertise and provide follow-up assessments, or they may act as consultants to the case manager, the client, or the client's family. Consultation includes providing services in such a way that families, service providers, and other professionals can provide the needed services themselves. For example, the case manager may consult with a neurologist about anticonvulsant medications for a client with seizures or arrange for the nurse specialist to provide technical assistance in suctioning or feeding techniques to a family.

The case manager must be able to work with professional groups who may have conflicting ideas and ideals as well as personality differences. A medical model of case managment may impose additional role strains because of its focus on deviance or sickness. Under the developmental model of case management advocated here, the focus is on the optimum development of the client, which enhances the role and status of the case manager. The developmental model encourages cooperative methods of aiding the client through understanding and communication among various professionals.

Consumer Advocacy Issues

The Constitution guarantees certain human rights to all people. In addition, persons with developmental disabilities have other rights specified in federal and state legislation. However, most of these rights are not self-enforcing. People must be aware of their rights and speak up in their own behalf. Since most developmentally disabled persons have difficulty both knowing and exercising their rights, they often need an advocate to speak for them and to represent their rights and interests. This function is logically performed by the case manager, whether the case manager is the parent or the professional.

The laws establishing the regional center system require programs to advocate and protect the rights of all developmentally disabled citizens. Although regional centers have a designated "clients' rights advocate" who acts as a consultant to the case manager and who works on problems that may arise, the primary advocate for the developmentally disabled person is the case manager. The parents (or other family members) are also effective advocates for their children, especially if they have been trained in case management. Both the family and the professional case manager should ensure that the client receives the services appropriate to his or her needs.

Although the concept of normalization is incorporated into federal and state legislation for the developmentally disabled, there is still a long way to go to implement normalization fully. Despite all the recent strides in legislation, the provision of services, and the education of the public, stigmatization still exists. The client, the client's family, and the case manager must always be on the alert in protecting the client's legal and human rights and implementing programs that enhance the client's growth and development.

For example, although Public Law 94-142 assures the right to a free and appropriate public education, one cannot assume that this will be guaranteed by a local school district. A case manager must therefore be an advocate for a developmentally disabled client to ensure that the proposed school program is appropriate for that client. This means that the case manager must know the client's functioning levels and must be familiar with local school programs. With that knowledge, the case manager may accompany the client and/or the client's family to the educational planning meeting at the local school district. If an appropriate school program cannot be agreed upon at that meeting, then the case manager will be involved with the appeal process, including testifying, gathering appropriate documentation, counseling the family and clients, and taking steps necessary to ensure provision of the proper services.

All case managers will be involved in the client advocacy just described. However, there is also class advocacy, which many staff are and should be involved in. In the first instance, case managers need to document service delivery problems and work to remedy them through advocacy, revising service agreements, and making changes in organizations, programs, or policies. When clients can express realistic goals, the case manager should assist in achieving those goals; when the client is severely handicapped, impaired, or noncommunicative, the case manager must obtain the services that are in the best interest of the client.

In addition to advocacy within the service system, professionals have the opportunity to train and assist clients, their families, and volunteers in class advocacy for the welfare of persons with developmental disabilities. Prejudice against people with mentally handicapping conditions has not evaporated, and communities and service systems often resist the concept of normalization. Community-based care is far from a universally accepted concept. Case managers need to challenge institutions or residences where the practice and living conditions are harmful to clients. Frequently case managers need to advocate access to and development of more appropriate habilitation services (Herr, n.d.). Issues concerning education, employment, and housing require organized advocacy, as do issues related to civil rights and confidentiality. Advocacy work needs to be geared to improving current conditions and services, but it should focus on future needs just as much. Continued involvement with self-help and parent and citizen advocacy groups can provide a means of charting direction and determining advocacy priorities.

Training and Education Needs of Case Managers

The case manager in services for the developmentally disabled usually has a master's degree in a social, behavioral, or life science and two years of professional experience, including work with developmentally disabled persons. Some service programs may substitute experience for the master's degree. These bachelor-level case managers may be designated differently and receive less pay, and their clients may be less severely impaired.

Besides prerequisite professional education and experience, continuous, organized staff training is necessary "to prepare new employees to perform their assigned duties competently, and to maintain and improve the competencies of all employees" (Accreditation Council for Services for Mentally Retarded and Other Developmentally Disabled Persons, 1977, Standards 4.8). Ongoing staff training includes orientation of new employees, in-service training to keep abreast of expanding knowledge in their field, and supervisory and management training. Training to improve competencies may consist of staff meetings, seminars, conferences, workshops, and college courses; visiting other agencies; participating in professional organizations; conducting research; publishing studies; and having access to a professional library.

Current Problems

The number one problem in the field of developmental disabilities, as well as in other human services fields, is money. Despite the fact that there are legislative mandates to provide certain services, it is often difficult to anticipate the rising costs of providing those services and the needs of an expanding population.

Related to this problem is the current conservative trend throughout the country. Demands for cutting costs and reducing budgets are periodically imposed upon the system without considering the effects on vulnerable clients. These demands are accompanying attempts to change legislation through budgetary means rather than through careful policy studies. Consumers and their representatives must constantly be on the alert to oppose changes in legislation or regulations that can weaken services provided for the developmentally disabled by not granting enough money. A related danger if budget cuts continue is the likelihood of deprofessionalization of staff. The complex needs of the developmentally disabled must be handled by a highly trained and professionally competent staff.

Future Directions

If the current conservative trend continues, the focus in the next few years will be to safeguard the achievements already gained during the last two decades in coordinating comprehensive services for the developmentally disabled. "Without a background of moral and financial support for the variety of programs needed to serve handicapped individuals, no further progress can be made and recent gains will be lost" (Stedman and Wiegerink, 1979, p. 163).

Further budget cuts will increase case managers' caseloads and consequently decrease client contact. Services for clients will be reduced, and the recent strides toward normalization will be difficult to maintain. Program development will be stifled, and the quality of services will probably decline. In other words, the future looks bleak unless the interest and concern of the 1960s and 1970s are revived. To maintain quality of service, consumers and their families as well as professionals need to oppose threats to services.

Vigilance and continued advocacy will be required to maintain the current level of services and to develop new services that persons with developmental disabilities need.

Suggested Readings

Adams, M. *Mental Retardation and Its Social Dimensions.* New York: Columbia University Press, 1971.

Braddock, D. "The Deinstitutionalization of the Retarded: Trends in Public Policy." *Hospital and Community Psychiatry,* 1981, *32* (9), 5–12.

Herr, S. S., Arons, S., and Wallace, R. E., Jr. *Legal Rights and Mental Health Care.* Lexington, Mass.: Heath, Lexington Books, 1983.

Kindred, M., Cohen, J., Penrod, D., and Shaffer, T. (Eds.). *The Mentally Retarded Citizen and the Law.* New York: Free Press, 1976.

Noble, J. H., Jr. "New Directions for Public Policies Affecting the Mentally Disabled." In J. J. Bevilacqua (Ed.), *Changing Policies for the Mentally Disabled.* Cambridge, Mass.: Ballinger, 1981.

Roos, P., McCann, B. M., and Addison, M. R. (Eds.). *Shaping the Future: Community-Based Residential Services and Facilities for Mentally Retarded People.* Baltimore: University Park Press, 1980.

Scheerenberger, R. C. *Deinstitutionalization and Institutional Reforms.* Springfield, Ill.: Thomas, 1976.

Summers, J. A. "The Definition of Developmental Disabilities: A Concept in Transition." *Mental Retardation,* 1981, *19* (6), 259–265.

Wiegerink, R., and Pelosi, J. W. (Eds.). *Developmental Disabilities, the DD Movement.* Baltimore: Paul H. Brookes, Publishing, 1979.

References

Accreditation Council for Services for Mentally Retarded and Other Developmentally Disabled Persons. *Standards for Services for Developmentally Disabled Individuals.* Springfield, Ill.: Joint Commission on Accreditation of Hospitals, 1977.

Adams, M. *Mental Retardation and Its Social Dimensions.* New York: Columbia University Press, 1971.

American Academy of Pediatrics, Committee for the Handicapped Child. *Normalization: A Guide to Services for Handicapped Children.* New York: American Academy of Pediatrics, 1973.

Attkisson, C. C., Hargreaves W. A., Horowitz, M. J., and Sorensen, J. E. (Eds.). *Evaluation of Human Service Programs.* New York: Academic Press, 1978.

Bandura, A. *Principles of Behavior Modification.* New York: Holt, Rinehart and Winston, 1969.

Bandura, A. "Vicarious and Self Reinforcement Processes." In Robert Glassen (Ed.), *The Nature of Reinforcement.* New York: Academic Press, 1971.

Bernstein, C. "Rehabilitation of the Mentally Defective." *Journal of Psycho-Asthenics,* 1919-1920, *24,* 3-12.

Boulding, K. E. "General Systems Theory: The Skeleton of a Science." In W. Buckley (Ed.), *Modern Systems Research for the Behavioral Scientist.* Hawthore, N.Y.: Aldine, 1968.

Bowen, M. *Family Therapy in Clinical Practice.* New York: Aronson, 1978.

Brown, E. G. "Governor's Charge to the Study Commission on Mental Retardation," dated October 30, 1963. In The Study Commission on Mental Retardation, *The Undeveloped Resource.* Sacramento: State of California, January 1965.

Chapman, J. E. "The Developmental Model: A Basis for Social Services Delivery to Developmentally Disabled Persons." Unpublished manuscript, San Bernardino, Calif., March 1979.

Children's Bureau, Social and Rehabilitation Services, U.S. Department of Health, Education and Welfare. "History of Children's Bureau Activities in Behalf of Mentally Retarded Children." In *Historical Perspectives on Mental Retardation During the Decade 1954-1964.* Publication no. 426. Washington, D.C.: Children's Bureau, Social and Rehabilitation Services, U.S. Department of Health, Education and Welfare, 1964.

Community Services Division, Department of Developmental Services, State of California. *Regional Center Operations Manual.* Sacramento: Community Services Division, Department of Developmental Services, State of California, 1980.

Davies, S. P. *The Mentally Retarded in Society.* New York: Columbia University Press, 1959.

Fernald, W. E. "The Inauguration of a Statewide Public School Clinic in Massachusetts." *Journal of Psycho-Asthenics*, 1921–1922, *27*, 25–34.

Germain, C. B. *Social Work Practice: People and Environments.* New York: Columbia University Press, 1979.

Germain, C. B., and Gitterman, A. *The Life Model of Social Work Practice.* New York: Columbia University Press, 1980.

Goddard, H. H. *The Kallikak Family: A Study in the Heredity of Feeblemindedness.* New York: MacMillan, 1912.

Golan, N. *Treatment in Crisis Situations.* New York: Free Press, 1978.

Herr, S. S. "From Rights to Realities: Advocacy by and for Retarded People in the 1980s." Publication no. (OHDS) 80-21026. Washington, D.C.: Department of Health and Human Services, n.d.

Human Relations Agency, State of California. *Lanterman Mental Retardation Services Act* (booklet). Sacramento: Human Relations Agency, State of California, n.d.

International League of Societies for the Mentally Handicapped. "Report of the Frankfurt Conference." *The Record,* June 1971.

Itard, J. M. G. *The Wild Boy of Aveyron.* (G. and M. Humphry, Trans.) New York: Century, 1932.

Kanner, L. *A History of the Care and Study of the Mentally Retarded.* Springfield, Ill.: Thomas, 1964.

Kennedy, J. F. *A National Plan to Combat Mental Retardation.* Washington, D.C.: Government Printing Office, 1961.

Kennedy, J. F. "Message from the President of the United States." *Congressional Record,* February 1963.

Kerlin, I. M. "Editorial." In *Proceedings of the Association of Medical Officers of American Institutions for Idiotic and Feebleminded Persons,* Nos. 11–19, 1888.

Kline, G. "Accomplishments and Immediate Plans in Massachusetts in Community Care of the Feebleminded." *Journal of Psycho-Asthenics,* 1923–1924, *29*, 7–18.

Kübler-Ross, E. *On Death and Dying.* New York: Macmillan, 1969.

Lensink, B. R. "Establishing Programs and Services in an Accountable System." In P. Roos, B. M. McCann, and M. R. Addison (Eds.), *Shaping the Future: Community-Based Residential Services and Facilities for Mentally Retarded People.* Austin, Tex: PRO-ED, 1980.

Leydorf, M. "The Seven Stages." In *We've Been There . . . Can We*

Help? Montclair, Calif.: Ontario Pomona Association for Retarded Citizens, 1978.

Mental Health Services Subcommittee, Assembly Ways and Means Committee, State of California. *A Redefinition of State Responsibility for California's Mentally Retarded.* Mental Health Services Subcommittee, Assembly Ways and Means Committee, State of California, Sacramento, 1965.

Meyer, C. H. *Social Work Practice: The Changing Landscape.* New York: Free Press, 1976.

Minuchin, S. *Families of the Slums.* New York: Basic Books, 1967.

Minuchin, S. *Families and Family Therapy.* Cambridge: Harvard University Press, 1974.

National Association for Retarded Citizens. *Residential Programming for Mentally Retarded Persons.* Arlington, Va.: National Association of Retarded Citizens, 1972.

Nirje, B. "The Normalization Principle and Its Human Management Implictions." In R. Kugel and W. Wolfensberger (Eds.), *Changing Patterns in Residential Services for the Mentally Retarded.* Washington, D.C.: U.S. Government Printing Office, 1969.

Parad, H. J. "Brief Ego-Oriented Casework with Families in Crisis." In H. J. Parad and R. R. Miller (Eds.), *Ego-Oriented Casework: Problems and Perspectives.* New York: Family Service Association of America, 1963.

Parad, H. J. (Ed.). *Crisis Intervention: Selected Readings.* New York: Family Service Association of America, 1965.

Parad, H. J. "Crisis Intervention." In *Encyclopedia of Social Work.* Vol. 1. (16th ed.) New York: National Association of Social Workers, 1971.

President's Panel on Mental Retardation. *A Proposed Program for National Action to Combat Mental Retardation.* Washington, D.C.: U.S. Government Printing Office, 1962.

Perlman, H. H. *Social Casework, A Problem-Solving Process.* Chicago: University of Chicago Press, 1957.

Ross, P. "Misinterpreting Criticisms of the Medical Model." *Mental Retardation,* 1971, *9* (2), 22–24.

Sampson, A. H. "Developing and Maintaining Good Relations with Parents of Mentally Deficient Children." *American Journal of Mental Deficiency,* 1947, *12* (2), 32–41.

Satir, V. *Conjoint Family Therapy.* Palo Alto, Calif.: Science and Behavior Books, 1964.

Satir, V. *Peoplemaking.* Palo Alto, Calif.: Science and Behavior Books, 1972.

Scheerenberger, R. C. *Deinstitutionalization and Institutional Reform.* Springfield, Ill.: Thomas, 1976.

Segal, R. M. *Mental Retardation and Social Action.* Springfield, Ill.: Thomas, 1970.

Silberstein, R. M., and Irwin, H. "Jean Marc-Gaspard Itard and the Savage of Aveyron: An Unsolved Diagnostic Problem in Child Psychiatry." *Journal of the Academy of Child Psychiatry,* 1962, *1* (2), 314-322.

Stedman, D. J., and Wiegerink, R. "Future of Service Delivery Systems for Handicapped Individuals." In. R. Wiegerink and J. W. Pelosi (Eds.), *Developmental Disabilities, the DD Movement.* Baltimore: Paul H. Brookes Publishing, 1979.

Stewart J. A. In *Proceedings of the Association of Medical Offices of American Institutions for Idiotic and Feebleminded Persons,* Nos. 1-10, 1882, p. 236.

Stewart, J. A. In *Proceedings of the Association of Medical Officers of American Institutions for Idiotic and Feebleminded Persons,* Nos. 11-19, 1888, pp. 54-56.

Study Commission on Mental Retardation, State of California. *The Undeveloped Resource: A Plan for the Mentally Retarded in California.* Sacramento: Study Commission on Mental Retardation, State of California, 1965.

Summers, J. A. "The Definition of Developmental Disabilities: A Concept in Transition." *Mental Retardation,* 1981, *19* (6), 259-265.

Talbot, M. E. *Edouard Seguin: A Study of an Educational Approach to the Treatment of Mentally Defective Children.* New York: Bureau of Publications, Teachers College, Columbia University, 1964.

Varela, R. A. "Changing Social Attitudes and Legislation Regarding Disability." In N. M. Crewe, I. K. Zola, and associates, *Independent Living for Physically Disabled People: Developing, Implementing, and Evaluating Self-Help Rehabilitation Programs.* San Francisco: Jossey-Bass, 1983.

Vaux, C. L. "Family Care of Mental Defectives." *Journal of Psycho-Asthenics,* 1934–1935, *40,* 44–56.

von Bertalanffy, L. "General Systems Theory." In N. J. Demerath and R. A. Peterson (Eds.), *System Change and Conflict.* New York: Free Press, 1967.

Wolfensberger, W. "The Origin and Nature of Our Institutional Models." In R. B. Kugel and W. Wolfensberger (Eds.), *Changing Patterns in Residential Services for the Mentally Retarded.* President's Commission on Mental Retardation. Washington, D.C.: U.S. Government Printing Office, 1969.

Wolfensberger, W. *The Principle of Normalization in Human Services.* Toronto: National Institute on Mental Retardation, 1972.

Wolfensberger, W. "The Normalization Principle, and Some Major Implications to Architectural-Environmental Design." Reprint. Georgia Association for Retarded Citizens, Atlanta, October 1978.

Zilboorg, G. *A History of Medical Psychology.* New York: Norton, 1941.

10

<!-- decorative border -->

People with Physical Disabilities and the Independent Living Model

June Isaacson Kailes, Marie Weil

This chapter addresses case management with the physically disabled person as conceptualized and practiced in the unique setting of the Independent Living Center. The center is presented as a social movement springing from civil rights developments in the 1960s. Emphasis is on client self-direction and control in contrast to the more traditional rehabilitation model in which the client is highly dependent on experts. Case management practice is founded on the principle of client self-determination. Hence, case management is the responsibility of the client and is performed by the client to the greatest extent possible. The center's role is to provide relevant training in problem solving and acquiring and using services: Professional case management staff serve as managers only until the client is self-reliant. They then assume a consultive and supportive role. The methods used in this process are described in detail and graphically illustrated.

Public policy is traced from the Vocational Rehabilitation Act of 1918 through many amendments to those of 1973, which gave the greatest incentive to development of Independent Living Centers. The impact of the 1968 Architectural Barriers Act and the 1970 Developmental Disabilities Act is also noted.

Problems in implementing this type of case management system center on agency reaction to assertive self-management. Within the centers, the roles of peer counselors, paraprofessionals, professional counselors, and families are difficult to balance in a philosophy that needs knowledgeable and skilled help but without the elitism and authoritarianism of the medical model.

New variations in case management practice are being developed in a relatively new area of human services: Independent Living Centers (ILCs) serving people with physical disabilities. This chapter traces the history of the social movement for Independent Living (IL), describes the theoretical and ideological base for independent living programs and discusses policy changes affecting people with physical disabilities. General models for case management in ILCs are presented, and the components of specific programs are used to illustrate the range of services needed for a successful program supportive of independent living. The models and approaches in ILCs have a great deal to offer clients and consumers in other human services areas because the IL approach emphasizes consumer participation and decision making with regard to services and care.

Although program emphasis varies considerably throughout the nation within the IL Movement, an ILC can best be defined as "a community-based program with substantial consumer involvement that provides directly or coordinates indirectly, through referral, services severely disabled individuals need to increase their self-determination and to minimize dependence on others" (Frieden, 1983, p. 62). The goal of such programs is to increase the abilities of people with disabilities to control their own lives.

The concept of self-direction and self-control, which is a basic value in the social services (National Association of Social Workers, 1980) and is grounded in the value of self-determination, is nonetheless a relatively new operational concept in work with people with physical disabilities. The IL Movement, in fact, is a developing social movement that challenges the older models for working with people who have disabilities.

Although the IL Movement is a recent development in the human services originating in the 1960s and gaining visibility and momentum in the 1970s, it is a rapidly growing sector. Currently there are approximately 300 throughout the United States.

Case Management in Independent Living Programs

The wide range of disabilities and of severity of disabilities and the resulting range of services needed by people with disabilities indicate the complexity of case management tasks and functions in ILCs. Underlying this considerable diversity of need, however, are several unifying principles for case management practice. At ILCs, decisions regarding goals and objectives are ideally made by the clients themselves rather than service providers. Once clients indicate that they have made a choice to achieve, enhance, or maintain an independent life-style, the ILC provides the support that enables them to live in the community free from the threat of costly and unnecessary institutionalization.

The first priority in case management in this field is to develop independence in the clients. The primary focus of staff, then, is teaching clients to arrange and control their lives efficiently rather than just providing the clients with services. Since many clients may be quite accustomed to assuming a dependent role to receive services, the educational process for self-advocacy and self-determination may sometimes appear slow and inefficient (Nosek, Dart, and Dart, 1981). Staff must constantly weigh when and when not to give assistance. Giving assistance prematurely may ultimately retard the development of the client's own independence.

Case management in the movement is the process of assuring that people with disabilities receive and are able to use the services and opportunities that they need to develop and maintain an independent life-style. The range of services and educational, social, and employment opportunities that are available will depend on the nature and severity of a person's disability. Many consumers will need some combination of medical, rehabilitation, and IL support services. In addition, many people with disabilities seeking to maintain or develop an independent life-style may well need supportive service (assistance with daily life tasks, such as transportation or personal care) and may need specialized employment preparation and placement services. Social and emotional support as well as individual, system, and class advocacy are basic elements in case management for this diverse population.

The answer to the question "Who is the case manager?" in IL settings depends on the client. The IL philosophy stresses that clients who have the ability or potential should be in charge of their own case management. If clients lack this ability, then one goal is to help them get to the point where they have it. Case management skills are important and useful for people with physical disabilities who may intermittently be using supportive IL services throughout their lives. When clients are unable or not yet ready to assume case management responsibility, then a service provider in an ILC typically assumes the role, gradually becoming less involved in decision making and planning as the client becomes more capable of taking over these tasks and responsibilities.

Theoretical and Ideological Base

While independent living as a concept has been defined in a variety of ways, it essentially means control over one's own life. Such control means having a choice "of acceptable options that minimize reliance upon others in making decisions and performing everyday activities. This includes managing one's own affairs, participation in day-to-day activities in the community, fulfilling a range of social roles, and making decisions that lead to self-determination and the minimization of physical or psychological dependence on others" (Frieden, 1983, p. 63). Independent living also implies freedom from social and physical isolation and from institutionalization. Its philosophy and ideology are grounded in people with disabilities having choices and opportunities available. Although many people without disabilities can take the presence of choices and opportunities for granted, choices and opportunities must be created for people with disabilities by changing policies, attitudes, physical structures, and social interactions. The IL Movement is grounded in an ideology that fosters risk taking rather than protection, that supports access and opportunity, and that defines independence in terms of social participation and not just physical mobility. An objective of independent living is to move away from pejorative labeling and a continuum of services based on dependency and toward a range of services based on personal decision making and social integration.

Independent living is an ideology that has spawned both a political movement and a new, nontraditional service delivery system. In the past, rehabilitation professionals were trained primarily to ascertain the degree of disabilities as malfunctions of bodily systems. People who live with physical disabilities know that the actual physical condition is not the most significant problem. The IL Movement has taken a new approach to the problem from an ecological perspective. Basically, the problem is being disabled in our society. This means living in a world as someone who is labeled as "different" and often thought of as abnormal, inferior, or defective. This ecological perspective recognizes that the individual not only must find ways to cope with and physically compensate for the disability but must contend with and overcome such social attitudes and behaviors as avoidance, pity, rejection, overprotection, discrimination, prejudice, and various physical barriers. Being disabled is not just a deficit of the body, it is a complex of social, psychological, and political barriers that people with disabilities must learn to contend with and to change.

The ideology and developing theoretical basis for the IL Model are grounded in three principal concepts that can alter the attitudes and behavior of society and the disabled community regarding physically limiting conditions. Deinstitutionalization, normalization, and mainstreaming are three ideas that support the development of personal choice, decision making, and social integration. Deinstitutionalization refers to the relocation of people with physical disabilities from institutional settings to community living arrangements. It also relates to a philosophical and social concern that moves away from a medical model of treatment for persons with physical disabilities and toward a model of community-based services and supports for independent living. This shift also indicates a rejection by the IL Movement of the medical and rehabilitation models of treatment. This rejection is based on (1) the reality that many physical disabilities are not curable and that the person should not be required to take on a lifelong sick role, (2) a concern for elevating the individual's role in self-care and to deemphasize the authoritarian role of the physician in diagnosis, and (3) treatment. The community model emphasizes self-care—putting the person in charge of her or his own plans and treatment, providing mutual assistance through support groups and providing peer counseling, and developing the individual as his or her own case manager.

The community model emphasizes social services personnel working with clients to foster greater self-reliance in all aspects of life and supports peer counseling as a process of modeling independent living. It postulates that client-consumers of services at an ILC can and should take control of making decisions about and planning their own lives. The use of medical terminology is downplayed, and information about service consumers relates to total functioning and not just physical evaluations (Baum, 1983). Clients are trained in problem-solving processes and assisted to gain maximum functioning with simulations of actual activities. Necessary resources are located throughout the community, and the client (or, where needed, the ILC staff) applies case management techniques to gain access to and monitor her or his own services. Service consumers connected to an ILC will learn, insofar as they are able, to use community resources. The staff emphasizes the educational role and provides assistance as needed.

The ability to use community resources lies at the heart of the concept of mainstreaming, which pertains to moving people with physical disabilities into the full flow of community life. This shift necessarily implies risks and gives rise to the particular set of services that typically comprises the mix offered in ILCs. DeJong (1983), who developed the basic analytic paradigm of the IL Movement, states, "The dignity of risk is the heart of the IL Movement. Without the possibility of failure, the disabled person lacks true independence and the ultimate mark of humanity, the right to choose" (p. 20). DeJong's IL paradigm creates a new way to work with people who have physical disabilities, and that paradigm leads to new ways of solving problems and of viewing these people and redirects ideas about technology. In contrast to the rehabilitation paradigm, which typically defines problems as being in the individual and relating to difficulties in performing activities of daily life, the IL paradigm locates the problem in the person-environment interaction and in notions of dependency. The new paradigm supports the general ideas related to community-based services, supports the consumer role as opposed to the sick role, and supports basic services grounded in advocacy, self-help, peer counseling, barrier removal, and consumer control.

Table 1. A Comparison of the Rehabilitation and Independent Living Paradigm.

Item	Rehabilitation Paradigm	Independent Living Paradigm
Definition of problem	Physical impairment; lack of vocational skill; psychological maladjustment; lack of motivation and cooperation	Dependence on professionals, relatives, and others; inadequate support services; architectural barriers; economic barriers
Locus of problem	In individual	In environment; in the rehabilitation process
Social role	Patient-client	Consumer
Solution to problem	Professional intervention by physician, physical therapist, occupational therapist, vocational counselor, and others	Peer counseling; advocacy; self-help; consumer control; removal of barriers and disincentives
Who controls	Professional	Consumer
Desired outcomes	Maximum ADL; gainful employment; psychological adjustment; improved motivation; completed treatment	Self-direction; least restrictive environment; social and economic productivity

Source: DeJong, 1983, p. 22. Used by permission of the publisher.

History of the IL Movement

A physical disability can be defined as a condition of the body that necessitates specialized support, frequently of a nonmedical nature. Persons with disabilities may be quite healthy, but in the past they have inevitably been cast in a sick or patient role and expected to behave in the dependent ways associated with this role. The medical model has been deeply ingrained in the world of disability. Often people with disabilities have had to be "legitimized" by a doctor who verified that they were indeed disabled. This verification process, dependent on the opinion of a physician, continues to support the notion that people with disabilities are sick, and sick people are (1) exempt from normal social activities and responsibilities, (2) exempt from any responsibility for their illness and often not held accountable for their condition, (3) not expected to become better by sheer will, and (4) obligated to accept society's definition that the state of being sick is not desirable (DeJong, 1983, pp. 14–19).

Because for many people disability is a constant state, there is no getting better; thus there is no getting away from the sick role under the medical model. This role is unacceptable to people with disabilities who are within the IL Movement.

The prevalence of the medical model has been associated with the institutionalization of many people with physical disabilities. Under this model, many healthy individuals have been hospitalized or placed in long-term care facilities because of their physical disability. Quite often, there is no real need for these people to be in institutions. They do, however, need nonmedical support services in order to live successfully in the community.

Historically, before the advent of ILCs, it was nearly impossible to meet these needs outside of institutions. Many people with severe disabilities were forced to live in routinized, other-directed environments, that is, institutions managed by others where decisions were made for people and where personal growth was difficult. The development of a philosophy and a social action movement for independent living grew out of concern for the rights and opportunities of people living with physical disabilities but is rooted in other rights movements, such as the civil rights movement, the consumer movement, the self-help movement, the "de-medicalization" or self-care movement, and the related movements for deinstitutionalization, mainstreaming, and normalization (De-Jong, 1983, pp. 11-20).

During the 1960s, like blacks, antiwar demonstrators, and women, people with disabilities felt dissatisfied, disenfranchised, and discontented. They began to change from being silent and passive to becoming activists about their cause. They began to question their roles as second-class citizens. They began to organize and develop their own ideology.

From the civil rights movement, the incipient IL Movement built its own concerns with both civil and benefit rights and was instrumental in changing public policy on employment and access (DeJong, 1983, p. 12). The campaign to render public buildings barrier free reflects an aspect of basic rights to mobility. Following the organizing for benefits and rights related to the National Welfare Rights Organization, disabled people became more cognizant of benefits that are necessary to support independent living in the community. Benefits of particular importance relate to attendant care, transportation, and income assistance (DeJong, p. 12). From the civil rights movement, members of the disabled community learned techniques of lobbying, court action, campaigning, and protesting such as sit-ins and demonstrations (DeJong, p. 13).

The efforts of black people to achieve social equality and equal rights with an emphasis on "black pride" grew out of the civil rights movement and provided a critical lesson for pioneers in efforts to promote independent living. As blacks indicated that the root cause of their problems was white racism, members of the activist disabled community recognized "that prejudice against disability is rooted in our culture's attitudes about youth and beauty, and in the able-bodied person's fear of vulnerability to physical disability" (DeJong, 1983, p. 12).

The consumer movement has also had a great effect on the social change orientation of the IL Movement. The consumer movement has attempted to clarify and define the rights of consumers of goods and services, which have been expressed most publicly in the work of Ralph Nader and the staff of the Research in the Public Interest Group. The consumer movement sprang from a growing distrust of producers of goods and services because of the questionable quality and safety of products and services. Within the disability community, the consumer movement has spawned a redefinition of service users, from the notion of patients to that of active consumers who are able to assess and make judgments about their own needs and services.

Previously people using rehabilitation and medical services related to physical disabilities were usually subject to the judgment of "experts" in regard to their treatment, supports, and life-styles. Frequently these authorities did not support ideas related or leading to independent living. The consumer movement within the disabled community rather naturally developed a distrust of providers of medical, social, and rehabilitation services. This distrust was almost revolutionary in its challenge to the concept that the provider—that is, the professional—knows best.

The IL Movement began to challenge the sanctity of professional judgment and to encourage people with disabilities to challenge such messages as: "I'm going to tell you how to feel"; "I'm going to tell you what you need to study and what you can be, what your scores indicate, and what you can and cannot do"; and "I'm going to tell you how you are going to live." The challenges to these traditional means of handling people with disabilities were also taken up in the protest against the medical model of treatment and in the developing self-help movement.

The self-help movement and the challenges to the medical model of service delivery counter the traditional notions of passive, dependent patients. The self-help movement emphasizes the active participation by people in their own care and moves away from the older, traditional dictums such as "the doctor knows best," "you need to be taken care of," "you are helpless and thus you need to be a good patient and a good patient waits." The consciousness raising and activism of the various social movements promoted the philosophy that people need to take greater responsibility for their own health and medical care. People, according to these movements, need to question what they are being told (DeJong, 1983).

A final social force that lent impetus to the IL Movement was the social movement for deinstitutionalization and related concerns for mainstreaming and normalization (see Chapter Nine). IL Movement advocates have continually struggled to convince service delivery providers that people can live outside of institutions without a nurse and without a doctor. Employing a personal care attendant in an accessible apartment is an acceptable and adequate option. Independent living is a viable option for many persons with disabilities. Although having a family to assist is helpful, it is not necessary. Concerns for self-determination, development of community-based services, choice, development of skills, and self-care coalesced into a social movement.

On the West Coast, some people feel that the spirit of the IL Movement can be traced back to 1958, when the state of California initiated what today is called the In Home Support Services Program. One hundred and fifteen people who were dependent on respiratory equipment were able to leave Rancho Los Amigos, a large Los Angeles County rehabilitation facility, and live in their own homes. They were given $10 each a day to support a personal care attendant.

The early IL Movement got much of its energy from older adolescents, college-age people, and young adults with physical disabilities. The movement evolved on college campuses, where in the late 1960s and early 1970s more and more people with disabilities were going to school, meeting each other for the first time, and encountering and struggling against an array of physical and attitudinal barriers. Universities including Illinois, Hofstra, Long Island, and the University of California at Berkeley and at Los Angeles developed large programs for people with disabilities. Berkeley, for example, had students with disabilities who attended classes during the day but returned to the hospital in the evening.

The movement grew out of the energies expended by these people. Although they could be independent students and part of the mainstream during the day, this gain was sacrificed at night when they reverted to the role of being a patient. This California group formed the Physically Disabled Students Program, offering services to other students with disabilities on the Berkeley campus. Gradually the program grew into the Center for Independent Living in Berkeley, the first of California's twenty-two ILCs. A similar experience took place almost simultaneously at the University of Illinois. Other programs developed in Boston and Houston (Varela, 1983).

One of the strengths of the movement is that it brought together a whole range of disability groups, not just people with spinal cord injuries, cerebral palsy, or multiple sclerosis. The movement took into consideration issues affecting all people with disabilities and struggled against barriers that all people with disabilities face.

Legislative History and Social Policy

The major goal of the IL Movement has been legislative reform and the establishment of rights for people with physical disabilities. One of the legislative goals was the approval of the Vocational Rehabilitation Act. The early legislation affecting the lives of people with physical disabilities was similar to that affecting people with conditions of mental retardation, mental illness, epilepsy, and sensory impairments. The negative effects of mass institutionalization on this population are described in Chapter Nine. All these categories of people were simply termed defective, and the influence of social Darwinism encouraged the building of large-scale institutions, usually in rural areas, which segregated the unfit from the fit.

The history of the creation of the asylum has been documented by Rothman (1971), Grob (1973), and Wolfensberger (1969), who illustrate the subordination of care and protection for people with physical and mental handicaps to the protection of society from "defectives."

The public view of physical disabilities shifted in response to veterans of World War I who suffered amputations and sensory impairments (Varela, 1983). The difficulties experienced by these veterans touched the lives of thousands of American families—these men could not simply be discarded and classified as unfit. Congress enacted measures, principally the National Defense Act of 1916, to provide veterans with vocational training and in 1917 amended that act to assist disabled veterans. The earliest Vocational Rehabilitation Act was passed by Congress in 1918, and its provisions were broadened in the National Rehabilitation Act of 1920. These acts set the pattern for a federal-state partnership in providing rehabilitation services. When the Rehabilitation Act was amended in 1936 to provide training for people who were blind, another shift in ideology took place. From the earlier emphasis on segregating people with physical and sensory handicaps, the emerging ideology emphasized a belief that such persons could be employed, if not economically self-sufficient, if they received appropriate training.

While these changes created opportunities for some, there were inherent problems in the scope and design of programs (Varela, 1983): (1) Congress became the principal arena for debates about provisions for disability, and (2) the population of people with disabilities far exceeded the available programs, which were geared almost exclusively toward the labor market and focused on the most employable or least disabled. This final aspect, often called "creaming," has remained a problem.

In spite of these problems, the legislative developments also opened opportunities and encouraged advocacy for the physically disabled community. Other expansions of benefits included amendments to the Rehabilitation Act in 1943 that provided limited medical benefits for people in vocational rehabilitation programs. In 1954, additional amendments to the Vocational Rehabilitation Act expanded rehabilitation services, authorized training and research, and allotted modest funds for improving and extending programs. Although much criticized for being underfunded and too restrictive, these amendments also spurred advocacy in the voluntary sector. Disabled veterans of World War II and their families and supporters formed an active constituency for these concerns. Accessibility to public buildings, public transportation, bathrooms, and other business and recreational structures became an important issue, leading to the establishment of the National Commission on Architectural Barriers to the Rehabilitation of the Handicapped in the 1965 amendments to the Vocational Rehabilitation Act. Although these amendments only applied to access to federal facilities, they focused attention on the right to access for the disabled community. This interest culminated in 1968 in the Architectural Barriers Act, which mandated that all facilities using federal funds had to be accessible to disabled people. Unfortunately, the provisions of this act calling for research and compliance activities, as well as later actions of the Architectural and Transportation Barriers Compliance Board (Section 502 of the Rehabilitation Act 1973), were not adequately funded and not stringently enforced. Even following amendments in 1974 and 1978, this board remained underfunded and unable to investigate consumer complaints (Cleland and Elisburg, 1981). The Developmental Disabilities Act of 1970 (discussed in detail in Chapter Nine) covered many people with physical handicaps under the terminology of "severe disability" and spurred action for developing and coordinating services for the underserved and at-risk population.

Lobbying for Independent Living

During the late 1960s, disability advocates lobbied in Washington for the extension and expansion of the Vocational Rehabilitation Program. They were also developing ideas for independent living services and were determined to achieve significant changes in policy. Earlier attempts to include funds for independent living services in the federal funding package in the late 1950s, and in 1961 had failed (Urban Institute, 1975, pp. 4–10).

The extant Vocational Rehabilitation Act was due to expire in 1972, and in that year Congress passed H.R. 3495, which revived the act and offered provisions for independent living services for people whose disabilities were so severe as to render a vocational training program infeasible. A major proponent, Sen. Alan Cranston, stated that the bill would "eliminate the creaming and shift the focus to harder cases in order to serve individuals with more severe handicaps" (Pflueger, 1977, p. 10). It would have been a major step toward developing community-based living and services. President Nixon vetoed the bill twice stating that its passage would undermine the traditional vocational rehabilitation goals of the bill and duplicate existing services. These vetoes galvanized the growing community-based disability service advocates and brought them together as a lobbying force.

In 1973, a compromise was reached. Congress agreed to authorize six research and demonstration projects as part of a Comprehensive Service Needs Study, which while not designated as independent living programs, established projects for community-based services supportive of independent living. The 1973 act thus set into motion a whole new set of service initiatives that affected the lives of the entire disabled population. It broadened the focus of service and mandated that severely disabled people not be bypassed (Varela, 1983). Disability rights activists seized the opportunity offered by the demonstration grants and began to use those funds for seed money for ILCs and for services for the disabled community that were not based on vocational training.

The most visible feature of the 1973 act is Section 504, which prohibits discrimination on the basis of handicap in any program or activity benefiting either directly or indirectly from federal financial assistance. This section is often referred to as the civil rights act for people with physical disabilities, because for the first time it legally recognized people with disabilities as a minority group that needed protection from discrimination. Section 504 has emerged as one of the most controversial and litigated pieces of legislation related to the disabled community (Kailes, 1983a).

The passage of this act broadened the base of advocacy for community-based services, but the essence of the movement continued to be individual choice, the dignity of risk, and the need for self-determination. The Rehabilitation Act of 1973 had several provisions that were vital to the development of the IL Movement. It established a priority of services for the severely handicapped and, through Title V, and the Architectural and Transportation Barriers Compliance Board, extended the legal rights of people with disabilities with regard to employment and public access (DeJong, 1983).

Despite passage of the Rehabilitation Act in 1973, actual administrative policies and practice changed little until disability advocates mounted a major campaign in the spring of 1977. President Carter had issued an executive order demanding that the Department of Health, Education and Welfare (HEW) do two things: issue regulations implementing the 1973 act and set guidelines and regulations for all other agencies that grant federal assistance. This executive order was not carried out, and during that spring hundreds of people with disabilities demonstrated at the HEW offices, at the Capitol, and eventually at the home of HEW Secretary Joseph Califano. Disability advocates filed a class action suit in Washington against Califano to compel him to issue regulations implementing the Rehabilitation Act. When Califano failed to do so, he was held in contempt of court by the district judge. Within a few days of the nationally publicized picketing around Califano's home by disability advocates, he finally issued a set of administrative regulations to implement Section 504 of the act, which banned discrimination on the basis of handicap (Bowe, Jacobi, and Wiseman, 1978). People from disabled communities all over the nation participated in these demonstrations.

Findings of the demonstration studies funded in the 1973 legislation and increased activism by leaders within the disabled community resulted in more favorable treatment of the IL philosophy in 1978 legislation, the Rehabilitation, Comprehensive Services, and Developmental Disabilities Amendments (PL 95-602).

The impact of advocacy by leaders in the disability movement is evident in the 1978 legislation. Two features in particular reflect the ideology of the IL Movement: Congress gave approval to community-based services and required (1) that nonprofit agencies seeking federal grants for ILCs involve "handicapped individuals . . . in policy direction and management of such center[s]" and (2) that such centers employ people with handicaps. These provisions established the IL Movement as a force to be contended with on both national and local levels.

Although this brief history of lobbying efforts and legislation indicates far-reaching advances for the IL Movement, problems remain: insufficient funding, an unwillingness to enforce regulations, and efforts to shift funding to the states in the form of block grants, which would weaken the national lobbying efforts of disability coalitions.

Case Management Models in Independent Living

Case management models for ILCs depend on the particular mix of services needed by members of the disabled community. The services usually needed are presented in Figure 1. All ILCs typically offer the core services shown, and each ILC offers some or all of the services listed under "Other Common Services." In addition, all ILCs are responsible for assisting service consumers in gaining access to and monitoring the community services listed.

Figure 1. Services Needed by People with Disabilities.

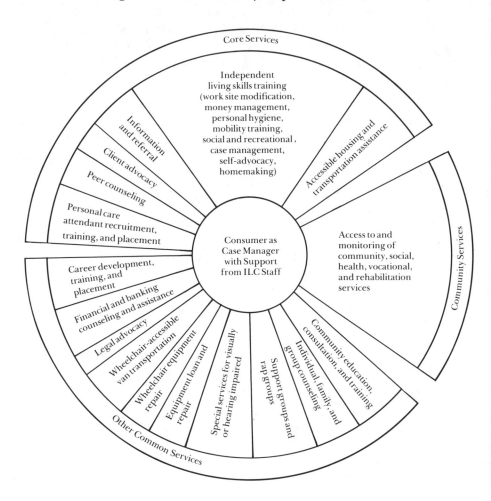

The needs and preferences of service consumers will determine the individual service plans that they will design in collaboration with ILC staff. Independent living service supports are
offered and provided in the community rather than in an institution
and are coordinated by the client and staff of the ILC in a manner
that increases the consumer's knowledge and abilities to make her
or his own decisions about treatment, rehabilitation, and life-style.

The ILC model for service delivery and case management is based on the belief that the individual should become her or his own case manager and advocate. This orientation contrasts sharply with earlier models, which stressed professional expertise and guidance in decision making. Along with the concept of individual self-determination, the IL model calls for consumer control of services; this concept requires ensuring that at least 51 percent of an ILC's board of directors, and a like percentage of the ILC's staff, are people with disabilities. This distribution is considered a means of ensuring that services are indeed accountable to the disabled community and that staff are sensitive to disability issues.

Although clients vary greatly in their ability to assume the rather complex role of case manager, ILCs are committed to helping clients develop these skills. Clients enter ILC programs with greatly differing levels of preparedness. Some fully understand their own goals, interests, and abilities and simply need assistance to attain their goals and obtain support services to live independently.

Older ILCs are seeing an increasing number of clients who have lived in overprotective institutions or homes that did not encourage self-determination. Such programs are also serving more adolescents who are just beginning to be self-directing. These clients need considerable support and training before they can become their own case managers. This move from dependence on staff to self-direction marks the shift from a client mentality to a consumer mentality, the latter involving individual goals and personal choices regarding life-style and vocation. Whatever the previous experience of a new client, the goal of IL program staff is to assist her or him in attaining IL skills. Figure 2 presents the progression of client and staff responsibilities toward independent living; it illustrates increased personal decision making and advocacy and decreased staff involvement in case management.

For each ILC client, a staff member must assess the services and skills needed. The client will take as active a role in this assessment as possible and work out a mutual agreement with the IL staff member for a service plan. The IL staff will either assist in obtaining or directly obtain access to needed services and programs

**Figure 2. Progression of Client and Staff Responsibilities
in an IL Program.**

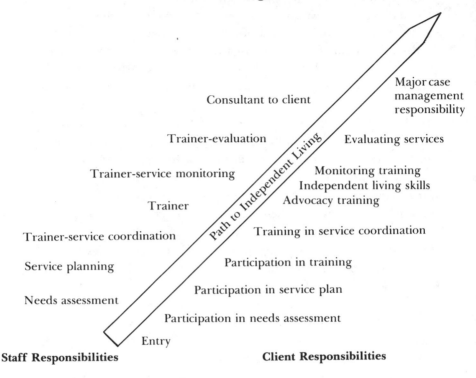

both within and outside of the ILC. Both consumer and staff will be involved in service monitoring and in assessing changing needs or interests. Within the ILC, the client might work with a team of staff members or meet with staff from other community agencies and programs to develop a total service plan to support independent living. If the client is not able or not yet ready to assume the responsibilities for this kind of case management, the staff will assist and provide training until the client can do so. For ILC service consumers, the process of learning to be their own case managers becomes a skill and tool to be used throughout life.

The client-as-case-manager model is complemented by the ILC management system, which must account for the service outcomes for all clients and evaluate service integration. The management of an ILC service system is comparable to the case management system for each client. The service needs for the entire disabled community in the service area must be assessed. This process can be very complex because of the difficulty in locating clients who have been isolated and those who are in long-term care facilities and institutions. Identifying needy clients is itself very complicated because of the range and number of disabilities that people needing ILC services may have. In addition to identifying the needs in the community, existing services and service gaps must also be determined. When services are coordinated through an ILC, participating agencies may have to work with clients, peer counselors, and ILC staff differently than they had in the past. This is particularly true for staff of a department of vocational rehabilitation, whose standards for clients eligible for vocational and skills development programs may be quite unlike the standards set by ILCs and their clients. In fact, advocacy for needed services and renegotiation of service delivery may be necessary.

After the needs have been assessed, the case management process moves within the ILC. A service plan is developed with clients enabling them to use particular services offered by the ILC and the community. Service planning and changing the ways other programs interact with clients form a major part of case management for both the client and the staff. If the ILC contracts out for particular services, such as attendant care or wheelchair-accessible van transportation, consumer feedback as well as staff evaluation of the services is critical. Because many ILC clients will be inexperienced, it is important that the ILC staff monitor services and teach clients how to monitor and evaluate services themselves.

Program evaluation by clients and staff completes the cycle of case management and leads to a new round of specifying needs and identifying problems in the service network for people with physical disabilities. Figure 3 presents a general model for class management for clients of an ILC. Any of the levels of client participation shown at the left of Figure 3 may apply throughout

Figure 3. Case Management Model for Clients of ILCs.

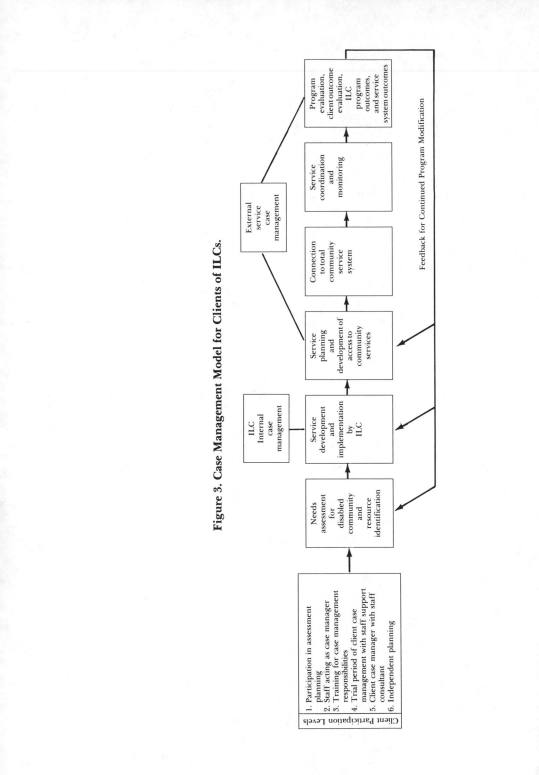

the case management process. Levels are numbered sequentially from the lowest to highest client involvement.

Independent Living Programs

According to a survey of 450 programs providing independent living services (residential, transitional, and nonresidential) conducted in 1978 by the Independent Living Research Utilization (ILRU) Project, only 35 programs actually fit the strict definition of consumer control (Frieden, 1983, p. 63). According to this definition, centers are controlled by consumers when over 51 percent of the board of directors and staff are people with disabilities. These findings indicate that the ideal ILC model is not yet prevalent. Yet the large number of programs providing some IL services grew remarkably in a short period of time. The three basic types of programs will differ in emphasis, but each requires attention to case management processes within the program and in the external service network.

A residential program is a live-in program that provides and coordinates attendant care, transportation, and a variety of other services. The Boston Center for Independent Living (BCIL) offers a residential program staffed by two full-time people. A transitional program is one that helps clients and people with disabilities move from rather dependent life-styles to independent living situations. Training in a variety of independent living skills is offered. A nonresidential program coordinates a variety of services for clients who live in the community.

An example of a transitional program is Rolling Start's transition living centers in San Bernardino, California. The program offers an environment for learning about, exploring, and experiencing independent living. The average client stays approximately six months. The models focus on deficient skills in areas such as attendant and financial management, socialization, and personal care. The lack of skills in attendant management and budgeting often results in institutionalization or long-term hospital care; thus, it is important that people with disabilities have expertise in the management areas.

The BCIL also conducts transitional programs in integrated residential developments in the Boston area. Two models are used, one in which participants handle their own transition to dwelling units in the community and one in which staff initially live in program units and move after the program is completed while the clients remain in the apartments. Both programs offer physical and occupational therapy and training in independent living skills.

An example of a nonresidential consumer-controlled program is the Westside Community for Independent Living (WCIL) in Los Angeles. The WCIL is one of the largest ILCs in the nation. The WCIL has three offices staffed by approximately forty employees who serve more than 1,000 people per month. It offers a full range of service programs to meet the needs of people with a wide variety of disabilities in all age groups. The programs offered are representative services needed by users of independent living services. These program components are typical of many ILCs.

Personal Care Attendant Recruitment and Placement. The ability to perform the basic activities of daily living—bathing, dressing, shopping, and cooking—are beyond the physical limitations of a substantial number of people with disabilities. This service enables people to maintain their independence by providing them with attendants who can give personal assistance in the clients' own homes. The WCIL recruits, screens, and refers attendants; advises clients about issues in paying for personal care attendants; and maintains a registry of volunteers available to read for people who are blind or visually impaired. Clients are responsible for hiring and paying their attendants.

Accessible Housing Information. The WCIL maintains up-to-date information on available, affordable housing by working closely with city and county housing authorities, landlords, and property managers. This program also provides information on housing subsidy programs.

Client Advocacy and General Advocacy. Advocates in the WCIL assist clients in obtaining benefits and services through various agencies, particularly the Social Security Administration and the Department of Rehabilitation; arrange for legal representation for clients; assist clients in the transition to the working world; promote the development of client self-advocacy skills; and assess the financial needs of clients and advise them on managing their money. General advocacy involves speaking for the needs of the total population and working for administration and policy changes.

Peer Counseling. Professional peer counselors who have a disability work with individuals, families, and groups. Direct-support and peer rap groups are also held. Clients learn to deal with personal and social adjustment, sexual concerns, interpersonal relationships, and other matters of independent living.

Information and Referral. The WCIL matches clients with disabilities with useful resources in the community, maintains files on agencies and equipment suppliers, and maintains a reference library.

Independent Living Skills Training. The WCIL helps clients improve their skills in personal hygiene, grooming, dressing, homemaking, community mobility, and social and recreational activities. Services are provided at the WCIL, in clients' homes, in the community, and at job sites.

Wheelchair-Accessible Van Transportation. The WCIL provides clients with transportation to and from its offices. Priority is given to those people with the most severe mobility impairments.

Community Education. Through educational programs for the general public and for human service professionals, the WCIL seeks to educate and sensitize the nondisabled community to the needs of persons with disabilities. One major focus of community education is to change the negative and demeaning stereotypes that are built into our language, from the word *handicapped* to such phrases as "confined to a wheelchair" (Kailes, 1984). The development of more positive images and nonstereotypical language is a significant task in community education. To promote more accurate and less stigmatizing language, the IL Movement discourages the use of such expressions as "wheelchair bound" or "cripple." It is, after all, only from the perspective of a nondisabled person that a wheelchair is a confinement or that a disability is seen before the person. In the view of members of the IL Movement, a person *uses* a wheelchair and is not bound to it. In fact, the wheelchair provides mobility and greatly increases freedom. A major effort in the public education campaign of the IL Movement is to change the public perception from a "cripple" to a person with a disability.

Computer Training Project. This WCIL project trains and finds jobs for people with disabilities as computer programmers. It combines the expertise of both rehabilitation professionals and the business community to prepare its students. The data processing field pays high salaries and offers excellent opportunities for advancement, giving persons with disabilities stable incomes and the potential for career growth.

Community Volunteer Program. The WCIL provides opportunities for community members to participate in direct client services, fund-raising activities, and special projects. Volunteers contribute at least four hours a week, and orientation and training are provided. The program emphasizes providing prevocational work experience to volunteers with disabilities.

The three basic types of program centers (residential, transitional, and nonresidential) are similar in several significant ways (Frieden, 1983, p. 65). They are all community based, involve consumers, and provide services designed to foster independent living for people with disabilities. However, they differ with regard to the extent of consumer control. Many have substantial consumer involvement without having consumer control (Frieden, 1983). "These differences may seem subtle and unimportant to the uninitiated observer. In fact, however, these differences are extremely significant, often prompting heated debate among supporters of Independent Living" (Frieden, 1983, pp. 65–66). Many leaders and founders of the movement argue that ILCs must be controlled by consumers. Others argue that consumer involvement on a lesser scale is adequate. Some founders of the movement hold that residential programs are institutional, segregated, and reflect the ghettoization of people with disabilities. Other leaders argue that residential programs provide important alternatives to institutionalization for people with severe disabilities and represent one point on a continuum of independent living services.

Another controversy centers on the charge that transitional programs are simply residential programs in disguise and are too much like traditional rehabilitation programs. According to this argument, transitional programs do not offer the necessary long-term support that is needed by people with disabilities in order to live productively in the community.

Such disagreements about service models reflect the vitality of a growing and changing IL Movement.

Practice Issues

Various issues are emerging in case management practice in IL programs. The very newness of the IL Model and the altered relationships between agencies elicit questions on how to improve service delivery and how to maximize the service consumer's role as a case manager. How will older, established agencies react to assertive self-management by the clients? How should ILC staff train service consumers to be their own case managers? Where full or major client responsibility seems infeasible, what should the nature of case management partnership between staff and consumers be? What is the best role for the peer counselor, and how should peer counseling be defined? What is the appropriate role for paraprofessional and professional counselors. Issues of service network integration and collaboration also come up.

There are various ways to deal with the issues concerning case management and direct service delivery. The three basic program types identified by Frieden (1983) must work out different solutions based on the chosen model and particular community conditions. Pflueger (1977) identifies the primary variables to be considered in tailoring an IL program to community needs as:

1. *Service setting.* Should the program be nonresidential or residential?
2. *Service delivery method.* Should services be provided by the IL program directly, contracted for by the IL program, or handled indirectly through referral?
3. *Helping style.* To what extent should consumers and other people with disabilities provide help? To what extent should the program rely on peer counseling or a mutual self-help approach? To what extent should professionals with or without a disability provide services and counseling?
4. *Vocational emphasis.* How much of a role should vocational preparation and training play in the IL program?
5. *Goal orientation.* Is the program geared to long-term case management or a short-term transitional process?
6. *Disability type served.* Should the program serve a specific category or set of disability categories? Should it be designed to

serve people with all types of physical disabilities? Should it serve people with developmental or emotional disabilities?

Each new program must be designed to fit its own community. These variables and the variety of possible service approaches underscore the importance of a careful assessment of needs and resources for people with disabilities in each locale.

Two central case management issues will apply regardless of the model used for a program: first, the nature of the case management partnership between consumers and staff and the means of training consumers to be their own case managers, and second, how peer counseling and professional counseling is balanced, that is, the extent to which professional counseling is used. The role of the staff person as educator has frequently been overlooked or taken for granted in professional human services training programs. Teaching someone how a service system operates and how to secure access to services is not a simple task. Each type of disability or combination of multiple disabilities requires a particular service network, which increases the complexity of case management. Although many clients may need two or three primary services, their other needs and interests will require social, health, rehabilitation, recreational, and vocational services of a community. The teaching role in IL programs is even more challenging because of the movement's special emphasis on training consumers in case management and advocacy skills. Finding ways to teach clients to use complex service systems is difficult in itself, but the difficulty is compounded because many clients who want to develop independent living and case management skills have previously been denied even basic training in decision making and planning by overprotective institutions and families. This special teaching function must be carried out by staff, peer counselors, or volunteers in very concrete and supportive ways.

The role of peer counseling in the IL movement is also a multifaceted issue. Early in the movement, great emphasis was placed on peer counseling in its basic form; that is, a person with a disability who has developed and maintained an independent lifestyle through an IL program helps others do the same. Life experience as a person with a disability is the primary qualification for peer counseling in ILCs. At the present time, however, "peer counseling" seems to have taken on several meanings. The peer counselor may be a volunteer who has been a client of the IL program, a paraprofessional staff member, or a professional staff member who has a disability.

The concept of a peer counselor as a role model has been a primary component in the case management and service delivery model for IL programs. Such counseling experience has a tutorial rather than a therapeutic purpose (Kailes, 1983b). Individual- or group-focused peer counseling has been designed to be a supportive experience that offers service consumers an opportunity to "compare notes" on such issues as how to handle driving or bathing or how to work with an attendant (Kailes, 1983b). In this situation, a peer counselor is generally a person with a disability who has achieved a substantial level of independent living and a sound emotional adjustment to his or her physical disability. In some cases, the peer counselor might not have a disability but be closely involved with someone (a child, spouse, or parent) who does (Kailes, 1983b).

Selecting and screening peer counselors is of extreme importance. Having a disability in itself does not qualify someone as an effective peer counselor. As in other peer support programs (such as drug abuse counseling), the counselor must have moved beyond concern with her or his own situation and be emotionally and intellectually able to teach, assist, and support others. The peer counselor must recognize that although many people may have similar reactions to a disability, there will be significant differences and varying approaches to assuming more responsibility for case management.

Possessing the basic qualities needed to develop helping relationships—warmth, genuineness, and empathy (Truax and Carkhuff, 1967)—is essential for effective peer as well as professional counseling. Screening for these abilities as well as other skills and attitudes has proven effective in selecting peer counselors (Kailes, 1983b). It is important to assess potential peer counselors' reasons for being interested in such a program and their reactions to their own disabilities and their relations with others who have physical disabilities.

Areas covered in the training of peer counselors should include the following: history of the IL Movement and the peer counseling model, dealing with feelings, maintaining confidentiality, developing rapport and supportive relationships, verbal and nonverbal communication with an emphasis on the effects of physical disability on communication patterns, respect for clients and their world views, development of self-awareness and the ability to be nonjudgmental; counseling skills, conducting counseling sessions, collaboration with one's own and other agencies and case management and service coordination, problem-solving techniques, developing plans and goals, relating to families and natural support systems, sexuality, and managing the counseling relationship.

The peer counseling role has been particularly important because the IL Movement has emphasized moving away from the medical and rehabilitation models. A major part of the need for a new model was the conviction that traditional, professionally based medical, rehabilitation, and social services had not been responsive to or supportive of the goals of independent living (Whitaker, Rochman, and Tso-Kosheri, 1984). Reliance on the self-help, self-health-care, and consumer movements was based partly on a distrust of service providers and a definite rejection of the idea that the provider knows best. However, because of the complexity of coordinating service needs for the disabled community, professionals must be involved in counseling, service coordinating, and administration.

The experience at WCIL illustrates the reintegration of professionals into the IL model while still focusing on self-determination by service consumers. Three factors spurred the employment of professionally trained counselors who themselves have physical disabilities instead of continuing to rely on the peer counseling model. It became painfully apparent that many entering clients had complex mental health difficulties. Complex disability and service integration problems had been anticipated, but the more difficult issues involved emotional and mental health. Although the well-trained peer counselors were equipped to deal with service needs and setting goals, they could not be expected to cope with emotional problems ranging from stress to psychosis and substance abuse. Consequently, the WCIL deployed two professionally trained counselors in response to this need. The professional counselors, freed from major supervisory and training responsibilities, could see more clients and deal more effectively with the range of emotional and mental health issues presented by consumers.

A problem that occasionally occurs with peer counselors or paraprofessionals is that their aspirations increase with their skills. Volunteer or low-paying work becomes less appealing as opportunities for more lucrative employment arise. The WCIL experience demonstrates the need to clarify roles and expectations. The roles of volunteers, paraprofessionals, and professional counselors should be clearly defined. Peer support, peer tutoring and assistance, and counseling on concrete service, planning, and life adjustment issues are reasonable duties for volunteer peer counselors. Complex mental health and emotional problems require professional intervention. Because of the specific issues pertaining to the interaction of mental health problems and physical disabilities, the WCIL found it best to have professional counselors who have themselves adjusted to living with a physical disability or sensory impairment. In fact, the IL program staff can be of immense assistance to the entire mental health practice and education community in documenting and exploring the complexity of functional and dysfunctional mental and emotional responses to disability.

Training and Education for Case Management in IL Programs

In training a new employee (or volunteer) for an IL program, an extremely important characteristic is whether the person has a disability or a close relationship with someone who does. All staff need to understand and subscribe to the philosophy of independent living and understand the methods for translating the philosophy into practice. Most new staff will also need training in methods of advocacy and means of assisting service consumers to become their own advocates.

New staff in IL programs generally fall into four categories: (1) previous volunteers; (2) graduates of human services, social work, or rehabilitation programs who have a disability or a special commitment to working with people with disabilities; (3) staff from a traditional rehabilitation, health, or human services program who want to be involved in the IL Movement; or (4) individuals with a particular interest in working with people who have disabilities.

Training needs for these four groups will differ. The training needs of peer counselors who are promoted to staff positions center on developing skills to deal with emotional problems and varying reactions to disabilities. Graduates of professional programs need a thorough grounding in IL philosophy, counseling, and case management practices. New staff coming from more established settings such as hospitals or nursing homes often have rather traditional approaches to client management and sometimes find the IL approach difficult to integrate into practice. They may need intensive training and supervision before they can use the IL Model effectively. All staff members must learn when to help clients help themselves and when to lend support or assistance.

In the early years of the IL Movement, a number of service and academic professionals with disabilities as well as other people with disabilities provided significant leadership in policy making and program development. Within IL programs, however, little emphasis was placed at first on academic or professional credentials. A distrust of professionalism within the movement was the major reason. Service orientation and commitment to the IL Model were the primary principles. For the movement to maintain its strength, that philosophical commitment must be maintained. However, as the movement develops and as programs grow and become more sophisticated, more emphasis will likely be placed on professional knowledge and skills needed for program and case management, intervention in mental health and emotional problems, and case and class advocacy. The trend at present seems to be for larger centers to have more staff who are peers in that they have disabilities but who also have specialized education in counseling or social work.

If this trend holds, it will be important for professional schools to incorporate the philosophy of the IL Movement and its case management methods into their curricula. Much of the IL approach is compatible with the value that counseling and social work place on client self-determination and client advocacy. In fact, the IL ideology could strengthen teaching methods in these areas.

In addition, professional schools need to give more attention to the effects of physical and developmental disabilities on individuals and their family systems and to investigate the interactions between physical disabilities and emotional responses. Finally, IL programs should encourage gifted staff to enter professional training programs so that leadership in programs and services can be maintained with the disabled community. Professional schools should not only include more counseling and case management issues related to independent living in their curricula but also actively recruit people with disabilities into their programs. A basic goal of IL programs is to increase the number of people with disabilities occupying staff and decision-making positions.

Consumer Advocacy

In spite of the clear intent of Congress in passing the 1973 Rehabilitation Act, the status of people with disabilities remains uncertain, in large part because recent federal administrations have been reluctant to enforce the new laws. There are also signs of a public backlash against increasing opportunities for the disabled community. After an initial period of little opposition to improved physical access to buildings, rights, and programs for people with disabilities, the nation seems to have entered a period of increased doubt, particularly over the cost of making the physical environment more accessible to people with disabilities. Given the widespread retrenchment in government expenditures for social programs, people with disabilities are finding themselves increasingly on the defensive during the 1980s (DeJong, 1980).

Independent living programs have always faced a dilemma in how much time to spend on advocacy activities and how much on basic service delivery, since either could absorb all available resources. But that dilemma has become increasingly intense. It is difficult to find the most workable approach to both movement advocacy and service provision. Our "society has traditionally used an extensive and sophisticated program of psychological, physical, and economic threats, punishments, and barriers combined with rewards that force people with disabilities into segregated situations and subservient roles" (Nosek, Dart, and Dart, 1981). It remains critical for IL programs as well as others in the disability rights movement to devote a portion of their resoures to client and public education and client and class advocacy in order to abolish these disincentives to independent living (Nosek, Dart, and Dart, 1981).

Broadly speaking, the central advocacy issues include, but are not limited to, the following concerns:

1. *Changing the focus of government benefit programs and policies from caring for people with disabilities in institutions toward maintaining them as productive, functioning members of the community.*

2. *Removing work disincentives that people with disabilities experience when attempting to return to or begin work.* Financial and policy disincentives continue to block many members of the disabled community from returning to work and consequently restrict people to a very small economic base. Because of the tremendous expenses for care and medical treatment that many people with severe disabilities incur, these individuals must be allowed more income without losing Social Security benefits. Entitlement programs need to be made more flexible and responsive to people with disabilities who want to live and work in the community.

3. *Making the environment accessible.* Now that building codes, regulations, and laws that have accessibility requirements exist, enforcement is needed at all levels of government. In addition, accessible transportation must be provided to support community-based independent living. Transportation remains one of the major advocacy issues facing the IL Movement. In addition to accessible public transportation, people with mobility impairments need para transit (that is, pickup service to take people from their homes or institutions to fixed-route public transportation) and transportation systems in rural areas.

Advocacy in these areas will need to be supported with continual efforts to develop policies and programs supporting independent living. One basic goal is to create a viable political force. In addition to political advocacy, it is crucial for the IL

Movement and its programs to maintain their commitment to individual client advocacy and class advocacy for the disabled community. Constant attention to evolving advocacy issues is necessary for the survival of IL programs and for the increased welfare of members of the disabled community.

Professional Roles and Collaboration

Issues relating to the appropriate roles and relations between professional and paraprofessional staff were presented earlier in the chapter. However, there is a need to clarify functions and responsibilities for each group. Although there is a continuing need for peer counseling in IL programs, the increasing sophistication of programs and the need to deal with complex mental and emotional problems necessitate increased involvement of professional staff. For ILCs, in addition to employing professional staff who either have disabilities or have a real sensitivity to them, it is necessary to ensure that professional staff do not assume an elitist attitude toward paraprofessionals and peer counselors. This sensitive issue needs to be dealt with in recruitment and selection and therefore in training, teamwork, and supervision (Whitaker, Rochman, and Tso-Kosheri, 1984).

In the past, ILCs and professional communities in general have felt threatened by and competitive toward each other. Competition was based on attracting and keeping clients. Some reasons why traditional rehabilitation services did not wish to establish strong links with ILCs were the following: (1) a sense that ILCs were ineffective and a low regard for ILCs because they were not professional organizations; (2) the "pigeonhole effect," that is, a difficulty of some rehabilitation professionals in dealing with a person with a disability as other than a subservient patient; and (3) the ambivalent feelings that rehabilitation professionals sometimes have when hearing positive feedback from clients about ILCs (Kailes, 1983c). Reports of the beneficial effects of ILCs can be a frustrating reminder of the ineffectiveness and fragmentation of services that rehabilitational professionals encounter.

On the other hand, ILCs may avoid stronger links with

rehabilitation and other professionals because of a reluctance to give up any autonomy and the strong distrust that many ILC founders had of inadequate, inappropriate, or unsuccessful service interventions. Although the strength of these negative responses has abated, more productive collaboration is still needed (Kailes, 1983c).

In order to build more mutual support and collaboration between ILCs and traditionally based rehabilitation and human services agencies, the sense of competition over clients must be eliminated or at least reduced. In addition, ILC staff and other professionals need to talk with each other, to examine the nderlying fear that one group is going to take over the other group, and to be more open with and trusting of each other, increasing communication and respect. Staff members of ILCs also need to remember the basic movement principle of channeling rage toward constructive service change, which includes building more collaborative interprofessional communication and service delivery.

Improving communication and collaboration includes sharing in-service training programs, involvement in feedback and monitoring of each other's service components, sharing research and technical expertise, use of each other as consultants for improving programs, and seeing that members of each group serve on the other's advisory boards and task forces. Creating opportunities to work together and to focus on the well-being of clients and the target population can help in developing more productive methods of collaboration.

Current Issues and Future Directions

Over the last decade "the Independent Living Movement has grown from a small band of people with disabilities struggling for simple rights to a significant political force shaping the future of disability policy" (DeJong, 1983, p. 25). ILCs as dynamic experiments in human development have recorded impressive results during this period (Independent Living Research Utilization, 1982, p. iii). The movement has given people with disabilities a significant voice in their own future and has engendered a new sense of worth, dignity, and pride that for too long was denied people with disabilities. On the basis of an extensive empirical study and projected growth rates, Frieden (1983) has predicted that by 1985 there will be about half a million people with disabilities living more independent and self-determining lives by participating in community-based IL programs. This projected growth will inevitably produce challenges and changes. ILCs as a new and important nontraditional service delivery system will face a number of challenges in the future. Many of these challenges have been discussed in this chapter, and several will be highlighted here.

The collection of nationwide data and outcome measures for ILCs is becoming increasingly urgent as programs must justify their existence. Funding cutbacks in federal social programs endanger the evolution of IL programs. Careful program research and evaluation can be used to document the benefits of ILCs and to at least maintain current funding levels. A sophisticated nationwide evaluation and data collection system can be used to justify increased federal funding for all ILCs.

The federal administration of the 1980s and the downturn in the economy have both delayed the advancement and expansion of IL programs. Policies to contain social program costs have hurt IL programs, which are not yet part of the mainstream of social programs. Federal and state funding bases need to be institutionalized throughout the nation.

To deal with this adverse climate, the movement and individual programs will need to make a variety of changes and take bold steps to maintain programs and increase service to the disabled community. Programs may have to institute fees for services that were previously supported by tax funds. In addition, ILCs will need to develop aggressive marketing programs like those already employed by health maintenance organizations. Under such a revamped funding structure, an ILC client could be eligible to receive a wide range of IL services for either a monthly or annual fee based on a sliding scale. Another way to handle increased costs is to increase the billing to insurance companies for ILC services for individual clients. The chief risk in shifting to fee for service or insurance coverage is that many lower-income clients and clients dependent on government benefit programs will not be able to afford the full range of services needed to maintain independent living.

Alternatively, ILCs might move more into economic development beneficial to clients and programs. For example, they might develop client-run or agency-run profit-making businesses, such as wheelchair repair and sales, custom van modification, and home health services. They might also develop other programs, services, or businesses that are not disability related. The risks of such programs are a displacement of the original service goals and the basic hazards that economic development corporations face which lack high levels of risk capital. The experiences of successful and unsuccessful community development corporations founded as part of the social programs of the 1960s can provide valuable lessons to ILCs entering these entrepreneurial areas.

ILCs will have to enter the world of charitable fund raising and competitive foundation and government grants. To maintain the positive focus of the IL Movement, it will be necessary to pursue funding and grants without engendering guilt, sympathy, or fear toward people with disabilities. The IL Movement has already illustrated that disability can be presented constructively when the dignity of the individual with a disability and the collective strength of the disabled community are stressed.

As the movement grows larger, ILCs are rapidly shedding their grass roots beginnings and developing a more professional image regarding the structure of their service delivery, their forms of case management, and staff expectations of competitive salaries, training, and benefits packages. This is a natural result of growth, but it is also a struggle. Can these changes take place without endangering the unique qualities of an ILC? The fear is that these changes could turn ILCs into just another part of the social services bureaucracy.

Formalization of organizational structure and professionalization of staff are characteristic of all organizations as they move through the stages of the organizational life cycle (Kimberly, 1980). However, these changes are more difficult for organizations that develop out of a social change movement. Institutionalization may—and does in the IL Movement—raise fears of the loss of the original sense of purpose and a displacement of goals, as well as the fear that organizational survival transcends concerns for client welfare. To maintain its vitality, the IL Movement will have to preserve its central mission to promote independent living by developing internal and external structures and employing professionals that support this mission.

Such vigilance is a form of internal advocacy within IL programs. Continued client advocacy through sound case management, legal class advocacy for the disabled community, and political advocacy for the IL Movement and its programs will be required to maintain the gains made for people with disabilities.

Suggested Readings

Brightman, A. J. (Ed.). *Ordinary Moments: The Disabled Experience.* Baltimore: University Park Press, 1984.

Crewe, N. M., Zola, I. K., and associates. *Independent Living for Physically Disabled People: Developing, Implementing, and Evaluating Self-Help Rehabilitation Programs.* San Francisco: Jossey-Bass, 1983.

Rehabilitation Gazette.

Varela, R. A. *Self-Help Groups in Rehabilitation.* Washington, D.C.: American Coalition of Citizens with Disabilities, 1979.

A computerized list of all Independent Living programs is available for $10.00 from the Institute of Independent Living Research Utilization, Texas Institute of Rehabilitation and Research, 133 Moursurd Avenue, Houston, Texas 77030.

References

Baum, S. "Two Perspectives on Rehabilitation Practice in Physical Disabilities." Paper presented at the American Occupational Therapists Association Conference, Chicago, April 1983.

Bowe, F. G., Jacobi, J. E., and Wiseman, L. D. *Coalition Building.* Washington, D.C.: American Coalition of Citizens with Disabilities, 1978.

Clark, G. M., and White, W. J. *Career Education for the Handicapped: Current Perspectives for Teachers.* Boothwyn, Pa.: Educational Resources Center, 1980.

Cleland, M., and Elisburg, D. Statements for the oversight hearing on the Architectural and Transportation Barriers Compliance Board, given before the Subcommittee on Select Education, House Committee on Education and Labor. 97th Cong., 1st sess., June 31, 1981, pp. 2–22, 88–114.

Dart, J. W., Jr., Dart, Y., and Nosek, P. "A Philosophical Foundation for the Independent Living Movement." *Rehabilitation Gazette*, 1980, *23*, 16–18.

DeJong, G. "The Historical and Current Reality of Independent Living: Implications for Administrative Planning." *Proceedings of the Policy Planning and Development in Independent Living.* East Lansing: University Center for International Rehabilitation, Michigan State University, 1980.

DeJong, G. "Defining and Implementing the Independent Living Concept." In N. M. Crewe, I. K. Zola, and associates, *Independent Living for Physically Disabled People: Developing, Implementing, and Evaluating Self-Help Rehabilitation Programs.* San Francisco: Jossey-Bass, 1983.

Dybwad, G. *Is Normalization a Feasible Principle of Rehabilitation? Models of Service for the Multihandicapped Adult.* New York: United Cerebral Palsy of New York City, 1973.

Frieden, L. "Understanding Alternative Program Models." In N. M. Crewe, I. K. Zola, and associates, *Independent Living for Physically Disabled People: Developing, Implementing, and Evaluating Self-Help Rehabilitation Programs.* San Francisco: Jossey-Bass, 1983.

Frieden, L., Richards, L., Cole, J., and Bailey, D. *ILRU Source Book: A Technical Assistance Manual on Independent Living.* Houston: Institute for Rehabilitation and Research, 1979.

Grob, G. *Mental Institutions in America: Social Policy to 1875.* New York: Free Press, 1973.

Independent Living Research Utilization. *On the Right Track: Foundations for Operating an Independent Living Program.* Houston: Independent Living Research Utilization, 1982.

Institute for Information Studies and Independent Living Research Utilization. *New Life Options.* Falls Church, Va.: Institute for Information Studies, 1979.

Kailes, J. I. "Independent Living Overview." Paper presented at Los Angeles Area Symposium on Independent Living: Project MIA, Los Angeles, October 11, 1983a.

Kailes, J. I. "Peer Counseling in Independent Living Centers." Paper presented at "Beyond Survival," a conference on Independent Living, Denver, Colo., August 13, 1983b.

Kailes, J. I. "The Role of the Social Worker in the Independent Living Process." Unpublished manuscript, Westside Community for Independent Living, Los Angeles, 1983c.

Kailes, J. I. "Watch Your Language, Please." Unpublished manuscript, Westside Community for Independent Living, Los Angeles, 1984.

Kimberly, J. R. "Initiation, Innovation, and Institutionalization in the Creation Process." In J. R. Kimberly, R. H. Miles, and associates, *The Organizational Life Cycle: Issues in the Creation, Transformation, and Decline of Organizations.* San Francisco: Jossey-Bass, 1980.

National Association of Social Workers. *NASW Code of Ethics.* Washington, D.C.: National Association of Social Workers, 1980.

Nosek, P., Dart, J. W., Jr., and Dart, Y. "Independent Living Programs: A Management Perspective." Unpublished manuscript, 1981. Available from Justin W. Dart, Jr., 2012 Lear Lane, Austin, Texas 78745.

Pflueger, S. *Independent Living.* Washington, D.C.: Institute for Research Utilization, 1977.

Rothman, D. *The Discovery of the Asylum.* Boston: Little, Brown, 1971.

Truax, C. B., and Carkhuff, R. R. *Toward Effective Counseling and Psychotherapy: Training and Practice.* Hawthorne, N.Y.: Aldine, 1967.

Urban Institute. *Report of the Comprehensive Needs Study.* Washington, D.C.: Department of Health, Education and Welfare, 1975.

Varela, R. A. "Changing Social Attitudes and Legislation Regarding Disability." In N. M. Crewe, I. K. Zola, and associates, *Independent Living for Physically Disabled People: Developing, Implementing, and Evaluating Self-Help Rehabilitation Programs.* San Francisco: Jossey-Bass, 1983.

Whitaker, J., Rochman, A., and Tso-Kosheri, S. Interview with authors. Westside Community for Independent Living, Los Angeles, February 17, 1984.

Wolfensberger, W. "The Origin and Nature of Our Institutional Models." In R. B. Kugel and W. Wolfensberger (Eds.), *Changing Patterns in Residential Services for the Mentally Retarded.* Washington, D.C.: President's Committee on Mental Retardation, January 1969.

11

Adapting Case Management to Specific Programs and Needs

Marie Weil

This chapter applies the knowledge and theory discussed in previous sections to the process of developing a case management system for a specific population. It serves as a guide to developing and implementing a case management program tailored to the needs of a specific agency, service network, or population. Common themes and issues that must be addressed in system design are examined, including the needs of clients and staff as well as the impact of organizational life stage on the structuring or restructuring of a case management system. The critical steps in the process of developing a case management system are delineated. The process of needs identification and assessment for a target population is presented, and issues related to setting appropriate goals and objectives and selecting an appropriate case management service delivery model are discussed. System design factors, including program staffing and case management roles are analyzed; issues of information collection and management within the case management agency and within the service network are discussed. The chapter concludes with a discussion of interorganizational management issues including service monitoring, accountability, and program evaluation.

Common Themes in Developing Case Management Systems

Although every case management system needs to be designed to meet the service, information, and accountability needs of its target population and its service providers, some questions need to be addressed in developing all such programs. In the preceding chapters, a number of themes recur that must be addressed in planning and updating case management systems.

Client Needs. First of all, any case management system must be designed to meet the service needs of its clients. Frequently, because target populations are vulnerable due to life stage, problem situation, or disability, the case management system must also be responsive to the needs of clients' families, advocates, and representatives. As Downing (Chapter Six) and Caires and Weil (Chapter Nine) have illustrated, clients' families may be extremely important in the following ways: (1) They can assure that clients receive and benefit from services; (2) they frequently are closest to the client's needs and can therefore serve as knowledgeable and sensitive advocates; (3) they can form support networks for their vulnerable member and for other people dealing with the same problem; (4) they can serve as excellent sources of feedback about the services provided; and (5) they can help the client take responsibility for his or her own case management and advocacy or, when that is not possible, perform either informal or formal case management functions. This involvement of clients and clients' families in the case management process can be a major factor in empowering clients and families and can contribute to client satisfaction. Clients or families joining together in self-help groups or mutual support groups can develop into more responsible, more sophisticated service consumers who can provide valuable feedback on services and policies. A central theme for developing a sound system of case management in any service program is to involve clients (and, where appropriate, their families or advocates) as much as possible to assure quality services and to uphold the rights of clients as articulated in legislation and professional codes of conduct.

Organizational Fit. A factor that is important to successful case management systems is discussed by Norman in Chapter Three and Honnard and Wolkon in Chapter Four and acknowledged in other chapters. The case management function must be suited to the organization as well as its clients. That is, the case management system must fit the organizational system and support desired patterns of organizational behavior. For example, case management systems designed for large, bureaucratic, multisited or nested systems, such as state mental health programs or public child welfare settings, will be different in scale, complexity, design, and sophistication from those of small voluntary agencies or a newly developing program such as a center for independent living.

In particular, the case management system must fit (1) the type of agency; (2) its service consumers; (3) the staff; (4) the level of technology available; (5) the organizational stage of development and the service network of the case management agency; and (6) the information, monitoring, and evaluation needs of the agency, its sanctioning body, and funding sources. Additionally, the methods and techniques of case management should fit the model of practice and the type of client-staff interactions needed to provide effective service. The case management system for children who are dependents of the court and for whom periodic court reviews are mandated will necessarily—by virtue of system size, bureaucratic regulations and procedures, and client needs—be a tightly structured, formalized process to safeguard vulnerable children. By contrast, case management in newly developing service areas, such as Independent Living Centers for people with physical disabilities, will be less formalized, involve more face-to-face contact with clients and other professionals, act more frequently on the basis of case conferences than court orders, and stress more client involvement.

The size of the staff and the number of staff roles will also vary depending on the service network and the complexity of the program responsible for case management. In very complex, large systems, such as state developmental disability or mental health systems, several levels of staff may be involved in case management regardless of the case management model used. When there is a primary therapist model, the therapist will be responsible for treatment and service integration, but other staff in clerical, technical, service delivery, and administrative positions will often be responsible for handling data, providing concrete services, reporting on quality assurance efforts, and evaluating programs and service outcomes.

In a community-based, advocacy-oriented program, the primary service provider, case coordinator, or service team may be responsible for planning, monitoring, and reporting. In such small programs, the administrative staff or consultants will frequently be responsible for reporting service outcomes and rates under treatment, quality control, and service monitoring and evaluation. Thus, the levels of staff involved in case management will vary, but all the principal functions of case management must be performed in a fashion that supports the general operation of the program. These functions include outreach and client identification, individual assessment, the development of individual service plans, establishing access to needed services, service coordination, tracking or monitoring the provision of services, client (and often family) advocacy, evaluation of service integration, and the reassessment of client needs.

Staff Needs. All case management systems must not only fit the needs of clients and administrators but also, and equally importantly, be designed to be a support service for staff. Ideally, case management systems should assist workers and supervisors in monitoring information about (1) what is happening with each client; (2) decisions concerning services for clients, and (3) case monitoring and evaluation. This is the area in which far too many systems fail, becoming instead technical toys of planners or administrators and evolving into technological wedges between staff and administrators. If systems for service integration do not help organize case planning, decision making, monitoring, and evaluating, it is quite likely that the system will be inconsistently adhered to and even sabotaged by workers.

Organizational Life Stage. A factor that affects the creation and implementation of all case management systems is the organizational life stage. Organizational needs and capabilities differ greatly depending on whether the program is new, institutionalized, being transformed, or in decline (Miles, 1980). As Chapter One indicates, incipient forms of case management have been in operation since the earliest days of Charity Organization Societies and have been a part of the human services literature since the writings of Mary Richmond and Mary Parker Follett. However, case management has only recently gained a separate identity as a function in the human services.

Although the hearts of planners and evaluators are gladdened by the all-too-infrequent opportunity to design a case management system, constraints in funding limit the pleasures of this challenge. Far more often, administrators, planners, evaluators, staff, and consultants face the task of updating or remodeling a primitive information management and service integration system so that case management activities meet current standards. The accelerating use of more formal reporting and charting systems and of computer-supported case management systems often places staff and administrators in difficult roles of adapting to technologies that seem to elevate the inhuman aspects of data management and downgrade the human interaction component of service provision.

Although organizations need to develop or restructure case management systems to meet service and accountability demands, the goals of the organization are displaced if the technology that was intended to be the servant becomes the master. This tension between focusing on people and focusing on data is a common problem in case management operations. What is needed is a design that is neither too burdensome nor too cumbersome to be useful to staff and yet is detailed enough to provide the information needed for client and service monitoring and program evaluation.

Whether a new case management system should be designed or an old one remodeled depends on the organizational life stage of the human services program. Although there is controversy about the nature and reality of organizational life cycles, as noted by Kimberly (1980b) there can be little doubt that reactions to a case management system that is an elemental part of a new program are different from reactions to a newfangled technology grafted onto an established program. All case management planners should anticipate problems in implementing a new plan, but the types of problems will differ depending on the internal life cycle stage of the case coordination agency and the life cycle issues of the organizations in the constituent service network.

For example, Independent Living Centers for people with physical disabilities evolved from social advocacy by and for that service population. Many leaders in the field have some type of physical disability or challenging condition themselves. These centers are just being developed and face all the problems of starting a service from scratch. The challenge for the relatively new organization or service system, as Kimberly (1980a, p. 30) notes, is that success may be paradoxical. As the number of service consumers and staff increase, so do program demands and accountability demands. The new agency necessarily becomes institutionalized and loses its flexibility and innovativeness: "Institutionalization is that process whereby new norms, values, and structures become incorporated within the framework of existing patterns of norms, values, and structures. This process is one that lends stability and predictability to social relationships and enables them to persist" (Kimberly, 1980a, p. 31).

During the process of institutionalization, an agency or organization must deal with three variables: (1) problems of internal social control, (2) problems related to formalizing the structure of work, and (3) problems relating to managing relationships with clients and other service organizations in the environment (Kimberly, 1976).

For example, likely problems in community and advocacy-based programs (such as programs for victims of family violence, shelters for battered women, and programs for persons with physical disabilities) will relate to the movement from early flexibility to more formal controls and structure. People who can tolerate uncertainty and ambiguity and who treasure flexibility and creativity are drawn to newly developing programs of community advocacy. A creative style of leadership is necessary in early program development. These earliest stages of the organizational life cycle, although they might be viewed as floundering efforts by the staff of established programs, promote experimentation, creativity, interaction, tolerance, and growth among staff, administrators, and clients. Face-to-face interactions between staff and clients and between staff members frequently become more impersonal as a program grows.

Informal planning and decision-making processes shift to the routines of business as usual emphasizing record keeping, efficiency, and accountability.

As new programs attract funds from various sources (which they must do to survive), there will be increasing demands for strict evaluation procedures. This change, as well as organizational growth, frequently accelerates structural differentiation within the program. Instead of program founders doing everything (often including the custodial work), new staff members are hired to carry out specific tasks with varying levels of responsibility. Inevitably this process leads to role differentiation and the bureaucratization and formalization of programs.

Organizational Relations with the Service Network. Managing relationships in the service network is a major factor in making or breaking case management systems in new agencies. Especially for the advocacy or community-based program, the service model chosen may have resulted from dissatisfication with the existing organizational network. However, if the new organization is to integrate services for a vulnerable or at-risk population, it must interact with older, institutionalized services in ways that help its clients. For example, a health maintenance or long-term care program may have been set up because the community's agencies and institutions failed to deal with the needs of the frail elderly or people who have chronic, severe medical conditions. Still, the new program—perhaps a day treatment center or a respite care program for frail elderly persons—must interact with and secure services from the older, less responsive institutionalized services and programs in the community. The ability of new programs, such as Independent Living Centers, to obtain cash benefits and the training needed by clients may depend on developing positive, reciprocal relationships with staid, highly bureaucratized, older programs, such as departments of vocational rehabilitation.

Managing relationships with other organizations, community groups, and consumer groups is also frequently complex in work with the chronically mentally ill. Direct service staff in public mental health agencies must deal with a variety of board and care programs, community treatment programs, and other community services. Staff of mental health agencies, both public and voluntary, frequently have to be involved with the temporary rehospitalization of chronic clients.

Since the essence of case management is the effective integration of services to meet clients' needs, interventions in the service network and the community are particularly critical in developing services, facilitating interagency coordination, and assuring the quality of services.

Structuring or Restructuring a Case Managment System. Instituting a new or revised form of case management in an established human services program presents its own set of difficulties. Change is threatening, and the introduction of more sophisticated, technological means for reporting and service coordination and evaluation is often viewed as a threat to therapeutic aspects of work and personal attention to individual clients. Staff may fear that they will spend their time filling out forms rather than assisting or counseling clients.

It is important to note, however, that organizations may go through processes of creation and innovation at many stages of their life cycle. Even if they are old and well established, new policies, new legislative mandates, new administrators, improved technologies for treatment, and new practice models may all induce a period of regeneration and innovation. In fact, the ability to take on a new mission or new approaches may be real factors in an organization's ability to survive in a changing social and economic environment. The essential distinction between old and new organizations can be described as follows: "Change in existing organizations has to come in the context of an established culture and an institutionalized set of norms, values, and procedures, whereas in the creation of new organizations, new cultures develop and new norms, values, and procedures are established" (Kimberly, 1980a, p. 42).

Planning Case Management Systems

A new or restructured case management system must adapt to its operating conditions. As noted, the system for service integration should meet the needs of clients, staff, and administrators for service quality, effectiveness, efficiency, and accountability. Whatever the type of agency or program, however, a basic process must be followed in developing a case management system. Figure 1 presents a flowchart that delineates this process. The tasks of system development are fairly complex, but the possible pitfalls in developing interagency coordination and cooperation are even more problematic. Therefore, this process should employ the best research and social measurement tools available and the best possible critical and analytic judgment of the people involved in planning and implementing the system. Careful analytic attention should be given to the following areas: (1) clients' needs; (2) information needs; (3) resource and service needs; (4) staffing needs; (5) system administration and management needs; (6) interagency coordination and service integration; and (7) accountability, documentation, and evaluation needs.

Case management systems operate at several levels—state, regional, and local. Each of these levels of operation has its own issues and problems. In this book and especially in this chapter, the local system is emphasized, where an agency or a network of agencies identifies, coordinates, and integrates human services in a particular community for a particular client population.

The most critical steps in the process of developing any case management system are:

1. conduct an in-depth assessment of client needs;
2. assess existing and needed resources;
3. identify problems likely to occur because of gaps or deficiencies in services;
4. create an interagency coordination mechanism, such as a task force, to plan the case management system, and assign responsibilities for specific case management functions;
5. determine interagency contractual arrangements for service coordination and monitoring;
6. determine goals and objectives for the case management system within the primary case management agency and for the total service network;
7. set priorities for case management service, if that is necessary, among members or subgroups of the target population (Levine and Fleming, 1984);
8. analyze information and information management needs;

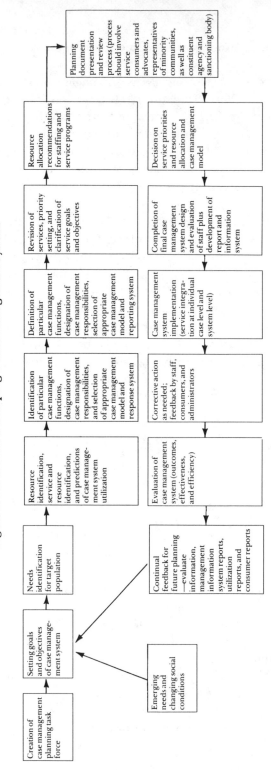

Figure 1. Process for Developing a Case Management System.

9. analyze costs and benefits of available information manage-
    ment and reporting systems;
10. determine the most appropriate (optimal) case management
    model for client and system needs;
11. determine the methods of coordination, monitoring, and
    collaboration among professionals and programs in the ser-
    vice network; and
12. determine the most appropriate means of monitoring services
    and of evaluating outcomes for both individual cases and the
    case management system as a whole.

This process clarifies issues requiring planning and guides
planners through the essential steps of case management system
development. Once the system is designed, an appropriate training
and staff development program can be implemented to support the
system. An essential part of staff development is instruction in the
use and application of information management and reporting
techniques and any other technological changes that accompany
the system. Before implementing the case management system, it is
important to identify potential problems and possible negative
consequences so that corrective actions can be undertaken. Following intensive preparation, the case management system can be
implemented. Procedures for monitoring, feedback, and corrective
action must be in place as well as procedures for evaluating the
system to facilitate comparison of actual program effects with
intended outcomes. This process of planning, implementing, and
evaluating will enable staff and administrators to assess and modify
the overall system so that it meets client and system needs more
effectively.

Levine and Fleming (1984, p. 61) identify a critical element
in describing the early need to establish an interagency task force
to plan for service network cooperation and collaboration. This task
force should be made up of persons who make decisions within
their own programs and can make commitments for their agencies.
Such a task force will need to hammer out a consensus on client
needs and service delivery and monitoring, plan the implementation of the case management system, and determine interagency
relationships and decision making within the case management

system. It is important that one agency be primarily responsible for case management so that these functions can be accounted for (Levine and Fleming, 1984). An interagency task force is needed to plan, test ideas, conduct the needs assessment and resource inventory, develop support for the case management system, and anticipate probable difficulties in implementation and evaluation. It is quite useful to maintain such a task force to serve as an interagency coordinating body.

Any interagency committee that is formalized as an ongoing monitoring component of the system should have staff representation and consumer representation. In particular, minority and client groups should be represented. An early task for planners of case management systems is to identify the programs that affect their target population and to involve these potential clients as well as members of service consumer groups in the planning process. In designing case management systems for the chronically mentally ill, Levine and Fleming (1984, p. 61) note that such a task force should include "representatives of vocational rehabilitation, social services, public welfare, public health, housing, and other local agencies whose programs are significant to the lives of chronically mentally ill persons." For other target populations, case management planners must identify the agencies and resources needed to constitute a viable service network for those populations.

Such a task force can provide an important feedback mechanism. Levine and Fleming (1984, p. 62) comment: "As the case management system is designed and subsequently implemented, consideration should be given to maintaining the task force as a means of monitoring the systems and identifying problems before they occur." The interagency planning task force, because of its representatives and knowledge of resources, is a logical work group to conduct the needs assessment for the case management system. If the group needs assistance in instrument design or data analysis, researchers, program evaluators, or social planners can be used as consultants.

Needs Identification and Assessment

Needs assessment is a complex function of human services planning whereby needs are identified and service priorities are set.

This function involves collecting and analyzing information to identify the needs of the target population, assess available services, and assess the gaps in service or problems in the service system. The phase after needs assessment, setting service priorities, is equally complicated. Because a service system seldom has the funds and personnel available to meet all identified needs of any population, it usually must set priorities favoring the resolution of certain problems or favoring particular subgroups of the target population. For example, state programs for children with developmental disabilities frequently target those children with the most severe or numerous handicapping conditions. Independent Living Centers have often targeted for job training services those persons who are highly motivated and could be trained in a growing job area, such as computer programming.

Setting priorities is obviously a political process. Sometimes legislative bodies set the priorities by law; sometimes states or counties do so by regulation. In other situations, planners or administrators may set the priorities, guided in many instances by available funding from governments or foundations for particular groups or problem areas.

Needs Identification. Identifying needs and resources also involves choices about how to collect information and from which sources. These choices influence the resulting recommendations for service. A frequent problem in conducting needs assessments is that it is much easier to collect information about who is already being served than to determine unmet needs (that is, identifying the people eligible for and in need of service who are not involved in or are unknown to the service network). The most active and able members of a target population or members who have the most active personal or group advocates are likely to receive whatever services are available. Many other people who are just as needy or needier than the people being serviced may not have similar access to services. For this reason, it is very important to consult multiple data sources in order to identify the unserved and underserved target population (Weil, 1979b).

Siegel, Attkisson, and Carson (1978, p. 228) describe the following methods for collecting needs assessment data: "(a) indi-cator approaches utilizing social and health indicator analyses; (b) social area survey approaches utilizing (1) demands for service, (2) analysis of service providers and resources, and (3) citizen surveys; and (c) community group approaches utilizing (1) community forums, (2) nominal group techniques, (3) delphi techniques, and (4) community impressions." These writers carefully analyze each of these assessment methods, sources of information, the methods of data analysis and the expertise required, and the time and resources required for each method.

Each of these methods of needs identification can supply valuable information, and a general rule of thumb is to seek multiple sources of data (Siegel, Attkisson, and Carson, 1978; Weil, 1979b). Needs assessment involves research and planning activities to ascertain service needs and service utilization patterns in a specific area of the human services. Warheit, Bell, and Schwab (1974) note that a needs assessment program should provide data so that planners and decision makers will be able to identify the extent and kinds of needs in the community, systematically evaluate the existing programs, and plan new programs. Introducing a new case management system may require a second round of needs identification. It is also necessary to know how the available services mesh together and what services are lacking in the service network or for specific subpopulations.

Analyzing data to determine needs and priorities entails a process of convergent needs analysis. Convergent needs analysis is a process of identifying high-priority needs using multiple research methods and multiple data sources to ascertain which needs consistently emerge from all sources (Siegel, Attkisson, and Carson, 1978; Weil, 1979b). These needs can then be justifiably targeted for service.

Needs Assessment Process. The process of needs assessment is illustrated in Figure 2. As can be seen, it is a complex process requiring a skilled and representative task force. The complexity of needs assessment for case management is stressed here because in addition to identifying the service needs of the target population, the actual operations of agencies in the service network must be evaluated, and the gaps in service and problems in service coordination and interagency collaboration must be carefully analyzed. Identifying services needs is difficult, and information needed to

Figure 2. Needs Assessment Process for Developing
Case Management Systems.

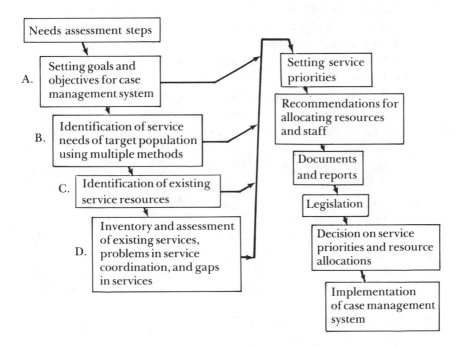

evaluate services and gaps in services may be closely guarded or even lacking. These problems heighten the need for high-level administrative collaboration in system planning.

Designing a Case Management System

No one model or approach to case management is universally applicable. The major planning task for developers of a system is to match target population needs with service network resources in order to provide as comprehensive a means of case management as possible. The negotiation of this match will largely determine the appropriate model.

The following questions will need to be answered to assess the service network and its abilities to support a case management system:

1. What services and resources are available?
2. What gaps in services and problems in the service network are known or anticipated?
3. What will the nature of the case management system be in the service network—voluntary, contractual, or mandated?
4. What history is there of interagency linkage and cooperation?
5. What steps are needed to create an effective working collaboration among agencies in the service network?
6. What programs and agencies and what type of staff will have primary responsibility for carrying out case management functions?
7. What interagency agreements are needed for staff to carry out the case management function?
8. What is the nature and source of authority for the agency primarily responsible for case management?
9. What feedback structure will be needed to react to individual or network problems in coordination and service integration?
10. What record-keeping and reporting systems will be needed within the designated case management agency and among the agencies of the service network?
11. What level of technology or computer support is available for the case management system?
12. What degree of support prevails in the service network for a case management system? How can this support be increased?
13. What is the nature of the exchange relationships that will develop between the case management agency and other programs in the service network and among the programs in the service network? Will the exchanges be mutually beneficial to organizations as well as to clients?
14. What time table seems realistic to implement the case management system? In what order will the steps be implemented? What formats (Program Evaluation and Review Techniques [PERT] or others) will be used to track implementation? What positive outcomes are anticipated? What negative outcomes are anticipated?
15. What type of monitoring and evaluation plan will be needed to receive feedback and plan corrective action for the new system?

16. What model of case management is most appropriate for the client population, case management staff, and service network? What are the benefits of and anticipated problems with this model?

All plans for case management systems should attend to the following issues:

1. goal setting with clear indications of benefits for clients, staff, and participating organizations;
2. the fit between technological processes and staff capabilities;
3. staff training and development and hiring of additional personnel;
4. effects of the case management system on the structure of work in the designated agency and other participating programs, the internal control systems and communication patterns within the case management agency and each of the participating agencies, and the service network and the relationships and reporting systems among the participating agencies; and
5. development of interagency policies and contracts that legitimate the intervention of case managers in service monitoring throughout the service network.

If the case management system is to be restructured in an existing agency, the following questions must be answered:

1. What will the relative costs and benefits be of the new case management system?
2. What internal organizational problems may arise in implementing and operating the new system? What vested interests, norms, values, and organizational behaviors will be problematic?
3. What internal benefits will be realized by the case management agency, staff, administrators, and clients as a result of the new system? How can these benefits be stressed and maximized? What internal systems, norms, values, and organizational behavior are supported by the new system?
4. What alterations in reporting channels and procedures will be needed?

5.   What staff training will be needed? How can staff input in the planning process be maximized?
6.   What effect will the new technology have on staff and on clients? How can these groups be prepared for these changes?
7.   What service network obstacles are anticipated? What history of interagency collaboration does the agency have? Are there problems in existing relationships? What changes in interagency communication, reporting, and collaboration will be needed?

Information collected in this analysis provides background knowledge needed to guide model selection and determine appropriate goals and objectives for a case management system.

Setting Goals and Objectives

The mission statement of a case management program is a broad statement of purpose. The mission statement then needs to be broken down into specific, measurable goals, and those goals broken down into discrete, measurable service objectives. The objectives can then be analyzed and divided into tasks and assigned for both the planning and implementation process. At the earliest point in planning, in conjunction with needs assessment, the first major decision must be whether, given the services, resources, and needs of the community or area, a case management system is of the greatest priority. If a community has very few services and considerable duplication in those that are available, case management may not be the best strategy to cope with serious gaps in the service network (Beatrice, 1979). However, Steinberg and Carter (1983, p. 68), who had assumed that "there is no point in coordinating incompetent and irrelevant services," found through their reserach that the assumption did not hold up. Administrators and planners reported a number of reasons why case management was a useful strategy, even when the service system was quite incomplete. "The case management program helps to obtain more appropriate utilization of what does exist, including institutions . . . [and] assists in documenting service gaps and in developing new, needed services"

(Steinberg and Carter, pp. 68–69). Therefore, if there is growing community support for the needs of the target population and funding for a case management program can be obtained, case management may indeed be used to identify needs and develop service integration plans that can be lobbied for in social and political forums.

Once the decision to proceed with a case management program is made, the broad goals for the program must be stated. These will obviously depend upon the needs and problems of the target population, but all case management programs will need to establish goals in the following areas: developing a more functional and collaborative human services system, developing service contracts with the participating agencies, establishing the importance of advocacy (both individual and class) for the target population, defining successful outcomes of service for clients and for the system as a whole, establishing systems that will measure outcomes, and developing a service network that is comprehensive, accountable, and able to meet the needs of the target population.

The objectives of the program specify parts of goals. Each of the goals is broken down into multiple objectives, which, achieved in combination, fulfill the goal. For example, goals for an Independent Living Center might include increasing (by a certain amount or percentage) the number of people with disabilities living independently and increasing (by a certain amount or percentage) the number of Independent Living Center clients who are participating in vocational training programs and getting jobs. In child welfare, an objective might be to make decisions regarding permanency planning within the mandated time frame so that children do not drift under foster care but are planfully reunited with their families or placed with adoptive families. These objectives would need to be stated in measurable form so that the program can be evaluated.

Objectives can then be operationalized through task analysis, whereby the tasks are broken down so that the appropriate personnel performs different functions. In developing a case management system, as in most other complex systems, tasks relate to data, things, and people. Tasks involving data include collecting and analyzing information needed to design the system and make it work. Tasks related to things include designing forms for reporting, monitoring, and evaluating programs and forms for assessing clients' needs and outcomes. Tasks related to people involve building relationships with the agencies in the service network, outreach to the target population, and developing ongoing communication processes with both agencies and clients.

The more thoroughly goals, objectives, and tasks are planned and associated with measurable outcomes, the clearer planners, administrators, and staff will be about what steps, corrective actions, and modifications are needed in the program plan. Program evaluation is built into such a plan when goals, tasks, and objectives are clearly and measurably specified (Fink and Kosecoff, 1978; Brekke, 1984). A number of good handbooks are available to assist in planning programs and evaluations (Attkisson, Hargreaves, Horowitz, and Sorensen, 1978; Fink and Kosecoff, 1978; Morris and Fitz-Gibbons, 1978; Rossi, Freeman, and Wright, 1979).

It may be helpful to use some of the system development and management tools that have been adapted to the human services in designing the case management system. Management by objectives (MBO) may be quite useful in planning case management systems by formalizing missions, goals, and objectives and incorporating a philosophy, a process of work, and a system to accomplish work (Raia, 1974). However, to make the MBO approach as discussed by Drucker (1981), Gruber (1981), and others useful in human services systems, some modifications are necessary (Ford, 1983). The interactive process of the case management system "allows for the integration of various management processes and techniques into a logical, coherent whole" (Ford, 1983, p. 4). The management processes that need to be considered in design include "strategic planning and organizational control; organizing and assigning workloads and tasks; problem solving and decision-making; and motivation and self-control" (Ford, 1983, p. 4).

In the human services, participatory management approaches are useful (Spano and Lund, 1981). In designing an information management and reporting system for a social services hospital unit, Spano and Lund made the following adaptations of the traditional MBO format: (1) They derived the mission statement from the existing departmental philosophy of service to clients: (2)

they included the departmental functions in their MBO plan; and (3) they included in their accountability procedures interactions with professional and community subsystems as well as the customary administrative reporting procedures. These ideas can readily be used in introducing a new case management system or adapting an old one.

Examples of statements for program philosophy, missions, and goals and objectives taken from the Senior Care Action Network training manual by Stumpf (1981) and from Spano and Lund (1981) are presented in Table 1.

Determining the Appropriate Case Management Model

After needs have been assessed, service priorities set and the mission, goals, and objectives agreed upon, the most appropriate and most feasible model for case management can be soundly determined. Issues that must be considered in model selection are the preferred or possible staffing patterns, funding constraints, and the limitations of the case management agency. After considering the available resources, population needs, available staff, and organizational constraints, the most optimal model can be identified and selected. The optimal model will be the one that best accommodates the resources of the organization and the service network and client's needs. The optimal model might be any one of the models described in detail in Chapter Two: (1) generalist or broker, (2) primary therapist, (3) interdisciplinary teams, (4) comprehensive service center, (5) family, (6) supportive care, and (7) volunteer. Who will serve as case managers and the particular case management functions that are emphasized will depend on personnel and clients' needs as well as the preferences of planners and administrators.

However, the model ultimately worked out to fit an individual program and community is not determined simply by who will provide the case management services. The functional emphasis and the degree of comprehensiveness of the prevailing and desired service network must also be considered in creating a model tailored to the capabilities, needs, and resources of the community.

The functional emphasis should be based on the needs of the target population. The degree of comprehensiveness represents a

Table 1. MBO Format for Human Services Programs.

Sample Program Philosophy

  1.   An awareness of the needs of the frail elderly with a caring attitude and a belief that this population's multiple needs can be served by a coordinated case management approach

  2.   A recognition that this alternative to institutional care is of value and warrants the expenditure of limited resources

  3.   A community attitude that agencies are part of an interdependent network and an awareness of the value of sharing authority and responsibility in order to develop a coordinated system of care (Stumpf, 1981, p. 25)

Sample Mission Statement

"To develop a single-entry-point service delivery system for the frail, vulnerable, and at-risk elderly that maintains these elders in their own surroundings as long as appropriate, thus preventing inappropriate and unnecessary institutionalization" (Stumpf, 1981, p. 7).

Sample Functions

  1.   Provision of case management activities, including case finding, prescreening, assessment, case planning, implementation, reassessment, and termination
  2.   Information and referral services
  3.   Resource development and liaison with community agencies
  4.   Research and evaluation
  5.   Supervision of case managers
  6.   Fiscal duties and monitoring of contracts
  7.   Education and training of staff and community agencies (Spano and Lund, 1981, p. 90)

Sample Objectives and Goals

  1.   Goal: "To develop the client's ability to manage once again on one's own."

        Objective: To assess each client's medical, social, and functional situation and arrange for assistance in the specific areas that will enable the client to live independently, within three days of client's contact with the agency.

  2.   Goal: "To provide the necessary services, not all desired services, aimed at making life more healthy, more socially connected, more manageable, and with more self-esteem."

Table 1. MBO Format for Human Services Programs, Cont'd.

Objective: To prioritize the ten greatest needs of the client to maintain independence, and to begin the termination process within one month after meeting the first five needs.

3.   Goal: "To develop a collaborative network of health and social services capable of responding effectively to the frail elderly."

Objective: To contact at least 80 percent of the currently existing health and social services within the geographical boundaries of the agency, and to develop in writing interagency referral agreements with those who choose to cooperate within the first six months of the agency's operation (Stumpf, 1981, p. 9).

compromise between what the service network currently has to offer and what it would offer to service the full range of needs. Intagliata (1981, p. 106), drawing from Ross (1980), presents three degrees of comprehensiveness for case management systems (Table 2). Grisham, White, and Miller (1983) present a more elaborate continuum

Table 2. Three Models of Comprehensiveness for Case Management Programs.

Services Included in Minimal Model	Services Included in Coordination Model	Services Included in Comprehensive Model
Outreach	Outreach	Outreach
Client assessment	Client assessment	Client assessment
Case planning	Case planning	Case planning
Referral to service providers	Referral to service providers	Referral to service providers
	Advocacy for client	Advocacy for client
	Direct casework	Direct casework
	Developing natural support systems	Developing natural support systems
	Reassessment	Reassessment
		Advocacy for resource development
		Monitoring quality
		Public education
		Crisis intervention

Source: Adapted from Ross, 1980.

of program comprehensiveness that assists in making fine distinctions about model feasibility given differences in authority to command resources and responsibility for clients.

The comprehensiveness of services is an inescapable part of the process of selecting an appropriate model for case management. Figure 3 presents the factors in choosing a model: case manager role, population type, and comprehensiveness of service system. It illustrates the possible combinations of case management provider models with different vulnerable populations and indicates that any one of these combinations can be organized as a minimal, coordinated, or comprehensive system of case management. The figure can also help in shifting from a minimal system to a more sophisticated, comprehensive one. The design and plan for growth can then be used to identify service gaps and to lobby for a more responsive service (Steinberg and Carter, 1983). Long-range planning can then realistically document what the existing case management system is and what it needs to be to meet the needs of the target population.

There are additional factors to consider in adapting models for particular needs. In some programs, services exist in various parts of the community; in other programs, such as long-term care facilities or comprehensive senior service centers, a variety of programs are housed under one roof; in yet other programs, especially those serving rural and suburban areas, services may be dispensed from mobile units (Weil, 1980, 1984). Another option for remote areas is to provide transportation to services and to arrange for clients to receive a variety of services on one day.

Wherever the case management system is located, it is important to look beyond the major social, mental health, and health agencies of the community and to identify other resources that may also be needed by the target population. Frequently, securing basic necessities (shelter, food) or access to general community services can pose significant problems for clients. Examples of difficult situations include locating apartments for clients of the mental health system who have recently been released from institutions; moving clients into their own apartments from board and care homes so that they can live independently; locating vocational training programs that are wheelchair accessible; locating home

Figure 3. Case Management System Design Choices.

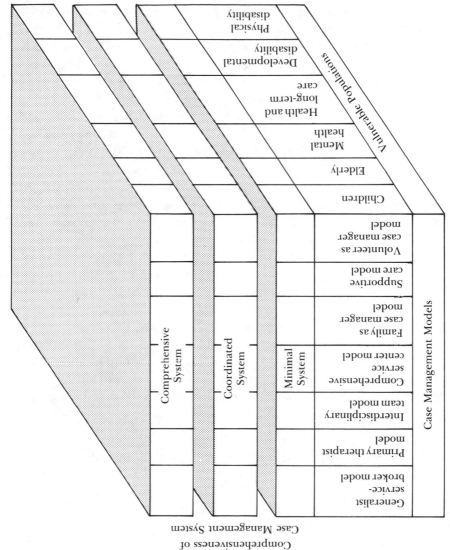

health attendants; finding appropriate employment for adults with developmental disabilities; building supportive community services for children in foster care or who are newly adopted; and locating daycare or respite care for children, elderly, or severely handicapped persons. These services are frequently needed as well as basic health, dental and eye care, entitlement programs, and concrete services such as transportation, socialization, and recreation. There may also be needs for formal advocacy support, such as legal assistance services, as well as mutual support groups or counseling services.

Not only must these services be identified, but program planners or staff also need to build cooperative relations with the people offering these services. Perhaps program planners will negotiate service contracts and develop agreements for service linkage, monitoring, and evaluation, which will be necessary parts of the case management system.

Along with identifying the range of services needed, planners must carefully document gaps in services. The needs assessment methodologies presented earlier can be applied to this part of the planning process, which might utilize personal or telephone interviews with both service providers and potential clients, mail or telephone surveys of agencies and potential clients, community meetings, or service network and community organization workshops. If used skillfully, these processes can begin to build support for the needs of the target population and for the case management system.

Design, Implementation, and Accountability

Regardless of the model chosen, certain issues must be dealt with in designing and implementing a case management system. These relate to personnel; data and information management; and reporting, monitoring, and accountability.

Personnel. The model chosen broadly determines the role of the case manager, but the background, training, and experience required for this position must be specified. Some of these decisions can be facilitated if the case management functions are carefully delineated and cleared with the service network members. In any program, the core case management functions (outreach, assessment, planning, linking, monitoring, evaluation, and advocacy) must be clearly specified so that the major tasks of the case manager are agreed upon. The range of activities to be included in each of the case functions and the case manager's ability to command resources and monitor service must be specified and contractually agreed upon by the participating agencies (Levine and Fleming, 1984).

When the emphasis on each function is decided, decisions must be made about siting case managers and case management functions. Although a single agency should serve as the core case management agency, certain functions might be delegated. The issue of program clout must also be considered in the relations of the case management program with the service network, planning bodies, and local policy makers (Intagliata, 1982). Staff should be assigned according to their roles. Detailed job descriptions that describe the functions and responsibilities of the case managers should be proposed and circulated in the service network. In an appendix to their manual on case management, Levine and Fleming (1984) present several model job descriptions.

Information Collection and Management. Collecting and managing information is a major function of any case management system. Information is always collected at two levels: the individual and the system. At the individual client level, formats need to be developed for collecting information about client assessment, service planning, outreach documentation, referrals and linking to services, monitoring service delivery, and evaluating progress and system responsiveness to client needs. These formats should be tools that improve and support direct case management services, not just instruments to document activities for administrators or funding sources (Weissman, 1978). Boserup and Gouge (1980), the National Conference on Social Welfare (1981), Stumpf (1981), Steinberg and Carter (1983), and Weissman (1978) offer examples of documentation and information collection in the fields of child welfare, developmental disability, and services for the elderly.

Each form used, whether in paper-and-pencil form or computer printout, should have clearly specified purposes and be designed to meet information management and decision making needs of the case managers, supervisors, administrators, and evaluators. Careful planning of these forms can make or break a system. It may be necessary to work with social planners or information management consultants to see that the forms fulfill these multiple functions.

The importance of this issue can be documented by an example. During the implementation of a computerized case management program for child welfare in a major metropolitan area, the author was involved in training direct service workers. In the course of the needs assessment process and training implementation, it became obvious that many on the staff so resented the imposition of the computerized system (neither workers nor unions participated in the planning process) that they had gone so far as to misreport information (such as by checking inapplicable boxes) or to enter erroneous information in order to sabotage the new computerized system. The trainer was hard pressed to illustrate at that late date the possible benefits for clients and workers of an efficient information management system. In contrast, at about the same time, the author served as a consultant for a demonstration project seeking to reduce the incidence of placing children from severely stressed multiproblem families in out-of-home care. In this program, a simple management information reporting system was designed that provided administrators and program evaluators with the information needed to take corrective action and assess program effectiveness. Significantly, the system was also designed as a planning tool for each individual worker. Therefore, the basic case management reporting form focused on client problems, worker decisions, and planned intervention steps, which were updated in the reporting system as the situation changed. In this instance, case managers were not only willing to use the system but excited about its utility in assisting them in case planning, decision making, and taking on another worker's case when that worker was absent or on vacation. The differences in the two experiences speak for themselves and indicate the significant impact that designing forms which provide feedback useful to staff can have on clients and systems.

Schoech and Schkade (1980) have illustrated how an automated, computerized management information system in a large child welfare bureaucracy can aid direct service workers in decision making and problem solving. They describe a system that allows "easy query of highly flexible and well-managed groups of data pertinent to the situation" (p. 567). A good management information system (MIS) can: "(1) assist case managers in their decision processes in semistructured tasks; (2) support, rather than replace, professional judgment; and (3) improve the effectiveness of the decison making rather than its efficiency" (p. 568).

To develop an MIS as part of a case management program, it is important to see that the system supports decision making and to recognize that the computer does not magically make decisions for the case manager (Ford, 1983). Steinberg and Carter (1983) and the National Institute of Mental Health's (1980) report on management information systems for mental health organizations also support this point.

The MIS for a case management program can assist in service delivery and monitoring client progress by establishing points for periodic client reevaluation (Schoech, 1982). The system can also establish specific time lines for periodic review like those built into the permanency planning legislation at federal and state levels for child welfare case review. If the MIS is designed to meet worker needs, it will generate monthly reports indicating recent and upcoming reevaluation points for clients (Ford, 1983). Information on problems in service delivery or changes in the client's status or situation can also be incorporated into the MIS. The case managers should help decide what information to include in MIS programs.

The MIS for a case management program should relate not only to internal decision making but also to changes in the community service system. The system should assist administrators and evaluators in monitoring interagency collaboration and service delivery. Agency relationships are just as important to monitor as client pathways (Ford, 1983). Programs should be monitored to determine whether they are operating as designed, whether service integration is occurring as planned, and whether the target population is being reached and adequately served (Rossi, Freeman, and Wright, 1979; Brekke, 1984).

The MIS should also indicate organizational network, community, and agency system changes. The previously recommended interagency task force can monitor and evaluate interagency service delivery and collaboration problems. Such a task force can focus both on the management and administrative problems in the case management program and on client problems (Ford, 1983). In addition, the task force becomes a means of implementing program changes and new ideas for service delivery as a result of improved information management and reporting. As Ford (1983, p. 9) notes: "This kind of networking solidifies the concept of community collaboration and cooperation for the benefit of agency staff as well as clients who have acesss to a more coordinated system." Where interagency contracts are used, the MIS can provide reports and updates on services rendered and problems to be corrected.

An analysis of the program's mission, goals, objectives, and functions and of the types of clients served and agencies involved will indicate basic information needs. It is important to look at the information needs for each level of program involvement, "starting with the information needed by the administrative, community, and professional networking levels, and going on down through the management levels" to actual worker tasks (Ford, 1983, p. 10). The flow of information upward as well as downward in the hierarchy should be documented to establish a full information feedback loop. At each step in this process, "the information needs should be identified as well as the source of information" (Ford, 1983, p. 10).

An MIS for a case management program can be strengthened by enlarging the information system in ways that are consistent with an MBO process, creating what Weiner (1982) describes as a "goal-oriented management system." This kind of management technique pulls together and orders the following management processes: programming, budgeting, operating and measurement, and reporting and analysis. Thus, combining MBO techniques with MIS and management control techniques creates a comprehensive management system.

Priorities for information must be established, since it is unlikely that all information desired can be collected in a timely and efficient fashion. The cost-effectiveness of information processing is an important managerial consideration. If certain information is needed only infrequently or only for a few cases, it may be simpler and more cost-effective to collect and record such information manually rather than by means of the computer (Cotter, 1981).

In designing an appropriate MIS for a case management program, decisions must be made regarding the trade-offs between the need for information and the cost of obtaining the information. Weiner (1982) recommends that the costs of system design, development, and maintenance be compared with the potential return on the investment. Instead of comparing the costs of instituting an automated MIS with continuing manual collection of data, "the focus should be on the greater effectiveness of the organization in achieving its mission or providing higher-quality services, and on greater productivity through avoiding future costs" (Ford, 1983, p. 11; Weiner, 1982). This idea can help in incorporating the MIS into the case management system, and it can assist direct service case managers in performing their tasks. As Ford (1983, p. 11) notes: "Utilizing an automated MIS can be viewed as taking advantage of the increased sophistication of the technology available to assist case managers in providing high-quality, comprehensive services to the community."

Service Network: Interorganizational Issues. Interorganizational relations must be considered from the earliest point in planning a case management system. All of the models for case management discussed, even the comprehensive service center model, will depend on reciprocal relationships with community agencies and services. Most case management programs depend on other agencies to see that clients get access to and receive needed services. Even before the case management program begins, most proposed programs need the backing of the service network leaders. Throughout its life, a case management system will depend on the collaboration of members of the service network.

As has been noted, other programs should be involved in the needs assessment process through an interagency task force. This task force should become an ongoing part of the planning, operating, and monitoring structure of the case management program. It is the vehicle through which information needs can be identified and information can be collected and updated. It can also engage in troubleshooting at the case or system level. Obviously, then, attention to the service network is of prime importance in maintaining a responsive case management program.

Where possible, formal interagency service contracts should be drawn up to clarify obligations and reciprocal arrangements. The positive benefits of the exchange can be documented from administrative levels down, thus assuring cooperation within the case management system while focusing on client well-being. The use of service contracts for individual clients is also recommended to clarify responsibilities and to hold all parties, including the client, accountable for tasks (Weissman, 1978). Such contracts can minimize possible problems with monitoring and evaluation. They can also be an invaluable aid in clarifying advocacy issues and developing procedures to redress problems. Building a cooperative network of colleagues is essential in making a case management system work effectively; however, this effort must not sabotage client advocacy (Weil, 1979a; Mailick and Ashley, 1981). Interagency communication and cooperation will also have to be established to support information management, data collection, and evaluation functions, which are often the most problematic functions in the service network.

Monitoring, Accountability, and Evaluation. Service monitoring is a primary function of a case management program that can combine worker activities and judgments with automated systems. This combination can bring about the following benefits: assisting in program effectiveness and achieving organizational goals, improving working conditions by reducing the need for repetitive tasks and organizing work, encouraging the broader use of data in program modification, and encouraging participatory management (Weiner, 1982).

Sound monitoring procedures that document client progress and pinpoint service delivery problems or issues that require worker advocacy are essential for assuring that clients receive quality service. Such procedures are also necessary to provide administrators with the information needed to determine whether the target population is being reached to document program effectiveness, to indicate points for corrective action, and to provide information for justifying continued program funding and resources. Evaluators need a sound monitoring system for the same reasons as administrators; in addition, evaluators need a data base at both client and system levels.

Although the needs and benefits of service monitoring are usually most visible at client and administrative levels, the system is not likely to be truly effective unless it also meets the needs of the staff. These staff needs pertain to case documentation, assessment and decision making factors, and an evaluation of both a client's progress and his or her problems with the service network. Attuning the monitoring system to address all these levels can be extremely beneficial. Administrators can receive needed data for strategic planning and corrective action, while supervisors can use data concerning operations and case load management, and case managers have a decision-making and scheduling tool (Bowers and Bowers, 1977).

Evaluation as a core function always operates at two levels, the client and the system. At the client level, the essential question is whether the client is receiving and benefiting from needed services. Evaluation questions will relate to whether the client is making the expected progress toward individual goals, what the actual service outcomes are compared with the expected outcomes, whether the client is receiving services in a timely and efficient manner, what the assessment of quality of services received is, whether the client's needs change, whether the service plan should be continued or modified, and whether the client is ready to be terminated from the case management program.

At the system or program evaluation level, both formative and summative evaluations need to be conducted. The formative evaluation assists in program monitoring and in identifying problems and taking corrective action. The summative evaluation builds on baseline data established at the beginning of the program through the needs assessment and by comparing the current situation to the initial one. Baseline data include information from the needs assessment and resource identification processes and information obtained in the MBO statements of goals and objectives. At the systems level, the following questions will be useful in evaluation: "How is the system working?; How well is it meeting [clients'] needs?; What benefits are being derived from it?; How appropriate are the forms and reports that have been designed?; How efficiently does the system run?; What are the costs, and is it staying within a predetermined budget?" (Ford, 1983, p. 13). As in needs assessment, various data sources should be used to answer these questions. Relevant sources include records from the system, interviews with clients and service providers from the network agencies, the interagency task force, and questionnaires to clients staff.

Case management programs must account for the quality and efficiency of their services to several sources. Usually evaluative information on service quality and cost-effectiveness must be provided to funding sources and legitimating bodies such as agency boards. However, it is equally important to be accountable to clients, consumer groups, the public, the professional community, members of the service network, and most assuredly the staff. Monitoring and evaluating both program effects and effectiveness ensure accountability within and outside of the case management program.

Suggested Readings

Attkisson, C. C., Hargreaves, W. A., Horowitz, M. J., and Sorensen, J. E. (Eds.). *Evaluation of Human Service Programs.* New York: Academic Press, 1978.

Gruber, M. L. (Ed.). *Management Systems in the Human Services.* Philadelphia: Temple University Press, 1981.

Morris, R. L., and Fitz-Gibbons, C. T. *How to Measure Program Implementation.* Beverly Hills, Calif.: Sage, 1978.

National Institute of Mental Health. *The Design of Management Information Systems for Mental Health Organizations: A Primer.* DHHS Publication no. (ADM) 80-333. Washington, D.C.: U.S. Government Printing Office, 1980.

Rossi, P. H., Freeman, H. E., and Wright, S. R. *Evaluation: A Systematic Approach.* Beverly Hills, Calif.: Sage, 1979.

Schoech, D. *Computer Use in Human Service Organizations.* New York: Human Sciences Press, 1981.

Stumpf, J. *Case Management with the Frail Elderly: A Training Manual.* 2 vols. Case Management Model Project, Senior Care Action Network (SCAN), Long Beach Area Geriatric Health Care Council, Long Beach, Calif., 1981.

References

Attkisson, C. C., Hargreaves, W. A., Horowitz, M. J., and Sorensen, J. E. (Eds.). *Evaluation of Human Service Programs.* New York: Academic Press, 1978.

Beatrice, D. F. "Case Management: A Policy Option for Long-Term Care." Unpublished manuscript, University Health Policy Consortium, Brandeis University, 1979.

Boserup, D. G., and Gouge, G. V. *The Case Management Model: Concept, Implementation, and Training.* Athens, Ga.: Regional Institute of Social Welfare Research, 1980.

Bowers, G. E., and Bowers, M. R. *Cultivating Client Information Systems.* Human Services Monograph Series, Project Share 5. Rockville, Md.: Project Share, June 1977.

Bramhall, M. "Case Management Program." Unpublished manuscript, Montgomery County Mental Health Association, Kensington, Md., n.d.

Brekke, J. S. "A Monitoring Evaluation of PACT: A Community Support Program for Young Adult Schizophrenics." Unpublished doctoral dissertation, School of Social Work, University of Wisconsin-Madison, 1984.

Brill, N. I. *Team Work: Working Together in the Human Services.* Philadelphia: Lippincott, 1976.

Cannady, D. "Chronics and Cleaning Ladies." *Psychosocial Rehabilitation Journal,* 1982, *5* (1), 6–19.

Cotter, B. *Planning and Implementing Social Service Information Systems: A Guide for Management and Users.* Human Service Monograph Series, Project Share 25. Rockville, Md.: Project Share, September 1981.

Drucker, P. F. "What Results Should You Expect? A User's Guide to MBO." In M. L. Gruber (Ed.), *Management Systems in the Human Services.* Philadelphia: Temple University Press, 1981.

Fink, A., and Kosecoff, J. *An Evaluation Primer.* Beverly Hills, Calif.: Sage, 1978.

Folkenberg, J. "Compeer Provides Help for Patients Returning to Community." *ADAMHA News,* 1982, *8* (20), 1–5.

Ford, K. "Process and Tasks in Developing a Management Information System in a Case Management Agency." Unpublished manuscript, School of Social Work, University of Southern California, May 2, 1983.

Gilbert, N., and Specht, H. *Planning for Social Welfare.* Englewood Cliffs, N.J.: Prentice-Hall, 1977.

Grisham, M., White, M., and Miller, L. "An Overview of Case Management." MSSP Evaluation Unit, University Extension, University of California, Berkeley, 1983.

Gruber, M. L. (Ed.). *Management Systems in the Human Services.* Philadelphia: Temple University Press, 1981.

Hays, P. "Models of Case Management for the Chronically Mentally Ill." In H. Marlowe and R. Weinberg (Eds.), *Proceedings of the 1982 Florida Conference on Deinstitutionalization.* Tampa: University of South Florida, 1982.

Intagliata, J. "Operationalizing a Case Management System: A Multilevel Approach." In National Conference on Social Welfare, *Case Management: State of the Art.* Grant no. 54-P-71542/3-01. Washington, D.C.: Administration on Developmental Disabilities, U.S. Department of Health and Human Services, April 15, 1981.

Intagliata, J. "Improving the Quality of Community Care for the Chronically Mentally Disabled: The Role of Case Management." *Schizophrenia Bulletin,* 1982, *8,* 655–674.

Intagliata, J., and Baker, F. "Factors Affecting the Delivery of Case Management Services for the Chronically Ill." *Administration in Mental Health,* in press.

Kahn, A. J. "Institutional Constraints to Interprofessional Practice." In Helen Rehr (Ed.), *Medicine and Social Work.* New York: Prodist, 1974.

Kazdin, A. E. *Research Design in Clinical Psychology.* New York: Harper & Row, 1980.

Kimberly, J. R. "Organizational Size and the Structuralist Perspective: A Review, Critique, and Proposal." *Administrative Science Quarterly,* 1976, *21,* 571–597.

Kimberly, J. R. "Initiation, Innovation, and Institutionalization in the Creation Process." In J. R. Kimberly, R. H. Miles, and associates, *The Organizational Life Cycle: Issues in the Creation, Transformation, and Decline of Organizations.* San Francisco: Jossey-Bass, 1980a.

Kimberly, J. R. "The Life Cycle Analogy and the Study of Organizations: Introduction." In J. R. Kimberly, R. H. Miles, and
associates, *The Organizational Life Cycle: Issues in the Creation,
Transformation, and Decline of Organizations.* San Francisco:
Jossey-Bass, 1980b.

Lamb, H. R. "Therapists-Case Managers: More Than Brokers of
Service." *Hospital and Community Psychiatry,* 1980, *31,* 762–764.

Lamb, H. R. *Treating the Long-Term Mentally Ill.* San Francisco:
Jossey-Bass, 1982.

Lauffer, A. *Social Planning at the Community Level.* Englewood
Cliffs, N.J.: Prentice-Hall, 1978.

Levine, I. S., and Fleming, M. *Human Resource Development:
Issues in Case Management.* Baltimore: Center of Rehabilitation
and Manpower Services, University of Maryland, 1984.

McMahan, L., and associates. "Case Management/Systems and
Strategies." Unpublished manuscript, Department of Training,
State of California, Sacramento, 1982.

Mailick, M. D., and Ashley, A. A. "Politics of Interprofessional
Collaboration: Challenge to Advocacy." *Social Casework,* 1981,
62 (3), 131–137.

Miles, R. H. "Findings and Implications of Organizational Life
Cycle Research: A Commencement." In J. R. Kimberly, R. H.
Miles, and associates, *The Organizational Life Cycle: Issues in
the Creation, Transformation, and Decline of Organizations.* San
Francisco: Jossey-Bass, 1980.

Morris, R. L., and Fitz-Gibbons, C. T. *Evaluating Outcomes of
Social Programs.* Beverly Hills, Calif.: Sage, 1978.

Mosher, L. R., and Keith, S. J. "Research on the Psychosocial
Treatment of Schizophrenia: A Summary Report." *American
Journal of Psychiatry,* 1979, *136* (5), 623–631.

National Conference on Social Welfare. *Case Management: State of
the Art.* Grant no. 54-P-71542/3-01. Washington, D.C.: Administration on Developmental Disabilities, U.S. Department of
Health and Human Services, April 15, 1981.

National Institute of Mental Health. *The Design of Management
Information Systems for Mental Health Organizations: A Prim-
er.* DHHS Publication no. (ADM) 80-333. Washington, D.C.:
U.S. Government Printing Office, 1980.

Raia, A. P. *Managing by Objectives*. Glenview, Ill.: Scott, Foresman, 1974.

Ross, H. *Proceedings of the Conference on the Evaluation of Case Management Programs* (March 5-6, 1979). Los Angeles: Volunteers for Services to Older Persons, 1980.

Rossi, P. H., Freeman, H. E., and Wright, S. R. *Evaluation: A Systematic Approach*. Beverly Hills, Calif.: Sage, 1979.

Schoech, D. *Computer Use in Human Service Organizations*. New York: Human Sciences Press, 1982.

Schoech, D., and Schkade, L. L. "Computers Helping Caseworkers: Decision Support Systems." *Child Welfare*, 1980, *59* (9), 566-576.

Schwab, J. J., Warheit, G. J., Fennell, E. B., Stewart, R., and associates. "Needs Assessment Methods for the Community Mental Health Center." *Evaluation*, 1975, *2* (2), 64-76.

Schwartz, S. R., Goldman, H. H., and Churgin, S. "Case Management for the Chronically Mentally Ill: Models and Dimensions." *Hospital and Community Psychiatry*, 1982, *33* (12), 1006-1009.

Siegel, L. M., Attkisson, C. C., and Carson, L. G. "Need Identification and Program Planning in the Community Context." In C. C. Attkisson, W. A. Hargreaves, M. J. Horowitz, and J. E. Sorensen, *Evaluation of Human Service Programs*. New York: Academic Press, 1978.

Spano, R. M., and Lund, S. H. "Management by Objectives in a Hospital Social Service Unit." In Murray L. Gruber (Ed.), *Management Systems in the Human Services*. Philadelphia: Temple University Press, 1981.

Steinberg, R. M., and Carter, G. W. *Case Management and the Elderly*. Lexington, Mass.: Heath, 1983.

Stumpf, J. *Case Management with the Frail Elderly: A Training Manual*. 2 vols. Long Beach, Calif.: Case Management Model Project, Senior Care Action Network (SCAN), Long Beach Area Geriatric Health Care Council, 1981.

Test, M. "Continuity of Care in Community Treatment." In L. I. Stein, (Ed.), *New Directions for Mental Health: Community Support Systems for the Long-Term Patient*, no. 2. San Francisco: Jossey-Bass, 1979.

Thwing, E., and Cannady, D. "Community Support Care." Unpublished manuscript, Human Service Center, Rhinelander, Wis., 1979.

Turner, J. C., and Shifren, I. "Community Support Systems: How Comprehensive?" In L. I. Stein (Ed.), *New Directions for Mental Health: Community Support Systems for the Long-Term Patient*, no. 2. San Francisco: Jossey-Bass, 1979.

Warheit, G. J., Bell, R. A., and Schwab, J. J. *Planning for Change: Needs Assessment Approaches*. Gainesville, Fla.: J. Hillis Miller Health Center, University of Florida, 1974.

Weil, M. "Social Services in a Housing Authority Setting." Unpublished manuscript, School of Social Work, Hunter College, New York, 1975.

Weil, M. "Interprofessional Work in Adoptions—Collaboration and Beyond." *Social Work Papers*, 1979a, *15*, 46–54.

Weil, M. *Needs Assessment in the Context of California Social Service Planning*. Los Angeles, Calif.: South West Regional Laboratory, 1979b.

Weil, M. *Senior Centers in a Comprehensive Service Delivery System for Orange County: Report and Recommendations of the Orange County Senior Citizens Council—University of California at Irvine Study Team*. Irvine: Orange County Senior Citizens Council and University of California Extension, Irvine, July 1980.

Weil, M. "Report on Fiesta Educativa." Unpublished manuscript, School of Social Work, University of Southern California, 1981.

Weil, M. "Research on Issues in Collaboration Between Social Workers and Lawyers." *Social Service Review*, 1982, *56*, 393–405.

Weil, M. "Involvement of Senior Citizens in Needs Assessment and Service Planning." In Florence S. Schwartz (Ed.), *Voluntarism and Social Work Practice: A Growing Collaboration*. Lanham, Md.: University Press of America, 1984.

Weiner, M. E. *Human Services Management: Analysis and Applications*. Homewood, Ill.: Dorsey Press, 1982.

Weissman, H. H. *Integrating Services for Troubled Families: Dilemmas of Program Design and Implementation*. San Francisco: Jossey-Bass, 1978.

Weissman, H. H., and Weil, M. "Successes and Failures in Integrating Services and Helping Families." In H. H. Weissman, *Integrating Services for Troubled Families: Dilemmas of Program Design and Implementation.* San Francisco: Jossey-Bass, 1978.

Wilmington Housing Authority. *The Wilmington System.* Wilmington, Del.: Wilmington Housing Authority, 1972.

Zuboff, S. "New Worlds of Computer-Mediated Work." *Harvard Business Review,* September-October 1982, *60,* 142-152.

12

Professional
and Educational Issues
in Case Management
Practice

Marie Weil

This concluding chapter presents organizational, professional, and educational issues in case management practice. The particular nature of human services organizations determines the technology and frames organizational concerns in developing functional case management systems. While the plan of a case management system may be impeccable, the manner in which it is introduced is of paramount importance in how it will be received by staff and clients. A variety of issues that affect the development of case management programs are discussed to indicate areas of concern and areas of rapid growth in case management methods. The critical nature of interprofessional and interdisciplinary teamwork and collaboration is highlighted. Issues and concerns regarding the education and training of case managers are delineated, and general principles and recommendations for case management system development are presented. Finally, directions for case management

357

are indicated noting particularly the unique role that case managers can play in the empowerment of clients.

Case management as a process of planning, monitoring, and accounting for services is here to stay. The complexities of clients' needs, organizations, and organizational networks and the increasing demands for accountability combine to give case management a central role in the provision of services to vulnerable populations. Case management systems have emerged from earlier service planning designs and have formalized recording and decision making. The inherent rationality of social planning, however, must always accommodate the realities of life in human services organizations. This is not to indicate that human services organizations operate irrationally, but rather to acknowledge some of the realities of their missions, technologies, and resources.

Organizational Issues

By definition, case management systems will involve the workings not only of an organization but of a network of organizations, each of which has its own goals, organizational culture, and means of operation. The case management program must relate to other components of its own agency and take on the herculean task of coordinating and monitoring the activities of a particular and sometimes unique set of agencies, services, and programs for each one of its clients. To coordinate, monitor, and evaluate the direct services provided to each client, a pattern of relationships and service processes must be established that will foster collaboration and minimize competition among the agencies.

To build a collaborative network, a case management development team must be aware of the political economy of each of its constituent agencies and of the environmental factors affecting the interactions among the members of the service network (D. Austin, 1981). The politics of interagency interaction relate to perceptions of and competition over dominance and degree of influence and the economics of acquiring and using resources that are usually inadequate to meet the needs of the total target population. The central political issue that affects the development of a case management system is the tension between the case management program's need to exercise authority in the service network—to ensure that clients' needs for service are met at an adequate level—and each participating agency's concern for maintaining organizational autonomy. The need for case management programs to monitor and evaluate all services received by their clients clearly challenges the independence of the evaluated agencies and their domains of operation and influence. The case management program may depend on other programs and organizations to provide clients, and it will definitely depend on the governmental or private group that funds it and the groups that sanction it. These groups as well as the organizations that provide complementary service, competing organizations, and clients form the task environment of the case management program (Hasenfeld, 1983).

In order to function, a case management program must be able to cross boundaries between agencies, intervene in the internal workings of other organizations, and have the sanction to do so. To carry out its functions, the case management program must convince agencies in the service network that they and their clients will benefit from its activities. The service network agencies will be more accepting of case management if they share a service philosophy and if the case management program can provide demonstrable benefits, such as smoothing the operations of the service system, strengthening the expertise and domain of participating agencies, sharing the work with especially difficult clients, increasing collaboration and reducing competition with other network agencies, and adding new resources or increasing access to existing resources (Hasenfeld, 1983).

Negotiating the access needed to monitor and evaluate services will frequently require formal agreements or contracts between the case management program and the participating agencies. The political and economic balances among constituent agencies will affect all of the case management operations. If the case management program has legal responsibility for the client, as in child dependency cases, interagency relationships will be built around that responsibility.

In the language of organizational behavior, developers of case management programs are building an interorganizational network. The case management agency clearly depends on this

network to provide services that clients need. The service network
will be much more efficient and productive if a positive interdependence can be built. Especially at a time when resources for social
services are shrinking and client needs and target populations are
increasing, it is important to identify mutually beneficial exchanges
of resources. Interdependence means that the agencies need each
other to accomplish their own goals. When client populations are
shared and resources are shared to the benefit of agencies as well as
clients, the case management program is much likelier to be
successful.

Another tension that can arise in case management programs
is between the need to set up routines (time lines, procedures for
reporting, and information management procedures), specify tasks,
and set standards for making service decisions and the realities
posed by clients and their actual needs, which vary and are
frequently unique. The process of establishing time lines for
making certain decisions may be routinized, but the content of the
decisions, the particular service mix, and the means of working with
each client will be specific and certainly not routine. The variability
of client needs points up the fact that much of what is undertaken
in the human services involves risk and uncertainty (Perrow, 1967;
C. Austin, 1981). Direct cause-and-effect relationships of many
interventions are not clear. Since people are the raw material and
products of human services systems as well as the instruments of
change, staff and administrators must inevitably deal with many
value choices and must make decisions in the face of the individual
uniqueness of clients, the complexities of their situations, and
limited knowledge (Hasenfeld, 1983).

The tension often felt between line staff and administrators
in case management programs arises from administrative pressure
to routinize and standardize tasks versus staff desire for clinical
autonomy. This effort is usually prompted by the desire to increase
efficiency by processing more clients. In contrast, staff members'
clinical interest is in accommodating the unique needs of each
client, and they fear that standardization leads to doing the same
thing for all clients rather than planning individually for unique
needs (Schoech, 1982). Thus, the staff's wariness toward standardization is based on serious concern for client welfare as well as a

defense of professional judgment and autonomy. Professional judgment is the antithesis of routine, requiring the application of knowledge, values, and skills to analyze a case and to make decisions about the services that clients will receive in "situations that are often complex and ambiguous and whose outcomes are difficult to predict" (C. Austin, 1981, p. 10). This tension between routine and professional judgment is the heart of much staff resistance to case management systems.

To overcome this resistance, planners and implementers of case management systems must appreciate the variability of individual cases, recognize the value of professional judgment, and construct the case management system especially its reporting and decision-making components so that it will be genuinely useful to staff. Boserup and Gouge (1980) discuss the need to develop two-way accountability in case management systems so that not only are workers responsible for completing case management tasks, but administrators are responsible for creating the conditions through policy, organization of work, and supports to ensure that case management tasks can reasonably be carried out.

Introducing the Case Management System

Despite all possible planning, a series of problems should be anticipated when implementing a case management system in a service network. Robert Burns could have been discussing case management systems when he observed that "the best laid plans of mice and men gang aft aglae." It is very important for administrators, task force members, and planners to anticipate any problems that may arise. This preparation will not prevent problems from occurring, but it gives time to plan strategies and remedial action. An anticipated problem is almost always easier to handle than an unanticipated one. (Happily, there are also unanticipated benefits as well as the expected ones used to market the program.) Problems should be anticipated in introducing the case management system to staff, clients, supervisors, and members of the service network. Although one can never plan for all possible problems, it is important to isolate problem categories and set up the means of resolving these difficulties.

Staff. It is reasonable to expect that a fair number of the staff will be resistant if not downright hostile toward a new or computer-assisted case management system. Staff reaction is often, "But I'm a professional, don't you trust me to do my job and to work for the client's benefit?" Staff members may feel that Big Brother is peering at them constantly and interfering with their work. They may bring up the issue of professional autonomy, hoping to deflect administrators from their intention. However, MISs do not replace professional judgment; they are information tools that should be used to support and formulate it (Schoech, 1982). However, if administrators are going to use this argument, they had better be sure that they design an MIS that *does* aid and support professional judgment. User-oriented or "user-friendly" computer software is rapidly being developed for microcomputer systems. However, computer specialists should never be turned loose to design systems on their own. Administrators, evaluators, and staff must be represented when designing information and reporting systems and when identifying critical components of the program's and service network's decision-making system. In using consultants, it is important to find someone with a knowledge of human services agencies as well as of bits, bytes, and software. The clearer administrators are about their information needs and their reporting requirements, the more successful they will be in working with consultants. If staff are represented in the design of the system and are provided with information during the development of the system, they are much likelier to be cooperative if not enthusiastic.

What administrators and planners often overlook is that staff may have very good reason to be resistant. While planners may visualize a problem-oriented and decision-making system as being a magnificent improvement, staff members are not likely to welcome the change if they have been schooled to agonize over detailed, diagnostic process recording. Even though the MIS and other case management procedures may support staff decision making and eliminate time-consuming, repetitive forms of record keeping, it does two things that are discomforting: (1) It replaces a known process with an unknown process, and (2) it moves concrete reporting tasks to a more abstract and conceptually oriented level (Zuboff, 1982).

Staff members need to be assisted in preparing for such changes. As noted, they should be involved in the planning and implementation of the system. In addition they need to participate in monitoring the effects of the system on clients and themselves and in pinpointing problems and planning corrective actions. Through such processes, the system can truly become their instrument as well as that of administrators. In addition, it is critical that staff receive careful, supportive training in operating and understanding the system and in appreciating its benefits for their clients and themselves. Ford (1983, p. 13) sounds the proper note for staff involvement:

> There is a need to be sensitive to how the use of computers in an automated MIS (and case management system) affects staff relationships and the accomplishment of their jobs. One rule of thumb is that everyone who puts information into the system (and line staff are essential for maintaining the flow of accurate updated information) must get something out of it. There must be a reason for line staff to fill out the extra forms. Additionally, it is important to emphasize the use of their skills and professional judgment when assessing the importance of the information provided as it pertains to a unique situation. The increased quantity and accessibility of information can be used to increase feedback, learning, and self-management as opposed to depersonalizing and routinizing the work place.

Supervisors should be trained to handle not only their own learning needs but also those of their staff. It is always necessary to prepare supervisors for the changes that they will have to enact and defend.

Service Network Members. When initiating a new case management program or radically restructuring an old one, it is of course important to have representatives from all the service network members involved in planning and setting up the system. But that is not sufficient. Invariably it will be agency leaders who are involved in the planning task force, and it is very important before instituting the new system to provide training for staff of all involved agencies in the system's purpose, methods of work, collaboration patterns, and advocacy provisions so that they will know about the changes. Such training can help pave the way for the case manager when he or she spans the boundaries of service programs, asking for more effective interagency collaboration and serving as advocates for the clients.

Clients. From the first contacts in outreach and needs assessment, the case management system's goals and objectives should be explained to clients. Setting out general goals can help clients participate more effectively in developing their own service plans. Nothing in a new system replaces the client's relationship with his or her case manager. The case manager should be the resource that assists the client in finding and making linkages with needed services. The case manager needs to be there for the client when things go awry and needs to work with the client in monitoring and evaluating the services that the client receives. Careful work of this kind can help to empower clients and can enable them to learn from and use services more effectively. When this occurs, many of the goals of any case management system are achieved.

Issues in Program Analysis

The previous chapter and Chapter Two discussed models for case management systems. Any of the models—generalist, primary therapist, interdisciplinary team, comprehensive service center, family, supportive care, or volunteer—must be adapted to fit target population needs, organizational capabilities, and service network capabilities and environment. The model chosen will determine the kind and quality of organizational relations as well as the task and functional emphasis in the case management system. However, choosing a model is not the end of the analytical and adaptation process. Plans to assess service efficiency, service effectiveness, and cost-effectiveness are major features of the program and must be scrutinized. These structural elements will have a major influence on the process and tasks of service integration.

In addition, when planning a case management system, the process requirements of the selected case management model must be compared with organizational and interorganizational realities. Boserup and Gouge (1980, p. 35) recommend using a "process analysis matrix," by which each major case management function can be compared with the major determining factors, specifically policies, resources, the case management organization, and the interorganizational system. The authors also include a category for analyzing the staff training needs for each of the major sets of functions.

The major functions of case management are: (1) client identification and outreach, (2) individual assessment and diagnosis, (3) service planning and resource identification, (4) linking the client to needed services, (5) service implementation and coordination, (6) monitoring, (7) advocacy, and (8) evaluation. To apply the process analysis matrix, each of these functions should be analyzed by administrators and staff in terms of prevailing policies, available resources, and intra- and interorganizational issues. For example, the new monitoring procedures for the system will probably institute more stringent monitoring policies for both the case management agency and the participating agencies. The members of the service network will need to alter policies so that staff from the case management agency can monitor clients' progress. Resources, in terms of personnel, facilities, and funds, will definitely affect the case management system. There may be a shortage of appropriately trained staff, or the existing staff may not wish to alter their work methods to accommodate a more formal case management process. The case management program will have to document service monitoring carefully and foster cooperation with the members of the service network to ensure compliance with its strictures regarding time, decision making, and documentation.

A tool such as the process analysis matrix can be quite useful for planners, but more important, it can be used by staff to identify probable agency and system effects and needed modifications. It can also be used in teaching staff practice approaches that will be supportive both to clients and to the case management system. This matrix can also be useful in stimulating discussion and in developing a consensus for supporting the case management system.

Equally important, the matrix can help to identify areas in which staff must be trained so that they can adapt to and adopt the new system.

For the system to be successful, the preferred outcomes for clients, staff, the program, and the service network must be identified first. If overall goals can be set for each of these categories to operationalize the preferred outcomes, it becomes much simpler to develop strategies as well as to measure the differences between objectives and achievements. Achieving program objectives will largely depend on how successfully people (clients and staff) are matched with technology.

Staff and Technology

Coordinating staff with the technological requirements of the case management system involves a variety of program development issues. Decisions must be made about auspices; service plans, reporting, and contracts; essential services; staffing patterns; supervision; the size and mix of case loads; and the types of decisions case managers must make. These decisions will vary with the demands of each program but must be considered by all.

Auspices. Decisions about the auspices under which a case management program will function are often complex. Case management programs have frequently been funded at the state level and administered locally (White and Grisham, 1982). They might also be funded and administered by the state or county or administered by a local voluntary agency using multiple funding sources. Auspices may be dictated by funding sources, but the local program must ensure that it has sufficient program autonomy to develop a case management system that is responsive to local needs. Frequently auspices are a major determinant of program design, the case management model, and service priorities.

Service Plans, Reporting, and Contracts. Client assessment and service planning based on clearly defined service objectives are becoming embedded in case management systems in most fields. In work with the educationally handicapped, the objective-oriented format is called the individual educational plan (IEP); in work with the developmentally disabled, it is called the individual development plan (IDP); in work with the mentally disordered, the individual program plan (IPP); and in work with people with physical disabilities, the individual habilitation plan (IHP). These models of service planning are so far some of the strongest and best-developed aspects of case management systems (Karls, 1983).

In human services programs and in mental health education, the major focus has frequently been on the process of work rather than on clearly specified objectives and measurable outcomes. Case management differs in focus from case load. As Boserup and Gouge (1980) comment, the phrase "carrying a case load" evokes an image of a worker laboring under a heavy burden, holding it aloft, and perhaps like Tantalus, always pushing the case load uphill. By contrast, case management emphasizes decision making, moving people through a service system, and removing them from the service system when possible. Movement through and beyond is the image rather than holding. The change to case management challenges methods, ideologies, and work patterns in many human service fields as it seeks to move away from a focus on the process to an orientation toward service provision based on the attainment of specific objectives and goals for clients.

The problem-solving process between client and worker lies at the heart of case management and must be supported, not undercut, by goal setting and monitoring. The case-recording system in particular should be structured so that it both supports the decison-making, planning, and evaluation process undertaken by the client and worker and meets the information requirements of program monitoring and evaluation. Case recording should take place at least as each major function in the case management process is concluded. More formal reports may also have to be made for supervisory, information management, or evaluation purposes at these points. Staff frequently encounter difficulties in fulfilling the recording and reporting functions because of the need to move from a process-oriented, descriptive method of recording to a method that focuses on goals and objectives at each step. Process records tended to focus on client problems; Boserup and Gouge (1980, p. 93) illustrate that the objective-oriented method provides the "flip side" of problem focus, because each problem that the client has should generate an objective, that is, what the client, worker, or other staff person will do to remedy the problem.

Service plans are the instruments that enable a case management system to focus on goals and outcomes. The case manager's work in developing a service plan focuses on the managerial skills of organizing, directing, and coordinating (National Association of Social Workers, 1982). To develop a service plan, the case manager must interview and assess the client's problems and then using forms and increasingly making use of computerized planning systems, the worker along with the client develops an initial problem list that becomes the basis of the service plan (National Association of Social Workers, 1982). Because of the orientation toward objectives, even the first problem list presents not only a listing of problems but also the "desired results of service" for each problem listed, records preservice activities to be undertaken by the case manager or client, and notes the agreed-upon priority of each problem (p. 8). The case manager then completes the preliminary resource assessment and determines client eligibility and can then proceed to develop the formal service plan. It is important to note that in an objective-oriented case management system the emphasis is on desired outcomes even at the earliest stages of client-worker interactions (National Association of Social Workers, 1982).

The service plan goes further than the problem list in that it not only lists problems, and the expected or desired results of service, but also specifies the intervention strategy, the steps to be taken, and the projected dates for achieving goal milestones (National Association of Social Workers, 1982). The specificity of the service plan makes it a useful therapeutic and planning tool for the client, involving him or her deeply in problem solving and decision making. This involvement is the earliest step toward client empowerment in the case management process. As White (1983) indicates, a service planning format that uses forms and sometimes computer entries assists in both organizing data collection and partializing problems.

Setting goals with clients is critical to assessing client progress over time. Carefully formatted service plans enable case managers to clearly specify goals and expected completion times for each of a client's problem areas. Boserup and Gouge (1980, pp. 171–172) offer the following guidelines for developing appropriate objectives for clients:

- Is the objective statement constructed properly (action verb plus single key result plus target date)?
- Does its achievement relate clearly to the case manager's and the client's responsibilities?
- Can it be understood by those who will play a role in its implementation?
- Is the objective realistic and attainable? Does it represent a significant challenge to the client and the case manager?
- Will the result, when achieved, justify the expenditure of time and resources required to achieve it?
- Is the objective consistent with basic agency policies and practices?
- Can the accountability for final results be clearly established?

After the service plan has been established, the case manager may use a variety of recording tools and documents to record client progress and needed service modifications. In addition, the case manager may also need to file and use documents that relate to legal aspects of a case, such as a court report in a child dependency case or medical or fiscal records for an elderly person. Most case management systems will also record information on all client contacts (and contacts with service network agencies). The case recording system should document client progress and problems and provide the requisite information for the management information system or modular design reporting requirements (Taylor, 1981). Steinberg and Carter (1983) indicate three levels of information that should be reported: (1) the client-worker level, (2) the agency or program level, and (3) the service system level. For each level, information on resources, performance, and outcomes should be recorded.

With the addition of case recording and management information or modular design reporting systems, the specific case management model for an agency should be complete. The credibility (from both organizational and professional viewpoints), relevance, and practicality of the selected model should be analyzed (Boserup and Gouge, 1980). If the system does not seem credible, agencies and staff will not support it. If it is irrelevant, it will be undermined or ignored, and future prospects for case coordination will be damaged. If it is impractical, that is, if the reporting requirements are so cumbersome that this function usurps other major activities, it will be discarded. An analysis of credibility, relevance, and practicality are means of reality testing and providing answers to the question "Will this system and model design work with the sponsoring agency and the service network?" Problems identified will indicate needs for system modification, simplification, or training or organizational changes that will make case management possible.

One means of preventing interagency problems of credibility and relevance and of specifying the patterns of interaction among agencies in the service network is to develop interagency contracts at the inception of the case management system. These contracts should spell out the nature of the work, the services to be included or exchanged, the procedures for monitoring, and the plans for evaluating the case management program. Such contracts must be negotiated by system administrators who can set policy and see that agreements are adhered to. The nature of the contracts will differ greatly depending on whether they are voluntary agreements or formal purchase-of-service contracts, but in either instance a written document forms a useful basis for interaction.

Contracts might also be used for service agreements for particular clients. The Lower East Side Family Union used service contracts with a variety of agencies to ensure that multiproblem families received needed services (Weissman, 1978). When such contracts are used, a major part of the case managers' responsibility is to monitor the contract and see that services are being delivered as planned. The contract can be a useful planning and decision-making tool and can also serve as a means of identifying service problems and indicating needs for corrective action.

Essential Services. Case management programs will either provide services or be involved in brokering services for clients. For any case management program, it is critical to identify the services essential for the target population. Services will vary in accordance with the needs and problems of the target population. The needs assessment process described in Chapter Eleven is the means by which the unique needs of a population can be identified and the existing and needed services can be assessed. Using this process, planners would also identify unmet needs and any general resistance that the target population may have toward a particular type of service or a particular agency (White and Grisham, 1982). This information will be a valuable tool in building a functional and collaborative service network. Where essential services are lacking, planners and administrators will have to determine if they or the case managers or supervisors need to be involved in resource development. This might take forms varying from lobbying for funds for needed services to providing technical services to assist local agencies in learning to serve new populations.

Staffing. One issue is quite problematic: "Who should do case management" (Grisham, White, and Miller, 1983, p. 10)? In what discipline should the case manager be trained? What disciplines are most effective for each field and model? Should case management be handled by a team or an individual? Should case management staff have advanced graduate degrees (Grisham, White, and Miller, 1983)?

Who will be the practitioner in the developing field of case management? None of the major helping professions yet claim case management to be under their purview. In fact, case management is sometimes relegated to clerks or lesser technicians in the human services. When the emphasis in case management is primarily on locating and using community resources to facilitate the client's return to social functioning, people who are trained to use the community's social services on behalf of the client dominate. In the helping professions, the social worker and the public health nurse most commonly conduct this type of case management. The psychiatrist, psychologist, and other mental health professionals usually work as primary therapists and case managers who focus on the internal resources of a client. In case management with the elderly, where health care and socialization needs are most important, "78 percent of the programs reported principal occupational identity of their coordinators was social workers and 21 percent nurses" (Steinberg, Carter, and White, 1979, p. 15). Who functions best as a case manager in specific systems must be studied.

These issues elicit strong feelings, but at present there is little research on which to base decisions. In the field of chronic mental illness, Intagliata and Baker (in press) report that no field of preparation is correlated with superior performance of case management functions. However, they did note that the more highly educated therapists tend to spend less time in case management. Levine and Fleming (1984) report that one university offers a master's degree in developmental disabilities that stresses competency-based education in case management. The authors favor professionally trained case managers who understand the roles of advocacy, expediting, assessing, planning, coordinating, and evaluating. Skills in facilitating and mediating groups and in interprofessional collaboration are also needed regardless of the field of practice. Because all human services organizations operate as "loosely coupled systems in which work units preserve considerable autonomy" (Hasenfeld, 1983, p. 150), it is particularly important for case managers to be able to function with professional autonomy in their own agencies and to command respect based on expertise within the service network. All the mental health and human services fields need to incorporate more case management methodology into their curricula. Whether professionals or paraprofessionals are used as case managers, it is of greatest importance that they receive substantial training.

Supervision. Related to staffing is the question of who should supervise and what models of supervision should be employed in a case management program. The roles of supervisors and case managers must be clearly described and distinguished. The model of supervision depends on the relationship between the case manager and the supervisor. Austin and Caragonne (1981) has found that vague roles and poorly defined responsibilities result in a greater emphasis on direct service functions and a deemphasis on case management functions. The direct service function of people trained in counseling or therapy will be particularly emphasized unless these people have an opportunity to learn the role and tasks of the case manager. If case managers are unsure about what to do or how to do it, they "will probably do that with which they are most comfortable" (Levine and Fleming, 1984, p. 31).

Kadushin (1976) has described the basic roles in supervision in the human services as administrative, including evaluating, providing support, and educating. These roles are present in case management, but special attention may need to be given to the teaching role with regard to "interpreting the service delivery system" (Caragonne, 1983, p. 72). Grisham, White, and Miller (1983, p. 11) note that the operations of case management systems might be improved if the more traditional models of individual supervision were replaced by models of accountability based on "appropriate team leadership." These authors see team leadership as better than traditional supervision, especially in multidisciplinary teams. In the team model, leadership is a major factor and team leaders must have skills in group facilitation and management.

Case Load Size and Mix. Like many other workers, case managers typically feel overworked. The principal areas of complaint relate to the size of case loads and the amount of paperwork required to fulfill case management functions (White and Grisham, 1982). Case load size is a problem in most agencies that serve vulnerable populations. Particularly in periods of declining service resources, the staff of case management programs are likely to find themselves trying to work with more and more clients with fewer and fewer community resources. Even in the best of times, however, many case managers will feel that they could provide better quality services with smaller case loads. For any new program, the work load will need to be monitored to gather data on reasonable case load size. Somewhat ironically, program success can cause very large case loads. If satisfied clients and community agencies broadcast the virtues of a case management program, it is likely to find its efficiency and quality limited by rapid increases in service demands with no accompanying increase in staff and other resources.

An even more complex problem in case load management has to do not with numbers of clients but with severity of problems. In their study of the Multipurpose Senior Services Project, White and Grisham (1982) found that case load mix was of great concern to a number of the program staff that they interviewed. "It was suggested that case load size should be directly linked to the mix of client conditions in that case load since the amount of effort involved with any given client varies with the condition of that client. Thus, a case load consisting of clients with more severe conditions should be smaller than a case load made up of 'healthier' clients." (White and Grisham, p. 255).

Types of Decisions. As examination of service plans reveals, case management is largely a process of decision making. One of the crucial elements in designing a case management system is to carefully determine what types and what range of decisions case managers will have responsibility for. The types of decisions will be governed by the needs and special problems of the target population. For example, in child welfare the needs of children for adult care and nurturance and the timing mandates of permanency planning legislation will shape the decision-making process regarding family reunification, foster care, or adoption planning. In programs serving the frail elderly, White and Grisham (1982, p. 37) found that staff reported that their decisions related to eight major areas: "level of care, emergencies, direct client aspects, time management, living arrangements, personal worker aspects, providers, and significant others." Clarification of expected decision areas and decision-making patterns is important for any case management system. Regardless of the special needs of the target population, general areas that will need to be considered in formulating decision-making areas are the "functional ability of clients and the amount of informal support available to them. In addition, client wishes are important in the decision-making process" (White and Grisham, 1982, p. 41). The importance of decisions reached by case managers highlights the necessity of collecting accurate and complete data during the assessment of client needs. As White and Grisham (p. 41) point out, case managers usually have time to review reports and meet with team members before making decisions; "however, there are instances . . . when a worker must make a decision 'on the spot.' At these times, workers must rely solely on their knowledge of the client, the community, and their own experience and background to make decisions. For this reason, the ability to solve problems and think independently is crucial."

Performance Issues

Various issues affect job performance in case management. Problems with "burnout" have been reported, caused either by stress from dealing with specific populations or dissatisfaction with routine work. A lack of career advancement is a frequent cause of staff unrest in large case management systems. The size of the case load also affects worker performance. Although different sizes are optimal in different fields, an overload of cases will significantly depress job performance (Levine and Fleming, 1984; Intagliata and Baker, in press; Steindorff, Lannon, and Soldano, n.d.).

In one study (White and Grisham, 1982), job satisfaction in case management has been related to contributing to the program's mission, being committed to working with the frail elderly, reducing dependence, developing new methods for serving the elderly, and enjoying working with other case management staff. "The opportunity to work as a team is perceived by many staff as a learning experience in which knowledge and expertise is shared" (White and Grisham, 1982, p. 62).

Autonomy and Clout. As previously noted, case managers must often function autonomously as boundary spanners as they intervene on behalf of clients in a variety of service settings. Their ability to act autonomously within their own setting in other agencies will depend on the kinds and degrees of authority or control that they have with regard to service provision for clients. Advanced training or status as an expert or an experienced worker can assist in developing clout, but actual authority related to service delivery, decision-making contracts, or reimbursement is the bottom line. Scott and Cassidy (1981) state that case managers need administrative support, and numerous authors cite the need for clout (Minnesota Department of Public Welfare, 1980; Platman and others, 1982; Schwartz, Goldman, and Churgin, 1982).

Interagency contracts, case conferences, or policies that specify that case managers have the authority to monitor services are all ways to provide clout to the case manager and ensure that the difficult functions of service monitoring and evaluation can be carried out. Other possible solutions to this problem include making the case management system the only entry point for core services (Intagliata, 1982), and giving case managers purchase-of-service power (Schwartz, Goldman, and Churgin, 1980). With purchase-of-service power, case managers can arrange services for clients and pay for them. The issue of conflict between outside coordination and professional autonomy, which has already been discussed, is a pervasive problem in the field. Schwartz, Goldman, and Churgin (1982, p. 32) define four kinds of authority that can assist case managers in fulfilling their duties: administrative, legal, fiscal, and clinical. In Chapter Eight, Ron Honnard provides a detailed discussion of these types of authority and their importance for case managers.

Time Management. Efficient management of time is a factor that affects all case managers. The ability to juggle the demands of various clients in a case load, monitor services for all clients, participate in case conferences and counseling sessions make heavy demands and require skills in decision making and scheduling. The needs of the target population and the specific case management model will shape the particular issues relevant for time management in any system, but in all programs successful case managers are likely to be those who have skills in planning, scheduling, and managing time.

Cost-Effectiveness. The issue of cost-effectiveness was discussed in the previous chapter, but it is valuable to note that the ability to document cost-effectiveness (for example, through reduced hospitalization, or limiting the time a child spends in foster care) is a major measure of the success of any case management system. Weiner (1982) has noted that it is important to document not only the costs of instituting a new system but the costs and risks to clients if it is not implemented.

Service Quality, Service Availability, and Resource Development. The quality and availability of services are perennial issues for all case management programs. Service availability concerns the existence and accessibility of services needed by the target population. If the services are used by the general community, the case manager will need to assure that case management clients are receiving adequate and nondiscriminatory service. If the services are specifically designed for the target population, the case manager will need to ascertain whether they in fact meet client needs and are delivered in appropriate and supportive ways.

Service quality is often a sore point. A case manager may have a long list of resources but be unwilling to use many of them because he or she deems the service quality unacceptable or the service delivery and client-worker interaction inappropriate. Service quality is particularly problematic since the monitoring procedures

of a case management program may identify numerous problems in service quality or gaps in the service network but will usually not be accompanied by the financial resources or staff capability to remedy such problems. Often social action, training, and education are needed to remedy deficiencies in the service system for vulnerable populations, and these are often long-term solutions. The involvement of case management program staff in resource development raises other types of problems. White and Grisham (1982) cite numerous questions related to whether case managers should be directly involved in resource development, whether case management programs should establish internal or new services that compete with established but poor quality community services, and whether case management programs "should provide the means for expanding existing services or developing new services" (p. 257). As Ron Honnard noted in Chapter Eight, case managers should be responsible for identifying gaps in service but should not be held accountable for resolving service problems when they do not have the means and resources to do so.

Interprofessional Relationships, Teams, and Collaboration

Interprofessional or interdisciplinary involvements are inevitable in case management practice. The needs of vulnerable populations require the skills and services of a multitude of diverse helping professions and service providers. One of the central skills of case management practice is the ability to work effectively with members of other professions, disciplines, and agencies for the common good of a client. Frequently there are many difficulties in interdisciplinary communications and involvements because in addition to personal, class, and ideological interests, members of different professions will have quite different (though sometimes overlapping) professional value bases, knowledge bases, and practice methodologies. Central skills for a case manager, therefore, are to articulate client needs to a wide variety of service providers, develop common interests and commitments to client service despite different auspices and approaches, and to manage, sequence, and orchestrate service delivery from various agencies and profes-

sionals in ways that are beneficial to the client and supportive of the case management system's goals and objectives.

Case managers may be involved with a variety of service delivery teams. In large, comprehensive service centers, they may be a part of (or leader of) an interdisciplinary team from within the agency. In many situations, however, the case manager will have to form a new "team" to work with each new client. Such teams are formed to provide the services needed by the client. The divergent interests of members of different disciplines can obviously cause numerous difficulties in communication and service planning, and the policies, constraints, and differences in purpose can create numerous problems in developing interagency teams to be involved with particular clients. Where the case management program is able to establish interagency contracts that specify case conferences, client service contracts, and responsibilities for communication and service monitoring, then case coordination can become a viable reality and interprofessional collaboration can greatly strengthen the services provided to clients.

An important element of education and training for case managers, therefore, should involve means and methods of interdisciplinary collaboration, group leadership, and facilitation and group decision making.

Training and Education for Case Management

Case Managers. Each of the eight major functions of case management require specific knowledge and skills. Outreach and determination of eligibility requires knowledge of the criteria and skills in contacting agencies, clients, consumer organizations, and community groups to explain program purposes and the potential benefits of participation in the case management program. In assessment and diagnosis, some knowledge and skills will be general, but some will be specific to the target population. Generally, the case manager will need to understand biopsychosocial functioning and have the skills for assessing client abilities to function in community life, in family life or intimate relationships, in service networks, and in social interactions. In most fields, case management is intended to improve functioning and to foster physical, psychological, emotional, and social wellness. A client's

level of functioning and ability to be actively involved in the case management process is also part of the assessment of functioning. Increasingly, the professional ideologies related to case management stress client participation and client independence. Empowering clients to take charge of their own lives and their own case management is increasingly stressed. To assist in this process, case managers also need knowledge and skills that foster independence and self-advocacy in clients rather than passivity. Thus, a mix of clinical, assessment, and advocacy skills are required.

Service planning requires a knowledge of the resources available in the community and of specialized resources and services that members of the target population may need. Also, the case manager must know how to design a service plan and combine resources that will benefit the client most. In addition, logical and analytical thinking is needed to develop a sequence of services and interventions that will help the client. Planning also involves skill in developing a service combination that will, within the limits of the available resources, optimally meet a client's needs. Skills in helping the client to make plans and in developing contingency plans are also important.

The linking function stems from planning and requires knowledge of the service system and the ability to work with clients and service network agencies and staff. Managing, sequencing, and relationship skills are needed to make the linkages work.

Service implementation and coordination requires that the worker (1) intervene to ensure that services are provided, (2) assist the client in using services, and (3) solve problems in service delivery, coordination, and client receptivity. Monitoring requires knowledge of the service delivery processes and skill at analyzing service delivery problems and interprofessional collaboration. The case manager must also know when to move from collaboration to advocacy (Mailick and Ashley, 1981; Weil, 1979). For evaluation, a case manager must understand procedures for assessing a client's progress and for using information systems.

Additionally, all case managers must know task group processes and have group facilitation and decision-making skills. The complex set of responsibilities illustrates the range of skills required to handle the various case management roles: advocate, broker, diagnostician, planner, community organizer, service organizer, service monitor, record keeper, evaluator, colleague, consultant, service coordinator, counselor, therapist, expeditor, and problem solver. Knowing how to order roles and how to move from one to another illustrates another level of skill.

In a survey of case coordination programs, Bertsche and Horejsi (1980, p. 96) identified the following areas as needing emphasis in training and supervising case managers:

> advocacy principles, the broker role, the mediation model, crisis intervention, systems of record keeping, state and federal regulations regarding the handling of client data, the consultation process, informal resource systems in the community, prevailing community attitudes towards various client groups, the normalization principle, public relations, principles of organizational behavior and change, and approaches to organizational management. Skills of special importance include helping the client to communicate with professionals and assert wants and needs, writing behavioral objectives, preparing written reports for professionals and lay persons, abstracting and summarizing data drawn from diverse sources, verbal transmission of information, public speaking and dealing with the media, and using supervision and consultation effectively. An additional skill is maintaining a degree of autonomy within one's own organization.

Supervisors. Supervisors in case management systems must fully understand the roles, functions, and knowledge and skill requirements for case managers. They need to be able to teach the case management staff how to sequence and carry out these functions. In addition, supervisors must know how to use a management information system, how to assess worker and program responsiveness to clients' needs, and how to evaluate efficiency and effectiveness. Supervisors will also need skills in group facilitation and decision making and may be involved in internal planning and evaluation as well as interagency contracting and negotiation to set up workable service arrangements. Finally, supervisors need expertise in leadership skills as well as a knowledge of management and workflow control.

Administrators. Administrators must have sound conceptual and practical knowledge of how the case management system functions and its relationships to network agencies. They will need skills in administration, program planning and evaluation, and information management and skills in interprofessional collaboration and negotiation to establish interagency contracts. Also important to administrators are the basic functions of managing, controlling, directing, and evaluating the internal operations of the agency and understanding the means of building effective interagency networks. In addition, administrators must be greatly involved in designing and developing information management and reporting systems. Leadership abilities are also required to keep a case management program on track.

Education for Case Management. Although case managers enter programs from many different disciplines, most have background in one of the mental health or health professions: social work, nursing, psychology, or psychiatry. Each of these disciplines should include more information on case management in their curricula. If professionals are not trained to carry out these functions, it is unlikely that they will fully integrate case management functions into their professional role. When this occurs, case management functions are often viewed as secondary. Case management will be taken more seriously if it is an integral part of one's professional education.

Currently, most professionals enter case management programs inadequately prepared. Consequently, agencies must make a considerable investment in training to assure competency and effectiveness in case management principles, methods, and techniques.

General Principles and Recommendations for Case Management Programs

In the extensive study of case coordination programs for the elderly undertaken at the Social Policy Laboratory of the Andrus

Gerontology Center at the University of Southern California, Raymond Steinberg and his colleagues collected exhaustive information about case management, analyzing over a thousand earlier programs that could provide guidelines for developing case management programs (Steinberg, White, and Carter, 1980). Most of their conclusions were "lessons" supported by the extensive survey of current programs that Steinberg's research team conducted (Steinberg and Carter, 1983). The following is a list of these guidelines for case management programs (Steinberg, 1978, pp. 5-6):

1. No one program model suits all communities.
2. The majority of users of innovative multipurpose or case coordination projects are not the at-risk populations for which that particular program was designed.
3. The agency that coordinates other agencies should not operate direct services.
4. Coordination is very expensive, as well as difficult. Don't try to coordinate too many agencies at once.
5. Public/voluntary agency funding contracts can work, but successful coordination requires moderate stress.
6. Consumer and community involvement is difficult, takes time, and is a two-edged sword. Different degrees of community control are indicated for different kinds of objectives.
7. Colocation does not equal coordination. Unification of different services under one administration does not guarantee coordination.
8. Authority helps but does not guarantee coordination. Purely cooperative models rarely succeed.
9. Accountability mechanisms are hellish to install and maintain, but can be productive in time.
10. A coordination system should be evolutionary and cumulative.
11. The potential efficiency and effectiveness of a coordination program cannot be evaluated during the first and second years. (This does not preclude performance monitoring and documenting the experience and the rate of progress.)
12. The leader of a coordination project must be a super being with optimum political skills, ad-

ministrative competence, missionary fervor, and familiarity with the entire range of professional interventions and management techniques. In addition, the leader must, during the early phases of the new project, be primarily process-oriented and in later phases, be primarily task-oriented.

13. At all levels of coordination, it is crucial that there be frequent and genuine interpersonal contact between representatives of agencies who are essential to the program's success.

One assumption based on research of the past literature (Steinberg, White, and Carter, 1980) did not hold up in the program research conducted by Steinberg and his research team. Current program managers reported that it was worth trying to coordinate even "incompetent and irrelevant services" (Steinberg and Carter, 1983, p. 68). These people felt that case management maximized the benefits that clients received even from an inadequate system; in addition, case management provided a means of lobbying for improved services.

These guidelines were developed from a study of programs for one population, the elderly. They constitute one of the areas that would be valuable for further research in case management to test their applicability to different population groups. In general, however, the organizational literature tends to support these guidelines; thus, they merit consideration and scrutiny for case management program planning and development.

Empirical study of Multipurpose Senior Services Programs brought White and Grisham (1982, pp. 261–265) to the following recommendations that may well have application to other service populations.

- The project should clearly define its approach to case management.
- A period of at least one year should be allowed for the start-up phase of a case management project.
- The preimplementation phase should include a public relations effort to inform the service community and the target population of the project's goals and operations.
- Project policy and procedural manuals should be

developed before site operations are implemented. Subsequent changes, directives, and decisions should be communicated in writing.

- A functional MIS should be in place at the time of project implementation with capacity for change and expansion over time.
- It is essential that communication between the central administrative agency and the local sites be frequent and open and include consultation, technical assistance, problem solving, and feedback.
- When implementing case management in multiple sites, sufficient flexibility should be incorporated into project design to accommodate to various local communities.
- Site selection should include careful examination of the impact that host agency requirements will have on the site's ability to function effectively.
- In the design of a broker-model case management program, some purchase of service capacity shoud be incorporated.
- Agreements for service referrals and contracts should include unambiguous standards for quality of service provision and procedures addressing problems of compliance.
- Contracts for purchase of services and agreements for service referrals should be established before clients are taken on.
- Access to a minimal set of services should be ensured before taking on clients.
- Serious consideration should be given to what role local sites should take in developing resources in response to identified service gaps.

Directions in Case Management Practice

This book has examined case management practice in six major fields of human services practice and has presented general issues in the organization, evaluation, and development of case management systems. This material presents the state of the art in case management practice. Case management will become more sophisticated in the coming years, as computerized systems of data management and service tracking become more "user-friendly." As a result, case managers are likely to need more skills in data management while maintaining their skills in clinical areas and general systems management. However, the available computer technology, although sophisticated, is not yet attuned to many of the issues of service quality with which case management systems must deal. Much more work is needed to maximize the contributions that automated data systems can make and to address the quality as well as quantity issues related to service delivery and outcome evaluations. Model testing and further research may also improve the means of monitoring client services. Monitoring methods, as well as the area of service implementation, need further conceptual and methodological development.

Case management has developed fairly rapidly in the fields of child welfare, care of the developmentally disabled, care of the elderly, health care, and mental health care. It is needed in other areas of human service as well. For example, case management could be very useful in working with battered women and their children by preparing them through counseling and skill development to work out more independent life-styles. Programs for ethnic populations or populations with special needs could also benefit. For example, refugee families usually connect to a principal agency with regard to resettlement and community adjustment. Case management could not only assist specific families but indicate problems and gaps in the network of services available to these populations and provide advocates who would work toward more responsive services and a more comprehensive service network. In general, any population that is vulnerable or at risk is likely to be in need of case management services.

Weissman, Epstein, and Savage (1983, p. 105) note that "it is the depth of skill in planning, coordinating, and monitoring that distinguishes the case manager from the ordinary clinician." Weick (1977) comments that the essential skill of the case manager relates to his or her involvement in keeping the service network agencies up to date on what is happening with the client. Far from being routinized automatons, case managers are in the forefront of an area of service provision that can be of major significance to clients of human services agencies. They can see to it that clients are viewed holistically; they can create individualized service systems; and they can intervene with clients, their personal support networks, and the service network to see that clients receive needed services, that they benefit from services, and that they move toward higher, more productive, and more satisfying levels of functioning. Case managers have a unique role to play in the empowerment of clients. The potential for healing, development, growth, and empowerment is exciting, and case managers need to claim the very special values and skills of this complex service function.

Suggested Readings

Austin, D. M. "The Political Economy of Social Benefit Organizations: Redistributive Services and Merit Goods." In H. D. Stein (Ed.), *Organization and the Human Services.* Philadelphia: Temple University Press, 1981.

Bertsche, A. V., and Horejsi, C. R. "Coordination of Client Services." *Social Work,* 1980, *25,* 94–98.

Brill, N. I. *Team Work: Working Together in the Human Services.* Philadelphia: Lippincott, 1976.

Schoech, D. *Computer Use in Human Service Organizations.* New York: Human Sciences Press, 1982.

Steinberg, R. M., and Carter, G. W. *Case Management and the Elderly.* Lexington, Mass.: Heath, 1983.

Weil, M. "Research on Issues in Collaboration Between Social Workers and Lawyers." *Social Service Review,* September 1982.

White, M., and Grisham, M. *The Structure and Processes of Case Management in California's Multipurpose Senior Services Project—Final Report.* Berkeley, Calif.: Multipurpose Senior Services Project Evaluation (MSSP Evaluation UNEX), University Extension, University of California, June 1982.

References

Austin, C. D. "Client Assessment in Context." *Social Work Research and Abstracts,* 1981, *17,* 4–12.

Austin, D. M. "The Political Economy of Social Benefit Organizations: Redistributive Services and Merit Goods." In H. D. Stein

(Ed.), *Organization and the Human Services.* Philadelphia: Temple University Press, 1981.

Austin, D. M., and Caragonne, P. *A Comparative Analysis of Twenty-Two Settings Using Case Management Components.* Austin: Case Management Research Project, School of Social Work, University of Texas, 1981.

Bertsche, A. V., and Horejsi, C. R. "Coordination of Client Services." *Social Work,* 1980, *25,* 94–98.

Boserup, D. G., and Gouge, G. V. *The Case Management Model: Concept, Implementation, and Training.* Athens, Ga.: Regional Institute of Social Welfare Research, 1980.

Caragonne, P. *A Comparison of Case Management Work Activity and Current Models of Work Activity Within the Texas Department of Mental Health and Mental Retardation.* Report for the Texas Department of Mental Health and Mental Retardation, April 1983.

Ford, K. "Process and Tasks in Developing a Management Information System in a Case Management Agency." Unpublished manuscript, School of Social Work, University of Southern California, May 2, 1983.

Grisham, M., White, M., and Miller, L. "An Overview of Case Management." Multipurpose Senior Services Project Evaluation (MSSP Evaluation UNEX), University Extension, University of California, Berkeley, 1983.

Hasenfeld, Y. *Human Service Organizations.* Englewood Cliffs, N.J.: Prentice-Hall, 1983.

Intagliata, J. "Improving the Quality of Community Care for the Chronically Mentally Disabled: The Role of Case Management." *Schizophrenia Bulletin,* 1982, *8,* 655–674.

Intagliata, J., and Baker, F. "Factors Affecting the Delivery of Case Management Services for the Chronically Mentally Ill." *Administration in Mental Health,* in press.

Kadushin, A. *Supervision in Social Work.* New York: Columbia University Press, 1976.

Karls, J. M. "Case Management Issues." Unpublished manuscript, 1983.

Levine, I. S., and Fleming, M. *Human Resource Development: Issues in Case Management.* Baltimore: Center of Rehabilitation and Manpower Services, University of Maryland, 1984.

Mailick, M. D., and Ashley, A. A. "Politics of Interprofessional Collaboration: Challenge to Advocacy." *Social Casework,* 1981, *XX,* 131–137.

Minnesota Department of Public Welfare. "Case Management." *Community Support Project Newsletter,* 1980, *3* (4), 1–10.

National Association of Social Workers. *Practice Digest,* 0161-0287/82/0404-0007. New York: National Association of Social Workers, 1982.

Perrow, C. "A Framework for the Comparative Analysis of Organizations." *American Sociological Review,* 1967, *32,* 194–208.

Platman, S. R., and others. "Case Management of the Mentally Disabled." *Journal of Public Health Policy,* 1982, *3* (3), 302–314.

Schoech, D. *Computer Use in Human Service Organizations.* New York: Human Sciences Press, 1982.

Schwartz, S. R., Goldman, H. H., and Churgin, S. *Manpower Issues in the Care of the Chronically Mentally Ill.* Sacramento: Department of Mental Health, State of California, 1980.

Schwartz, S. R., Goldman, H. H., and Churgin, S. "Case Management for the Chronically Mentally Ill: Models and Dimensions." *Hospital and Community Psychiatry,* 1982, 33 (12), 1006–1009.

Scott, R., and Cassidy, K. "The Case Management Function: A Position Paper." Unpublished manuscript, 1981. (Available from K. Cassidy, New Jersey Division of Mental Health and Hospitals, Trenton, N.J.)

Steinberg, R. M. "Case Coordination: Lessons from the Past for Future Program Models." Paper presented at the National Conference on Social Welfare, 105th annual forum, Los Angeles, May 1978.

Steinberg, R. M., and Carter, G. W. *Case Management and the Elderly.* Lexington, Mass.: Heath, 1983.

Steinberg, R. M., Carter, G., and Kuna, J. "Essentials of Program Design and Practice in Case Coordination with the Vulnerable Elderly." Paper presented at 32nd annual meeting, Gerontological Society, Washington, D.C., November 26, 1979.

Steinberg, R. M., Carter, G. W., and White, M. "National Survey of

Current Case Coordination Programs for the Elderly: Preliminary Findings." Paper presented at the 32d annual meeting of the Gerontological Society of America, Washington, D.C., November 24, 1979.

Steinberg, R. M., White, M., and Carter, G. (with the assistance of N. E. Cutler, R. A. Downing, N. Grant, D. O. Hutson, J. Kuna, and V. Jurkiewicz). *Extracts from the Literature: A Compendium of Findings and Recommendations for Planners and Implementers of Coordination Programs for the Elderly. Alternative Designs for Comprehensive Delivery Through Case Service Coordination/Advocacy: Learnings from the Past and Models for the Future* (AoA Grant 90-A-1280). Los Angeles: Social Policy Laboratory, Andrus Gerontology Center, University of Southern California, August 1980.

Steindorff, S., Lannon, P., and Soldano, B. "Case Management Evaluation: A Review of Factors and Findings in New York." Unpublished manuscript, State University of New York, Albany, n.d.

Taylor, J. B. (with J. Gibbons). *Using Microcomputers in Social Agencies.* Beverly Hills, Calif.: Sage, 1981.

Thompson, J. D. "Organizations and Output Transactions." *American Journal of Sociology,* 1962, *68,* 309-324.

Weick, K. "Organizational Design: Organizations as Self-Designing Systems." *Organizational Dynamics,* 1977, *6,* 31-46.

Weil, M. "Interprofessional Work in Adoptions—Collaboration and Beyond," *Social Work Papers,* 1979, *15,* 46-57.

Weil, M. *Senior Centers in a Comprehensive Service Delivery System for Orange County: Report and Recommendations of the Orange County Senior Citizens Council—University of California at Irvine Study Team.* Irvine: Orange County Senior Citizens Council and University of California Extension, Irvine, July 1980.

Weil, M. "Southeast Asians and Service Delivery," In *Bridging Cultures: Social Work with Southeast Asian Refugees.* Los Angeles: Asian American Mental Health Training Center, 1981.

Weil, M. "Research on Issues in Collaboration Between Social Workers and Lawyers." *Social Service Review,* 1982, *56,* 393-405.

Weil, M. "Involvement of Senior Citizens in Needs Assessment and Service Planning." In Florence S. Schwartz (Ed.), *Voluntarism and Social Work Practice: A Growing Collaboration.* Lanham, Md.: University Press of America, 1984.

Weiner, M. E. *Human Services Management: Analysis and Applications.* Homewood, Ill.: Dorsey Press, 1982.

Weissman, H. H. *Integrating Services for Troubled Families: Dilemmas of Program Design and Implementation.* San Francisco: Jossey-Bass, 1978.

Weissman, H., Epstein, I., and Savage, A. *Agency-Based Social Work.* Philadelphia: Temple University Press, 1983.

White, M. "The Care Plan Meeting in MSSP: Utilization and Usefulness of the Care Plan MIS Package." Berkeley, Calif: Multipurpose Senior Services Project Evaluation (MSSP Evaluation UNEX), University Extension, University of California, January 11, 1983.

White, M., and Grisham, M. *The Structure and Processes of Case Management in California's Multipurpose Senior Services Project—Final Report.* Berkeley, Calif.: Multipurpose Senior Services Project Evaluation (MSSP Evaluation UNEX), University Extension, University of California, June 1982.

Zuboff, S. "New Worlds of Computer-Mediated Work." *Harvard Business Review,* September-October 1982, *60,* 142–152.

Name Index

Subject Index

Academy of Sciences (France), 235
Access program, 153, 156, 184, 185–186
Accountability: defined, 64–65; in design implementation, 342–350; goals and objectives of, 17; and information management, 61–65; roles related to, 22–23; in team model, 50
Accreditation Council for Services for Mentally Retarded and Other Developmentally Disabled Persons, 258, 264, 268, 270
Administration on Aging, 186
Administrator: role of, 17; training of, 381
Adoption Assistance and Child Welfare Act of 1980 (PL 96-272), 120, 124, 134, 143
Advocacy: case and class types of, 220; for chronically mentally ill, 219–221; concepts of, xi; for developmentally disabled, 266–268; for elderly, 163–165, 191–194; and exchange relationships, 42; function of, 39–42; legal and service

types of, 219; levels of, 39–40; for people with physical disabilities, 298–299, 307–309; questions in, 41; role of, 20, 131, 136–137, 148, 163–165
Agencies, cooperation by, 81–82
Aid to Families with Dependent Children, 178
Alameda project, 130, 132, 134
Alternative Health Services (AHS) Project, 154, 184, 187–188
American Academy of Pediatrics, Committee for the Handicapped Child of, 252, 271
American Association of Mental Deficiency, 239
American Health Planning Association, 149, 167, 168
American Public Welfare Association, 64–65, 67
Architectural and Transportation Barriers Compliance Board, 289, 290
Architectural Barriers Act, 277, 288–289

397